PAUL IN THE
Summa Theologiae
❋

PAUL IN THE
Summa Theologiae

MATTHEW LEVERING

THE CATHOLIC UNIVERSITY
OF AMERICA PRESS
Washington, D.C.

To Jörgen Vijgen

Copyright © 2014
The Catholic University of America Press
All rights reserved

Cataloging-in-Publication Data available from the
Library of Congress
ISBN: 978-0-8132-2597-5

CONTENTS

Acknowledgments	vii
Introduction	ix

PART 1. THE ORDER OF THE *Summa Theologiae*

1. The Triune God	3
2. The Passion of Christ	49
3. Baptism	76

PART 2. THE ORDER OF THE PAULINE LETTERS

4. The Mosaic Law	109
5. Grace	153
6. The Virtue of Religion	186

PART 3. TRACING PAULINE TEXTS IN THE *Summa Theologiae*

7. Romans 1:20 in the *Summa Theologiae*	219
8. 1 Corinthians 13 in the *Summa Theologiae*	236
9. Philippians 2:5–11 in the *Summa Theologiae*	267
Conclusion	283
Works Cited	293
Index	303

ACKNOWLEDGMENTS

Sustained engagement with scripture needs to be a distinguishing mark of contemporary Thomist theology. But what kind of engagement with scripture does Aquinas's *Summa theologiae* actually exhibit? The present study seeks to answer this question by means of a painstaking survey of the *Summa*'s use of Pauline texts. When I began this project four years ago, I was inspired and buoyed by the collegial friendship of Jeremy Holmes, now dean of Wyoming Catholic College. Another crucial impetus was the friendship of Charles Raith II, now assistant professor of theology at John Brown University. Jeremy and Chad read this manuscript and contributed major improvements.

Three excellent doctoral students at the University of Dayton helped with this project. After I had gone through the *Summa* and noted each place where it quoted a Pauline text, Alan Mostrom took my handwritten notes and turned them into a Word document with helpful tabulations. Jason Heron put together the bibliography at the end of the book, researched the *Summa fratris Alexandri*, and offered excellent suggestions for the introduction. Lastly, Elizabeth Farnsworth assisted in the preparation of the manuscript for publication with her typical thoroughness and precision. At Mundelein Seminary, my research assistant David Augustine, whose help has been invaluable, prepared the index. Christopher Baglow, who reviewed the book for the Catholic University of America Press, also merits thanks, not least for his own groundbreaking scholarship in Aquinas's exegesis. He expertly grasped the book's purpose and appreciated the rationale of its plodding method. Jim Kruggel of the Catholic University of America Press guided the book through to publication; once again I am indebted to this extraordinary editor and friend.

Acknowledgments

Mary Catherine Sommers graciously invited me to deliver the 2012 Aquinas Lecture at the University of St. Thomas in Houston, where I presented a version of the seventh chapter. Many thanks to friends who entertained me there, including Thomas Osborne, Ed Houser, Christopher Martin, John Hittinger, Steven Jensen, and Jeremy Wilkins. Many other friends contributed in various ways, often unbeknownst to them, to the making of this book. I cannot here name them all, but they include John Boyle, Daniel Keating, Reinhard Hütter, Tim Gray, Bruce Marshall, Gilles Emery, OP, John Kincaid, and Thomas Joseph White, OP. Thanks to the generosity of James and Mary Perry and to the friendship of Robert Barron, I am now privileged to serve as the Perry Family Foundation Professor of Theology at Mundelein Seminary, for which I am deeply grateful. To my beautiful wife, Joy, I cannot thank you enough and I rejoice in everything you are and do; thanks be to God for our children and our life together.

Two chapters in the book have been previously published, and I thank the editors of these journals—Pablo Zambruno, OP, and Joseph Mangina. Chapter one appeared as "Paul in the *Summa theologiae*'s Treatise on the Triune God," *Angelicum* 90 (2013): 87–127. Chapter seven appeared as "Variations on a Theme by Paul: Romans 1:20 in the *Summa Theologiae*," *Pro Ecclesia* 22 (2013): 153–66.

I dedicate this book to Jörgen Vijgen. Jörgen is a dear friend of many years and a superb Thomist scholar. The manuscript benefited tremendously from his careful suggestions regarding content and organization. I am so grateful to have received his friendship, instruction, and encouragement over the years. May God abundantly bless him and his family!

INTRODUCTION

THE IDEA for this book began with a question generated by my interest in Thomas Aquinas and scripture: what would I find if I tracked each citation of Paul in the *Summa theologiae*? Put another way, how would examining Aquinas's Pauline citations enhance our understanding of the ways in which scripture informs the *Summa*? Underlying this question, of course, is the difference between the genre of Aquinas's commentaries on scripture and the genre of the *Summa theologiae*. Whereas the former exposit God's scriptural Word verse-by-verse, the latter undertakes the task that we today associate with dogmatic theology and that Aquinas called "sacra doctrina."[1] The content of *sacra doctrina* is the salvific realities revealed by God in history and known in faith as taught by the church under the guidance of the Holy Spirit. Specifically, *sacra doctrina* contemplates and communicates the truth about the triune God and other things in relation to God (who is also the primary teacher of *sacra doctrina*).[2] In this task, the theologian investigates the "onto-

---

1. On *sacra doctrina* see Thomas Aquinas, *Summa theologiae* I, q. 1, in Aquinas, *Summa Theologica*, trans. Fathers of the English Dominican Province (Westminster, Md.: Christian Classics, 1981). On dogmatic theology, see for example Pope John Paul II, *Fides et Ratio*, no. 66, in *The Encyclicals of John Paul II*, ed. J. Michael Miller, CSB (Huntington, Ind.: Our Sunday Visitor, 2001), 888.

2. I cannot here address the longstanding debate about whether sacred doctrine consists more in a communicative disclosure or in a body of knowledge, other than to indicate that I think both viewpoints are right. This debate has generated a number of important studies of Aquinas's theological approach and of the purposes of the *Summa theologiae*. See in this regard G. F. Van Ackeren, SJ, *Sacra Doctrina: The Subject of the First Question of the Summa Theologica of St. Thomas Aquinas* (Rome: Catholic Book Agency, 1952); Victor White, OP, *Holy Teaching: The Idea of Theology according to St Thomas Aquinas* (Oxford: Blackfriars, 1958); Per Erik Persson, *Sacra Doctrina: Reason and Revelation in Aquinas*, trans. J. A. R. Mackenzie (Oxford: Blackwell,

logical, causal and communicative structures" of the realities revealed in scripture.[3] Thus the Pauline references in the *Summa theologiae* should be expected to serve the purposes of contemplation of the realities of faith, rather than simply reprising the content of Paul's letters.

The tasks of the biblical commentaries and of the *Summa* are complementary. Both seek to understand the salvific realities that Paul proclaimed. In the *Summa*, however, Paul's voice is present in the service of contemplative wisdom about God and his works, rather than as the driving voice of the text.[4] Because of his convictions about the unfolding of

---

1970); James A. Weisheipl, OP, "The Meaning of *Sacra Doctrina* in *Summa Theologiae* I, q. 1," *The Thomist* 38 (1974): 49–80; Cornelius Ernst, OP, "Metaphor and Ontology in *Sacra Doctrina*," *The Thomist* 38 (1974): 403–25; T. C. O'Brien, "'Sacra Doctrina' Revisited: The Context of Medieval Education," *The Thomist* 41 (1977): 475–509; Jean-Pierre Torrell, OP, "Le savoir théologique chez saint Thomas," *Revue Thomiste* 96 (1996): 355–96; Brian J. Shanley, OP, "*Sacra Doctrina* and the Theology of Disclosure," *The Thomist* 61 (1997): 163–88; Mark F. Johnson, "God's Knowledge in Our Frail Mind: The Thomistic Model of Theology," *Angelicum* 76 (1999): 25–45; Lawrence J. Donohoo, OP, "The Nature and Grace of *Sacra Doctrina* in St. Thomas's *Super Boetium de Trinitate*," *The Thomist* 63 (1999): 343–402; R. Francis Martin, "*Sacra Doctrina* and the Authority of Its *Sacra Scriptura*," *Pro Ecclesia* 10 (2001): 84–102; Anthony Keaty, "The Demands of Sacred Doctrine on 'Beginners,'" *New Blackfriars* 84 (2003): 500–509; A. N. Williams, "Argument to Bliss: The Epistemology of the *Summa Theologiae*," *Modern Theology* 20 (2004): 505–26; Peter M. Candler, Jr., "Reading Immemorially: The *Quaestio* and the Paragraph in the *Summa Theologiae*," *American Catholic Philosophical Quarterly* 78 (2004): 531–57; Henry Donneaud, OP, *Théologie et intelligence de la foi au XIIIe siècle* (Les Plans, Switzerland: Parole et Silence, 2006).

3. Pope John Paul II, *Fides et Ratio*, no. 97, in *The Encyclicals of John Paul II*, 907. Pope John Paul II observes, "The interpretation of sources is a vital task for theology; but another still more delicate and demanding task is the *understanding of revealed truth*, or the articulation of the *intellectus fidei*. The *intellectus fidei*, as I have noted, demands the contribution of a philosophy of being which first of all would enable *dogmatic theology* to perform its functions appropriately. The dogmatic pragmatism of the early years of this century, which viewed the truths of faith as nothing more than rules of conduct, has already been refuted and rejected; but the temptation always remains of understanding these truths in purely functional terms" (ibid.). For a similar contemporary vision of dogmatic theology, see Reinhard Hütter, "Transubstantiation Revisited: *Sacra Doctrina*, Dogma, and Metaphysics," in *Ressourcement Thomism: Sacred Doctrine, the Sacraments, and the Moral Life*, ed. Reinhard Hütter and Matthew Levering (Washington, D.C.: The Catholic University of America Press, 2010), 21–79.

4. For further reflection on scripture and the *Summa theologiae*, see John F. Boyle, "On the Relation of St. Thomas's Commentary on Romans to the *Summa theologiae*," in *Reading Paul with St. Thomas Aquinas*, 75–81; John F. Boyle, "St. Thomas Aquinas and Sacred Scripture," *Pro Ecclesia* 4 (1995): 92–104; Michael M. Waldstein, "On Scripture in the *Summa Theologiae*," *Aquinas Review* 1 (1994): 73–94; Thomas Prügl, "Thomas Aquinas as Interpreter of Scripture,"

sacra doctrina in the church, Aquinas is willing to use Paul to address issues that certainly did not occur to Paul. Aquinas's perspective on the realities of faith is nonetheless deeply Pauline, as one would expect from his constant recourse to Paul's letters. Aquinas has a keen sense for the specific Pauline texts that illumine each theological topic. The study of how Paul's voice is present in the *Summa*, therefore, should exemplify Aquinas's understanding of the relationship of *sacra doctrina* and *sacra scriptura*.[5]

The recent recovery of Aquinas's biblical commentaries has made Aquinas's use of scripture something of a hot topic.[6] Already in 1950,

trans. Albert K. Wimmer, in *The Theology of Thomas Aquinas*, ed. Rik Van Nieuwenhove and Joseph Wawrykow (Notre Dame, Ind.: University of Notre Dame Press, 2005), 386–415; Otto Hermann Pesch, "Paul as Professor of Theology: The Image of the Apostle in St. Thomas's Theology," *The Thomist* 38 (1974): 584–605; Matthew Levering, "A Note on Scripture in the *Summa Theologiae*," *New Blackfriars* 90 (2009): 652–58; Matthew Levering, "Aquinas," in *The Blackwell Companion to Paul*, ed. Stephen Westerholm (Oxford: Wiley-Blackwell, 2011), 361–74.

5. See Leo J. Elders, SVD, "Aquinas on Holy Scripture as the Medium of Divine Revelation," in *La doctrine de la revelation divine de saint Thomas d'Aquin*, ed. Leo J. Elders, SVD (Vatican City: Libreria Editrice Vaticana, 1990), 132–52; J. Mark Armitage, "Why Didn't Jesus Write a Book? Aquinas on the Teaching of Christ," *New Blackfriars* 89 (2008): 337–53.

6. See for example the essays in *Reading Paul with St. Thomas Aquinas*, ed. Matthew Levering and Michael Dauphinais (Washington, D.C.: The Catholic University of America Press, 2012) and the essays in *Aquinas on Scripture: An Introduction to His Biblical Commentaries*, ed. Thomas G. Weinandy, OFM Cap., Daniel A. Keating, and John P. Yocum (London: T. and T. Clark International, 2005). See also Charles Raith II, "Abraham and the Reformation: Romans 4 and the Theological Interpretation of Aquinas and Calvin," *Journal of Theological Interpretation* 5 (2011): 280–300 and "Theology and Interpretation: The Case of Aquinas and Calvin on Romans," *International Journal of Systematic Theology* 14 (2012): 310–26; Thomas F. Ryan, "The Love of Learning and the Desire for God in Thomas Aquinas's *Commentary on Romans*," in *Medieval Readings of Romans*, ed. William S. Campbell, Peter S. Hawkins, and Brenda Deen Schildgen (New York: T. and T. Clark International, 2007), 101–14; Thomas Domanyi, *Der Römerbriefkommentar des Thomas von Aquin: Ein Beitrag zur Untersuchung seiner Auslegungsmethoden* (Bern: Lang, 1979); Steven Boguslawski, OP, "Thomas Aquinas," in *Reading Romans through the Centuries: From the Early Church to Karl Barth*, ed. Jeffrey P. Greenman and Timothy Larsen (Grand Rapids, Mich.: Brazos Press, 2005), 81–99; Steven Boguslawski, OP, *Thomas Aquinas on the Jews: Insights into His Commentary on Romans 9–11* (New York: Paulist Press, 2008); Leo J. Elders, SVD, "The 'Lecturae' of St. Thomas Aquinas of the Letters of the Apostle Paul to the Philippians and Colossians," *Doctor Communis*, n.s. 9 (2009): 131–49; Antoine Guggenheim, *Jésus Christ, grand prêtre de l'ancienne et de la nouvelle Alliance. Étude du Commentaire de saint Thomas d'Aquin sur l'Épître aux Hébreux* (Paris: Parole et Silence, 2004); Angus Paddison, *Theological Hermeneutics and 1 Thessalonians* (Cambridge: Cambridge University Press, 2005), 69–99. For background in the patristic period see, for example, *Paul and the Legacies of Paul*, ed. William S. Babcock (Dallas, Tex.: Southern Methodist University Press, 1990).

Marie-Dominique Chenu remarked about Aquinas's use of scripture that at times "the citations from the Bible with which his writings are sown are no more than ornamental. Yet the very pith of his work was scriptural, and his theology had at its roots the Gospel movement of his day."[7] According to the influential work of Chenu, Aquinas's "systematic *Summa* is implanted in and fed with a continuous study of Scripture," so that "its most perfect rational structures are never an end, but a means to arrive at a better knowledge of the Word of God."[8] More recently, Jean-Pierre Torrell has emphasized that "Sacred Scripture intimately penetrates Thomas's work."[9] Torrell observes that the *Summa theologiae* and the *Summa contra Gentiles* together contain around twenty-five thousand explicit citations of the Bible.

Torrell, however, calls for "more careful studies" to establish "the familiarity and the affection with which Thomas holds certain books."[10] The present work answers this call by means of painstaking investigation of Aquinas's use of the Pauline letters in the *Summa theologiae*. Modern New Testament scholars generally consider the following seven New Testament letters to have been written by Paul: Romans, 1 and 2 Corinthians, Galatians, Philippians, 1 Thessalonians, and Philemon. According to some scholars, Paul also is the likely author of Ephesians, Colossians, and 2 Thessalonians. Most scholars do not think that Paul wrote 1 and 2 Timothy or Titus, and almost no scholar thinks that Paul wrote Hebrews. Since Aquinas treats all fourteen of these letters as Pauline, I include them all in the present study.

For unsuspecting readers, let me make clear that I have presented

---

7. M.-D. Chenu, OP, *Toward Understanding Saint Thomas*, trans. A.-M. Landry, OP, and D. Hughes, OP (Chicago: Henry Regnery, 1964), 68.

8. Ibid., 322. See also, for similar interests around the same time, Charles J. Callan, "The Bible in the *Summa Theologica* of St. Thomas Aquinas," *Catholic Biblical Quarterly* 9 (1947): 33–47; Jacobus-M. Vosté, OP, "Exegesis Novi Testamenti et Sancti Thomae Summa theologica," *Angelicum* 24 (1947): 3–19; J. Van der Ploeg, OP, "The Place of Holy Scripture in the Theology of St. Thomas," *The Thomist* 10 (1947): 398–422; and J. R. Sheets, SJ, "The Scriptural Dimension of St. Thomas," *American Ecclesiastical Review* 144 (1961): 154–73.

9. Jean-Pierre Torrell, OP, *Aquinas's Summa: Background, Structure, and Reception*, trans. Benedict M. Guevin, OSB (Washington, D.C.: The Catholic University of America Press, 2005), 72.

10. Ibid., 73.

Introduction

Aquinas's Pauline citations in a purposively plodding fashion. This is because I am trying to exhibit Paul's voice as much as possible as it is actually heard in the *Summa theologiae*. It is one thing to say, with Torrell, that in the *Summa*: "When it comes to the Christo-forming character of grace, the connection with St. Paul is clear: Thomas merely states in theological language what he finds in the Pauline epistles."[11] It is another thing to examine each reference to the Pauline epistles that we find in the *Summa*'s actual treatise on grace.[12] This latter task involves identifying each reference, situating it within the broader topic of the article, and asking how it contributes to the argument of the article. A particular reference may contribute in a very small way, along lines that are tangential to Paul's own concerns. The article itself may be linked deeply with Pauline theology, or may be addressing a topic that arises only in patristic or medieval times. A quotation from Paul may be central to both the article and to Paul's own theology, or it may simply be a quick way of finding a biblical authority for an ingenious objection. An article may also quote Paul simply in order to show that scripture does not contradict the properly philosophical argumentation that Aquinas's *respondeo* develops.[13]

Just as it would be a mistake to try to evaluate Paul's voice in the *Summa theologiae* without contextualizing this voice in terms of its actual role in the arguments of particular articles, so also one should keep in view the broader context of each article, insofar as each article belongs within a *quaestio* and within a treatise (a set of *quaestiones* on a specific topic). Aquinas's individual quotations from Paul can seem to be of disparate val-

---

11. Ibid.

12. Waldstein cautions against the use of the term "treatise" on the grounds that this plays into the hands of those who view the *Summa theologiae* as a rationalistic system. I occasionally use the term, for lack of a better one, in order to describe how Aquinas takes up a unified sets of questions. See Waldstein, "On Scripture in the *Summa Theologiae*," 73–75.

13. In studying Paul in the *Summa theologiae*, I am not claiming that every time Paul makes an appearance Aquinas is thereby undertaking theological rather than philosophical argumentation. In this regard Ralph McInerny warns against "flawed understandings of the nature of Christian philosophy, a tendency to disparage the natural in favor of the supernatural, [and] the suggestion that the philosophy of St. Thomas is to be found only in his theological works, and cannot be separated from them" (McInerny, *Praeambula Fidei: Thomism and the God of the Philosophers* [Washington, D.C.: The Catholic University of America Press, 2006], 32). The study of Aquinas need not be a competition between theologians and philosophers.

ue, but when his Pauline quotations in a particular *quaestio* or treatise are seen as a whole, one recognizes more easily that Aquinas has provided a full-bodied Pauline theology of the topic. Even the Pauline citations that help Aquinas to formulate very minor objections turn out to have an integral place within Aquinas's assemblage of the most important Pauline texts on a given theological topic.

WILHELMUS VALKENBERG'S *WORDS OF THE LIVING GOD*

Although there are a number of studies of Aquinas's biblical commentaries, as well as numerous studies of Aquinas's theology that take seriously his engagement with scripture, there are almost no studies that track and evaluate Aquinas's biblical citations in the *Summa theologiae*. The major exception is Wilhelmus Valkenberg's *Words of the Living God: Place and Function of Holy Scripture in the Theology of St. Thomas Aquinas*. Distinguishing between the "place" and the "function" of biblical texts in the *Summa theologiae*, Valkenberg develops both a quantitative and a qualitative assessment of Scripture's role in the *Summa*. He explains: "The term 'place' refers to a quantitative analysis in which the contribution of all sorts of quotations from Scripture to the theological text can be measured. The term 'function' refers to a qualitative analysis of the role Scripture plays in the text, not only as a contributing factor in its surface structure, but also as the main source in its deep structure."[14] He focuses on the *tertia pars* of the *Summa theologiae*, in particular questions 53–56 on Christ's resurrection. Testing Michel Corbin's thesis that Aquinas's theology became more biblical as Aquinas became more aware of Aristotle's philosophy, Valkenberg compares questions 53–56 with Aquinas's treatment of Christ's resurrection in his *Commentary on the Sentences*. He finds that Aquinas's theology did indeed become significantly more biblical. Thus Aquinas's commentary on distinctions 1–22 of Book III of the *Sentences* contains 164 references to Paul, whereas Aquinas refers to Paul 502 times in questions 1–59 of the *tertia pars*. In both the *Commentary on*

14. Wilhelmus G. B. M. Valkenberg, *Words of the Living God: Place and Function of Holy Scripture in the Theology of St. Thomas Aquinas* (Leuven: Peeters, 2000), 2.

the Sentences and the *Summa theologiae*, Paul is the most frequently cited biblical author (followed by John). In distinctions 1–22 Aristotle is cited 209 times in comparison with 164 for Paul, whereas in questions 1–59 Aristotle is cited 128 times in comparison with 502 for Paul.

Valkenberg criticizes the early-twentieth century research of Georg Graf von Hertling, who classified Aquinas's citations of Augustine and established standards for evaluating these citations as informative, confirmative, decorative, and so forth.[15] In Hertling's work, Valkenberg fears, Aquinas's citations come to be seen as proof texts rather than as giving voice to the "auctoritas" that Aquinas is citing. Valkenberg explains that "a distinction was drawn between valuable and void quotations. According to this point of view, quotations that are actually used to prove something in the text were opposed to quotations that do not have such a function."[16] Aquinas, however, often uses biblical texts for purposes that go beyond proving a particular point. Valkenberg therefore warns against envisioning scripture "solely as an element in logical argumentation, while the function of Scripture as encompassing source and framework for theology is left out of consideration."[17] Aquinas's use of scripture aims to give full expression to the "auctoritas" of the Word of God and not simply to prove particular theological points. Quotations that might at first appear merely "decorative" in fact serve to shape the cumulative impact of Aquinas's biblical citations in a particular treatise.

Valkenberg contrasts biblical citations that have a "theologically primary function" with biblical citations that have a "theologically secondary function."[18] Biblical citations with a "theologically secondary" function "do not directly bear upon the *quaestio* and its solution itself, but upon the several aspects considered in the *quaestio* as a literary form."[19] By contrast, biblical citations that possess a "theologically primary" function have "a determinative function with regard to the *quaestio* itself."[20] Examples of a theologically primary function include when the scriptural

15. See Georg Graf von Hertling, "Augustinus-citate bei Thomas von Aquin," in *Sitzungsberichte der philosophisch-philologischen und der historischen Klasse der Königlichen Bayerischen Akademie der Wissenschaften zu München* (Munich: 1904), 535–602.
16. Valkenberg, *Words of the Living God*, 46.
17. Ibid., 47.
18. Ibid., 134–40.
19. Ibid., 139.
20. Ibid.

citation originates the problem or topic of the *quaestio*; when the biblical citation, located in the *sed contra*, provides the path along which the *quaestio* is to be answered; and when the biblical citation, at the end of the theological argumentation, confirms the position taken by Aquinas. As Valkenberg observes: "The theologically primary function of Scripture will be found everywhere in Aquinas' theology, because it is essential to a theology proceeding from the principles of faith known through revelation."[21]

In this regard Valkenberg offers something of a correction of Chenu's theory of "biblical zones" in the *Summa theologiae*. Chenu raised a significant question: "Can the study of the economy of salvation, can the doctrinal interpretation of the biblical narrative in which this economy is unfolded, take on the shape and structure required by science, without the nature of sacred history being altered?"[22] According to Chenu, the answer is yes, for two reasons. First, Aquinas explores the contingent events of sacred history insofar as they open onto the divine Wisdom, that is to say "the divine reasons that govern such an economy."[23] Precisely because God is at the center of *sacra doctrina*, theology "returns always to the Gospel, to the word of God, because it is fulfilled in the thought of God."[24] Second, in order that *sacra doctrina* not lose touch with the concrete history of salvation, the *Summa theologiae* includes "biblical zones" such as "the three elaborate blocks of questions in which Saint Thomas develops what Scripture says about the six days of creation (*Ia Pars*, q. 67–74), the old law (*Ia-IIae*, q. 89–106), the life and mysteries of Christ (*IIIa Pars*, q. 27–59)."[25] In these "biblical zones" the biblical narrative governs the ordering of topics. For his part, Valkenberg agrees that some topics of the

21. Ibid.
22. Chenu, *Toward Understanding Saint Thomas*, 303.
23. Ibid., 307.
24. Ibid., 309. It follows that God can be contemplated in a manner that cannot be reduced solely to tracing and retracing the biblical-historical narratives. In scripture, God invites us to rise in and through our participation in the temporal realities of biblical revelation (the history of creation and redemption) to their revealed source, the infinitely transcendent wisdom and love of the triune God. In the *Summa theologiae*, scripture provides not only the framework and content of theological pondering, but also the entire *telos* of theology as a finite participation in God's own knowledge and a deepening of our friendship with the Trinity.
25. Ibid., 316.

Summa are more directly dependent on scripture, but he holds that the "theologically primary function" of scripture is present in the whole of the *Summa*.[26]

Turning to Aquinas's theology of Christ's resurrection in his *Commentary on the Sentences* and *Summa theologiae*, Valkenberg finds that "the number of explicit quotations per 1,000 words is 14 in *in III Sent.* 21.2, and 24.3 in *STh.III* 53–56."[27] Even so, in both the *Commentary on the Sentences* and the *Summa theologiae*, Aquinas uses scripture more often in a "theologically secondary function" than in a "theologically primary function."[28] With regard to Paul, Valkenberg states that "Aquinas uses the letters of saint Paul not as a source of data but as a source for his own theological insights. Consequently, he is the main source for Aquinas when considering the soteriological value of the resurrection of Christ. He considers Paul as the first and foremost of all theologians."[29]

THE APPROACH OF THE PRESENT BOOK

Much as I admire Valkenberg's approach, I have not followed his technical apparatus in the present book. I do not categorize the Pauline quotations in terms of whether their theological function is primary or secondary, nor do I compare the *Summa* with the *Commentary on the Sentences*. Rather than burdening the reader with theoretical apparatus, I simply

---

26. Christopher Baglow is likewise concerned to call into question Chenu's opposition between the "biblical zones" with their narrative ordering and the other sets of *quaestiones* with their sapiential-scientific ordering. Baglow follows André Hayen's proposal that understanding the structure of *sacra doctrina* in the *Summa theologiae* benefits from attending to Aquinas's prologues to the *Compendium theologiae* and the *lectura* on John's Gospel, both written during the same time period as the *Summa theologiae*. See Christopher T. Baglow, "Sacred Scripture and Sacred Doctrine in Saint Thomas Aquinas," in *Aquinas on Doctrine: A Critical Introduction*, ed. Thomas Weinandy, OFM Cap., Daniel Keating, and John Yocum (New York: T. and T. Clark, 2004), 1–25. See also André Hayen, *Saint Thomas d'Aquin et la vie de l'église* (Louvain: Publications Universitaires, 1952), as well as Christopher T. Baglow, *"Modus et Forma": A New Approach to the Exegesis of Saint Thomas Aquinas with an Application to the* Lectura super Epistolam ad Ephesios (Rome: Pontifical Biblical Institute Press, 2002) and John F. Boyle, "The Twofold Division of St. Thomas's Christology in the *Tertia Pars*," *The Thomist* 60 (1996): 439–47.

27. Valkenberg, *Words of the Living God*, 128.

28. See ibid., 134.

29. Ibid., 133.

move through the citations of Paul and discuss each one in relation to the topic that Aquinas is addressing in the article. I generally arrange this material into sections, and at the end of each section I draw some conclusions about how Aquinas is using Paul in the articles and questions under consideration. I purposefully keep the interpretative framework quite spare, in hopes of focusing attention on the work that the Pauline quotations do. So that readers can easily recognize these quotations from Paul, I use the Revised Standard Version rather than the Douay-Rheims translation of the Vulgate or a direct translation from Aquinas's Latin version.[30] When Aquinas relies upon a variant reading from that found in the RSV, I am careful to point this out.

My book approaches Aquinas's use of Paul in the *Summa theologiae* by means of three interpretative methods, which I have distinguished as three parts, each with three chapters. These three parts respond to three basic scholarly questions that arise when one seeks to understand how Aquinas employs Paul in the *Summa*: first, how does Aquinas use Pauline texts within the flow of his speculative or sapiential exposition; second, how does Aquinas use each of Paul's letters within his treatises; third, how do specific Pauline texts appear in different ways throughout the various treatises of the *Summa*? In the first two parts, I have been careful to include treatises from the *prima pars* (the triune God, questions 2–43); the *prima-secundae pars* (the Mosaic law, questions 98–105, and grace, questions 109–14); the *secunda-secundae pars* (the virtue of religion, questions 81–89); and the *tertia pars* (Christ's passion, questions 46–49, and the sacrament of baptism, questions 66–69). The first part follows the order of the *Summa theologiae* and has chapters on the triune God, Christ's passion, and baptism. The second part follows the order of Paul's letters and has chapters on the Mosaic law, grace, and the virtue of religion. The third part traces particular Pauline texts throughout the *Summa* and has chapters on Romans 1:20, 1 Corinthians 13, and Philippians 2:5–11. In short,

---

30. Thomas Gilby, OP, remarks: "St. Thomas's text was the Latin Vulgate according to the early thirteenth-century Paris exemplar; it seems likely that he consulted the corrected version, the Jacobin Bible, edited in his own community of Saint-Jacques" (Gilby, "Appendix II: The *Summa* and the Bible," in St. Thomas Aquinas, *Summa theologiae, vol. 1 (Ia.1): Christian Theology* [Cambridge: Cambridge University Press, 2006], 134). Gilles Emery, OP, has noted to me in conversation that identifying Aquinas's exact text is not so simple.

without offering an exhaustive treatment, I provide various lenses for understanding Aquinas's use of Paul in the *Summa theologiae*, and I focus on treatises and texts that should be of wide theological interest.

Since my case for the value of Aquinas's Pauline citations rests partly on the sheer cumulative impact of these citations, it is worthwhile to include, at the end of this introduction, some rough statistical data concerning Aquinas's use of Paul in the *Summa*. This statistical data helps to contextualize the more specific studies that follow in my chapters. The data show both that Aquinas cites Paul frequently and that Aquinas cites each of Paul's letters extensively. Pauline citations appear most regularly in the *tertia pars*, as we would expect. By my count, 67 of the 119 questions of the *prima pars* have Pauline citations. This is also the case for 78 of the 114 questions of the *prima-secundae pars*; 160 of the 189 questions of the *secunda-secundae pars*; and 84 of the 90 questions of the *tertia pars*.

Where is Paul's voice least present? In the *prima pars*, questions 2–11 and 15–18 treat the divine attributes and quote Paul only six times; questions 27–31 and 34–42 on the Trinity quote Paul only thirteen times; questions 44–55 and 59–61 on creation and the angels quote Paul only five times; and questions 96–102 on Adam and Eve quote Paul only three times. In the *prima-secundae pars*, questions 6–27 and 29–61 treat human actions, passions, and the nature of habits and virtues; these questions have only forty Pauline citations. This is not surprising, as these questions are highly philosophical, drawing heavily upon Aristotle. In the *secunda-secundae pars*, questions 137–45 treat perseverance, fortitude, and temperance; these questions, perhaps surprisingly, have only six Pauline citations. In the *tertia pars*, the six questions that lack Pauline citations are scattered widely, and almost every question has a large number of Pauline citations. Of the *Summa*'s 512 total questions, 123 have no citations of Paul. Thus three quarters of the questions of the *Summa theologiae* contain Pauline quotations.

How many times is Paul cited in the *Summa theologiae*? This question does not allow for an exact answer. Aquinas sometimes quotes Paul solely in order to quote the gloss's commentary on the particular Pauline verse, and in these cases one has to make a judgment call regarding whether or not the Pauline citation is worth noting. Each enumerator will make different judgment calls. In my research, I undertook a rough tabulation of all the Pauline citations in the *Summa* and identified around 2,198 citations, 600 of which come from Romans; 480 from 1 Corinthians; 168 from 2 Corinthians; 145 from Galatians; 183 from Ephesians; 72 from Philippians; 71 from Colossians; 20 from 1 Thessalonians; 18 from 2 Thessalonians; 117 from 1 Timothy; 44 from 2 Timothy; 23 from Titus; 1 from Philemon; and 256 from Hebrews. Nearly half of the citations, then, come from Romans and 1 Corinthians. This is what we would expect given the length and theological significance of these two letters.

It is worth noting that Aquinas does not use only a few favored verses from each Pauline letter or from certain favorite letters. Rather, he uses a wide range of verses and quotes proportionately from almost every Pauline letter. Leaving room for some imprecision, we can say that in the *Summa theologiae*, Aquinas quotes 203 of the 433 verses of Romans; 210 of the 437 verses of 1 Corinthians; 88 of the 257 verses of 1 Corinthians; 50 of the 149 verses of Galatians; 89 of the 155 verses of Ephesians; 30 of the 104 verses of Philippians; 37 of the 95 verses of Colossians; 13 of the 89 verses of 1 Thessalonians; 12 of the 47 verses of 2 Thessalonians; 49 of the 113 verses of 1 Timothy; 21 of the 83 verses of 2 Timothy; 16 of the 46 verses of Titus; 1 of the 25 verses of Philemon; and 115 of the 303 verses of Hebrews. Put another way, of the 2,336 verses that are contained in the fourteen letters that Aquinas counts as Pauline, he quotes 934 verses (40 percent). This is indeed a broad sampling of verses, especially since he quotes some verses repeatedly.

Even so, Aquinas certainly does have favorite Pauline chapters, and it may be of use to identify at the outset the chapters from which Aquinas quotes the highest percentage of verses. Among his favorite chapters are Romans 1 (21 of 32 verses), Romans 5 (14 of 21), Romans 6 (15 of 23), Romans 7 (14 of 25), Romans 8 (27 of 39), 1 Corinthians 2 (10 of 16), 1 Corinthians 13 (12 of 13), 1 Corinthians 14 (27 of 40), Galatians 5 (16 of 26), Ephesians 1 (19 of 23), Ephesians 4 (20 of 32), Colossians 3 (14 of 25), 1 Timothy 5 (14 of 25), Hebrews 1 (9 of 14), and Hebrews 2 (12 of 18). Commentators on the Pauline letters will recognize here many of the chapters that scholars of Paul's theology have long found most fascinating.

Before proceeding, I should observe that the present study does not argue that Aquinas is more biblical than his medieval contemporaries. By way of comparison, the roughly contemporaneous Franciscan compendium, the *Summa fratris Alexandri*, quotes Paul 161 times in its massive treatise on the triune God; Aquinas's shorter treatise on the triune God cites Paul ninety-three times. The *Summa fratris Alexandri* contains a brief treatise on Christ's passion that contains forty-three Pauline citations, while Aquinas's treatise on Christ's Passion quotes Paul fifty-nine times. So far as I can tell, Aquinas's use of Paul does not separate him in any striking way from his contemporaries. Not only Aquinas, but also other mid-thirteenth century *magistri*, quote Paul much more than Peter Lombard had done (and thus much more than commentators on Lombard's *Sentences* had the opportunity to do). Since Lombard was writing in the context of compendia of patristic sayings such as Peter Abelard's *Sic et Non*, it is no wonder that his *Sentences* focused on the church fathers and especially on Augustine.

Having noted the "impression of overriding rationality" that Aquinas's writings give, Yves Congar adds nonetheless that "it is impossible to avoid being struck by his masterly knowledge and use of Scripture."[31] If this is true about Aquinas's use of Paul, how and why is it true? Given the significance of Aquinas's theological achievement, concentrated attention upon how he cites Paul is long overdue. Studies of Aquinas's commentaries on Paul's letters need now to be complemented by turning directly to the *Summa theologiae* with the goal of tracking and evaluating Aquinas's Pauline citations. This is the task—admittedly a rather plodding one—to which we now turn. It is my hope that this approach to Aquinas's use of Paul will bear fruit in a deeper awareness of the strengths and limitations of Aquinas's integration of the Pauline letters into the *sacra doctrina* of his *Summa theologiae*.

---

31. Yves Congar, OP, *I Believe in the Holy Spirit* (3 vols. in one), trans. David Smith (New York: Crossroad, 1997), 3:116.

PART I

THE ORDER OF THE
Summa Theologiae

CHAPTER 1

THE TRIUNE GOD

GILLES EMERY has provided a careful exposition of the doctrine of the Holy Spirit in Thomas Aquinas's *Commentary on the Letter to the Romans*. Emery notes that Aquinas's biblical "commentaries do not offer a different doctrine from his synthetic works. Rather, their genre is different. By means of direct contact with the biblical text whose words they explain and whose profound meaning they seek to expose, these commentaries offer another access to the thought of St. Thomas."[1] Emery shows how Aquinas, in his commentary on Romans, reflects extensively on the person and mission of the Holy Spirit.[2] The influence of Paul on Aquinas's theology of the triune God in the *Summa theologiae*, however, has not yet been studied, although in recent years a number of excellent works on Aquinas's theology of God have appeared.[3]

---

1. Gilles Emery, OP, "The Holy Spirit in Aquinas's Commentary on Romans," in *Reading Romans with St. Thomas Aquinas*, ed. Matthew Levering and Michael Dauphinais (Washington, D.C.: The Catholic University of America Press, 2012), 127–28. On this point see also Gilles Emery, OP, *The Trinitarian Theology of Saint Thomas Aquinas*, trans. Francesca Aran Murphy (Oxford: Oxford University Press, 2007), 19–22.

2. See also Emery's "Biblical Exegesis and the Speculative Doctrine of the Trinity in St. Thomas Aquinas's *Commentary on John*," in *Reading John with St. Thomas Aquinas: Theological Exegesis and Speculative Theology*, ed. Michael Dauphinais and Matthew Levering (Washington, D.C.: The Catholic University of America Press, 2005), 23–61.

3. The presence of Scripture in Aquinas's theology of the triune God certainly has not been ignored: see for example Emery, *The Trinitarian Theology of Saint Thomas Aquinas*, 9–17; more broadly see Emery's *The Trinity: An Introduction to Catholic Doctrine on the Triune God*, trans.

Aquinas's debts to Augustine and Aristotle in his theology of God are well known and have received extensive attention, but the role of Paul requires examination.

Biblical scholars debate whether Paul thinks of the Father, Son, and Holy Spirit as "of one 'essence,' one in 'being.'"[4] Aquinas, of course, assumes that Paul does so—or at least that Paul has a basic understanding that the Father, Son, and Holy Spirit are distinct yet one in divinity. In his theology of the triune God in the *Summa theologiae* (questions 2–43 of

---

Matthew Levering (Washington, D.C.: The Catholic University of America Press, 2011), 12–50. Further recent studies of Aquinas's theology of the triune God include Gilles Emery, OP, *Trinity in Aquinas* (Ypsilanti, Mich.: Sapientia Press, 2003); Emery, *Trinity, Church, and the Human Person: Thomistic Essays* (Naples, Fla.: Sapientia Press, 2007); Bruce D. Marshall, "Aquinas the Augustinian? On the Uses of Augustine in Aquinas's Trinitarian Theology," in *Aquinas the Augustinian*, ed. Michael Dauphinais, Barry David, and Matthew Levering (Washington, D.C.: The Catholic University of America Press, 2007), 41–61; Bruce D. Marshall, "What Does the Spirit Have to Do?," in *Reading John with St. Thomas Aquinas*, 62–77; Harm Goris, "Theology and Theory of the Word in Aquinas: Understanding Augustine by Innovating Aristotle," in *Aquinas the Augustinian*, 62–78; Rudi A. Te Velde, *Aquinas on God: The 'Divine Science' of the Summa Theologiae* (London: Ashgate, 2006); W. J. Hankey, *God in Himself: Aquinas' Doctrine of God as Expounded in the Summa Theologiae* (Oxford: Oxford University Press, 1987); Matthew Levering, *Scripture and Metaphysics: Aquinas and the Renewal of Trinitarian Theology* (Oxford: Blackwell, 2004). For a brief introduction to Aquinas's approach, see Gilles Emery, OP, "Contemporary Questions about God," *Nova et Vetera* 8 (2010): 799–811.

4. Michael J. Gorman, *Cruciformity: Paul's Narrative Spirituality of the Cross* (Grand Rapids, Mich.: Eerdmans, 2001), 74. Without using the language of being or essence, Gorman wants to affirm that "it is absolutely crucial for Paul—and for us—to keep the Father, Son, and Spirit united as one in relation to the cross. Otherwise, the cross becomes a place only for the outpouring of divine wrath on an innocent but passive 'son'; the 'spirit' of these two can hardly be one" (ibid.). For a Trinitarian reading of Paul, see especially Gordon D. Fee, *God's Empowering Presence: The Holy Spirit in the Letters of Paul* (Peabody, Mass.: Hendrickson, 1994). Influenced by Eberhard Jüngel and Jürgen Moltmann, Charles B. Cousar suggests that "the understanding of the attributes of God in much of western theology in fact represents a continuation of the thinking of the Corinthians against which Paul polemicizes. In both instances God is understood in light of human judgments as to what God must be and do if God is to be really God, and in many cases such judgments merely mask the desire for control, for moral superiority, or for the maintenance of the status quo. Paul's alternative opens the door to an entirely different way of thinking about God and about God's (and therefore also genuinely human) power, righteousness, wisdom, faithfulness, freedom, and love" (Cousar, *A Theology of the Cross: The Death of Jesus in the Pauline Letters* [Minneapolis, Minn.: Fortress Press, 1990], 48). I wonder, however, whether Cousar understands the metaphysics he criticizes. See also my "God and Greek Philosophy in Contemporary Biblical Scholarship," *Journal of Theological Interpretation* 4 (2010): 169–85.

the *prima pars*), Aquinas provides ninety-three citations of the fourteen letters that he considers to be Pauline. This chapter will explore exactly where these quotations of Paul appear, and whether they can be said to play a significant role in informing Aquinas's arguments. Thirty of these citations are of Romans, and twenty-two are of 1 Corinthians. The dominant voice, then, is the Paul of Romans and 1 Corinthians. Aquinas cites Ephesians nine times, Hebrews nine times, 1 Timothy seven times, 2 Corinthians three times, 2 Timothy four times, Colossians three times, Philippians twice, Galatians twice, and 1 Thessalonians and Titus once each. The only Pauline letters that he does not cite in his treatise on the triune God, therefore, are 2 Thessalonians and Philemon. The passages that are most frequently cited include Romans 8:28–32 (nine times), Romans 9 (seven times), 1 Corinthians 2:6–12 (five times), Romans 1:19–21 (four times), and Hebrews 1:3 (three times).

Of the forty-two questions in Aquinas's treatise, only thirteen have three or more citations from Paul, and of these only nine have four or more citations from Paul. The nine questions with four or more citations of Paul are devoted to the following topics: how God is known by us (both now and in eternal life), God's knowledge, God's will, God's justice and mercy, God's providence, God's predestination, how we know the Trinity of persons, the person of the Father, and the missions of the Son and Holy Spirit. The four questions with three citations of Paul are devoted respectively to the names of God (analogy), the power of God, the Son's name "Image," and the persons in relation to the divine essence. Put another way, between question twelve (on how we know God) and question twenty-five (on the power of God), we find fifty-five of Aquinas's ninety-three citations of Paul. Fifteen of the forty-two questions have no citations of Paul, and a further ten questions have only one citation. In other words, seventeen of the forty-two questions contain almost all of the Pauline citations. The question with the most citations of Paul is the one on predestination, which contains nineteen citations. The next highest number of citations from Paul is found in the question on how we know God, which contains nine citations. Two questions thus have twenty-eight of the ninety-three citations of Paul in Aquinas's treatise on the triune God.

Not surprisingly, then, we can already say that Paul has much more of an impact in certain areas of Aquinas's treatise than in other areas. This is especially clear with regard to the questions related to God's will, where Paul plays a highly significant role. There is also a large number of questions in which Paul plays no role or almost no role. The task at hand, therefore, is to explore the major role that Paul plays in certain questions, while also inquiring into his influence in the questions that have only one or two Pauline citations. In examining Aquinas's Pauline citations in this treatise, I follow in the order that Aquinas provides, beginning with question two and ending with question forty-three.

PAUL IN QUESTIONS 2–12

Question two asks whether human reason can show that God exists. The pivotal article is the second one, in which Aquinas argues that God's existence can be demonstrated by human reason. The *sed contra* quotes Romans 1:20, "Ever since the creation of the world his [God's] invisible nature, namely, his eternal power and deity, has been clearly perceived in the things that have been made." Aquinas concludes that this could not be a true statement "unless the existence of God could be demonstrated through the things that are made; for the first thing we must know of anything is, whether it exists."[5] We could not clearly perceive God's "invisible nature" on the basis of created things, unless we could demonstrate on the basis of created things that God exists. Since Paul's statement belongs to divine revelation, it must be true, and the only way for it to be true is if God's existence can be demonstrated by reason.

Aquinas does not here take up the possibility of sin occluding the powers of human reason. Although he elsewhere affirms that sin can render our intellect ineffectual in knowing God, he is more concerned here about God's transcendence. How is it that we can demonstrate the existence of God, given that God is not a kind of being and that God's nature infinitely transcends any finite concept by which we might seek to express and characterize it? The word "God" refers to an infinite reality that as such cannot be conceptualized by a finite mind.

---

5. *ST* I, q. 2, a. 2, *sed contra*.

Indebted to Exodus 3:14 in its Latin translation, in which God names himself "I am who am," Aquinas holds that the way to demonstrate that God exists (as Paul indicates is possible) is to reason from finite, contingent, changing existents to infinite, sheer "to be." This is how God can be seen to be simply "I am." This path, Aquinas notes, was followed by Aristotle in his metaphysical demonstrations of God as pure act. In Aquinas's view, these demonstrations work as properly philosophical demonstrations that attain to truth about God. The importance of this is twofold: the God in whom Christians believe is pure act, and we can deduce from God's nature as pure act further implications about the nature of God ("his eternal power and deity"). The significant point is that Aquinas considers that there are two ways of reflecting about the Christian God—biblical revelation and (Greek) metaphysics or philosophy—rather than holding that there is only one way to know God, namely through the narrative of scripture. Aquinas considers the two ways to be complementary.

The use of both ways can be seen in the first article of question three. Aquinas points out in an objection that God appears to have a body, because this is a possible interpretation of Genesis 1:26, "Let us make man in our image, after our likeness."[6] Humans have bodies, and if humans are made in the image and likeness of God, then it would seem logical to conclude that God has a body. In the objection, Aquinas quotes Hebrews 1:3 in order to strengthen the view that the "image" of God means a bodily figure. Hebrews 1:3 states that the Son "reflects the glory of God and bears the very stamp of his nature." In Aquinas's version, "stamp" is *figura*. The objection suggests that Hebrews, too, has a bodily God in mind, on the grounds that "everything that has figure is a body, since figure is a quality of quantity."[7] In answer to this objection, Aquinas argues that humans are in the image of God not according to bodily attributes—since other animals also possess such attributes—but according to human possession of intelligence. He is aware that Scripture at times describes God by means of

---

6. *ST* I, q. 3, a. 1, obj. 2. For contemporary views along these lines, see Benjamin D. Sommer, *The Bodies of God and the World of Ancient Israel* (Cambridge: Cambridge University Press, 2009); Stephen H. Webb, *Jesus Christ, Eternal God: Heavenly Flesh and the Metaphysics of Matter* (Oxford: Oxford University Press, 2012).

7. *ST* I, q. 3, a. 1, obj. 2.

bodily imagery, but he denies that such imagery is found in Genesis 1:26 or Hebrews 1:3. In the *respondeo* of the article, Aquinas provides a philosophical demonstration of God's immateriality. He makes clear that this philosophical argumentation complements biblical revelation; the *sed contra* aptly quotes John 4:24, where Jesus tells the Samaritan woman, "God is spirit."

The second article of question three also includes a quotation from Hebrews in an objection. Aquinas quotes Hebrews 10:38, "My righteous one shall live by faith, and if he shrinks back, my soul has no pleasure in him." This passage implies that God has a soul, and, as Aquinas observes, "Whatever has a soul is composed of matter and form; since the soul is the form of the body."[8] Again Aquinas's answer depends on the view that the biblical application of corporeal attributes to God does not contradict statements in scripture that rule out such corporeal attributes. For both biblical and metaphysical reasons, we should hold that God is incorporeal, with the result that the attribution of a "soul" to God in Hebrews 10:38 must be seen as simply a way of speaking about his will. Aquinas concludes, "A soul is attributed to God because His acts resemble the acts of a soul; for, that we will anything, is due to our soul. Hence what is pleasing to His will is said to be pleasing to His soul."[9]

Question four, on God's perfection, has no references to Paul. The third article of question five inquires into whether being is convertible with goodness, and the *sed contra* quotes 1 Timothy 4:4, "For everything created by God is good." Paul says this in rejecting the view that Christians should abstain from marriage or abstain from certain foods. No food has been created evil, and as Paul adds, "Nothing is to be rejected if it is received with thanksgiving; for then it is consecrated by the word of God and prayer" (1 Tim 4:4–5). Aquinas uses this passage to support his contention that all of God's creatures are good, and that God is the infinitely good source of all created beings. He also employs the metaphysical argument that "all being, as being, has actuality and is in some way perfect; since every act implies some sort of perfection; and perfection implies desirability and goodness."[10]

---

8. *ST* I, q. 3, a. 2, obj. 1. 9. *ST* I, q. 3, a. 2, ad 2.
10. *ST* I, q. 3, a. 2.

Questions six and seven, on God's goodness and infinity, do not refer to Paul. The next citation of Paul is in the first article of question eight, on whether God is in all things. Paul is again used by Aquinas to pose a problem (in an objection), namely, how God can exist in things that are morally evil, such as demons. In 2 Corinthians 6:14, Paul warns Christians not to marry non-Christians, and in this vein Paul asks rhetorically, "For what partnership have righteouness and iniquity? Or what fellowship has light with darkness?" Aquinas reasons that God is perfect righteousness and light. How, then, can God be present in demons, whose wills are profoundly evil? The answer is a metaphysical one that is equally rooted in the biblical account of the freedom possessed by rational creatures: "In the demons there is their nature which is from God, and also the deformity of sin which is not from Him; therefore, it is not to be absolutely conceded that God is in the demons, except with the addition, *inasmuch as they are beings*."[11]

Paul is not mentioned in questions nine and ten, on God's immutability and eternity. He returns in article three of question eleven, on whether God is one. In an objection, Aquinas quotes a portion of 1 Corinthians 8:5–6, where Paul states that "although there may be so-called gods in heaven or on earth—as indeed there are many 'gods' and many 'lords'—yet for us there is one God, the Father, from whom are all things and for whom we exist, and one Lord, Jesus Christ, through whom are all things and through whom we exist." In Aquinas's Latin version, the scare quotes are not added, so that in the section quoted by Aquinas, Paul appears to be admitting that there are many gods and lords. If there are many gods, then, Aquinas reasons, there cannot be one God—since if God is one among many gods, then he cannot be the transcendent source of all being, but instead is a finite entity among other finite entities. In his response to the objection, he indicates that Paul means simply that the pagans think that there are many gods, whereas Christians know that "there is one God, the Father, from whom are all things and for whom we exist, and one Lord, Jesus Christ, through whom are all things and through whom we exist." In Aquinas's view, Paul decisively distinguishes the Father and the Son

---

11. *ST* I, q. 8, a. 1, ad 4.

from everything else ("all things"), so as to affirm that the Father and Son are the source of being and thereby to leave no room for the notion that the Father and Son are finite entities among other gods and lords. In this same article, Aquinas also defends God's unity—not a numerical unity (as if God were one limited thing among other things) but a transcendental unity (absolutely indivisible)—on metaphysical grounds rooted in God's simplicity as pure act.

Although the arguments in which Aquinas has thus far drawn upon Paul have not been negligible—having to do with God's existence, immateriality, goodness, immanence, and unity—the first place where he repeatedly quotes Paul is question twelve, on how we know God (both in this life and in eternal life). In article three of question twelve, Aquinas quotes Ephesians 1:17–18 in answering an objection regarding whether the bodily eye can see the essence of God. In Book XXIX of *City of God*, Augustine had suggested that something like this might be possible, and so Aquinas is compelled to take up the question. The objections quote Job 19:26 and Isaiah 6:1, both of which seem to speak of being able to see God with the bodily eye. Replying to the passage from Isaiah, Aquinas states again that "in divine Scripture divine things are metaphorically described by means of sensible things," so that Isaiah's image of God sitting on a throne should not be taken literally as a metaphysical claim that God is bodily.[12] Replying to the passage from Job, Aquinas argues that Job is describing intellectual vision rather than bodily vision of God (since the issue is not whether Christ's flesh can be seen, but whether the Godhead can be seen). Ephesians 1:17–18 helps Aquinas here by exemplifying such intellectual vision. In this passage Paul prays "that the God of our Lord Jesus Christ, the Father of glory, may give you a spirit of wisdom and of revelation in the knowledge of him, having the eyes of your hearts enlightened, that you may know what is the hope to which he has called you." As Aquinas says, it is by the "eyes of our hearts," our intellectual vision, that we will be able to see God.

The *sed contra* of the fourth article of question twelve quotes Romans 6:23, "For the wages of sin is death, but the free gift of God is eternal life

---

12. *ST* I, q. 12, a. 3, ad 3.

in Christ Jesus our Lord." Aquinas's version reads *gratia*, or grace, rather than "free gift." Guided by John 17:3, Aquinas adds that eternal life is the vision of God. If so, then the vision of God comes through grace rather than through the capacities of nature. The point is that by the natural powers of the intellect, we cannot see God's essence. This can be shown by philosophical reflection as well. Aquinas remarks, "If therefore the mode of anything's being exceeds the mode of the knower, it must result that the knowledge of that object is above the nature of the knower."[13] This is certainly the case with God's being as compared to the finite mode of knowing of both humans and angels.

The *sed contra* of article six includes a quotation from 1 Corinthians 15:41, "Star differs from star in glory." Aquinas uses this quotation to support his contention that eternal life is not the same for each of the blessed. Some experience the fullness of beatific vision more intensely than others, depending on the degree of charity that they achieved in their earthly lives by cooperating with the grace of the Holy Spirit. In this section of 1 Corinthians, Paul does indeed emphasize that "not all flesh is alike" (1 Cor 15:39) and that the celestial bodies differ not only from terrestrial bodies, but also from each other. On this basis he turns to his main argument, which is that the human body "is sown a physical body" and "raised a spiritual body" (1 Cor 15:44). Although he does not say it explicitly, it is possible that the diversity that he describes in the first half of the argument (including 1 Corinthians 15:41) implies a diversity among "spiritual bodies" and thus among the blessed.

Article seven asks whether the blessed, in seeing God's essence, comprehend or exhaustively understand the infinite God. An objection draws together two Pauline texts, Philippians 3:12 ("I press on to make it my own [*sequor autem si quo modo comprehendum*]") and 1 Corinthians 9:24–26 ("So run that you may obtain it ... I do not run aimlessly [*Sic currite, ut comprehendatis ... sic curro, non quasi in incertum*]"). The objector uses the presence of the Latin verb "comprehendere" in these two passages as an argument in favor of the view that Paul "presses on" or "runs," not aimlessly or with any doubt about the goal, in order to comprehend God in

---

13. *ST* I, q. 12, a. 4.

eternal life. Aquinas replies to the objection by stating that believers will attain to God but will not comprehend him in the sense of containing the infinite in our finite intellect.

Article nine asks whether the blessed see God's essence directly or through "similitudes" (as we understand things in this world through images and concepts). The problem is that if we see God through finite "similitudes," then we cannot truly be said to see the infinite God. Aquinas's conclusion is that God unites himself to the intellects of the blessed in such a way that the blessed have direct knowledge of God, rather than knowing God through similitudes. An objection quotes 2 Corinthians 12:4, "He heard things that cannot be told, which man may not utter." Augustine, in commenting on this Pauline text, considered that Paul had an experience of rapture in which he saw the divine essence. In his answer to the objection, Aquinas replies that while Paul may have experienced such a rapture, Paul's reflection on what he was seeing (a reflection that requires similitudes or concepts) could not have been the same as his seeing of God's essence.

The first objection of article eleven defends the claim that one can see God's essence in this life. Jacob seems to have done this, according to his words in Genesis 32:30, "I have seen God face to face, and yet my life is preserved." Such face-to-face knowledge, as Aquinas notes in the objection, seems to be what Paul promises that the blessed will receive in heaven: "For now we see in a mirror dimly, but then face to face. Now I know in part; then I shall understand fully, even as I have been fully understood" (1 Cor 13:12). Answering this objection, Aquinas follows Pseudo-Dionysius in holding that in the Old Testament, people are said to see God when "certain figures are formed in the senses or imagination, according to some similitude representing in part the divinity," as can happen in infused contemplation.[14]

Article twelve returns to a topic that Aquinas already treated in question two, namely whether in this life we can know God by "natural reason." In this article he adds an element that was not present in the earlier question: the problem of sin. Both the just and the unjust have use of the natural powers of the human mind, since sin does not remove our natural

---

14. *ST* I, q. 12, a. 11, ad 1.

powers. In Book I of *On the Trinity*, however, Augustine appears to say that only the just—that is, only those purified by faith—can know the divine light. In his *sed contra*, Aquinas cites again Romans 1:19–20, "For what can be known about God is plain to them, because God has shown it to them. Ever since the creation of the world his invisible nature, namely, his eternal power and deity, has been clearly perceived in the things that have been made." He affirms that although no one but the just can see God, nonetheless the unjust (demons and wicked humans) are able to know God by natural reason, since sin does not deprive the unjust of the ability to reason from effect to cause. Aquinas is not unaware of the problems that sin causes for the intellect's ability to know that God exists,[15] but neither can he admit that sin negates this ability. In his reply to the objection, Aquinas notes that Augustine, in his *Retractions*, retracts the strong form of his position.

Given the dark character of our knowledge of the infinite God in this life, Aquinas lastly inquires in question twelve, article thirteen whether grace really gives us a better understanding of God in this life than we can obtain from natural reason. Even by the light of grace, we cannot in this life know "what God is." Aquinas replies by observing that the grace of the Holy Spirit both strengthens our natural light, and adds significantly to our knowledge of God's effects (by which we come to know God). As he says, "Although by the revelation of grace in this life we cannot know of God *what He is*, and thus are united to Him as to one unknown; still we know Him more fully according as many and more excellent of His effects are demonstrated to us, and according as we attribute to Him some things known by divine revelation," as for example that God is triune.[16] The importance of the grace of the Holy Spirit for our knowledge of God in this life is confirmed by Aquinas in his *sed contra* through Paul's remark that what "God has revealed to us through the Spirit" (1 Cor 2:10) is something that "[n]one of the rulers of this age understood" (1 Cor 2:8), where these "rulers" are supposed by Aquinas (following the medieval gloss) to be the Greek philosophers.

---

15. On this latter point, see *ST* II-II, q. 1, a. 5; *ST* II-II, q. 2, a. 4; *ST* II-II, q. 15, aa. 1–3; *ST* I, q. 13, a. 9.
16. *ST* I, q. 12, a. 13, ad 1.

It is difficult to evaluate Aquinas's use of Paul in question twelve's investigation of how we know God. On the one hand, Aquinas makes use of Pauline texts that help us to understand what Paul experienced and hoped for as regards knowing God. Paul calls us all to receive from the Father "a spirit of wisdom and of revelation in the knowledge of him, having the eyes of your hearts enlightened, that you may know what is the hope to which he has called you, what are the riches of his glorious inheritance in the saints, and what is the immeasurable greatness of his power in us who believe" (Eph 1:17–19). Here and now, the grace of the Holy Spirit does indeed give us a much richer experiential knowledge of God. We rejoice in what "God has revealed to us through the Spirit" (1 Cor 2:10). Beyond what is available to us in simple faith, God can bestow upon us particular gifts, such as Paul's ecstatic experience in which he "was caught up into Paradise—whether in the body or out of the body I do not know, God knows—and he heard things that cannot be told, which man may not utter" (2 Cor 12:3–4). There is also a knowledge of God available to us through the use of created rationality, by which we can reason from finite and contingent beings to the creator. Idolatry involves not only in the rejection of the grace of the Holy Spirit but also the rejection of the created gift of reason: "For what can be known about God is plain to them, because God has shown it to them. Ever since the creation of the world his invisible nature, namely, his eternal power and deity, has been clearly perceived in the things that have been made" (Rom 1:19–20).

Regarding eternal life, Paul affirms that our knowledge of God then will be far greater than the knowledge we possess now. He says that "now we see in a mirror dimly, but then face to face. Now I know in part; then I shall understand fully, even as I have been fully understood" (1 Cor 13:12). Paul does everything in hope of attaining to this eternal union with God. For this reason it is appropriate that Aquinas in question twelve quotes Philippians 3:12, where Paul says, "Not that I have already obtained this or am already perfect; but I press on to make it my own, because Christ Jesus has made me his own," and 1 Corinthians 9:26–27, "I do not run aimlessly, I do not box as one beating the air; but I pommel my body and subdue it, lest after preaching to others I myself should be disqualified." It seems possible, too, that Paul's statement that "star differs from star in

The Triune God

glory" can be applied to the blessed in eternal life, since Paul is making an argument about the condition of the blessed in the resurrection and the kingdom of God.

On the other hand, we can also recognize that Aquinas's use of Paul in this question runs into certain problems. For one, in this condensed space he is not able to make a case that Paul does indeed look forward to the vision of the divine essence. Paul employs different language in this regard. Although I think that one can make the case that Aquinas's understanding of beatific vision articulates what is required by Paul's desire for "face to face" knowledge of God, Aquinas cannot make the case here. When Paul appears in the objections, Paul's meaning is sometimes distorted, as in the case where Aquinas's objector depends upon the Latin verb *comprehendere*. Similarly, Aquinas's reading of Romans 6:23, "the free gift of God is eternal life in Christ Jesus our Lord," significantly stretches Paul's meaning by applying this to the vision of the divine essence. Even so, when read in the context of Paul's other statements, one can agree that God's free gift of eternal life cannot be less than the filial knowledge of adopted sons in the Son, and thus cannot be less than beatific vision.

PAUL IN QUESTIONS 13–22

In question thirteen, on analogous naming of God, article five lays out Aquinas's central principles. Since his argument here relies upon the relationship of effect to cause, it is no surprise to find once more (in his *respondeo*) a quotation of Romans 1:20, "Ever since the creation of the world his invisible nature, namely, his eternal power and deity, has been clearly perceived in the things that have been made." Aquinas uses Paul's statement as a way of refuting the notion that our language refers to God only equivocally, as if God's transcendence meant that we can say nothing true about God. There are only two other quotations of Paul in question thirteen. In article six, asking whether the words that we apply to God (such as "good") are primarily predicated of creatures rather than of God, Aquinas in his *sed contra* quotes Ephesians 3:14–15 by way of showing that Paul considers certain names to be primarily predicated of God. In this passage Paul says that "I bow my knees before the Father, from whom every family in heaven and on earth is named." The name "father," in other words, applies first to God, because all families come from him, and only secondarily to human fathers. Paul's meaning may not be the philosophical one that Aquinas identifies, but Aquinas's interpretation is consonant with what Paul says.

In the ninth article Aquinas takes up the question of whether the name "God" can be shared, as seems to be the case since "God" (*deus*) and the "gods" (*dii*) share a name. Aquinas considers that "this name *God* is incommunicable in reality, but communicable in opinion; just as in the same way as this name *sun* would be communicable according to the opinion of those who say that there are many suns."[17] As an example of the use of the word "god" to designate things *believed* to be god, Aquinas quotes Paul's warning to the Galatians, "Formerly, when you did not know God, you were in bondage to beings that by nature are no gods; but now that you have come to know God, how can you turn back again to the weak and beggarly elemental spirits, whose slaves you want to be once more?" (Gal 4:8–9). Paul does not here suppose that there are many beings that by nature are gods, but instead Paul uses the term "gods" to register the belief in gods (which he connects with demon worship).

In question fourteen, on God's knowledge, Aquinas quotes Paul six times, though never more than once per article. The first quotation occurs in the *sed contra* of article one. He cites Paul's praise of God's wisdom, "O the depth of the riches and wisdom and knowledge of God! How unsearchable are his judgments and how inscrutable his ways!" (Rom 11:33). Paul means here to emphasize the mystery of God's plan of election, and it is evident that Paul considers God's will to be rooted in God's all-encompassing wisdom. Aquinas concludes from this that God must have perfect knowledge, a conclusion that he defends metaphysically as well. In article two, Aquinas considers God's knowledge of himself: can we say anything about how God knows himself, and specifically about whether God knows himself exhaustively? Paul's statement that "no one comprehends the thoughts of God except the Spirit of God" (1 Cor 2:11) constitutes the *sed contra* of this article. Whatever else Paul means to say, he

---

17. *ST* I, q. 13, a. 9.

certainly makes clear that God knows himself exhaustively. Articles five and six both quote Hebrews 4:12–13 in their *sed contra*. These articles ask whether God knows things other than himself, and if so how he could know them by his proper knowledge. This is a problem that Aristotle could not resolve, and it led Aristotle to assume that Pure Act can have no knowledge of the cosmos. Hebrews 4:12–13 says the opposite: "For the word of God is living and active, sharper than any two-edged sword, piercing to the division of soul and spirit, of joints and marrow, and discerning the thoughts and intentions of the heart. And before him no creature is hidden, but all are open and laid bare to the eyes of him with whom we have to do." Aquinas philosophically defends this claim in dialogue with Aristotle's *Metaphysics*.

In article eight of question fourteen, Aquinas investigates whether God causes things by his knowledge of them, or whether their existence is the cause of God's knowledge of them. He concludes that God's knowledge, joined to his will, is indeed the cause of all things. In an objection, Aquinas quotes Romans 8:30 in light of Origen's interpretation of this passage. Origen held that when Paul says that "those whom he called he also justified," Paul means that God knows future things not because he causes them but because they will happen. Aquinas argues that Origen's position can only be true in the sense that the future things that God knows certainly will happen. Does God know all things that could happen, including things that are not? Aquinas addresses this topic in article nine, and takes as his *sed contra* Romans 4:17, where Paul describes God as the one "who gives life to the dead and calls into existence the things that do not exist." If God did not know things that are not, he could not call them into existence. Aquinas reasons that anything that is or that could be in any way must be known by God, since God's actuality and power are infinite.

Questions fifteen, sixteen, and seventeen treat the divine ideas, truth, and falsity. These questions are highly philosophical and contain no quotations of Paul. Question eighteen asks whether God should be said to be "living," and it too does not cite Paul. Question nineteen, on God's will, contains fewer quotations of Paul than perhaps we might expect, but it does have five quotations of Paul (although never more than once in an article). Romans 12:2 provides the *sed contra* for the first article, on whether there is will in God. Here Paul exhorts his congregation, "Do not be conformed to this world but be transformed by the renewal of your mind, that you may prove what is the will of God, what is good and acceptable and perfect." It follows that will is in God, just as knowledge is—although as Aquinas hastens to add, God is supremely simple and therefore his knowledge and will are not different from his existence. The second article, which explores whether God wills things other than himself, also is anchored by a quotation of Paul in the *sed contra*. The text that Aquinas chooses is 1 Thessalonians 4:3, "For this is the will of God, your sanctification." Paul goes on to specify what God wills us to do in order to be holy. Aquinas takes the text to be clear evidence that God wills things other than God, and it certainly does show this (even if Paul was not intending to make the philosophical point). The *sed contra* of the third article again quotes Paul, this time Ephesians 1:11, where Paul speaks of "the purpose of him [God] who accomplishes all things according to the counsel of his will." Aquinas uses this passage to defend the view that no necessity constrains God's will as regards things other than God. Rather, as Paul makes clear, God accomplishes all things that he has freely willed to come to be. Aquinas observes that God necessarily wills only himself; creation and redemption are God's free acts.

Article six asks whether God's will is always fulfilled. Aquinas answers that as the universal cause of things, God's will cannot be frustrated, even if certain particular causes are frustrated (by other particular causes) in their effect. Here the most significant objection comes from 1 Timothy 2:4, where Paul states that God "desires all men to be saved and to come to the knowledge of the truth." Since it seems that not all humans are saved, at least if the testimony of Jesus is to be taken at face value, then it would appear that God's will is frustrated by permanently unrepentant sinners. Aquinas reviews various solutions to this dilemma and concludes that the best one is that of John of Damascus, who distinguishes between two aspects of God's eternal will: God's antecedent will, which wills that all be saved (and which does not come to pass), and God's consequent will, which takes into account permanent human rebellion and wills some to be punished in hell.

Article eight has to do with whether God's will, which cannot be ultimately frustrated, imposes necessity even on free creatures. Thus, for example, if God predestines a person from eternity, is that person truly free with respect to the choice of whether or not to love God? Aquinas answers that God wills that rational creatures be free, so that "God wills some things to be done necessarily, some contingently."[18] Again the most significant objection is taken from Paul, in this case Romans 9:19, where Paul asks, "For who can resist his will?" Paul makes clear that no one can, but this does not thereby deprive us of freedom. To account for this, Aquinas notes that it is God's will that some things happen through free causes.

Question twenty treats God's love, and its fourth and final article contains two citations of Paul. This fourth article is about whether God loves better things more. Aquinas answers yes, both because God's love is the cause of the goodness that things possess, and because better things are more lovable. As Aquinas puts it, "God's loving one thing more than another is nothing else than His willing for that thing a greater good."[19] Paul has a role in two of the objections. One objection concludes that God loves sinners more than he loves Christ, because God "did not spare his own Son but gave him up for us all" (Rom 8:32). Quoting Hebrews 2:16, "For surely it is not with angels that he [God] is concerned but with the descendants of Abraham," another objection observes that God loves humans more than angels, despite the fact that angels are ontologically better. Aquinas replies to the first objection by observing that God loved Christ above all things in two ways: by giving him the divine glory (as the incarnate Son) and by enabling him to conquer sin on behalf of all humankind. He replies to the second objection by noting that human nature and angelic nature are equal in terms of grace and glory, although human nature is privileged above angelic nature through the incarnation, a privilege that God gave humans because otherwise all of us would have been lost through sin.

Question twenty-one, on God's justice and mercy, has four articles

---

18. *ST* I, q. 19, a. 8.
19. *ST* I, q. 20, a. 4.

and five references to Paul, two of which are found in article one. Ephesians 1:11, where Paul states that God "accomplishes all things according to the counsel of his will," poses a problem for Aquinas's view that there is justice in God. It seems that God works simply according to his arbitrary will rather than in accord with any standard of justice. This problem is answered by Aquinas by means of a distinction: God acts toward creatures in accord with distributive justice but not in accord with commutative justice. The latter is not possible between God and creatures, because creatures do not stand before God as equals in an exchange of goods. Aquinas quotes Romans 11:35 in this regard, "Or who has given a gift to him [God] that he might be repaid?" Distributive justice is present in God, by contrast, because God gives to each creature what is proper to it. Through such justice, God does not place himself in the position of a debtor toward creatures, but instead gives himself what is due to himself. Aquinas explains, "It is due to God that there should be fulfilled in creatures what His will and wisdom require, and what manifests His goodness."[20]

Mercy consists in the removal of defects without requiring that justice be met. In article three, Aquinas notes that mercy is one of God's attributes, since he bestows good gifts, in particular the forgiveness of sins, in order to make up for the defects he finds in his rational creatures. Aquinas specifies that "God acts mercifully, not indeed by going against His justice, but by doing something more than justice."[21] In pardoning rebellion against himself, he does not act unjustly toward anyone, but instead bestows a gift upon the sinner. An important objection to this position comes from 2 Timothy 2:13 (to which I add verses 11–12): "The saying is sure: If we have died with him, we shall also live with him; if we endure, we shall also reign with him; if we deny him, he also will deny us; if we are faithless, he remains faithful—for he cannot deny himself." The objection quotes 2 Timothy 2:13 with the aim of arguing that God cannot deny his own justice, and therefore he can never act mercifully. We have already noted Aquinas's answer, which is that God's mercy goes beyond justice but does not violate it. He confirms this answer by means of Paul's command, "Be kind to one another, tenderhearted, forgiving one another, as

---

20. *ST* I, q. 21, a. 1, ad 3.
21. *ST* I, q. 21, a. 3, ad 2.

God in Christ forgave you" (Eph 4:32). We must imitate God in being merciful.

Article four asks whether each of God's works contains both justice and mercy. In an objection, Aquinas quotes Romans 15:8–9, where Paul seems to separate Christ's justice (or covenant fidelity) from Christ's mercy: "For I tell you that Christ became a servant to the circumcised to show God's truthfulness, in order to confirm the promises given to the patriarchs, and in order that the Gentiles might glorify God for his mercy." The same action of Christ, it seems, embodies truthfulness or justice with respect to the Jews, and mercy with respect to the Gentiles. Aquinas explains that every work of God is a work of justice, both because each work contains the good order and proportion that belong to distributive justice, and because in mercifully providing for us, God pays what is owed to himself as the good and wise creator. Similarly every work of God is a work of mercy, because creatures in themselves are owed nothing; all creatures are, at bottom, God's sheer gift. In reply to the objection from Romans 15:8–9, Aquinas observes that Christ's action is one of both justice and mercy toward Jews and Gentiles, but with a unique aspect of justice vis-à-vis Jews, namely the fulfillment of God's covenantal promises to Israel.

Question twenty-two treats God's providence. In the four articles of this question, Aquinas rather surprisingly quotes Paul only four times, three instances of which are found in article two. Article one addresses whether providence is indeed an attribute of God. Aquinas answers in the affirmative by defining providence as God's wise plan for the ordering of creatures to their ultimate end. The first objection argues that since God is eternal, he has no need to take counsel, and so he does not need prudence or practical wisdom (providence). Aquinas replies that God must have a wise plan for the ordering of things, a plan that is carried out by his command. This plan or wisdom regarding things to be done is his providence. Aquinas supports this claim about God's providence by quoting Ephesians 1:11, where Paul describes "the purpose of him who accomplishes all things according to the counsel of his will." This purpose is God's providence.

Article two asks the most pressing and difficult question, namely whether all things fall under God's providence. It would seem that there is too much evil for such to be the case, and there is also the issue of the freedom that God has given rational creatures to employ for better or worse. Furthermore, why would God's providence include irrational animals and other non-rational creatures? Maimonides had limited God's providence to human beings, and in an objection Aquinas makes the same point by quoting 1 Corinthians 9:9, where Paul asks rhetorically, "Is it for oxen that God is concerned?" In his *respondeo* Aquinas observes that God's providence must extend to all things, because "the causality of God, who is the first agent, extends to all being, not only as to constituent principles of species, but also as to the individualizing principles.... Hence all things that exist in whatsoever manner are necessarily directed by God towards some end."[22] He supports this position with Paul's statement that the authorities "that exist have been instituted by God" (Rom 13:1). In Aquinas's version, this text reads "*quae a Deo sunt, ordinata sunt*," conveying the sense that everything that is from God is well ordered. Whether the translation is "instituted" or "*ordinata sunt*," however, Paul has in view only the "governing authorities," the political rulers (such as the Roman emperor). Aquinas's use of this text here, while not original to him, is something of a stretch, although one might suppose that if even the Roman emperor is under God's providential order, then all things are.

Somewhat more successful, I think, is his quotation in the same article of Romans 8:28, "We know that in everything God works for good with those who love him" (Aquinas's version reads "*diligentibus Deum omnia cooperantur in bonum*" [to those who love God, all things work together for good]). In either translation, Paul's fundamental meaning is clear: God ensures that nothing thwarts the salvation of his elect. Aquinas concludes from this that God's providence extends uniquely over the just, whereas the wicked are in a certain sense abandoned to their rebellion. One can also see that if God fully ensures that nothing thwarts the salvation of his elect, it must follow that "everything happening from the exercise of free will must be subject to divine providence."[23]

Let us review the place of Paul in questions 13–22. Paul's place is significant, but is it central? Aquinas's treatment of analogy begins with Ro-

---

22. *ST* I, q. 22, a. 2.
23. *ST* I, q. 22, a. 2, ad 4.

mans 1:20 as a confirmation both of the cause-effect relationship required by analogy, and of the impossibility that our naming God is equivocal. When we name God, moreover, we do not simply name creatures primarily and God only in a derivative and secondary way. Rather, the names that we use apply primarily to God. In this regard Aquinas employs Ephesians 3:14–15, in which Paul, in a richly rhetorical passage, proclaims that all human families are named from the divine Father, who causes all humans to be; this passage requires that the name "father" apply primarily to God. Aquinas also finds help in Galatians 4:18 for explaining how the same word "god" can name both false gods and the living God.

It would be a stretch to identify Paul as a key source for Aquinas's theology of naming God, but nonetheless the ways in which Paul insists that God can be named—from "the things that have been made," from human paternity, and from reflection on the meaning of the word "god"—have significant value for the project of naming the creator God who reveals himself in Israel.

Aquinas employs Paul relatively frequently in his questions on divine knowledge and will, whereas his more philosophical questions on the divine ideas, truth and falsity, and the divine "life" do not need Paul. On the divine knowledge, Aquinas nicely puts together the key Pauline texts: God supereminently possesses wisdom and knowledge, in a manner that goes far beyond what we can comprehend (Romans 11:33); God's Spirit comprehends God, so that God fully knows himself (1 Corinthians 2:11); no creature is hidden from God's sight (Hebrews 4:13); God knows his elect from eternity (Romans 8:30); from eternity God knows things that are future in time and God brings them into existence (Romans 4:17). This Pauline portrait of God's knowledge is rich indeed in its scope and implications, which Aquinas develops and specifies through philosophical reflection. The same is true for Aquinas's selection of Pauline texts on God's will (question nineteen). God wills only "what is good and acceptable and perfect" (Rom 12:2); God wills our sanctification (1 Thessalonians 4:3); God's will is efficacious (Ephesians 1:11); God wills that all humans be saved, although as Aquinas says this seems to be God's antecedent will (1 Timothy 2:4); no one can resist God's will (Romans 9:19). Indeed, as this Pauline portrait of God's will shows, no one would want to resist God's will because his will is nothing other than infinite love and infinite goodness. In creating from eternity, God ensures that the infinite love and goodness with which he creates is not frustrated by the rebellion of his rational creatures. He ensures that, despite the sin and suffering so prevalent in our world, his good and loving purpose will be accomplished. Just as Aquinas manages to display the infinite range and personal intimacy of God's knowledge, so also he displays the goodness, power, and presence of God's will. These texts from Paul beautifully characterize the God whom Christians worship.

It seems fair to say, too, that the impact of Paul's portrait of God in Aquinas's questions on God's knowledge and will becomes more apparent when one lines up the various Pauline texts and notes how they complement each other. Together, they express a powerful doctrine of the transcendent God knowing and loving his people. In the individual articles, this cumulative power is not as visible, insofar as the various Pauline quotations have differing functions within the articles. There are a number of Pauline quotations that play a major and obvious role, and these quotations are generally in the *sed contra*. But there are also Pauline quotations that play a negligible role, and a few quotations are put to a use that is different from Paul's meaning. It is when they are seen as a whole that their full significance for Aquinas's portrait of God is manifest.

This is certainly the case for the quotations of Paul in questions 20–22, on God's love, justice and mercy, and providence. Aquinas's treatment of God's love in question twenty emphasizes that God's love is causal of created goodness. This emphasis accentuates the mystery of why God permits the permanent rebellion of some rational creatures, because God appears to withhold the causal love that would have saved these rational creatures. It is therefore noteworthy that Aquinas outlines the scope of God's love more fully by means of two quotations from Paul. God is the one who loves the human race so much that he "did not spare his own Son but gave him up for us all" (Rom 8:32), and God is the one who reaches out to the human race in Christ Jesus rather than uniting himself with the highest angels. Similarly, as we find in question twenty-one, God's will is just rather than arbitrary (Ephesians 1:11); God is supremely the giver, so that we stand in a position of gratitude rather than of pride in our own gifts (Romans 11:35); we must forgive each other as God in Christ has forgiven us (Ephesians 4:32); and in showing mercy in Christ to the human race, God demonstrates his justice toward Israel by keeping his covenants (Romans 15:8–9). The God of love, mercy, and justice is the covenantal God of Israel. He is the Giver of all gifts, not in an arbitrary fashion but in love guided by supreme wisdom and fidelity. He is profoundly forgiving, to the point of taking on human flesh and dying for us. This is Paul's portrait of God, and it is Aquinas's as well. As a further indication of Paul's significance here, the tensions in Paul's presentation of God with respect to election and predestination are also reflected in Aquinas.

Regarding God's providence (question twenty-two), Paul's major contribution to Aquinas's treatment is the text from Ephesians 1:11, which emphasizes "the purpose of him who accomplishes all things according to the counsel of his will." This passage has a Christological aspect in its context: Paul is arguing that "we who first hoped in Christ have been destined and appointed to live for the praise of his glory" (Eph 1:12). Aquinas similarly cites Romans 8:28, which holds that God ensures that nothing can thwart his elect from reaching their goal of union with him. These Pauline passages support the truth that Jesus Christ is at the center of God's wise ordering of all things toward their goal. Aquinas's account of providence is not a solely philosophical postulate. The role of Paul in Aquinas's theology of providence is therefore highly significant, despite the paucity of Pauline quotations in Aquinas's treatment of this theme.

Does Paul have a central place, then, in questions 13–22? Yes and no. On the negative side, when viewed in terms of particular quotations in this set of ten questions as a whole, Paul's letters cannot be said to possess a central place in Aquinas's argumentation, which after all is largely philosophical. Four of the ten questions have no Pauline citations. The presence of Paul in Aquinas's theology of divine naming, divine love, divine mercy and justice, and divine providence is too sporadic to be called central. This is especially the case in his question on divine providence, where Aquinas surprisingly quotes Paul in only two of the four articles. Yet, on the positive side, I note that eight times in these ten questions, a Pauline quotation anchors the *sed contra*, including four times in Aquinas's question on God's knowledge and three times in his question on God's will. These two pivotal questions (fourteen and nineteen) give a central place to Paul. Since these questions are central to Aquinas's exposition, then so, arguably, is Paul. Similarly, Paul appears at significant junctures of Aquinas's account of analogy. Aquinas's question on divine love includes Paul only in the fourth article, but the quotations from Paul manifest crucial aspects of God's love. The few quotations of Paul in Aquinas's question on providence serve to confirm the centrality of Jesus Christ in God's providential ordering, surely a significant point. The quotations of Paul in Aquinas's question on God's justice and mercy at first glance might seem rather minor in Aquinas's argument, but they show themselves to be more valuable when viewed as a whole (and together with earlier quotations). When all the quotations of Paul in these ten questions are gathered together, the impact of Paul's portrait of God becomes especially clear.

PAUL IN QUESTIONS 23–26

In question twenty-three, Aquinas treats predestination in eight articles. This question has by far the most Pauline quotations of any question in Aquinas's treatise on the triune God. Of the nineteen Pauline quotations in question twenty-three, five are from Romans 8:28–30 and another four are from Romans 9. The other ten come from Romans 11, 1 and 2 Corinthians, Ephesians, 1 and 2 Timothy, and Titus. Four of the eight articles have a quotation of Paul in the *sed contra*, and another one of the articles quotes Malachi 1:2–3, which Paul himself quotes in Romans 9:13. It will be clear that Paul's role is particularly important in this question, with Romans 8–9 being especially prominent.

Article one, on whether God predestines human beings, quotes Paul twice. The *sed contra* is Romans 8:30, "And those whom he predestined he also called." Aquinas recognizes that Origen and John of Damascus raise questions about the meaning of the predestination in this passage (the Greek verb is προώρισεν). I noted Aquinas's view of Origen's position earlier, when discussing question fourteen, article eight. In article one of question twenty-three, Aquinas responds to John of Damascus's *On the Orthodox Faith*, where Damascene emphasizes that God's foreknowledge does not predetermine anything. Aquinas observes that predestination does not in fact impose necessity on anyone, since God's predestination of his elect, by the grace of the Holy Spirit, ensures that they *freely* choose to embrace God. Predestination is nothing more than what is required by the fact that the end toward which God, in his eternal providence, orders some human creatures is an end that is attainable only by grace: for rational creatures to be united to the trinitarian life, God must draw us to himself in a manner beyond what our natural powers can accomplish. Predestination, therefore, is a special part of providence corresponding to the reality that some rational creatures have an end that can be obtained only with the help of the grace of the Holy Spirit.

In the same article, Aquinas also quotes in an objection 1 Corinthians 2:12, "Now we have received not the spirit of the world, but the Spirit which is from God, that we might understand the gifts bestowed on us by God." It seems to follow from this passage that if the Holy Spirit in us enables us to understand the gifts that God has given us, then the predestined would be able to know their predestination. Since no one can know whether he or she is predestined (except by a special divine revelation), the objection concludes that God does not give the gift of predestination. In his reply to the objection, Aquinas explains that the Holy Spirit does not allow us to understand whether God has given us the gift of predestination, because such knowledge would not serve the growth of charity in us: we would either despair or become presumptuous.

The second article asks whether God's predestination is in the predestined as well as in God. Aquinas answers that predestination is solely God's eternal plan for the ordering of some of his rational creatures to a supernatural end; predestination is not a temporal reality. Although this eternal plan therefore "does not put anything in the predestined," God's execution of this plan in time does have an effect in the predestined, namely the effect of grace. In this article Aquinas twice quotes Romans. First, in an objection, he quotes Paul's statement that Christ was "designated Son of God in power" (Rom 1:4). Aquinas's version of this verse reads that Christ was the predestined (*praedestinatus est*) Son of God. The point of the objection is to argue that only an existing person can be "destined" or "predestined," and so predestination cannot be God's eternal plan for his elect but instead can only characterize existing persons. Aquinas replies that from eternity God can predestine persons who do not yet exist in time. Second, Aquinas quotes Romans 8:30 in his *respondeo*, in order to describe the execution in time of God's eternal predestination. This execution consists in our being "called" and "justified."[24]

In article three, Aquinas asks whether God reprobates anyone. "Reprobation," he explains, "differs in its causality from predestination."[25] Predestination causes grace and glory in the human person, whereas reprobation does not cause sin but instead only causes what follows upon sin, namely the punishment of being abandoned to our sin (both now and forever). This article does not contain a direct quotation of Paul, but its *sed contra* is Malachi 1:2–3, "I have loved Jacob but I have hated Esau," which Paul quotes in Romans 9:13. For Aquinas, God's love for Jacob is God's predestination or election of Jacob, while God's hatred for Esau is God's reprobation or abandonment of Esau—an abandonment caused by Esau's freely chosen sins.

Article four inquires into whether God chooses the predestined. In an objection, Aquinas notes that it would seem that the answer is no, because as Paul says, God "desires all men to be saved and to come to the knowledge of the truth" (1 Tim 2:4). The objection concludes that if God truly willed that all humans be saved, then he could not choose only some as predestined from eternity for union with him. Yet in the *sed contra*, Aquinas quotes a passage from Paul that makes clear that from eternity God does choose some (not all) humans for union with him. Speaking specifically about Christian believers, Paul states that God "chose us in him [Christ] before the foundation of the world, that we should be holy and blameless before him. He destined us in love to be his sons through Jesus Christ, according to the purpose of his will, to the praise of his glorious grace which he freely bestowed on us in the Beloved" (Eph 1:4–6). Paul emphasizes that God makes this choice "before the foundation of the world," in other words from eternity. In his *respondeo* Aquinas comments that because predestination is a special part of providence, "Predestination presupposes election in the order of reason; and election presupposes

---

24. Aquinas's version has *magnificavit* here, but Aquinas interprets it in the sense of justification.

25. *ST* I, q. 23, a. 3, ad 2.

love."²⁶ God's choice or election means that he wills this particular good (beatific communion with God) to some humans. Since God's love causes good, his love is the reason for his choice (election), and his choice is the reason for predestination. In his love, he chooses the elect from eternity, so as to predestine them. As before, Aquinas handles 1 Timothy 2:4 by appealing to the distinction between God's antecedent and consequent will.

In the fifth article, Aquinas addresses the topic of whether God's foreknowledge of human merits is the cause of predestination, so that God's love and choice would not be rooted solely in the mystery of God's wisdom and will. This was the opinion of the semi-Pelagians, and many theologians over the centuries have shared this view. Aquinas shows that it is an untenable position, however, by quoting Paul's insistence that solely God's will is the cause of election: "When Rebecca had conceived children by one man, our forefather Isaac, though they were not yet born and had done nothing either good or bad, in order that God's purpose of election might continue, not because of works but because of his call, she was told, 'The elder will serve the younger'" (Rom 9:10–12). The point is that God's election is strictly "not by works but because of his call." Had God foreknown the works and elected Jacob for that reason, then God's election of Jacob would indeed have been "by works." Similarly, Aquinas quotes Paul's ruling out of human boasting: "Not that we are sufficient of ourselves to claim anything as coming from us; our sufficiency is from God" (2 Cor 3:5). Were God to elect anyone because of his or her foreseen merits, that person would have a right to claim a "sufficiency" based on his or her works.

Aquinas makes clear, then, that "why He [God] chooses some for glory, and reprobates others, has no reason, except the divine will."²⁷ We can understand God's will in this regard only so far as to be able to say that he manifests the goodness of his mercy in those whom he elects, and he manifests the goodness of his justice in those whom he permits to choose permanent rebellion. This is the way in which Aquinas makes sense of Paul's teaching that God "has endured with much patience the vessels of

---

26. *ST* I, q. 23, a. 4.
27. *ST* I, q. 23, a. 5, ad 3.

wrath made for destruction, in order to make known the riches of his glory for the vessels of mercy, which he has prepared beforehand for glory" (Rom 9:22–23) and, along similar lines, "In a great house there are not only vessels of gold and silver but also of wood and earthenware, and some for noble use, some for ignoble" (2 Tim 2:20). The latter passage belongs to an exhortation to purify oneself of sin and strive to be "a vessel for noble use" (2 Tim 2:21), but the fact remains that God has arranged the world so that there are these two kinds of vessels. If we are a "vessel for noble use," we cannot puff up with pride, because God's utterly free love and choice, from eternity, are the source of our goodness.

In article five's discussion of whether predestination is caused by God's foreknowledge of our merits, the *sed contra* rather surprisingly does not come from Romans. Instead it comes from Paul's statement in Titus 3:5 that God "saved us, not because of deeds done by us in righteousness, but in virtue of his own mercy." In context, Titus 3:5 is an encomium to the saving work of Christ and the Holy Spirit rather than a statement about God's eternal will. Yet the point is that had God saved us in Christ and the Holy Spirit because God foreknew our merits, rather than strictly out of his love and mercy, than our salvation would have its cause in ourselves. This is what Paul—and Aquinas—wish to rule out.

The objections in article five contain three quotations from Romans. The first objection quotes Romans 8:29, "For those whom he foreknew he also predestined to be conformed to the image of his Son," and Romans 9:15, "I [God] will have mercy on whom I have mercy." Ambrose, like many church fathers, drew these passages together by commenting that God will have mercy on those who, in God's foreknowledge, God knows will turn to him. Aquinas replies that God does not choose his elect on the basis of his foreknowledge of their merits, but rather their merits come because God eternally loves and chooses them. The third objection quotes Romans 9:14, "Is there injustice on God's part? By no means!" As the objection points out, humans are equal both with respect to the possession of human nature and with respect to the possession of original sin. It therefore seems unjust for God, from eternity, to plan to give some humans—but not all—the gift of eternal life in union with him. Aquinas answers that God has a plan for the participation of creatures in his goodness, and this plan includes a wide variety of degrees of participation: some manifest his goodness by means of his mercy, and others by means of his justice. God's goodness requires that he give all his creatures a share in his goodness, but God's goodness does not require that all creatures share equally or in the same way. Predestination to union with God is a sheer gift and therefore cannot be demanded in justice by any creature. This answer helps because it places the focus where it should be—God's goodness and the gratuity of his gifting—but it does not fully resolve the problem, which remains an inscrutable mystery.

The sixth article, on whether predestination is certain, quotes Romans 8:29 in the *sed contra*. Aquinas's goal in this article is to distinguish predestination from necessity, while also insisting that predestination infallibly takes effect. All those who are predestined from eternity will indeed be united to God forever. Yet this is not necessity, because, as Aquinas has already shown with regard to providence, God wills that some things take place through the action of free causes. The effect of predestination comes to be in a person through the exercise of (graced) free will. In the *sed contra*, however, Aquinas quotes Paul's remark that "those whom he foreknew he also predestined" (Rom 8:29) in order to cite the medieval gloss on this passage. The gloss states that all who are predestined to glory will certainly receive glory.

The seventh article takes up a similar question, whether the number of the predestined is certain. Since predestination is God's eternal plan, Aquinas affirms that the number of the predestined is indeed certain. He has a different point to make, however, when in his *respondeo* he quotes Romans 8:28, "We know that in everything God works for good with those who love him, who are called according to his purpose." Some theologians, such as Anselm, had speculated that God permitted a certain number of angels to fall and that these made room for an equal number of predestined humans. The reprobation of some angels, on this view, would work for the good of those humans whom God predestined in love. Aquinas does not accept this line of reasoning. He instead holds that the number of predestined humans is known to God alone and has no necessary relation to the number of the fallen angels.

In article eight, on whether the prayers of the saints can further the effect of predestination, Aquinas quotes Paul so as to show that nothing, including prayers, can change the eternal plan of God: "For the gifts and the call of God are irrevocable" (Rom 11:29). Although Paul obviously has in view God's faithfulness to the Jewish people rather than the abstract question of whether the plan of predestination can be changed by our prayers, Romans 11:29 certainly implies that even prayers cannot change God's plan. Aquinas does think however that prayers can further the effect of predestination. This is so because predestination's effect takes place through persons who exercise free will, including by their decision to pray that certain things might come about. The example that Aquinas gives is Isaac's prayer that his wife Rebekah might conceive a child. An objection raises the problem that if prayers can further the effect of predestination, then it would seem that God needs help in accomplishing his plan, which is contrary to Romans 11:34 in Aquinas's version (which differs from the RSV). Aquinas's version of this text reads, "Who has helped the Spirit of the Lord?" Aquinas replies to the objection by quoting 1 Corinthians 3:9: "For we are God's fellow workers." In this passage Paul is describing his apostolic ministry, but the point is clear: God's plan of predestination includes the ways in which humans, by their free actions, cooperate with God in bringing about the effect of predestination.

Question twenty-four discusses God's "Book of Life," which is mentioned a few times in scripture (for example, Psalm 69:28 and Revelation 3:5). Aquinas concludes that this book is God's knowledge of his plan of predestination. He quotes Paul only once in the three articles of this question. In the *respondeo* of the first article, on whether the book of life is the same thing as predestination, Aquinas observes that God's knowledge of predestination can be compared to a book. Just as a book stores knowledge, so also God contains within his knowledge the names of all the predestined. In this regard Aquinas cites 2 Timothy 2:19, "God's firm foundation stands, bearing this seal: 'The Lord knows those who are his.'"

Question twenty-five treats God's power. In the six articles, Paul appears only three times. Two of these references are in the third article, whose topic is whether God is all-powerful. Aquinas brings in Paul to formulate objections. Thus in 2 Timothy 2:13 Paul says that God "remains faithful—for he cannot deny himself." If he cannot deny himself, then it would seem that he is not all-powerful. Similarly, another objection cites 1 Corinthians 1:20, "Has not God made foolish the wisdom of the world?" This citation is buttressed by the gloss, which comments that the world imagined to be impossible what God has shown to be possible. The objection continues by noting that if possibility and impossibility were measured in relation to God rather than in relation to the world, then since everything is possible for God, nothing in this world would be truly impossible—and thus there would be no necessity in anything, which is false. To these objections Aquinas replies, first, that God is all-powerful with respect to active power, not to passive power, and so the fact that God cannot do some things (such as sin) does not negate his omnipotence. Second, God's omnipotence does not remove necessity from the order of created things, because possibility is said of something "in reference to its proximate cause."[28]

Article six of question twenty-five asks whether God can do better than what he actually does. The *sed contra* comes from Ephesians 3:20 (to which I add verse 21): "Now to him who by the power at work within us is able to do far more abundantly than all that we ask or think, to him be glory in the church and in Christ Jesus to all generations, for ever and ever." Paul is speaking here of the grace of the Holy Spirit in us, but it is evident that Aquinas's application of this text to God's power in general need not distort Paul's meaning. God is indeed more powerful than we can ever imagine, and so we cannot place limits on what God can do. Yet Aquinas adds two qualifications to this point. First, given the nature of a thing, God cannot make this nature to be better than it is without changing it to be another thing, and thereby destroying its present order; second, the mode of God's action can never be better than it is, because God does all that he does from infinite wisdom and goodness.

Question twenty-six addresses God's beatitude, his happiness. We find two references to Paul in the four articles. In article one, on whether happiness pertains to God, the *sed contra* consists of 1 Timothy 6:15, "This will be made manifest at the proper time by the blessed and only Sovereign, the King of kings and Lord of lords." Paul names God blessed, and, as Aquinas

---

28. *ST* I, q. 25, a. 3, ad 4.

observes, Paul does so for good reason, because true beatitude or happiness is the absolute perfection of an intellectual nature. God is infinite perfection of being and intelligence, and so he is supremely happy. Article three asks whether God is the beatitude of each of the blessed, since God is the supreme good of the blessed. Aquinas answers that the blessed each possess his or her own beatitude. The blessed do not acquire God's beatitude. Aquinas states that "as regards the act of understanding, beatitude is a created thing in beatified creatures; but in God, even in this way, it is an uncreated thing."[29] Nonetheless, the beatitude of the blessed is in fact to share to varying degrees in God. God is the beatitude of the blessed in the sense that God is the object of beatific vision. To support the view that the beatitude of the blessed consists in sharing in God (which the blessed do to varying degrees), Aquinas cites the passage we have seen above from 1 Corinthians 15:41, "Star differs from star in glory."

Let us pause to take stock of questions 23–26. What is the impact of Paul on Aquinas's treatment of predestination, the book of life, God's power, and God's beatitude? Clearly Paul plays the lead role in Aquinas's theology of predestination (although certainly not the only role, since Aquinas quotes other sources as well). The central texts are Romans 8:29, where Paul connects God's foreknowledge and predestination; and Romans 8:30, where Paul speaks of those who are predestined, called, justified. Paul teaches that God chose or predestined believers in Christ "before the foundation of the world" (Eph 1:4), and so predestination is from eternity and cannot be frustrated (Romans 11:29). Predestination is consistently positive: it is about being united to God in Christ, not about damnation. Paul addresses the possibility that God might seem to be unjust because he predestines some for mercy but does not predestine all (Romans 9:14–15, 22–23; 2 Timothy 2:20). Paul also underscores that predestination is not a reward for our goodness, but rather God is the cause of all our good. God predestines whom he wills, and the blessed owe their salvation not to their works (or to God's foreknowledge of their works) but strictly to God's all-sufficient mercy (Titus 3:14, 2 Corinthians 3:5). God, the giver of such great gifts, desires that all humans be saved (1 Timothy 2:4), and yet

---

29. *ST* I, q. 26, a. 3.

our cooperation with God is required for our salvation (1 Timothy 2:4, 1 Corinthians 3:9). That neither Paul nor Aquinas succeeds in resolving this mystery is further evidence of Aquinas's fidelity to Paul on this topic.

Regarding the book of life and God's power, Aquinas refers to Paul only in marginal ways. Certainly the quotation of 2 Timothy 2:19, "The Lord knows those who are his," is apropos to the book of life; and Aquinas takes two excellent examples of Paul's theology of God's power when he cites God's humbling of worldly wisdom (1 Corinthians 1:20) and the superabundant character of God's gifting in our lives (Ephesians 3:20). But these citations are few and far between. Nonetheless, Aquinas has already drawn heavily from Paul in his question on predestination, the themes of which are largely replicated by the question on the book of life, and in his question on God's will, the themes of which are closely related to God's power. It would be an exaggeration, then, to say that Paul plays no significant role for Aquinas's theology of the book of life and God's power. It does seem to me, however, that Aquinas's examination of God's beatitude (and ours) has little Pauline influence. Paul calls God "blessed" (1 Tim 6:15), but this is not much to go by, and Paul's usage is much less technical than is Aquinas's philosophical reasoning about what perfect beatitude involves. Even so, I cannot imagine that Paul would disagree with Aquinas here.

PAUL IN QUESTIONS 27–43

In Aquinas's treatise on the triune God, he first examines what is common to the divine persons (questions 2–26) and then what distinguishes these persons (questions 27–43). It seems clear that Paul has a fairly significant role in Aquinas's theology of what is common to the divine persons. Aquinas supports the trajectory of his thought by means of Romans 1:20, which establishes the mode of reasoning about God from effects to cause. Aquinas bolsters his theology of our knowing of God (both now and in eternal life) and of God's knowledge and will by means of relatively frequent citations of Paul. This is equally the case, as we have just seen, with respect to predestination, and Paul's influence appears also in Aquinas's theology of God's justice and mercy and (albeit less so) of God's providence. The places where Paul's influence can be most strongly found—God's knowledge, will, and predestination—are fundamental to Aquinas's portrait of what is one in God.

Regarding the distinction of divine persons, Paul's role is less than we might expect. In part this is because many of Aquinas's questions are highly technical and philosophical. They draw upon the gospels rather than Paul, and they seek to clarify the mystery of the Trinity by means of philosophical reasoning (about relation, for instance). Question twenty-seven, on the eternal procession of the Son and Holy Spirit, cites the Gospel of John twice and the First Epistle of John once, in addition to one reference to Paul. This reference aims to show that the Holy Spirit is truly God. In 1 Corinthians 6:19, Paul exhorts his congregation, "Do you not know that your body is a temple of the Holy Spirit within you, which you have from God?" The point for Paul has to do with how Christians should behave, especially in sexual matters. Aquinas, however, quotes this passage in order to support the Holy Spirit's divinity, because, as he says, only God has the right to have a temple. If the Holy Spirit can make of our bodies a "temple," then it must be that the Holy Spirit is God. Paul certainly does not have this conclusion in mind, but arguably Paul's understanding of a temple accords with Aquinas's reasoning. For Paul, too, a "temple" that is worthy of the name could hardly be indwelt by anything less than God.

In a somewhat roundabout way, then, Aquinas brings Paul in as a reference for the divinity of the Holy Spirit. The remaining four articles of question twenty-seven, however, do not quote Paul; instead, they quote the Gospel of John and the wisdom literature. Question twenty-eight, on relation in God, has no Pauline citations and in fact no biblical ones at all. Question twenty-nine, on the divine persons, is also highly philosophical and has only one quotation from Paul, namely 1 Timothy 6:20, where Paul cautions Timothy, "Avoid the godless chatter and contradictions of what is falsely called knowledge." In the context of question twenty-nine, the quotation serves to defend the use of the word "person," which is not found in scripture. Aquinas notes that such language is not "to be shunned ... for it does not lead us astray from the sense of Scripture."[30] But, while the quotation serves a useful purpose, it does not have much relation to

---

30. *ST* I, q. 29, a. 3, ad 1.

Paul's warning to Timothy and it does not do significant theoretical work in Aquinas's arguments for distinction in God.

Question thirty, on the number of divine persons, is again a very philosophical treatment; 1 John is quoted once but no other biblical texts appear. Question thirty-one has to do with how to speak about unity and plurality in God. The third article (of four) asks whether one can rightly say "God alone," since God is three persons. The *sed contra* of this article consists in 1 Timothy 1:17, "To the King of ages, immortal, invisible, the only God, be honor and glory for ever and ever." Paul's description of God as "the only God" helps Aquinas to affirm that we can rightly say "God alone." In his *respondeo*, he distinguishes grammatically between categorematical and syncategorematical terms. When "alone" is understood in the former sense, it cannot be applied to God. In the latter sense it can be applied to God, because it would then mean "nothing but God."

Question thirty-two examines how we can know that God is three persons. Although the question has four articles, all four of its citations of Paul appear in the first article. In this article Aquinas first argues that since creative power pertains to what is common to the persons, we cannot know that God is three from his effects. From his effects, we can only know that God is one. On this basis, Aquinas suggests that any attempt to demonstrate that God is three derogates from the dignity of faith, which is "the conviction of things not seen" (Heb 11:1). Among the things "not seen" by the natural powers of the intellect is the threeness of God. This is why Paul can also say that "among the mature we do impart wisdom, although it is not a wisdom of this age or of the rulers of this age, who are doomed to pass away. But we impart a secret and hidden wisdom of God, which God decreed before the ages for our glorification" (1 Cor 2:6–7). This "secret and hidden wisdom of God," Aquinas thinks, includes the revelation that God is Trinity. Although Paul's intended meaning in 1 Corinthians 2:6–7 is unclear, Aquinas's quotation of these verses, like his quotation of Hebrews 11:1, does not veer entirely away from the contextual meaning, since both 1 Corinthians and Hebrews speak of God the Father, Christ the Son, and the Spirit.

The two other Pauline quotations in this article appear in the response to the first objection. Arguing that the ancient philosophers had some idea of the Trinity, the first objection cites a passage from Aristotle's *De caelo et mundo* and Augustine's remarks in his *Confessions* about the Neoplatonists' understanding of the emanation of the word/mind. Aquinas explains that Aristotle was speaking of the use of the number three in sacrificial rituals, and that the Neoplatonists were speaking of the "word" as the "ideal type whereby God made all things," not as a distinct person.[31] Aquinas also faults the Neoplatonists for failing to recognize the Holy Spirit. He emphasizes that the ancient philosophers, whom he again equates with the "rulers of this age" about whom Paul speaks, knew some of the attributes of the one God and appropriated these to distinct emanations. They did so in such a manner that although in a certain sense they knew God, "they did not honor him as God" (Rom 1:21). The tension in Aquinas's description of the ancient philosophers is similar to what we find in Romans 1: they failed in understanding God, and yet they knew enough to be culpable.

Question thirty-three, on the person of the Father, contains five quotations from Paul, one in the second article and four in the third article. The second article asks whether "Father" is a proper or a metaphorical name of the divine person. In his answer to an objection, Aquinas draws upon his teaching on analogous naming to explain that paternity is applied primarily to God rather than to creatures "as regards the thing signified, but not as regards the mode of signification."[32] As we would expect, he quotes Ephesians 3:14 in support of his position that "Father" properly names the first person of the Trinity, who is the perfect generator or begetter of the divine Son: "I bow my knees before the Father, from whom every family in heaven and on earth is named."

The third article of question thirty-three asks whether "Father" is first applied to God as the name of the divine person or first as common to the whole creative Trinity. The third objection argues that paternity, as taken with respect to the first person, is conceptually the same as paternity as taken with respect to the whole creative Trinity. To bolster this position Aquinas quotes Colossians 1:15, "He is the image of the invisible God, the first-born of all creation." Paul here seems to equate the generation of the

---

31. *ST* I, q. 32, a. 1, ad 1.
32. *ST* I, q. 33, a. 2, ad 4.

Son with the generation of creatures, and so the name "Father" would apply equally to what is common to the persons and to what is distinct to the first person. In response Aquinas quotes John 1:18 and argues, "To *receive* is said [in Colossians 1:15] to be common to the creature and to the Son not in a univocal sense, but according to a certain remote similitude whereby He is called the First Born of creatures." In other words, Paul phrases it as he does because he wants to underscore our adoptive sonship in the Son.

Sketching the various ways that the creative Trinity is our Father, Aquinas remarks in the *respondeo* of article three that by grace we are adoptive sons, since "it is the Spirit himself bearing witness with our spirit that we are children of God, and if children, then heirs, heirs of God and fellow heirs with Christ" (Rom 8:16–17). Those who have attained to eternal glory through the grace of the Holy Spirit at work in them have God the Trinity as their Father even more fully. For this distinction, Aquinas quotes Romans 5:2, "Through him we have obtained access to this grace in which we stand, and we rejoice in our hope of sharing the glory of God" (Aquinas's version reads *"gloriae filiorum Dei"*). Paul also appears in Aquinas's answer to the first objection, which argues that the common name (Father as applied to the whole Trinity) should precede the particular name (Father as the name of the first person). Aquinas states that since the divine Word contains the ideas of how God can be participated in finite modes (creatures), the Word precedes creatures. Thus the begetter of the Word must be the one whom the name "Father" primarily signifies. As begotten by the creative Trinity, creatures have a certain likeness to the Word. This likeness is especially profound in rational creatures whom God predestines for eternal union with himself in the Son, as Paul suggests when he says that "those whom he [God] foreknew he also predestined to be conformed to the image of his Son, in order that he might be the first-born among many brethren" (Rom 8:29).

In question thirty-four, on the person of the Son, Aquinas investigates the name "Word" as a personal name of the Son and in relation to creatures. He quotes Paul only once, in an objection in the second article (which treats whether "Word" is a personal name of the Son). This quotation involves Basil's suggestion, in the fourth-century trinitarian controversy (*Contra Eunomius*), that the Holy Spirit can be called the Son's Word on the grounds that Hebrews 1:3 states that the Son upholds "the universe by his word of power." On this view, the Son's "word of power" could be construed to be the Spirit. In his reply to the objection, Aquinas considers that this might be so in a loose, figurative sense, insofar as the Spirit manifests the Son.

Question thirty-five treats the name "Image" in two articles. The second article has three quotations of Paul. In the second objection, Aquinas points out that Paul calls the human male "the image and glory of God" (1 Cor 11:7), which would appear to mean that the name "Image" is not a name that properly distinguishes the Son from all else. Aquinas replies that the Son alone is the divine image of the Father, whereas humans are images of God in an imperfect manner, given our finite nature. In his *respondeo*, he observes that the Greek church fathers applied the name "Image" to both the Son and the Spirit, whereas the Latin fathers applied it solely to the Son. In Aquinas's view, the latter is the correct course because "the Son proceeds as word, and it is essential to word to be of like species with that whence it proceeds; whereas this does not essentially belong to love, although it may belong to the love which is the Holy Spirit, inasmuch as He is the divine love."[33] The New Testament applies the name "Image" only to the Son, and both times this name is found in Pauline texts: the Son is "the image of the invisible God" (Col 1:15) and "reflects the glory of God and bears the very stamp of his nature" (Heb 1:3). In neither case is Paul aiming to apply what we would call a "name" to the Son, but Aquinas nonetheless can rightly (in my view) interpret this language as a description of what distinguishes the Son.

Question thirty-six focuses on the Holy Spirit, both with respect to his proper name and with respect to his procession, especially whether he proceeds not only from the Father but also from the Son. This question contains no quotations of Paul. The same is true for question thirty-seven on whether the Holy Spirit is properly named "Love" and question thirty-eight on whether the Holy Spirit is properly named "Gift." Questions 36–38 are dominated by quotations from the church fathers, most notably

---

33. *ST* I, q. 35, a. 2.

Augustine but also various Eastern fathers, due to the differences between East and West on the procession of the Spirit. In question thirty-nine, Aquinas turns to more technical trinitarian queries. The eight articles of this question investigate such issues as whether the divine essence is the same as the persons and whether attributes that belong to what is common in God can be appropriated to particular persons. Three of the eight articles contain one Pauline quotation each. In article four, on whether concrete, essential names (such as "God") can stand for one or more persons, the *sed contra* of the article points out that the Creed says "true God from true God." Here "God" stands both for the Father and for the Son. The word "God," Aquinas explains, "signifies the divine essence as in Him who possesses it."[34] There is no freestanding "God" that is other than the three persons. Even so, the word God is appropriate because by it we mean either what is common to the three persons (the divine essence, including creative power), or one, two, or three persons. Aquinas observes that in 1 Timothy 1:17—"To the King of ages, immortal, invisible, the only God"—"God" signifies the three persons, whereas "God" would signify only one of the persons if one said that "God begets" and only two of the persons if one said "God spirates."

Article seven of question thirty-nine asks whether names that refer to what is common to the persons, such as wisdom, can rightly be appropriated to a particular person. Aquinas considers that such appropriation can help to illumine our faith in the three divine persons. Wisdom, for example, helps us to understand the distinctiveness of the divine Word, even though we know that the infinite divine wisdom pertains equally to all three persons. This example comes to Aquinas from 1 Corinthians 1:24, where Paul proclaims "Christ the power of God and the wisdom of God." In this verse, which serves as the *sed contra* of article seven, Paul intends simply to praise Christ, rather than to exemplify the doctrine of appropriation. Nonetheless his application of these names can help us to see how appropriation works. Paul is not saying that God the Father is not wise, but rather he applies the name "wisdom" to Christ in order to help us understand the Son. The eighth article examines some examples

34. *ST* I, q. 39, a. 4.

of how the church fathers appropriated to distinct persons names that are common to the persons. For instance, Augustine linked power with the Father, wisdom with the Son, and goodness with the Holy Spirit. In an objection, therefore, Aquinas quotes 1 Corinthians 1:24 and asks why, given that Paul links the Son with power, Augustine links the Father especially with power. Aquinas replies that this can be considered in terms of causality: "*power* has the nature of a principle, and so it has a likeness to the heavenly Father, who is the principle of the whole Godhead."[35]

In question forty, Aquinas clarifies the relationship of "relation" to "person." The four articles of this question involve technical philosophical precisions, and do not quote Paul. Question forty-one takes up the similar topic of the relationship of "person" to "notional act." Of the six articles, only article two contains a Pauline quotation. An objection in this article is based on Colossians 1:13, "He [the Father] has delivered us from the dominion of darkness and transferred us to the kingdom of his beloved Son" (Aquinas's version reads "*in regnum Filii dilectionis suae*"). The objection interprets "beloved Son" or "Son of his love" as meaning that the Son's begetting takes place by the Father's will. Aquinas observes that the Father loves Christ, but this does not mean that the Father's love is the principle of the Son's being begotten.

Question forty-two has six articles, and of these the fourth contains two Pauline quotations. Quoting both John 14:28, where Jesus says "the Father is greater than I," and 1 Corinthians 15:28, "When all things are subjected to him, then the Son himself will also be subjected to him [God the Father] who put all things under him," Aquinas asks whether the Father and the Son are equal in greatness. He answers affirmatively, and in support of this view he employs as his *sed contra* Philippians 2:6, where Paul says that Christ was "in the form of God" but "did not count equality with God a thing to be grasped" (Aquinas's version reads, "*Non rapinam arbitratus est esse se aequalem Deo*"). The objection's use of John 14:28 and 1 Corinthians 15:28 reflects the use of these texts by Arian and semi-Arian theologians in the fourth century and displays the difficulty of the problem. Aquinas has already shown, however, that the Son is fully God, and

---

35. *ST* I, q. 39, a. 8.

he has done so using other biblical texts. The passage from Philippians 2:6 underlines this point, because if Christ had been a mere creature, then equality with God would have been simply out of the question. In his *respondeo*, Aquinas adds that the Father's generation must have been perfect and thus the Son whom the Father generates can hardly fail to share equally in the divine nature. Like the pro-Nicene fathers, Aquinas interprets 1 Corinthians 15:28 (and John 14:28) as referring to Christ in his human nature.

The last question in Aquinas's treatise on the triune God—question forty-three—pertains to the missions of the Son and Spirit in time. This question is not about the triune God in himself, but about the Father's sending of the Son and Spirit for the salvation of the world. Article two, on whether the missions are eternal or only temporal, quotes Galatians 4:4 in the *sed contra*: "When the time had fully come, God sent forth his Son." The key point is that the missions are not in the divine nature but in time, because the missions signify the entering of the Son and Spirit into time, and "that a divine person be possessed by any creature or exist in it in a new mode, is temporal."[36] In the third article, on whether the invisible mission is the gift of sanctifying grace, Aquinas includes in an objection Paul's remark that "God's love has been poured into our hearts through the Holy Spirit who has been given to us" (Rom 5:5). It would seem, then, that the Holy Spirit is the cause of sanctifying grace in us rather than being sent in sanctifying grace. Aquinas replies that both are true: the Holy Spirit causes sanctifying grace and is sent in sanctifying grace, which disposes us to receive the Holy Spirit. Another objection in the same article holds that the invisible mission is not only the gift of sanctifying grace, but also the gratuitous graces such as the gift of prophecy. Quoting 1 Corinthians 12:7, where Paul speaks of "the manifestation of the Spirit for the common good," Aquinas answers that normally the gratuitous graces are signs of the possession of sanctifying grace. When someone possesses gratuitous graces such as prophecy without sanctifying grace, the Holy Spirit has caused these graces but has not been sent into the person.

Article five, on whether the Son is sent invisibly, contains two quota-

---

36. *ST* I, q. 43, a. 2.

tions from 1 Corinthians, both of which are in the objections. The first objection cites 1 Corinthians 12:11, "All these are inspired by one and the same Spirit," to argue that the Son is not sent invisibly because sanctifying grace comes strictly from the Spirit. The second objection notes that the gifts that perfect the intellect can be present without charity, as 1 Corinthians 13:2 suggests: "If I have prophetic powers, and understand all mysteries and all knowledge, and if I have all faith, so as to remove mountains, but have not love, I am nothing." Since this is so, and since the Son proceeds by way of intellect (as the Word), it seems to follow that the invisible mission, as the gift of sanctifying grace, only involves the Spirit. In his *respondeo* Aquinas points out that sanctifying grace means that the whole Trinity dwells within the soul, including even the Father, although he is not "sent" because he is the source. When the Son is known by faith, he is sent into the soul in an invisible mission. As the Word who with the Father spirates Love, the Son "is sent not in accordance with every and any kind of intellectual perfection, but according to the intellectual illumination, which breaks forth into the affection of love."[37]

Lastly, the seventh article also has two Pauline quotations, both of which appear in the answer to the sixth objection. This objection held that the Holy Spirit is never sent visibly, since if the Holy Spirit were sent visibly it would seem fitting that this visible mission should occur frequently in order to make manifest the invisible mission. In response, Aquinas notes that the visible mission of the Spirit is needed only for the purpose of confirming and spreading faith, or as Paul puts it, "for the common good" (1 Cor 12:7). Since confirming and spreading faith is the task of Christ and the apostles, Christ received the visible mission of the Spirit at his baptism, and the apostles received the visible mission of the Spirit at Pentecost. In this regard Aquinas quotes Hebrews 2:3, which states that God's salvation "was declared at first by the Lord, and it was attested to us by those who heard him."

To review Paul's place in Aquinas's theology of the Trinity, is it possible to say that Paul has a significant role here? Paul is particularly present in Aquinas's theology of God the Father. Paul praises "the Father, from

---

37. *ST* I, q. 43, a. 5, ad 2.

whom every family in heaven and on earth is named" (Eph 3:14). The Son is the sustainer of the universe who shares in the divine nature, including the divine power and wisdom, and who is the Father's eternal image (Colossians 1:15, Hebrews 1:3, 1 Corinthians 1:24). The Son is the Father's equal in divinity, although he subjects himself (and his kingdom) to the Father in his humanity (Philippians 2:6, 1 Corinthians 15:28). In Christ, who is the incarnate Son of the Father, we are called to be adoptive children of the Father by grace and glory and to share in the kingdom of the Son (Colossians 1:13; Romans 5:2, 8:16–17, 8:29). Aquinas uses Paul to argue that the Holy Spirit is truly God, because our bodies are temples of the Spirit (1 Corinthians 6:19). Paul helps him to defend the status of the Trinity as a mystery inaccessible to natural reason (Hebrews 11:1, 1 Corinthians 2:6–7) and to critique the ancient philosophers' understandings of God (Romans 1:21). Aquinas distinguishes his use of philosophy in Trinitarian theology from Paul's warning against "godless chatter" (1 Tim 6:20). The "only God" is none other than Father, Son, and Holy Spirit (1 Tim 1:17). The sending of the Son for our salvation occurs in the fullness of time (Galatians 4:4). The members of the church possess various manifestations of the Holy Spirit whose purpose is to build up the church (1 Corinthians 12:7, 12:11). The descent of the Spirit upon Christ at his baptism and upon the apostles at Pentecost confirms their mission of declaring salvation (Hebrews 2:3).

Certainly, then, Aquinas employs Paul in order to speak about the Father, Son, and Holy Spirit, both in themselves and in their relation to us. At the same time, however, Aquinas's many theoretical precisions regarding the distinction of persons in God make generally little use of Paul. The main purpose of his treatise is to contemplate and defend the intelligibility of what has been revealed, so as to preserve the truth of God's triunity. For this task, Paul does not play much of a role. Instead, Paul serves Aquinas in manifesting the scriptural witness to the revelation of the Trinity and to the ways in which we are related to the Father through Christ and the Holy Spirit. Although this role does not require many quotations from Paul, it is nonetheless a major role for the success of his treatise.

CONCLUSION

What is the significance of the fact that Aquinas draws so much more heavily on Paul in certain questions, among them question twelve on our knowledge of God, question fourteen on God's knowledge, question nineteen on God's will, question twenty-three on predestination, question thirty-three on God the Father, and question forty-three on the missions of the Son and Spirit? It likely has to do with Aquinas's sense of Paul's own preaching, focused as it is on our salvation. Paul proclaims that in the Christ, through the Holy Spirit, we have been united to the Father. Indeed, this has been the plan of the Father from before the creation of the world. Our knowledge of God, then, is a dynamic one: we look forward the resurrection of the dead, and we rejoice in our adoptive sonship in the Son through the Spirit, precisely because we want to share in the "inheritance" (Rom 8:17) of the Son, which is nothing less than the Father's glory. Like Paul, we "count everything as loss because of the surpassing worth of knowing Christ Jesus my Lord" (Phil 3:8), and each of us can say with Paul that "I press on to make it my own, because Christ Jesus has made me his own" (Phil 3:12). We know that already, in Christ, God has revealed to us his wisdom, the wisdom of love. But it is the full, personal knowledge of God that we seek: "For now we see in a mirror dimly, but then face to face. Now I know in part; then I shall understand fully, even as I have been fully understood" (1 Cor 13:12). We shall commune intimately in "the depth of the riches and wisdom and knowledge of God" (Rom 11:33).

For God to save us in this way, he must know us; and his knowledge and plan must be transcendent and eternal. As Paul says about God, "before him no creature is hidden, but all are open and laid bare to the eyes of him with whom we have to do" (Heb 4:13). It is because God knows us from eternity that his knowledge can be so complete. Only a God who knows us from eternity, and whose knowledge (when joined to his will) is causal, can accomplish what Paul claims for God: "For those whom he foreknew he also predestined to be conformed to the image of his Son, in order that he might be the first-born among many brethren. And those whom he predestined he also called; and those whom he called he also justified; and those whom he justified he also glorified" (Rom 8:29–30). Furthermore, if God were not good, then we could hardly count on him as our savior. God wills only what is good, and God's purpose is our sanctification (Romans 12:2, 1 Thessalonians 3:3). God desires that we be saved (1 Timothy 2:4). His eternal purpose to save his people in Christ Jesus cannot be frustrated (Ephesians 1:11, Romans 9:19, Romans 11:29). At the heart of our predestination is the predestination of Jesus (Ephesians 1:4, Romans 1:4). It is God's election that makes us good, rather than our works eliciting God's election (Romans 9:11–12, 2 Corinthians 3:5, Titus 3:5).

The God who saves us is Father, Son, and Holy Spirit. This truth can only be known through revelation, since it is there that we discover the Son and Spirit leading us to the Father. To understand how this is so, without breaking the unity of God, is part of the task of trinitarian theology. But trinitarian theology is rooted in recognizing in faith, with Paul, that our bodies have become temples of the Holy Spirit (1 Corinthians 6:19) and that we are being configured to "the image of his Son" and thus to "the image of the invisible God" who "reflects the glory of God and bears the very stamp of his nature, upholding the universe by his word of power" (Rom 8:29, Col 1:15, Heb 1:3). We are to bow our "knees before the Father" as co-heirs with Christ the Son in the Holy Spirit (Eph 3:14, Rom 8:16–17). We have entered into the kingdom of Christ, the kingdom of the Trinity. We know this because "God's love has been poured into our hearts through the Holy Spirit who has been given to us" (Rom 5:5) and because we have received, as members of the body of Christ, the gifts of the Holy Spirit (1 Corinthians 12).

All these Pauline passages are quoted by Aquinas in his treatise on the triune God, which is an exercise in speculative theology, that is to say, faith seeking understanding. Aquinas begins with the principle that we can know that God is from his effects (Romans 1:20). Our minds were made to know God; the world itself bears witnesses to its Creator, "the King of ages, immortal, invisible, the only God" (1 Tim 1:17). Yet we have sinned against God by refusing to honor him (Romans 1:21). In order to see God properly, therefore, we need to be redeemed from sin and restored to God. In another passage quoted by Aquinas, Paul prays "that the God of our Lord Jesus Christ, the Father of glory, may give you a spirit of wisdom and of revelation in the knowledge of him, having the eyes of your hearts enlightened, that you may know what is the hope to which he has called you, what are the riches of his glorious inheritance in the saints" (Eph 1:17–18). This is what we need to know in order to know and love God as we should. We discover this God in Christ and the Holy Spirit. Aquinas helps us to speak rightly about this God, but he could hardly do so without Paul's voice guiding us through the treatise, calling us to seek eternal life with the Father, Son, and Holy Spirit, one God.

CHAPTER 2

THE PASSION OF CHRIST

WITH REFERENCE to Thomas Aquinas's use of 1 Corinthians 1:18 in *Summa theologiae* III, question forty-eight, article six, Thomas Joseph White observes that for Aquinas: "The human acts of Christ from the cross are the acts of the Word made flesh. Even amidst weakness and suffering, they can communicate effects of divine power."[1] Through the weakness of his cross, the Son of God re-

1. Thomas Joseph White, OP, "Kenoticism and the Divinity of Christ Crucified," *The Thomist* 75 (2011): 22. See also White's "Jesus' Cry on the Cross and His Beatific Vision," *Nova et Vetera* 5 (2007): 555–81. For further discussion of Aquinas's theology of the cross, see Romanus Cessario, OP, *The Godly Image: Christ and Salvation in Catholic Thought from Anselm to Aquinas* (Petersham, Mass.: St. Bede's Publications, 1990) and "Aquinas on Christian Salvation," in *Aquinas on Doctrine*, ed. Thomas G. Weinandy, OFM Cap., Daniel A. Keating, and John P. Yocum (London: T. and T. Clark International, 2004), 117–37; Jean-Pierre Torrell, OP, "The Priesthood of Christ in the *Summa Theologiae*," in Torrell, *Christ and Spirituality in St. Thomas Aquinas*, trans. Bernhard Blankenhorn, OP, et al. (Washington, D.C.: The Catholic University of America Press, 2011), 126–58; Rik Van Nieuwenhove, "'Bearing the Marks of Christ's Passion': Aquinas' Soteriology," in *The Theology of Thomas Aquinas*, ed. Rik Van Nieuwenhove and Joseph Wawrykow (Notre Dame, Ind.: University of Notre Dame Press, 2005), 277–302; Matthew Levering, *Christ's Fulfillment of Torah and Temple: Salvation according to Thomas Aquinas* (Notre Dame, Ind.: University of Notre Dame Press, 2002). Discussing medieval christology, with a particular focus on the knowledge and passions of Christ, Kevin Madigan argues that it serves as a counter-example to John Henry Newman's theory of development of doctrine: "Time and again, we have seen 'prima facie' dissimilitudes between an ancient christological doctrine and its medieval development. However, closer inspection and analysis have revealed,

deems us. Obviously the cross of Christ is a central theme for Paul, one that touches all aspects of his theology. Thus in his *A Theology of the Cross: The Death of Jesus in the Pauline Letters*, Charles Cousar treats the following themes: how Christ's cross reveals God's righteousness and love; how Christ's cross overcomes sin and reconciles us to God; how the cross relates to the resurrection; how the cross redefines the people of God; and how the church is conformed to Christ's cross.[2] For his part, Michael Gorman identifies thirteen "narrative patterns of Christ's death" in the Pauline letters: obedience/righteousness/faith (fullness); love; grace; sacrifice; altruism/substitution; self-giving/giving; voluntary self-humbling/abasement; culmination of a story that includes incarnation and suffering; paradoxical power and wisdom; interchange; apocalyptic victory and liberation for new life and transformation; reconciliation and justification; and prelude to resurrection/exaltation.[3]

Are these Pauline themes present in Aquinas's theology of Christ's passion? In the *Summa theologiae*, Aquinas devotes four *quaestiones* to the passion of Jesus Christ: questions 46–49 of the *tertia pars*. Aquinas quotes Paul fifty-nine times in these four questions. Another way to gauge Paul's presence in this section is to note that Aquinas cites Paul in twenty-four of the thirty articles contained in the four questions. He provides eighteen quotations from Romans, eight from 1 Corinthians, six from 2 Corinthians, four from Galatians, eight from Ephesians, five from Philippians, two from Colossians, one from 2 Thessalonians, one from 2 Timothy, and six from Hebrews (which Aquinas includes among the Pauline epistles). These four questions, then, lack only 1 Thessalonians, 1 Timothy, Titus, and Philemon. Among the most frequently quoted verses are Romans

---

in virtually all these cases, that the 'dissimilitude' was very far from superficial. Indeed, by Cardinal Newman's criteria, the conceptual differences between the early and late are, almost invariably, profound and unbridgeable" (Madigan, *The Passions of Christ in High-Medieval Thought: An Essay on Christological Development* [Oxford: Oxford University Press, 2007], 92). This may be the case for the passions of Christ, although even here I strongly doubt that the medievals are far from the Gospel of John. But it certainly does not hold with regard to the doctrine of Christ's cross.

2. Charles B. Cousar, *A Theology of the Cross: The Death of Jesus in the Pauline Letters* (Minneapolis, Minn.: Fortress Press, 1990).

3. Michael J. Gorman, *Cruciformity: Paul's Narrative Spirituality of the Cross* (Grand Rapids, Mich.: Eerdmans, 2001), 82–87.

3:24–25 (four times), Ephesians 5:2 (three times), and Philippians 2:8–10 (five times). Twelve of the fifty-nine citations appear in the *sed contra* of the article, which means that the crucial *sed contra* includes a quotation from Paul in almost half of the thirty articles. A further twelve of the citations appear in the *respondeo*, although an accurate understanding of the presence of Paul in the *respondeo* requires observing that nine of these citations occur in three questions.[4] Twenty-three citations are found in the responses to the objections, and twelve in the objections. This fits with the pattern of biblical citations in Aquinas's *Summa*: most are found in the *sed contra* or the objections and replies. The *respondeo* is where Aquinas synthesizes his sources.

Are the passages that Aquinas chooses to quote representative of the main lines of Paul's thought on Christ's passion? In what follows, I hope to obtain a clearer picture of the relationship of Paul's theology of the cross to Aquinas's. I hope also to clarify how Aquinas uses Paul in framing his theological reflection on Christ's passion. Clearly, Aquinas's mode of reflection is very different from Paul's. As a medieval theologian, Aquinas's perspective necessarily differs in significant ways from Paul's. The question then is whether Aquinas succeeds in understanding Paul and integrating Paul's theology of the cross into the *Summa theologiae*'s treatment of Christ's passion. To be of true value, Aquinas's use of Paul must illumine and clarify the things that Paul cared most about, so that the truth about Jesus Christ taught by Paul shines forth in Aquinas's theology.

In this chapter, I go through questions 46–49 and comment on the Pauline quotations as they appear. As in the previous chapter, I examine how each quotation functions within the article in which it appears. Since most articles have one or more citations from Paul, we should be able to gain a clear sense of how Aquinas's theology of Christ's passion employs Paul's teaching. By reflecting more synthetically on the use of Paul in the twelve articles of question forty-six and then on Paul's place in the eighteen articles of questions 47–49, I also hope to be able to provide a sense of how Paul's theology of the cross shapes the whole of Aquinas's theology of Christ's passion.

---

4. *ST* III, q. 46, a. 3; q. 47, a. 2; and q. 49, a. 6.

PAUL IN QUESTION 46 OF THE *TERTIA PARS*

In question forty-six of the *tertia pars*, Aquinas examines Christ's passion in itself (as opposed to the causes and effects of Christ's passion). He first asks whether, in order for the human race to be healed of sin and raised to eternal life in God, it was "necessary" for Christ to suffer (article one); whether deliverance from sin could have been accomplished in another way (article two); why, given that God could have delivered us in other ways, Christ's suffering was the best way (article three); and why Christ suffered specifically on a cross rather than undergoing another form of death (article four). These four articles have to do with the perennial question of why God's messiah suffered the ignominy and searing pain of death on a cross. If God were going to heal and transform us, why should God do so by such a gruesome death? The next four articles inquire into the nature and extent of Christ's passion: whether Christ endured every form of suffering (article five); whether he experienced the greatest possible pain (article six); whether he suffered in his whole soul (article seven); and whether someone who enjoys perfect intimacy with the Father can really be said to "suffer" (article eight). The purpose here is to reflect upon Christ's passion as a fully human suffering that is nonetheless unique, as befits the redemptive suffering of the incarnate Son of God. The next three articles involve external elements of Christ's passion: its time (article nine) and place (article ten), as well as the fact that Christ suffered alongside two thieves (article eleven). Finally, the last article asks whether we can say that the Son of God suffered on the cross (article twelve). Insofar as Christ's passion is the suffering of the incarnate Son, its uniqueness becomes clear.

In the first article, on the "necessity" of Christ's passion, Aquinas presents what may well be the central Pauline text on the passion: Romans 3:24–25, which underscores the saving power of Christ's shedding of his blood. Aquinas pairs this text from Romans with Ephesians 2:4, which places Christ's passion in the context of God's providential plan for the restoration and elevation of human beings to union with God in glory. Aquinas quotes these two texts in his answer to the third objection, which argues that Christ's passion was unfitting and unnecessary both with respect to God's mercy, which can free us from our debts without any act of "satisfaction," and with respect to God's justice, which mandates eternal punishment for our rebellion against God. Aquinas observes that if Christ's passion is necessary in any sense, it will be necessary in relation to God's mercy and justice. Romans 3:24–25 and Ephesians 2:4 suggest the kind of "necessity" involved. In Romans 3:21, we learn that "the righteousness of God has been manifested apart from law, although the law and the prophets bear witness to it." What is the righteousness of God? It is that by sending Jesus Christ as the redeemer, God proves "that he himself is righteous" (Rom 3:26) because he has fulfilled his covenantal promises. Those who have faith in Jesus are justified "through the redemption which is in Christ Jesus, whom God put forward as an expiation by his blood, to be received by faith" (Rom 3:24–25). The blood that Jesus shed on the cross, as the incarnate Son's self-offering out of love for us, paid the penalty of sin and thereby restored the relationship of justice between humans and God. For justice to be restored from the side of humanity (rather than merely by divine fiat), it was necessary that Christ suffer. This was not only an act of justice but also of supreme mercy, since justification in Christ is God's sheer gift to us: we "are justified by his grace as a gift" (Rom 3:24).

The same points about God's mercy and justice are found in Ephesians 1–2, although set more clearly in the context of God's eternal plan for his creation. Paul states that God "chose us in him [Christ] before the foundation of the world" and "destined us in love to be his sons through Jesus Christ, according to the purpose of his will, to the praise of his glorious grace which he freely bestowed on us in the Beloved" (Eph 1:4–6). From eternity, God's creative plan included his redemption of us in the incarnate Son. Redemption makes us God's adoptive sons, filled with grace, who are destined to live eternally with Christ Jesus in heaven, in accord with God's "plan for the fulness of time, to unite all things in him [Christ], things in heaven and things on earth" (Eph 1:10). It might sound as though Paul has in mind primarily Christ's resurrection, since Paul is speaking of God's plan for our glorification in Christ. But in fact Paul speaks explicitly of Christ's passion—his spilling of his blood out of love for us—as central to God's eternal plan (and thus "necessary" in the sense of willed eternally by God): "In him [Christ] we have redemption through his blood, the forgiveness of our trespasses, according to the riches of his grace which he lavished upon us" (Eph 1:7–8). God mercifully forgives our sins, and thereby lavishes grace upon us, when Christ pays the just penalty for sin by giving up his life out of supreme love. When humans turn away from God (the source of all life) through sin, the just penalty is death; Christ pays this for us because, as the sinless one, he does not owe it himself. God does not allow Christ to see corruption, but instead raises Christ from the dead and makes "him sit at his right hand in the heavenly places" (Eph 1:20). This reward, which God justly gives to Christ, God gives to all who are in Christ. As Paul says, "God, who is rich in mercy, out of the great love with which he loved us, even when we were dead through our trespasses, made us alive together with Christ (by grace you have been saved), and raised us up with him" (Eph 2:4–6). Aquinas concludes that although God could have forgiven our sins without satisfying his justice, it was more merciful that God accomplish justice through Christ's passion, because God thereby united humanity to himself through Christ's supreme act of human love. In this sense, as the superabundant fulfillment of God's mercy and justice, Christ's passion was "necessary."

The second article asks whether God could have redeemed us in some way other than Christ's passion. Aquinas quotes 2 Timothy 2:13 in the third objection. This verse is not directly about Christ's passion. Paul (or the author of 2 Timothy) states that "if we are faithless, he [God] remains faithful—for he cannot deny himself." Aquinas uses the text to argue, in the voice of the objector, that God could not have redeemed us without Christ's passion, since by his passion Christ fulfills God's justice. God is infinite justice, and so it would seem that if God had redeemed us without Christ's passion, God would be denying himself by denying his justice. For our purposes, this argument of the objector is not especially significant. In his reply, Aquinas dismisses it by saying that God can justly overlook sins committed against himself, since God is "the sovereign and common good of the whole universe," in contrast to the responsibilities of a judge who answers to a higher authority.[5] But the quotation from 2 Timothy 2:13

---

5. *ST* III, q. 46, a. 2, ad 3.

turns out to be more significant than would appear to be the case from the verse itself. It is part of a longer passage that runs as follows: "The saying is sure: If we have died with him, we shall also live with him; if we endure, we shall also reign with him; if we deny him, he also will deny us; if we are faithless, he remains faithful—for he cannot deny himself" (2 Tim 2:11–13). Christ's passion and resurrection are here the path by which God "remains faithful," in a manner quite similar to what we found in Romans 3:21–26. God is always faithful, and he has manifested this fidelity—this righteousness—in Christ Jesus, by whose passion we have been redeemed. United to his passion by faith, we are united to his resurrection and will "live with him." Second Timothy 2:11–13 thus echoes and augments the teaching of Romans 3:21–26 and Ephesians 1–2. The faithful God is the one who in Christ Jesus has died and risen from the dead. When we know God's faithfulness by our faith in Christ's passion and resurrection, our faith configures us to the God who is faithful.

In the *respondeo* of article three, on the fittingness of Christ's passion for delivering the human race, Aquinas quotes Romans 5:8: "But God shows his love for us in that while we were yet sinners Christ died for us." This passage adds to the emphasis on God's love and fidelity that we saw in Aquinas's first two articles. Aquinas reasons that Christ's passion is a means to an end, namely the salvation of sinners. Christ's passion takes away our sin, but we must be joined to Christ's passion by faith. Such faith is stimulated by the appreciation for God's love that we gain when we see in Christ how much God loves us. As Aquinas remarks, "[M]an knows thereby how much God loves him, and is thereby stirred to love Him in return, and herein lies the perfection of human salvation."[6] Our salvation is perfected when we are transformed from lovers of self to lovers of God. By revealing how much God loves us, Christ's passion stimulates our awareness of how lovable God is. God's fidelity stimulates our faith (2 Timothy 2:11–13), and God's love stimulates our love (Romans 5:8). This shows the mercy and righteousness of God, as well as the fact that salvation is God's gift (Romans 3:24–25 and Ephesians 2:4).

In the same *respondeo*, Aquinas goes on to quote 1 Corinthians 6:20

---

6. *ST* III, q. 46, a. 3.

and 15:57. In 1 Corinthians 6:20, Paul exhorts the Corinthians to avoid immoral behavior, and he urges them: "You are not your own; you were bought with a price. So glorify God in your body." In 1 Corinthians 15:57, Paul has been speaking of the resurrection of the dead at the end of time, when sin and death will be completely conquered. The cause of our resurrection is Christ's passion and resurrection, and so Paul praises God: "Thanks be to God, who gives us the victory through our Lord Jesus Christ." In both cases, Aquinas concludes that Christ's passion should inspire us to recognize our worth and to live accordingly. Because God paid a great price for us, we too should value our lives; and because God became human in order to save the human race, we should appreciate the dignity of being human. Christ's passion not only teaches us about the greatness of God's fidelity and love, but also teaches us about the importance of human, embodied fidelity and love. In thinking about the fittingness of Christ's passion, therefore, we should consider both its redemptive efficacy in itself and the way in which it inspires an appropriate response in us.

The fourth article contains four quotations from Paul. In the *sed contra*, he quotes the description in Philippians 2:8 of the humility of the divine Son: "And being found in human form he humbled himself and became obedient unto death, even death on a cross." He had already quoted Philippians 2:8 three previous times in the *tertia pars*, but this is the first time in his treatise on Christ's passion. The theme of Christ's humility accords with the topic of the article, namely whether it was fitting for Christ to die on a cross rather than not dying or dying in some other, more dignified way. In his *respondeo*, Aquinas takes up Augustine's suggestion that the shape of the cross gives a sense of the dimensions of Christ's teaching. Augustine, followed by Aquinas, refers to Ephesians 3:17–19, where Paul expresses the hope that "Christ may dwell in your hearts through faith; that you, being rooted and grounded in love, may have power to comprehend with all the saints what is the breadth and length and height and depth, and to know the love of Christ which surpasses knowledge, that you may be filled with all the fulness of God." This all-surpassing love of Christ is found in his humility, as well as in the other virtues stimulated by Christ's cross. Yet it would seem that Christ's humility went so far as

The Passion of Christ

to make him "to be sin" (2 Cor 5:21) and to be "a curse for us" (Gal 3:13). Aquinas quotes these two passages and replies that the point is that Christ, in his humility, bore our penalty, not that Christ actually became the sin and curse that alienate us from God.

This point becomes even clearer through Aquinas's reply to the second objection's statement (quoting John of Damascus) that Christ did not take on "dishonoring afflictions." Aquinas explains that Christ certainly did not experience sufferings that would have separated him from God, such as despair or sinful passions, but Christ did willingly suffer injuries that made manifest his profound solidarity with sinners, his taking on the full extent of our penalty out of supreme love for us. In this regard Aquinas quotes Hebrews 12:2, which urges us to look "to Jesus the pioneer and perfecter of our faith, who for the joy that was set before him endured the cross, despising the shame, and is seated at the right hand of the throne of God." Not only the physical suffering, but also the shame of being crucified as a disgraced criminal pertains to Christ's bearing the penalty of our sin through his passion.

Article five asks whether Christ endured, in some sense, all forms of suffering. Aquinas does not quote Paul in this article, but he does refer to Paul in answering the next article, regarding the extent of Christ's suffering. According to Aquinas, Christ endured not only the greatest sensible pain, but also the greatest interior pain or sadness. He was not sad for his own sins, as we are. Rather, he was sad for the sins of the entire human race. This sadness belonged to his act of satisfaction for sin. To help show this, Aquinas cites 2 Corinthians 7:10, "For godly grief produces a repentance that leads to salvation and brings no regret, but worldly grief produces death" (in Aquinas's version, 2 Corinthians 7:10 reads: "*Quae secundum Deum est tristitia, poenitentiam in salutem stabilem operator*"). Since godly sadness produces penitence or penance, Aquinas notes that godly sadness is "a useful means of satisfying for sins."[7] Christ is saddened also by the loss of his bodily life, since the rupture of death "is naturally horrible to human nature."[8] Thus Christ becomes "sin" or bears our "curse" not only

---

7. *ST* III, q. 46, a. 6.
8. Ibid.

through suffering physical pain but also through interior suffering. His satisfaction for sin is not simply an exterior offering, like the death of a sacrificial victim, but rather is a profoundly interior offering motivated by his love for us, a love that grieves over what our sins have done. His grief plays a role in healing the wound of sin from within, because he does penance for the evil deeds of the whole human race.

The next two articles, on whether Christ suffered in his whole soul even while possessing the beatific vision (his non-conceptual intimacy with his divine Father), have no quotations from Paul. In article nine, Aquinas cites Paul again in asking whether Christ suffered at a fitting time, that is, at Passover and while still a young man. In the first objection of article nine, Aquinas quotes 1 Corinthians 5:7: "For Christ, our paschal lamb, has been sacrificed." Since Christ's passion was foreshadowed by the Jewish sacrifice of the paschal lamb, it would seem that the passion should have occurred when the paschal lambs were slain. This took place, however, the day before Christ's passion; otherwise Christ would not have been able to eat the Passover meal with his disciples. Aquinas answers this problem through a complex examination of the timing of Christ's last supper as depicted in the synoptic gospels and the Gospel of John. The point for us is how Aquinas uses Paul to connect Christ's passion with the paschal lamb of Passover, and thereby to show how Christ is indeed the messiah by whose blood God spares all people.

In this same article, Aquinas also argues that Christ willed to die in the prime of life in order to give us a sense of the bodily perfection of risen bodies, that is, that we will not rise again in old age and decrepitude. He quotes Ephesians 4:13, where Paul speaks of the building up of believers in the body of Christ "until we all attain to the unity of the faith and of the knowledge of the Son of God, to mature manhood, to the measure of the stature of the fulness of Christ." This "stature" is obviously more that physical maturity and perfection, but also involves the perfect wisdom and love that Christ reveals on the cross.

Article ten asks whether Christ suffered in a suitable place. Rather than suffering outside the gate of Jerusalem, should Christ have suffered and died in the temple, for example, in order to show that he was the fulfillment of the temple sacrifices? Aquinas argues that by dying outside the gate of Jerusalem, Christ fittingly died in the city that God had chosen to house the temple, and also fittingly died outside the gate of this city so as to fulfill the symbolism of the scapegoat on the day of atonement.[9] He quotes Ephesians 5:2 in order to highlight that Christ's passion is indeed the fulfillment of the ceremonial precepts of the Mosaic law. In Ephesians 5:2, Paul exhorts us to "walk in love, as Christ loved us and gave himself up for us, a fragrant offering and sacrifice to God." Paul's language here draws upon, and shows the fulfillment of, the Mosaic law's precepts about the offering of animal sacrifices. This connection is made even more explicit by Hebrews 13:11, also quoted in this article by Aquinas. In Hebrews 13:10–12, Paul states, "We have an altar from which those who serve the tent have no right to eat. For the bodies of those animals whose blood is brought into the sanctuary by the high priest as a sacrifice for sin are burned outside the camp. So Jesus also suffered outside the gate in order to sanctify the people through his own blood." The fulfillment of Israel's law is a key element, then, in understanding the efficacy of Christ's passion. The Jewish messiah cannot be understood outside his fulfillment of the law given by God for his people Israel. It is through fulfilling this law that Christ makes us holy.

In article eleven Aquinas treats the fact that Christ's crucifixion took place next to the crucifixion of two thieves. He quotes two passages from Paul in his first objection. Both passages are intended by Aquinas to suggest the unfittingness of Christ and the thieves being crucified together, although Aquinas's own position is of course that it was fitting. In 2 Corinthians 6:14, Paul is warning against marrying non-Christians: "Do not be mismated with unbelievers. For what partnership have righteousness and iniquity? Or what fellowship has light with darkness?" By extension, Aquinas's objector thinks that Christ and the two thieves should have no partnership or fellowship. Similarly 1 Corinthians 1:30 calls upon the Corinthians not to boast about themselves or their righteousness, because their righteousness is strictly God's gift in Christ. God "is the source of your life in Christ Jesus, whom God made our wisdom, our righteousness and sanctification and redemption." Since Christ is our righteousness,

---

9. See Leviticus 16:27 and Hebrews 13:11.

then as 2 Corinthians 6:14 says, he has no fellowship with iniquity. Aquinas replies to this objection by explaining that Christ associates himself with our iniquity in order, through his righteousness, to conquer iniquity. This is indeed the central purpose of his cross: the one who does not owe the penalty of death takes on this penalty (as thus associates himself with sinners) for our sake. We have seen this same point in Paul's conviction that Christ has willingly borne the shame of the cross and freely become "sin" and "a curse" for us. He associates himself with sinners without being a sinner, and through his supreme love he redeems us.

Lastly, the twelfth article, on whether Christ suffers in his divinity on the cross, includes one quotation from Paul. In 1 Corinthians 2:8, Paul remarks about the "rulers of this age" that if they had understood the wisdom of God for the glorification of humans, "they would not have crucified the Lord of glory." The objector draws from this the conclusion that the divine glory is what suffers on the cross. By contrast, Aquinas—indebted to Athanasius and others—states that "the Lord of glory is said to be crucified, not as the Lord of glory, but as a man capable of suffering."[10] The point is that the incarnate Son suffers as man; his suffering in time is truly the suffering of the Son of God (as man), but it does not introduce change or sadness into the eternal God. For our purposes, the quotation has an added significance in filling out the portrait of Paul's theology of the cross. Paul recognizes that the wisdom of the cross is available to us only through the Holy Spirit and the gift of faith. The Son of God dying on a cross does not answer to what powerful people would expect from a powerful God. In redeeming us, the Son of God penetrates deeply into our condition and heals us from within. As Philippians 2 emphasizes, he is supreme humility, love, and obedience, and as such he reverses the false notion of divinity that imagines (as Adam and Eve did) that to grasp for power is to become God-like. Since God is love, obedience to him is love.

---

10. *ST* III, q. 46, a. 12, ad 1.

The Passion of Christ

SUMMARY

Arguably the nineteen quotations from Paul (including the two quotations from Hebrews) in question forty-six already present a full portrait of Paul's theology of the cross. Certainly the major elements of Paul's theology of the cross are present. Christ redeems us by his blood (Romans 3:24–25); his suffering pays our penalty and makes satisfaction for our sins (1 Corinthians 6:20, 2 Corinthians 7:10). As the divine Son, he reveals his divinity by his awe-inspiring humility, and by his obedient love he reverses the pride and grasping of Adam and Eve (Philippians 2:8). He bears the curse of sin and death for us (2 Corinthians 5:21, Galatians 3:13). He shows God's mercy and love for sinners (Ephesians 2:4, Romans 5:8). He shares in the ignominy that sinners experience (Hebrews 12:2). He embodies God's faithfulness and covenant righteousness (Romans 3:24–25, 2 Timothy 2:13). His cross should inspire us to imitate his love and faithfulness (Ephesians 2:4, 2 Timothy 2:13). He fulfills the Law that God gave Israel, as the perfect and once-and-for-all paschal sacrifice for sins (1 Corinthians 5:7, Ephesians 5:2, Hebrews 13:11). He is our righteousness, in the sense that we receive righteousness from him as a gift rather than by our own power (1 Corinthians 1:30). Even though he enters into our condition and bears the penalty of sin, he is perfectly righteous (2 Corinthians 4:21, 2 Corinthians 6:14). He reveals to us the scope of God's eternal plan for his elect people, its extraordinary wisdom and love (Ephesians 2:4, Ephesians 3:18, Ephesians 4:13). He calls us to imitate him and to attain to his fullness, so that we might share in his victory (1 Corinthians 15:57).

PAUL IN QUESTIONS 47–49
OF THE *TERTIA PARS*

In question forty-seven, Aquinas addresses in six articles the topic of who caused Christ's passion. Did Christ submit to it freely, or was he compelled by Pilate to die? If he submitted to it freely, did he essentially commit suicide? Did God the Father command that his Son die, and if so did the Father kill his own Son? In the same question, Aquinas also takes up the related issue of the diverse involvement of Gentiles and Jews (including the disciples) in the death of Jesus Christ. Did those who urged that he be executed, and those who executed him, have any knowledge of who he was?

The first article takes up the question of whether Christ caused his own death, so that his slayers really were not responsible for it. The issue arises especially from Christ's statement in John 10:18 (quoted by Aquinas): "No one takes it [my life] from me, but I lay it down of my own accord. I have power to lay it down, and I have power to take it again; this charge I have received from my Father."[11] Aquinas reasons that Christ, who had the power to do miracles, could have miraculously (by the divine power) prevented his slayers from killing him. Christ therefore had a certain freedom in accepting his death that others do not have. To accept one's death is quite different from killing oneself, however. Aquinas resolves this issue without the help of Paul.

By contrast, in the second article Aquinas cites Paul seven times, more than in any other article in his four questions on Christ's passion. The second article asks whether Christ died out of obedience to God the Father. Indeed, Paul says as much in Philippians 2:8, which Aquinas quotes in the *sed contra*: "And being found in human form he humbled himself and became obedient unto death, even death on a cross." Regarding Christ's obedience, Aquinas in the *respondeo* cites Romans 5:19, "For as by one man's disobedience many were made sinners, so by one man's obedience many will be made righteous." This obedience, Aquinas emphasizes, is hardly a passive submission to the will of a tyrannical Father. On the contrary, the Father and the Son are united in love, and so the Father's command and the Son's obedience (in the unfolding of his incarnate life) are moved by love. The incarnate Son actively loves us, and this love takes concrete shape through his obedience, in his passion, to the Father's will to save us from sin and death. Christ's obedience is a free act, motivated by wisdom and love. In his obedience to the command of his loving Father, Christ freely and actively dies out of love for us, in order to reverse the sin of Adam and Eve and to heal the wound of sin from within human nature.

In addition to quoting Pauline passages that manifest Christ's obe-

---

11. See *ST* III, q. 47, a. 1, obj. 1.

dience, therefore, Aquinas also quotes Paul to portray Christ's perfect freedom in giving his life for our sake. One such passage is Ephesians 5:2, which Aquinas cites both in the *respondeo* and in an objection (the objector argues that Christ gave his life out of charity rather than out of obedience, to which Aquinas replies that it is charity that produces Christ's obedience). Recall that in Ephesians 5:2, which Aquinas quoted already in article ten of question forty-six, Paul exhorts us to "walk in love, as Christ loved us and gave himself up for us." Because of his love for us, Christ freely died for us. In the *respondeo* Aquinas also cites Romans 5:10, which we can combine with Romans 5:8 (cited in article three of question forty-six) and 5:9: "God shows his love for us in that while we were yet sinners Christ died for us. Since, therefore, we are now justified by his blood, much more shall we be saved by him from the wrath of God. For if while we were enemies we were reconciled to God by the death of his Son, much more, now that we are reconciled, shall we be saved by his life." Christ's death reconciles us to God because of his obedient love, which is the inner reality that makes a sacrifice acceptable to God. As Aquinas points out, this truth was already apparent to the prophet Samuel who corrects Saul with the words, "Has the Lord as great delight in burnt offerings and sacrifices, as in obeying the voice of the Lord? Behold, to obey is better than sacrifice, and to hearken than the fat of rams."[12] Since Christ's love was perfect, his obedience was perfect in the offering of his life for our redemption.

As the true sacrifice, Christ fulfills the animal sacrifices of the Mosaic law. In this regard Aquinas quotes Colossians 2:16–17, "Therefore let no one pass judgment on you in questions of food and drink or with regard to a festival or a new moon or a sabbath. These are only a shadow of what is to come; but the substance belongs to Christ." He cites this passage by way of arguing (in the response to the first objection) that the Mosaic law itself, which Christ fulfilled, was the command of God that Christ obeyed. By his passion, Christ fulfilled the moral, ceremonial, and judicial precepts. In order to show that Christ by his passion obeyed the moral precepts, which are fulfilled by love, Aquinas quotes Galatians 2:20,

---

12. See *ST* III, q. 47, a. 2.

where Paul rejoices that he has found life and indeed shares in Christ's life "by faith in the Son of God, who loved me and gave himself up for me." Christ's passion was an act of free, powerful love.

Closely related to the second article, the third article asks whether God the Father handed over his innocent Son to be killed on the cross. This question, raised most forcefully in the medieval period by Peter Abelard, appears to be answered in the affirmative by Paul in Romans 8:32, which Aquinas quotes in the *sed contra*: "He did not spare his own Son but gave him up for us all." There is a moral problem here, since Judas and Pilate, among others, did evil by handing Jesus over to be killed. Does God the Father, then, share in the evildoing of Judas and Pilate? In an objection, Aquinas notes that God certainly cannot do evil, and he quotes once more the passage from 2 Corinthians 6:14 that we saw in the eleventh article of question forty-six, to the effect that "righteousness and iniquity" have no connection. How then to resolve this problem?

Aquinas answers by describing, in light of Isaiah 53, the ways in which God the Father delivered up Christ. He did so by eternal predestination (since this was God's plan from the beginning for our salvation), by infusing Christ's human nature with charity through the grace of the Holy Spirit, and by not preventing Christ's persecutors from killing him. In these three things the Father and the Son were in accord. Since the incarnate Son freely chose to die out of love for sinners, the Father certainly cannot be said to have killed his innocent Son. Nonetheless, Aquinas does see in Christ's passion both "the kindness and the severity of God" (Rom 11:22). He sees God's "severity" in that God required satisfaction for sin—although (as Aquinas earlier pointed out) God did so out of love for us, since it pertains to the dignity of human nature that sin be healed from the side of humans. The fact that God required satisfaction for sin is, according to Aquinas, what Paul means by saying that God "did not spare his own Son" (Rom 8:32). As for God's kindness, Aquinas sees it in the fact that no merely human satisfaction could have repaid the debt. This, for Aquinas, is what Paul means by adding in Romans 8:32, "but gave him up for us all," as well as by stating in Romans 3:25 that God put Christ "forward as an expiation by his blood." Only the satisfaction offered by the incarnate Son could pay the penalty owed for rebellion against God.

In other words, Christ's passion was an act of sheer mercy even as it restored justice.

The fourth article, on whether it was fitting that Christ suffer at the hands of gentiles, contains no quotations from Paul, and neither does the sixth article on whether the greatest possible sin was the crucifying of Christ, in which Aquinas explains that this sin was gravest for those who knew that Jesus was the messiah and also discusses the roles of Judas, the chief priests and the populace in Jerusalem, and Pilate and his Roman soldiers. The fifth article asks whether those who persecuted Christ knew who he was. In answering this question, Aquinas follows the passage from 1 Corinthians 2:8 that he quoted in the twelfth article of question forty-six: "None of the rulers of this age understood this; for if they had, they would not have crucified the Lord of glory." He pairs 1 Corinthians 2:8 in the *sed contra* with Acts 3:17, where Peter tells his Jewish brethren that "I know that you acted in ignorance, as did also your rulers," and Luke 23:34, where Christ says from the cross, "Father, forgive them; for they know not what they do." Even so, Aquinas adds that those who saw Christ's miracles and heard his teachings could not have been entirely ignorant, especially if they knew scripture well. He therefore supposes that the leaders of the people, who were learned and who had been following Jesus's career, must have been culpable, as Judas too most certainly was.

Question forty-eight examines the ways in which Christ's passion caused our salvation. Article one explores Christ's meriting of salvation for all who are joined to him by grace. In the *sed contra*, in order to show that Christ merited glory by his passion, Aquinas quotes Philippians 2:9, "Therefore God has highly exalted him and bestowed on him the name which is above every name." This exaltation is presented as Christ's reward for his humility and obedience "unto death, even death on a cross" (Phil 2:8). The exaltation of Christ in his human nature does not imply that Christ lacked the divine nature, since Philippians 2:6 portrays Christ as being "in the form of God" though he "did not count equality with God a thing to be grasped, but emptied himself."

Article two, on Christ's satisfaction for sins, does not repeat the Pauline quotations that Aquinas has already used to elucidate this reality. Article three is about the saving power of Christ's sacrifice, and the *sed contra* repeats the passage from Ephesians 5:2 that we found in both question forty-six (article ten) and question forty-seven (article two). Article four repeats Galatians 3:13 (question forty-six, article four) in order to show that Christ's Passion redeemed us from sin; recall that Galatians 3:13 reads, "Christ redeemed us from the curse of the law, having become a curse for us." He paid our penalty, or in other words redeemed our curse, by undergoing for us the penalty/curse through his suffering and death. Aquinas also uses Romans 8:9 in this article. An objection points out that Christ hardly needs to redeem us or buy us back, since we never ceased to belong to him. One does not need to redeem what one has in one's possession. God's providence and power do indeed extend to all humans, and in this regard no redemption is needed. But as Aquinas points out by means of Romans 8:9, there is an important sense in which redemption is necessary. Those who lack charity are alienated from God and need redemption. As Romans 8:9 puts it, "Any one who does not have the Spirit of Christ does not belong to him." To have the Spirit of Christ means to live in charity, focused on the things of God rather than on the things on this world. Christ is the redeemer of all humans by his passion, because his satisfaction for sins frees us from our state of sinful alienation.

Article five asks whether Christ alone is the redeemer. Why should not the entire Trinity be redeemer? Quoting Galatians 3:13 once more (again in the *sed contra*), Aquinas explains that Christ alone made superabundant satisfaction and so Christ alone is the redeemer, although the entire Trinity willed that the incarnate Son, in obedience to the Father and through the grace of the Holy Spirit, accomplish this redemption. Yet Aquinas notes in an objection that Paul seems to suggest that Christ's passion is not sufficient redemption: "Now I rejoice in my sufferings for your sake, and in my flesh I complete what is lacking in Christ's afflictions for the sake of his body, that is, the church" (Col 1:24). If anything is lacking in Christ's sufferings, then Christ would need the help of Paul (and others) to redeem the human race. Aquinas interprets this remark of Paul's by recourse to another Pauline statement: "If we are afflicted, it is for your comfort and salvation" (2 Cor 1:6) (in Aquinas's version, this verse reads, "*Sive tribulamur pro vestra exhortatione et salute*"). The "comfort" or "exhortation" described here constitutes the way in which Paul completes "what is lacking in Christ's afflictions." In itself, Christ's passion lacks nothing for our redemption, but the example of the saints (including Paul) exhorts us to desire to share in Christ's passion by faith and love. Through their sufferings and labors in union with Christ, the saints cooperate with Christ, the sole redeemer, by inspiring and guiding others to be united to him.

Article six, on whether Christ's passion is the efficient cause of our salvation, contains four citations of Paul. The central citation comes in the *sed contra*: "For the word of the cross is folly to those who are perishing, but to us who are being saved it is the power of God" (1 Cor 1:18). Faith in the gospel of Christ's cross connects us with God's saving power. In believing in Christ crucified, we find ourselves caught up by "the power of God." Christ's passion, then, is nothing less than the power of God for our salvation. The conclusion must be that Christ's passion causes our salvation as the efficient or agent cause. Aquinas adds that God alone can cause salvation in us, but God does this by working through Christ's human actions and sufferings.

An objection arises from 2 Corinthians 13:4, where Paul reminds the Corinthians that the risen Christ is powerfully at work in them and in Paul's apostolic ministry, which they neglect at their peril: "For he was crucified in weakness, but lives by the power of God. For we are weak in him, but in dealing with you we shall live with him by the power of God." From Paul's remark here, it would seem that the power of God in Christ comes about not through his passion, which is weakness, but through his resurrection. Aquinas replies to this objection by citing another passage from Paul, 1 Corinthians 1:25. In this passage Paul, having represented himself as preaching Christ crucified, assures the Corinthians that "the weakness of God is stronger than men." To be weak in Christ, to share in the weakness of his passion, is to share in the "weakness of God" that is "stronger than men" because of its power for salvation.

Another objection consists in the fact that Christ's passion was a bodily event, and as such it cannot be an efficient cause that touches all people. Aquinas replies that Christ's human sufferings were the sufferings of the incarnate Son, so that God works through Christ's passion. It is not only a bodily event which could directly impact only those who were physically present. Rather, as the bodily event through which the Son of God reconciled all humans to God, Christ's passion has a spiritual dimension that allows it to exercise efficient causality upon each human person through spiritual modes of contact, namely faith and the sacraments of faith. In this regard it differs from other merely human events, which have only a limited range of direct efficient causality, due to the limitations of corporeal existence. Aquinas comments that this is why Paul mentions faith when describing "the redemption which is in Christ Jesus, whom God put forward as an expiation by his blood, to be received by faith" (Rom 3:24–25).

Question forty-nine is Aquinas's final question on Christ's passion, and it focuses on the effects of Christ's passion in humans. Aquinas argues that Christ's passion delivers us from captivity to sin, from captivity to the devil, and from captivity to the punishment of sin. He also argues that Christ's passion reconciles us to God and opens the "gate" of the kingdom of heaven. By humbling himself so profoundly in his passion, Christ merits his exaltation to the right hand of the Father, so that his resurrection and ascension are intimately bound to his passion.

When Aquinas reflects in article one on how Christ's passion delivers us from sin, he employs Paul to explore the role of faith and charity in the forgiveness of sins. As the efficient cause of redemption, Christ's passion operates powerfully in those who are united to it by faith and charity. We would still be in our sins if we lacked charity, since charity is the bond that unites us to God (and frees us from sinful cleaving to creaturely things). In this regard Aquinas once more quotes Romans 5:8, "God shows his love for us in that while we were yet sinners Christ died for us." The point is that God's love causes our love. When we see how much God loves us, we are inspired to love him. He causes our love not by compelling it, but by inspiring it to move freely towards him. This emphasis on love need not lead to neglecting the role of faith. Faith unites us with Christ's passion, as Aquinas underscores by again quoting Paul's teaching that "God put forward [Christ Jesus] as an expiation by his blood, to be received by faith" (Rom 3:25). But such faith is lifeless if we lack charity. Aquinas comments that only through "faith living through charity" can Christ's passion "be applied to us, not only as to our minds, but also as to our hearts."[13]

---

13. *ST* III, q. 49, a. 1, ad 5.

The second article has to do with whether Christ's passion frees us from captivity to the devil. Aquinas holds that it does, on the basis of texts such as John 12:31–32, where Jesus says, "Now is the judgment of this world, now shall the ruler of this world be cast out; and I, when I am lifted up from the earth, will draw all men to myself." The devil has no power of his own but only exercises power over sinners who repudiate God. The punishment for repudiating God is to be left under the power of the devil, who himself most forcefully repudiates God. God permits this just punishment to take place, but through Christ's passion, God freed all sinners from the devil's power, because God thereby forgave all sins, reconciled all sinners to himself, and exposed once and for all the injustice of the devil (who conspired to cause Christ's death, which Christ did not owe). In an objection, however, Aquinas states that not all people were truly freed from the devil's power, because there are still many idolatrous regions of the world and because the time of the Antichrist will only worsen things. He quotes 2 Thessalonians 2:9, "The coming of the lawless one by the activity of Satan will be with all power and with pretended signs and wonders." It seems that the power of Christ's passion in delivering sinners from captivity to the devil is in fact rather severely limited, despite the claim of Hebrews 10:14 (quoted by Aquinas): "For by a single offering he has perfected for all time those who are sanctified." Aquinas replies to this objection by pointing out that although God mysteriously permits the devil's ongoing activity, nonetheless God has indeed given an all-sufficient remedy in Christ's passion, even if some people do not avail themselves of this remedy.

In the third article, Aquinas addresses the fact that we do not appear to have been freed from the punishment of sin by Christ's passion. In an objection he quotes Romans 6:23: "For the wages of sin is death." Since the time of Christ's passion, many people have died, and so it seems that we still do endure the punishment of sin, despite the superabundant satisfaction offered by Christ on the cross. In reply, Aquinas argues that those who receive the fruits of Christ's passion—exaltation to eternal life—must first be configured to him by enduring the passibility and mortality of the flesh. The lesson is summed up well by Paul (quoted by Aquinas): "When we cry, 'Abba! Father!' it is the Spirit himself bearing witness with our spirit that we are children of God, and if children, then heirs, heirs of God and fellow heirs with Christ, provided we suffer with him in order that we may be glorified with him" (Rom 8:15–17). This necessity that we suffer with Christ is all the more true if we sin after baptism. Baptism gives us a share in Christ's passion, by configuring us sacramentally to his death. Aquinas refers to Romans 6:4, "We were buried therefore with him by baptism into death, so that as Christ was raised from the dead by the glory of the Father, we too might walk in newness of life." If (or when) we sin after baptism, we are not re-baptized but we are configured afresh to Christ's suffering by means of penance. In this way we continue to suffer the punishment of sin in certain respects, while knowing that Christ has borne the full punishment in a manner far beyond our relatively small sufferings.

Paul provides the *sed contra* for Aquinas in article four, which asks whether Christ's passion reconciled us to God. In a passage that Aquinas also quoted in article two of question forty-seven, Paul affirms: "For if while we were enemies we were reconciled to God by the death of his Son, much more, now that we are reconciled, shall we be saved by his life" (Rom 5:10). Aquinas explains that sin is what makes us enemies of God, and so whatever takes away sin thereby reconciles us to God. Christ's passion takes away our sin by means of Christ's supreme love in paying the penalty of death. Christ's giving up of his life out of love for us is such a good act that it satisfies for the sins of all who are united to his passion.

The fifth article, on whether Christ opened the "gate" of the kingdom of heaven, is built around three quotations from the letter to the Hebrews. The *sed contra* quotes Hebrews 10:19, to which I add verses 20–22: "Therefore, brethren, since we have confidence to enter the sanctuary by the blood of Jesus, by the new and living way which he opened for us through the curtain, that is, through his flesh, and since we have a great priest over the house of God, let us draw near with a true heart in full assurance of faith." The "sanctuary" here is the heavenly sanctuary, where Jesus is at the right hand of the Father. By his passion, Jesus has opened the way into this heavenly sanctuary. Hebrews is using the imagery of the temple curtain that concealed the holy of holies and prevented the Israelites from entering. In this vein Aquinas further cites Hebrews 9:11–12, "When Christ appeared as a high priest of the good things to come, then through the greater and more perfect tent (not made with hands, that is, not of this creation) he entered once for all into the Holy Place, taking not the blood of goats and calves but his own blood, thus securing an eternal redemption." Yet this reliance on Hebrews also poses a problem for Aquinas, because Hebrews devotes much space to praising the faith of the saints from Abel to Daniel, who lived before Christ but who nonetheless (according to the passage quoted by Aquinas) "through faith conquered kingdoms, enforced justice, received promises, stopped the mouth of lions" (Heb 11:33). If people before Christ could by faith merit eternal life, how then can Christ be said to have opened the "gate" of the heavenly kingdom? Aquinas replies that their faith and charity cleansed them from their sins but not from original sin, which only Christ's passion removes. They were able to enter heavenly glory only after Christ's victorious passion.

Article six addresses Christ's passion as meriting his exaltation to the right hand of the Father. The previous five articles discussed the effects that Christ's passion causes in us. This final article, therefore, treats the effect that Christ's passion produces for himself, namely the merited reward of exaltation. Aquinas has treated this previously, but here he discusses it more extensively. In the *sed contra* he again quotes Philippians 2:8–9, "And being found in human form he humbled himself and became obedient unto death, even death on a cross. Therefore God has highly exalted him and bestowed on him the name which is above every name." In the *respondeo* Aquinas defines merit by appealing to Paul's explanation in Romans 4:4, "Now to one who works, his wages are not reckoned as a gift but as his due." Paul's point is that we, like Abraham, have received a gift (justification) that was not our due; we have been reckoned righteous by God because of our faith. Aquinas, however, employs Paul's statement in order to make clear that Christ has received a gift (exaltation) that is his due. He merited these "wages" by his passion.

With respect to Christ, Aquinas speaks in the *respondeo* of a fourfold self-humbling mirrored by a fourfold exaltation. The fourfold exaltation of Christ consists in his resurrection, ascension, sitting on the right hand of the Father, and judiciary power. In describing Christ's ascension as merited by Christ's death, Aquinas quotes Ephesians 4:9 (to which I add verse 10): "In saying, 'He ascended,' what does it mean but that he had also descended into the lower parts of the earth? He who descended is he who also ascended far above all the heavens, that he might fill all things." Paul makes clear that Christ ascends to the right hand of the Father in order to pour forth spiritual gifts upon his church. One can also see from Paul's language that by his descent, Christ truly merits the ascent. In addition, Aquinas quotes Philippians 2:8–9 once more, and this time he includes verse 10, "that at the name of Jesus every knee should bow, in heaven and on earth and under the earth." He uses the passage from Philippians to highlight that Christ's sitting at the right hand of the Father, where he receives divine honor, corresponds to the merit of Christ's humbling himself by accepting death on the cross.

SUMMARY

How does Paul's theology of the cross inform Aquinas's reflections on the cause of Christ's passion, on the causal power of Christ's passion, and on the effects of Christ's passion in humans (questions 47–49)? The first main issue was whether the Father commanded the death of his innocent Son. Aquinas answers that Christ certainly did die out of obedience (Philippians 2:8, Romans 5:19), but that this obedience was a free act of perfect love for us (Ephesians 5:2, Galatians 2:20). Christ's sacrifice, which fulfilled the sacrificial worship of the Mosaic law, could not have reconciled humans to God without the central element of interior obedience and love (Ephesians 5:2, Colossians 2:16–17, Romans 5:10). The commands of God to which Christ was obedient were the precepts of the Mosaic law, namely the moral (charity), ceremonial (sacrifice), and judicial (satisfaction and redemption) precepts that Christ fulfilled on the cross (Galatians 2:20, Colossians 2:16–17). Because Christ died freely out of love, the Father was not guilty of evildoing when he did not spare his Son from the cross (Romans 8:32). No satisfaction made by a mere human could have been sufficient, and so in sending the Son, the Father's supreme mercy shines forth precisely in the restoration of justice (Romans 8:32, Romans 11:22). Furthermore, Christ's persecutors—at least most of them—did not know who he was (1 Corinthians 2:8).

The second key issue was how to describe Christ's saving work and Christ's status as savior. By his passion, Christ merited exaltation both for himself and for us (Philippians 2:9). His passion works our salvation as a holy sacrifice and as redemption from sin (Ephesians 5:2, Galatians 3:13). He is the sole redeemer, although the saints can cooperate with his work by their example and exhortation (Galatians 3:13, Colossians 1:24). Although Christ dies in weakness, this very weakness reveals God's saving power (1 Corinthians 1:25, 2 Corinthians 12:4, 1 Corinthians 1:18). Because Christ is the divine Son, the saving power of his passion can be present to all times and places through faith and the sacraments of faith (Romans 3:25).

Third, Aquinas treated the issue of how Christ's passion changes our lives. Christ's passion shows us how much God loves us, so that God elicits our free love rather than compelling our love (Romans 5:8). We share in Christ's passion by faith living through charity (Romans 3:25, Romans 5:8). Christ's passion sanctifies us and reconciles us to God (Romans 5:10, Hebrews 10:14). Although God still permits the devil to be active in the world, Christ's passion redeems us from the captivity to the devil produced by our repudiation of God (2 Thessalonians 2:9). We no longer owe the debt of punishment for sin, now that Christ has paid it, but we still must suffer and die so as to be conformed to Christ's passion and thus to his glorious exaltation (Romans 6:4, Romans 8:17, Romans 6:23). By his passion, Christ opens the kingdom of heaven (Hebrews 9:11–12, Hebrews 10:19), not least for those who had faith in him before his coming (Hebrews 11:33). Christ merited his own exaltation, and so we can be sure that his passion and resurrection are intrinsically related (Philippians 2:8–10, Ephesians 4:9, Romans 4:4).

CONCLUSION

In my summaries of Aquinas's use of Paul in questions 46–49, I have already anticipated the conclusion of the chapter. But it seems to me that it might still be of help here to conclude by summarizing the things Aquinas learns from Paul. There are seven areas in which he learns most from Paul. First, Paul affirms that Christ's passion is the work of the incarnate Son of God. Second, Paul seeks to show that Christ's passion fulfills the Mosaic law, or in other words fulfills God's covenantal work in Israel. Third, Paul emphasizes that Christ's passion should be understood as a work of free obedience, humility, and love. Fourth, Paul does not wish to suggest that the power of Christ's passion comes solely from Christ's interior disposition; on the contrary, Christ's innocent shedding of his blood is also significant because it pays the penalty of sin, so that Christ's passion accomplishes the perfect sacrifice, redemption, and satisfaction for sin. Fifth, Paul makes clear that Christ merits his exaltation but that we receive salvation strictly as God's gift through Christ the sole redeemer. Sixth, Paul urges us to be configured to Christ's passion and to share in its fruits by faith and charity. Seventh, Paul holds that Christ's passion is intrinsically connected to his resurrection, and that Christ's passion opens the door to the kingdom of heaven.

In these fundamental areas, Aquinas's theology of the cross is profoundly Pauline, because of his range of Pauline quotations and the decisive character they have in shaping his arguments in each article of his treatise. One might ask, however, whether Aquinas's treatise suffers from being rooted in an Aristotelian procedure of investigation. Does the form of his treatise move him away from the historical Paul's theology of Christ's passion? Aquinas organizes his reflections by first studying Christ's passion in itself (the fittingness of its central elements), then the cause of Christ's passion (God the Father, Christ, and/or his persecutors), then the power of Christ's passion to liberate us from sin and to elevate us to eternal life, and then finally the effects that Christ's passion causes in us. These four questions do not correspond to the focus of any particular letter. Yet, it is notable that in each of the first three questions, Aquinas brings to his investigation quotations from Romans, 1 Corinthians, 2 Corinthians, Galatians, Ephesians, and Philippians. All of these letters are represented in each question. This is the mark of speculative theological engagement, which brings together and integrates texts from the most important Pauline letters. In his fourth question, Aquinas allows Romans and Hebrews to be the predominant voices, which is fitting given their importance for Christian theology of salvation.

In *A Theology of the Cross: The Death of Jesus in the Pauline Letters*, Charles Cousar divides his study into five chapters, "Jesus' Death and God," "Jesus' Death and Human Sinfulness," "Jesus' Death and the Resurrection," "Jesus' Death and the People of God," and "Jesus' Death and the

Christian Life."[14] The Pauline passages that Cousar singles out for particular attention are Romans 3:21–26, 4:24–25, 5:6–8, and 6:1–11; 1 Corinthians 1:18–2:5, 5:1–13, 11:17–34, and 15; 2 Corinthians 4:7–15, 5:14–6:2, and 13:1–4; Galatians 3 and 6:11–18; and Philippians 3:2–11. In his four questions in the *Summa theologiae*, Aquinas relies upon nine of these fourteen passages. The five passages that are not present in Aquinas's four questions include, first, Romans 4:24–25: "It will be reckoned to us who believe in him that raised from the dead Jesus our Lord, who was put to death for our trespasses and raised for our justification." Aquinas quotes this text three times in his questions on Christ's resurrection. First Corinthians 11:17–34, the next missing passage, appears fourteen times in Aquinas's questions on the eucharist. Second Corinthians 4:7–15, with its statement that Paul is "always carrying in the body the death of Jesus, so that the life of Jesus may also be manifested in our bodies" (2 Cor 4:10), and Galatians 6:11–18, where Paul says "far be it from me to glory except in the cross of our Lord Jesus Christ," do not appear in Aquinas's treatise, but Aquinas cites other passages that make clear our configuration to Christ's death. Aquinas cites Philippians 3 at a variety of points throughout the *tertia pars*. The other nine passages that Cousar privileges—Romans 3:21–26, 5:6–8, and 6:1–11; 1 Corinthians 1:18–2:5, 5:1–13, and 15; 2 Corinthians 5:14–6:2 and 13:1–4; and Galatians 3—appear a total of sixteen times. My point is that if we take Cousar's list of key passages as broadly representative of modern scholarship about Paul's theology of the cross, we find these central passages to be well represented indeed in Aquinas's theology of Christ's passion (not least in its connection with Christ's resurrection and the sacraments).

Cousar treats a number of other passages, including Philippians 2:6–11, in passing. His portrait of Paul's theology of the cross focuses on the seven letters that he considers authentically Pauline: Romans 1 and 2 Corinthians, Galatians, Philippians, 1 Thessalonians, and Philemon. He is thus unable to give a central place, as Aquinas does, to Ephesians or Hebrews. Insofar as these letters only strengthen Aquinas's penetration into the Pauline theology of the cross, I hope to have shown that the theologian or biblical scholar seeking a portrait of Paul's theology of Christ's passion would do well to read the *Summa theologiae*.

14. See Cousar, *A Theology of the Cross*.

CHAPTER 3

BAPTISM

IN A NICE IMAGE, Liam Walsh describes Thomas Aquinas's theology of the sacraments as "eschatology in the flesh ... [I]t is the way that Christians live the 'already' of Christ in the 'not yet' that waits the return of all things to God in the glory of the resurrection."[1] For Aquinas, Walsh observes, baptism establishes believers in the communion of the church. This point is made also by Colman O'Neill, whose *Sacramental Realism* owes a significant debt to Aquinas. The Holy Spirit can unite humans to Christ prior to their reception of baptism. By baptism, however, believers become full members of the eucharistic community of

---

1. Liam G. Walsh, OP, "Sacraments," in *The Theology of Thomas Aquinas*, ed. Rik Van Nieuwenhove and Joseph Wawrykow (Notre Dame, Ind.: University of Notre Dame Press, 2005), 328. For further discussion of Aquinas's sacramental theology and his theology of baptism, see Michael Dauphinais, "Christ and the Metaphysics of Baptism in the *Summa Theologiae* and the *Commentary on John*," in *Rediscovering Aquinas and the Sacraments: Studies in Sacramental Theology*, ed. Matthew Levering and Michael Dauphinais (Chicago: Hillenbrand Books, 2009), 14–27; Liam G. Walsh, OP, "The Divine and the Human in St. Thomas's Theology of Sacraments," in *Ordo sapientiae et amoris*, ed. C.-J. Pinto de Oliveira (Fribourg: Éditions universitaires, 1993), 321–52; Bernhard Blankenhorn, OP, "The Place of Romans 6 in Aquinas's Doctrine of Sacramental Causality," in *Ressourcement Thomism: Sacred Doctrine, the Sacraments, and the Moral Life*, ed. Reinhard Hütter and Matthew Levering (Washington, D.C.: The Catholic University of America Press, 2010), 136–49; Bernhard Blankenhorn, OP, "The Instrumental Causality of the Sacraments: Thomas Aquinas and Louis-Marie Chauvet," *Nova et Vetera* 4 (2006): 255–93; John P. Yocum, "Sacraments in Aquinas," in *Aquinas on Doctrine: A Critical Introduction*, ed. Thomas G. Weinandy, OFM Cap., Daniel A. Keating, and John P. Yocum (London: T. and T. Clark, 2004), 159–81.

the church: "Baptism itself, in its very performance in the name of the Trinity and as a profession of the community's faith in Christ, looks towards participation in the Eucharist."[2] When O'Neill goes on to describe the sacrament of baptism in detail, he relies heavily on the Pauline letters, especially Romans but also the Corinthian correspondence, Ephesians, Colossians, and Philippians. Baptism has a central place in Paul's theology, as befits one who, after his blinding encounter with the risen Christ on the road to Damascus, "rose and was baptized" (Acts 9:18) by Ananias.

In his four questions on baptism in the *Summa theologiae*, Thomas Aquinas quotes Paul eighty-nine times. As usual, the most cited epistle is Romans—although this time the disproportion is more than normal, with Romans appearing thirty-seven times and the second-most frequently cited epistle, Ephesians, appearing only about half as many times (seventeen). Aquinas refers to 1 Corinthians thirteen times, Galatians and Hebrews eight times each, Colossians three times, 1 Timothy twice, and 2 Corinthians and Titus once each. Certain verses are cited multiple times: Ephesians 4:5 appears eight times, Romans 6:3–4 eight times, Ephesians 5:26 five times, and Galatians 3:27–28 five times. The four questions contain a total of forty-two articles, and of these, thirty-six contain at least one quotation from Paul. Of the fourteen epistles that Aquinas considers to be Pauline, the four questions on baptism lack a reference only to Philippians, 1 and 2 Thessalonians, 2 Timothy, and Philemon. Since Aquinas cites only sparingly from 2 Corinthians, Colossians, 1 Timothy, and Titus, it can be seen that his four questions on baptism rely heavily on five of the fourteen epistles.

In accord with the procedure of the first part of this book, I move through Aquinas's Pauline quotations according to the order of the *Summa theologiae*'s questions and articles. This approach gives us an opportunity to see how various Pauline texts interact with each other in articles that contain more than one Pauline reference, as is the case for twenty-one of the forty-two articles. My goal in this chapter is to gain insight into how Pauline theology informs Aquinas's understanding of the sacrament of baptism.

2. Colman E. O'Neill, OP, *Sacramental Realism: A General Theory of the Sacraments* (Chicago: Midwest Theological Forum, 1998), 121.

QUESTION 66: OF BAPTISM IN ITSELF

The first article asks whether baptism is the mere washing by water. It might seem that Aquinas would answer no, but in fact he wishes to link the outward sacrament (the mere washing) and the inward effect (justification and the "character" that baptism inscribes) as tightly as possible. His *respondeo* builds upon Hugh of St. Victor's and Peter Lombard's definitions of the sacrament of baptism, both of which emphasize the washing by water. In his *respondeo*, Aquinas distinguishes between *sacramentum tantum*, *res et sacramentum*, and *res tantum*. The "sacrament alone" is visible and external: it is the washing by water. The reality or "res" is the internal effect. The *res et sacramentum*, then, is the unity of the sacrament's external and internal dimensions. In the reply to the first objection, Aquinas addresses John Damascene's way of defining baptism in terms of the inward effect, since the outward washing does not last whereas the inward effect can endure and in the case of the "character" does endure. Aquinas accepts this way of defining baptism, although he underscores that the outward and inward dimensions of the sacrament must be kept together. In the midst of his consideration of Damascene's definition, he examines the enlightenment brought by baptism. Baptism is called the sacrament of faith because it inaugurates our spiritual life, so that we are freed from sins and able to live by faith. In this regard Aquinas applies to baptism Hebrews 10:38, which itself is a quotation of Habbakuk 2:4: "My righteous one shall live by faith."

After this opening article in which Hebrews 10:38 serves to present baptism's relationship to faith, the second article quotes Romans 6:3: "Do you not know that all of us who have been baptized into Christ Jesus were baptized into his death?" This article asks whether baptism was instituted after Christ's passion. Aquinas answers that baptism was instituted by Christ at his own baptism. The first objection includes the reference to Romans 6:3 and argues that since the saving power of Christ's passion is operative in all the sacraments, and since the cause precedes the effect, baptism must have been instituted after Christ's passion so that we could be baptized into it. In reply, Aquinas says that Christ himself gave baptism its saving power. Baptism is a sacramental sign of Christ's passion and derives its saving power from it, but Christ could give this power to the sacrament even prior to his passion.

The third article bolsters the relationship of baptism to faith by quoting Romans 10:17, "faith comes from what is heard," in the reply to the first objection. The article asks whether water is the proper material element of baptism, or whether another material element (such as fire or oil) could be used. Aquinas considers that God chose water as the proper matter of baptism because of its unique ability to signify the nature of baptism (regeneration unto spiritual life) and the effects of baptism (cleansing from sins), along with its universality and its ability to signify our participation in Christ's pasch. In the reply to the first objection, he notes that fire would have not been an appropriate sign, since fire enlightens actively whereas in baptism we are passively enlightened. Why then does John the Baptist promise that Christ will baptize with the Spirit and fire? Aquinas observes that fire here may symbolize the Spirit, or it may symbolize purification by suffering or purification after death.

The fourth article asks whether plain water, rather than (for example) rose-water, should be used. This article lacks a citation of Paul, but the fifth article has three such citations. The topic of the fifth article is the "form" of baptism, the words spoken by the minister that express what the sacrament is and that consecrate the sacrament. Without these words, there is a washing with water but not a sacrament. The form of baptism, Aquinas says, needs to express the cause of baptism: the triune God (the principal cause) and the human minister (the instrumental cause). The proper form of baptism therefore is "I baptize you in the name of the Father, and of the Son, and of the Holy Spirit." Regarding why the sacrament of baptism needs words, Aquinas quotes Ephesians 5:26, where Paul states that Christ died for the church in order "that he might sanctify her, having cleansed her by the washing of water with the word." This passage seems to indicate clearly that absent the words, the washing alone does not suffice.

The church in the Greek-speaking East, however, uses a different form for baptism. The Orthodox baptize with water and the following words: "May the servant of Christ, _____, be baptized, in the name of the Father, of the Son, and of the Holy Spirit." Aquinas notes appreciatively that these words seek to ensure that the minister does not seem too powerful.

If believers imagine that baptismal grace depends on the human minister, there will be a recurrence of the unfortunate situation Paul describes in 1 Corinthians 1:12 (quoted by Aquinas): "Each one of you says, 'I belong to Paul,' or 'I belong to Apollos,' or 'I belong to Cephas,' or 'I belong to Christ.'" Aquinas gladly grants that the Orthodox form is valid, although he defends the active tense ("I baptize you") in the Latin rite because this form underscores the minister's intention to baptize. Every valid baptismal form must in some way express the intention to baptize. Simply to proclaim the name of the Father, Son, and Holy Spirit would be insufficient, because, as Aquinas says with reference to Colossians 3:17, everything that we do must be done in the divine name.

Article five thus emphasizes the role of the words in the sacrament, along with the need to avoid confusing the instrumental cause of baptism (the human minister) with God. The words must express the minister's intention and must invoke the holy Trinity who causes the baptismal effect. Thus far, then, we have had Pauline quotations about faith, Christ's passion, the words of baptism, the church, and the Trinity. The sixth article is about whether one can validly baptize in the name of Christ rather than in the name of the Trinity. In favor of this position, the first objection quotes Acts 8:12, which in Aquinas's version reads "in the name of Christ they were baptized, both men and women." Aquinas buttresses the objection by citing Ephesians 4:5, "one Lord, one faith, one baptism." If there is "one baptism," how could there have been baptisms in the early church that were in the name of Christ rather than in the name of the Trinity? Aquinas replies by suggesting that perhaps the apostles received a revelation permitting them, for a time, to baptize in Christ's name so as to increase reverence for the savior. In his *respondeo*, he makes clear that since Christ commanded that we baptize in the name of the Trinity, and since the Trinity causes our sanctification, baptism should be conferred in the name of the Trinity.

The seventh article also contains Ephesians 4:5 in the first objection. The topic is whether immersion is necessary for a valid baptism, and it seems that the answer must be yes since many churches practice immersion and there is only "one baptism." Replying to this objection, Aquinas observes that washing with water is a necessary material component of baptism, as shown by Ephesians 5:26's reference to "the washing of water [*lavacro aquae*]," but there are various valid ways in which this washing can be done. There are three other citations of Pauline texts in article seven. The second objection quotes Romans 6:3–4 to argue that the only way to be buried with Christ symbolically is to be immersed in water. Aquinas agrees that immersion most clearly signifies burial with Christ, but he argues that this can also be signified, in a lesser but real way, by washing with water any part of our body. The *sed contra* comes from Hebrews 10:22, "Let us draw near with a true heart in full assurance of faith, with our hearts sprinkled clean from an evil conscience and our bodies washed with pure water." In Aquinas's view, Hebrews's use of the image of sprinkling indicates that baptism can be validly done by sprinkling, which makes sense for a number of situations, such as when there is little water, or the baptized person is ill, or the minister is not strong enough to support the weight of the person being baptized. Lastly, Aquinas quotes Romans 4:11 in his reply to the third objection. The third objection argues that since original sin affects the whole body, baptism should be by immersion. Aquinas replies that in cases where baptism cannot be by immersion, the most appropriate part of the body to pour water upon is the head. This is the case even though circumcision, which "was a sign or seal of the righteousness which he [Abraham] had by faith" (Rom 4:11), involved the procreative member, since Christ was to be born of the seed of Abraham.

This seventh article therefore contains a variety of baptismal themes drawn from Paul: the unity of baptism, washing (or sprinkling) with water, sharing in Christ's passion, circumcision as a figure of baptism. The eighth article asks whether threefold immersion is necessary for baptism, in order to signify the three days of Christ's burial and the causality of the Trinity, as well as to make clear that the second and third immersions are not re-baptisms. Aquinas explains that for various reasons, the church over the centuries has practiced both single immersion and threefold immersion. Both are valid, although threefold immersion is now the required practice. Replying to the objection that if threefold immersion were not necessary then the second and third immersions would be re-baptisms, he quotes Jerome's comment on Ephesians 4:5–6, in which Jerome states that the three immersions are one baptism, because the intention is to confer one baptism with the three immersions, not to confer three baptisms.

In the ninth article, we find six citations from Paul, the first two of which are already familiar—Ephesians 4:5 and Romans 6:3–4. The ninth article addresses the topic of re-baptism, which Aquinas rejects. The *sed contra* is Ephesians 4:5, "one faith, one baptism." In the *respondeo*, Aquinas builds upon Paul's comments that we "were baptized into his [Christ's] death" (Rom 6:3) and that Christ has died "once for all" (Rom 6:10). Since Christ dies but once, never to die again, so also we should be baptized only once. Aquinas goes on to interpret Hebrews 6 as being about those who have been baptized, but who have then fallen away so as to "crucify the Son of God on their own account and hold him up to contempt" (Heb 6:6). Such persons cannot be restored or re-baptized (see Hebrews 6:4). Quoting Romans 5:18, Aquinas also argues that just as original sin cannot be renewed, so also baptism, which takes away original sin by applying the salvation won by Christ, cannot be renewed.

The final reference to Paul in this article occurs in the reply to the fifth objection. That objection proposed that since both baptism and the eucharist sacramentally represent Christ's passion, the fact that the eucharist (a "more perfect sacrament than baptism") is repeated daily means that baptism, too, can be repeated. Aquinas replies that baptism represents Christ's passion insofar as we die with Christ so as to be born into new life, whereas the eucharist represents Christ's passion so that we might share in his sacrificial body and blood at the eucharistic banquet. Just as we are born once and eat many meals, so also we should be baptized once and receive the eucharist frequently. To portray the eucharist, Aquinas quotes 1 Corinthians 5:7–8, "For Christ, our paschal lamb, has been sacrificed. Let us, therefore, celebrate the festival [*Pascha nostrum immolatus est Christus: itaque epulemur*]."

The tenth article, about the church's rite of baptism, includes four Pauline references. The first two have a minor role. In the third objection, Aquinas cites Galatians 3:28, "there is neither Jew nor Greek," and Colossians 3:11, "here there cannot be Greek and Jew, circumcised and uncircumcised, barbarian, Scythian, slave, free man, but Christ is all, and all in all." In themselves these passages are highly significant for the theology of the spiritual life bestowed by baptism. The objection, however, simply notes that if major differences such as Jew and Greek no longer matter, then minor differences such as changing into a white baptismal garment seem to be useless. In the reply to this objection, Aquinas notes that the white garment is not necessary, but it has the worthwhile purpose of symbolizing the glory of resurrection and the purity of life that should follow from baptism, as stated by Romans 6:4: "We were buried therefore with him by baptism into death, so that as Christ was raised from the dead by the glory of the Father, we too might walk in newness of life." Aquinas also cites Romans 6 in replying to the first objection. He observes that the church rightly celebrates solemn baptism on the eve of Easter rather than on the feast of the epiphany (when Christ was baptized), because baptism has its power from Christ's passion, with regard to which Aquinas quotes Romans 6:3: "Do you not know that all of us who have been baptized into Christ Jesus were baptized into his death?"

The three references to Paul in article eleven appear in the first objection, the *sed contra*, and the reply to the third objection. The article asks whether there are three kinds of baptism: baptism of water, baptism of blood, and baptism of the Spirit. The first objection quotes Ephesians 4:5, which we have seen repeatedly above, in order to argue that baptism is one, not three. Aquinas replies that the latter two baptisms are included in water baptism, because water baptism derives its power from Christ's passion (baptism of blood) and from the Holy Spirit. The *sed contra* quotes Hebrews 6:2, "with instruction about ablutions [*baptismatum doctrinae*]," for the purpose of citing the gloss on this verse, which highlights the plural "ablutions" (or "baptisms") and which suggests, rather implausibly, that the plural is used because of the three kinds of baptism. Aquinas's reply to the third objection remarks that John of Damascus lists various other (figurative) baptisms, such as the Israelites' crossing of the Red Sea, about which Paul says that "all were baptized into Moses in the cloud and in the sea" (1 Cor 10:2). This is Aquinas's first citation of 1 Corinthians 10, which plays an important role in typologically connecting the life of Israel with that of the church, but whose role in the article is not particularly significant. By now it should be clear that Aquinas takes care to quote the major Pauline baptismal texts, even if the place that these texts receive in a particular article may not seem important. By quoting these texts, Aquinas presents a biblical theology of baptism that operates both on the surface of the *Summa*'s narrative and, as it were, under the surface.

The twelfth and final article of question sixty-six contains two citations of Paul, in objections two and three, respectively. Objection two argues that baptism of blood (martyrdom) is *not* the most excellent form of baptism, because true baptism of blood is possible only with baptism of the Spirit (the infusion of charity). In defense of this position, the objection cites 1 Corinthians 13:3, "If I deliver my body to be burned, but have not love, I gain nothing." Objection three points out that Christ's passion, the model of baptism of blood, relied upon the Holy Spirit, as can be seen from Hebrews 9:14, "How much more shall the blood of Christ, who through the eternal Spirit offered himself without blemish to God, purifying your conscience." Aquinas replies to both objections by granting that baptism of blood must include baptism of the Holy Spirit, but he observes that the converse is not true, and so baptism of blood is more perfect. Through these Pauline citations, Aquinas underscores that possessing charity is necessary for baptismal grace to have its due effect. He makes clear that Christ's passion and the Holy Spirit are the sources of baptism's saving power.

Examination of each Pauline citation in these twelve articles shows, not surprisingly, that Aquinas's concerns regarding the sacrament of baptism often differ from those of Paul. Consider articles 10–12, on the Church's baptismal rite, the three kinds of baptism, and whether baptism of blood is the most excellent of the three kinds. To say the least, none of these are issues that Paul takes up. Yet Aquinas quotes Paul nine times in these three articles. Does this mean that Aquinas's use of Paul is artificial? I hope to have made clear that the answer is no, so long as one allows that Paul need not have treated the topics in order to illumine central aspects of the topics. For example, regarding the baptismal rite, the key question is what kind of rite would be appropriate for signifying the difference that baptism makes. Aquinas uses Paul—Galatians 3:28 and Colossians 3:11—to ensure that this difference is not conceived in any superficial way. With respect to whether the baptized person ought to put on a white garment in the baptismal rite, or when the church ought to hold its solemn baptismal ceremonies, it is a matter of symbolizing that "all of us who have been baptized into Christ Jesus were baptized into his death" so that "as Christ was raised from the dead by the glory of the Father, we too might walk in newness of life" (Rom 6:3–4). Similarly, in article eleven, regarding the three kinds of baptism, Aquinas uses 1 Corinthians 10:2 in order to show that he has not thereby excluded the Old Testament "types" of baptism: he does not look upon baptism solely in terms of the New Testament, cut off or isolated from the Old. And in article twelve on the superiority of baptism of blood, Paul serves to ensure that we understand baptism in terms of the centrality of charity (1 Corinthians 13:3) and in terms of the redemptive power of Christ's shedding of his blood on the cross through the Holy Spirit.

Most of the other topics of question sixty-six, likewise, cannot be considered ones that were pressing for Paul. Paul does not engage questions such as when Christ instituted baptism (article two), whether plain water is the required matter of the sacrament (articles three and four), whether the baptismal formula is suitable or whether baptism in the name of Christ suffices (articles five and six), whether full immersion and threefold immersion are needed (articles seven and eight), and whether baptism can be repeated. The articulation of these questions belongs to the later development of the sacrament in the church. Paul does not give detailed instructions about the administration of the sacrament of baptism, although he clearly presumes that it should be done with water. Similarly, Aquinas's first article in question sixty-six, regarding whether baptism is the mere washing, invokes a distinction between *sacramentum tantum*, *res tantum*, and *sacramentum et res* that obviously is not in Paul's vocabulary, even if Paul does make clear that we can receive the sacrament without receiving its saving effects.

If question sixty-six generally raises issues that arose well after Paul wrote his letters, is it appropriate for Aquinas to appeal to Paul so much in this question—nineteen times in articles 1–9, and nine more times in articles 10–12? The answer is yes. In article one, for instance, Aquinas's treatment of whether baptism is a mere washing is enhanced by Paul's connection between baptism and faith (and article three also makes this connection). Article two on the institution of baptism holds that Christ instituted the sacrament at his baptism, but nonetheless, by reference to Paul, also insists upon a profound connection to Christ's passion. This

Pauline contribution is absolutely necessary for understanding Christ's baptism—and ours—in relation to his passion. Aquinas's reflections on the baptismal formula rightly draw upon Paul's concern that Christians not suppose they were baptized into Paul or into any other disciple. Aquinas also benefits here from Paul's connection between the washing and the word (in Ephesians 5) and by Paul's reverence for the divine name (Colossians 3). The unity of baptism (Ephesians 4) is at stake when Aquinas inquires in article six whether baptism can be conferred in the name of Christ and when in article eight he wonders whether threefold immersion is tantamount to being baptized thrice. In article seven, the reasons for baptismal immersion become more apparent thanks to Paul's emphasis on being baptized into Christ's death, while at the same time Paul's connection between baptism and faith lends weight to the church's practice of baptizing both by full immersion and by washing the head. Last, the six references to Paul in article nine—which examines whether baptism can be repeated—help Aquinas identify the unrepeatable nature of baptism: since we are baptized into Christ's death and resurrection, which occurred but once (Romans 5–6), baptism should occur only once.

Theologically, then, Aquinas employs Paul to probe into the foundations of why the church does what it does with respect to the sacrament of baptism. By employing Paul so extensively, he not only answers the questions posed to him by later tradition, but also establishes important markers regarding the nature of the sacrament of baptism. It is clear, nonetheless, that Paul does not determine Aquinas's mode of treating "baptism in itself." Rather, Aquinas is guided by later controversies over the sacrament and its proper rite, among them the question of re-baptism, the question of whether water baptism is necessary for salvation (or whether baptism of blood and baptism of the Spirit suffice), the question of whether baptism could have been instituted before Christ's passion, the adequacy of the baptismal formula (especially given the difference between the East and West), whether baptism in the name of Christ is permissible (a controversy in which Pope Pelagius II was involved), the different practice among the churches regarding immersion, and so forth. To answer these later questions, as well as to formulate their central concerns with precision, Aquinas returns to Paul. Paul's connection of baptism with faith, his insistence on the centrality of charity, his development of baptism's link with Christ's pasch and the Holy Spirit, and his appreciation for the unity of baptism provide the core of Aquinas's theology of "baptism in itself" in question sixty-six.

QUESTIONS 67 AND 68: THE MINISTERS AND RECIPIENTS OF BAPTISM

Question sixty-seven, on the ministers of baptism, contains eight articles and thirteen references to Pauline texts. In general, these references are not especially significant, and so with a few exceptions, I will treat them more briefly. The second objection of article one notes that Pseudo-Dionysius includes the duty of cleansing among the responsibilities of deacons. Since Ephesians 5:26 shows that baptism is a washing or cleansing, it seems that baptism should be a duty of deacons. Following the instruction of Pope Gelasius I, however, Aquinas holds that deacons should baptize only in cases of urgency.

The second article argues that priests have the responsibility of baptizing. Aquinas quotes 1 Corinthians 10:17, "we who are many are one body, for we all partake of the one bread," by way of observing that the eucharist, the consecration of which is the central purpose of the ministerial priesthood, is the sacrament of unity. Since baptism enables a person to share in the unity of the church and to receive the eucharist, priests are therefore also called to baptize. In the reply to the first objection, Aquinas explains that while bishops (the successors of the apostles) can baptize, they are not called primarily to do so. As evidence, he recalls Paul's example: in 1 Corinthians 1:14 and 16, Paul names three Corinthians whom he baptized but emphasizes that "Christ did not send me to baptize but to preach the gospel" (1 Cor 1:17). The point is that bishops are too busy with other tasks to be primarily responsible for baptizing.

In the third article, Aquinas argues that laity can baptize in cases of necessity. His chief argument comes from God's mercy, since baptism is necessary for salvation and there are many cases—for example, if an infant is dying—when baptism is a matter of urgency and cannot wait for the arrival of a priest. Since God "desires all men to be saved" (1 Tim 2:4), says

Aquinas, God ensured that baptism can be performed not only by priests but also by laity.

The bulk of the Pauline references in question sixty-seven appear in article four, on whether a woman can baptize. Aquinas arrives at his answer by considering Colossians 3:11, "Here there cannot be Greek and Jew, circumcised and uncircumcised, barbarian, Scythian, slave, free man, but Christ is all, and in all," and Galatians 3:28 (to which I add verse 27), "For as many of you as were baptized into Christ have put on Christ. There is neither Jew nor Greek, there is neither slave nor free, there is neither male nor female; for you are all one in Christ Jesus." The power to baptize does not require the sacrament of orders, and so women can baptize just as validly as men. At the same time, Aquinas considers that no layperson should baptize if a deacon or priest is present, and also that a man should baptize rather than a woman if both are present and the situation is urgent. In this regard he quotes 1 Corinthians 11:3, "The head of every man is Christ, the head of a woman is her husband, and the head of Christ is God." Paul thinks that there is "neither male nor female" in Christ, but at the same time Paul still thinks that the head of the household is the husband. Aquinas also accepts other Pauline texts about the teaching and governing role of men in the church. Thus in objection one, we find 1 Corinthians 14:35, "it is shameful for a woman to speak in church," and in the second objection we find 1 Timothy 2:12, "I permit no woman to teach or to have authority over men."

The sixth article asks whether several people, at the same time, can baptize the same person. This topic gives Aquinas the opportunity to cite in the *sed contra* and in the *respondeo* one of his favorite passages, "One faith, one baptism" (Eph 4:5). He emphasizes that the form or words of baptism must reflect this unity, since the baptismal washing is integrally connected with the words—as he confirms by citing Ephesians 5:26, which in his version reads "that he [Christ] might sanctify her [the church] by the washing of water in the word of life." If the baptizers said, "We baptize you," then they would be failing to recognize and signify that it is the one Christ who baptizes, and that the minister of baptism must be one because he or she is acting as a minister or representative of Christ, who is one. If each of the baptizers said "I baptize you" at the same time, and the intention of each person was to baptize an unbaptized person, then there would be only one baptism, but the baptizers should receive punishment of some kind, Aquinas says, for baptizing improperly.

Lastly, article eight has to do with the responsibilities of the godparents. Aquinas says that they do not need to instruct their godchild in the faith, if they know that the parents are doing so. Yet by accepting the role of godparent, a person commits himself or herself to instructing the godchild in the faith, if necessary. In the reply to the second objection Aquinas argues that spiritual instruction differs from the instruction that we receive from our parents, because spiritual instruction comes from God. In this regard he quotes Hebrews 12:9, "We have had earthly fathers to discipline us and we respected them. Shall we not much more be subject to the Father of spirits and live?" This verse of Hebrews discusses the fact that God permits us to suffer in order to discipline us and prepare us for eternal life. As Aquinas employs it, the verse buttresses an argument for having instructors in the faith who are not our parents. This moves rather far from the verse's intended meaning, and yet one can see the point: our parents are not our only instructors in Christian faith.

Before evaluating the role of Paul in question sixty-seven on the ministers of baptism, let us survey Aquinas's Pauline quotations in question sixty-eight on the recipients of baptism. Paul appears twenty-one times in the twelve articles of question sixty-eight. Four of these citations are in the first article, which inquires into whether all people need to receive baptism. The purpose of baptism, Aquinas observes, is to unite us to the salvation won by Christ. Lacking union with Christ's saving work, we remain in our sins and cannot attain to eternal life. In this regard Aquinas quotes Romans 5:18, "Then as one man's trespass led to condemnation for all men, so one man's act of righteousness leads to acquittal and life for all men." To show that baptism incorporates us into Christ and thereby enables us to share in his "act of righteousness," Aquinas quotes Galatians 3:27, "For as many of you as were baptized into Christ have put on Christ." In the reply to the first objection, Aquinas cites two more Pauline texts, one from Romans and one from Ephesians. The objection pointed out that since people could be saved without baptism before Christ's coming, it would seem that after Christ's coming the same would be true. Aquinas answers that by implicit faith, and especially through the sign of circumcision, people were united to the future coming of Christ. Thus Abraham "received circumcision as a sign or seal of the righteousness which he had by faith while he was still uncircumcised" (Rom 4:11). After Christ's coming, too, people are united to him by faith, as Paul makes clear when he urges the Ephesians to pray to God the Father "that Christ may dwell in your hearts through faith" (Eph 3:17). The Mosaic sacrament of circumcision signified this faith prior to Christ's coming, and now the Christian sacrament of baptism signifies and causes the enlightenment of faith.

The second article continues the discussion regarding whether anyone can be saved without baptism. If a person has a desire (even an implicit desire) to receive baptism, the person can certainly be saved: indeed, God, "whose power is not tied to visible sacraments," can infuse this inward desire for baptism by faith and charity, and can thereby unite the person to Christ's saving work, even if the person is not in fact able to receive the sacrament. This is Aquinas's answer to the first objection's argument that a catechumen, despite having "faith working through love" (Gal 5:6), would be damned if he or she died before baptism. Quoting another Pauline text—"real circumcision is a matter of the heart, spiritual and not literal" (Rom 2:29)—Aquinas holds that such a catechumen would not be damned, since faith and desire for the sacrament have already incorporated him or her spiritually into Christ. Yet, in Aquinas's view, such a catechumen would have to undergo purgatory for sins that would otherwise have been purged by baptism. Along these lines, he interprets 1 Corinthians 3:15—"he himself will be saved, but only as through fire"—to refer to the situation of those who owe a debt of punishment for their sins but who are nonetheless imbued with faith and charity.

The third article is about deferring baptism, which Aquinas rejects for infants but accepts for adults who are preparing, as catechumens, to receive baptism. The only Pauline citation comes in the third objection and consists in Hebrews's warning against sins after baptism: "How much worse punishment do you think will be deserved by the man who has spurned the Son of God, and profaned the blood of the covenant by which he was sanctified, and outraged the Spirit of grace?" (Heb 10:29). Aquinas replies to this objection by pointing out that baptism gives us the grace not to sin. If we sin after baptism, furthermore, we can have recourse to the sacrament of penance. The fourth article inquires into whether sinners who intend to remain in their sins should be baptized, so as to justify them at least for the time being. Aquinas answers that if by "sinners" we mean those who have guilt for past sins, then sinners should be baptized, just as Ephesians 5:26 describes. But if by "sinners" we are talking about those who intend to continue sinning, then the sacrament of baptism will impress the baptismal character but, until the person repents, will lack the effect of removing sin. No one who intends to continue sinning can "put on Christ" (Gal 3:27) in the sense of sharing in his righteousness. In this regard Aquinas once more quotes 2 Corinthians 6:14, "For what partnership have righteousness and iniquity?" In his reply to the third objection, he adds that as the sacrament of faith, baptism's salvific effects can only build upon "faith working through love" (Gal 5:6).

The fifth article asks whether baptism should be followed by an act of penance on the part of the newly baptized sinner. In the *sed contra* Aquinas cites the remarks of Ambrose on Romans 11:29, "For the gifts and the call of God are irrevocable." Commenting on this verse, Ambrose states that in baptism God remits all punishment for sin, so that no acts of penance are needed. In his *respondeo* Aquinas likewise argues that when we are incorporated into Christ's passion and death, we receive the satisfaction that he makes and we do not need any of our own. To buttress this point, he quotes Romans 6:3–4, "Do you not know that all of us who have been baptized into Christ Jesus were baptized into his death? We were buried therefore with him by baptism into death."

The *sed contra* of the sixth article also refers to Ambrose's remarks on Romans 11:29. This article asserts that the sacrament of penance, and in particular the confession of sins, is not needed prior to baptism, since baptism itself forgives all sins. Nonetheless those who are preparing to be baptized should confess their sins interiorly and repent of them before God.

The seventh article investigates whether the recipient of baptism must intend to receive the sacrament. In his *respondeo* Aquinas refers to one of his favorite texts, Romans 6:4, in order to show that baptism entails leaving one's old life behind so as to lead a new life. This requires the intention to receive baptism, at least for an adult who possesses the use of free will. Along similar lines, the eighth article addresses the question of whether the sacrament of baptism requires that the one seeking baptism possess right faith. Aquinas argues that in order to receive the grace of baptism, one must possess faith, even though the baptismal character is imprinted by the power of God whether or not the baptized person possesses faith. In his *respondeo*, he cites Romans 3:22—"the righteousness of God through faith in Jesus Christ"—in support of the view that the effect of baptism, namely righteousness, can only be had with faith. He makes the same point in an objection by quoting Ephesians 3:17, "That Christ may dwell in your hearts through faith." The objection raises the problem of infant baptism, a problem that is made more difficult by Aquinas's strong affirmation of the necessity of intending to be baptized and of having faith.

The ninth article addresses infant baptism directly. With the help of Augustine, Aquinas defends the view that infants should be baptized, despite their lack of both intention and faith, on the grounds that "as the child while in the mother's womb receives nourishment not independently, but through the nourishment of its mother, so also children before the use of reason, being as it were in the womb of their mother the Church, receive salvation not by their own act, but by the act of the Church."[3] The intention and faith of the infant's baptismal sponsors make up for the infant's inability to make use of reason. Romans 5:17 and 5:12 appear in the *respondeo* in order to show that just as infants receive condemnation in Adam, so also infants surely should be able to receive the remedy in Christ through the sacrament of baptism. Building upon Romans 5:12, verse 17 states, "If, because of one man's trespass, death reigned through that one man, much more will those who receive the abundance of grace and the free gift of righteousness reign in life through the one man Jesus Christ." With assistance from John 3:5, Aquinas reasons that this free gift must be available through baptism to all who are affected by the transmission of sin, including infants.

The eleventh article contains the final two references to Paul in question sixty-eight. The topic of this article is whether an infant, even while

---

3. *ST* III, q. 68, a. 9, ad 1.

still in his or her mother's womb, can be baptized. Aquinas responds that an infant in the womb can be sanctified directly by God, but cannot receive a sacrament, since sacraments depend upon bodily actions involving not only the recipient's soul but also the recipient's body. In favor of the view that an infant can be baptized in the womb, the first objection quotes Romans 5:15, which observes that God's free gift in Christ is far greater than the trespass of Adam. To this objection, Aquinas replies that God need not work through the sacrament. God can also sanctify directly, as in the case of John the Baptist. The third objection has to do with difficult births in which both infant and mother are likely to die. Can the mother's womb be opened, thereby hastening her death, so that the infant might be baptized while he or she is still alive? Citing Romans 3:8, where Paul says that we must not "do evil that good may come," Aquinas answers no.

There are various ways to approach the significance of Pauline citations in questions 67–68. We might first note the Pauline citations that, in their own context, actually have to do with baptism, such as Ephesians 5:26, "having cleansed her [the church] by the washing of water with the word"; 1 Corinthians 1:17 (as well as 1:14–16), "For Christ did not send me to baptize but to preach the gospel"; Ephesians 4:5, "one Lord, one faith, one baptism"; Galatians 3:27, "for as many of you as were baptized into Christ have put one Christ"; and Romans 6:4, "we were buried therefore with him by baptism into death, so that as Christ was raised from the dead by the glory of the Father, we too might walk in newness of life." These five passages, which we found already in question sixty-six, provide a scriptural foundation for Aquinas's baptismal theology. In conjunction with these foundational passages, he brings in other texts that relate to the ministers and recipients of baptism. For example, Colossians 3:11 and Galatians 3:28 help to show that women can baptize; Ephesians 3:17, Galatians 5:6, and Romans 3:22 serve to emphasize the connection between faith and baptism; Romans 2:29 and 4:11 highlight the link to circumcision; and Romans 5:12, 15, and 17 undergird Aquinas's argument for why baptism must be available to infants.

Other than in 1 Corinthians 1:12–17, Paul does not say much about the ministers of the sacrament of baptism, which is the topic of question sixty-seven. It is no wonder that in this question, Aquinas relies heavily on canon law and cites Isidore, Pope Gelasius I, Pope Urban II, Pope Nicholas I, and Pope Gregory III. The topics are largely technical ones that would not have occurred to Paul, but to which Aquinas applies certain foundational principles drawn from Paul. Question sixty-eight is much different, because Paul does have a good bit to say about the recipients of baptism. In the first article of question sixty-eight, for example, the use of Romans 5:18 and especially Galatians 3:27 to explain why all humans are now called to baptism clearly resonates well with Paul's own concerns. Similarly, the second article's inquiry into whether anyone can be saved without baptism benefits from Romans 2:29, and the fourth article's discussion of whether baptism should be given to people who intend to remain in their sins makes excellent use of Galatians 3:27 and 2 Corinthians 6:14. Even in question sixty-eight, however, many issues arise that belong to later sacramental theology rather than to Paul, such as article five's treatment of whether baptized adults should be asked to do penance for the sins they committed prior to baptism, and article six's treatment of whether confession of sins should be required for adults prior to baptism. Romans 11:29 plays a role here, mainly to emphasize the sheer gratuity and finality of God's gifting, but Paul's voice is not a major one on these topics.

Aquinas makes good use of Romans 6:4 and Romans 3:22 in showing that an intention to be baptized, as well as right faith, is necessary in the recipient of baptism. Paul would certainly agree, but this only increases the difficulty of the issue of infant baptism. The apostles generally baptized adults, but they also baptized whole households. Aquinas builds his argument in favor of infant baptism partly upon Romans 5, where Paul describes what might be called the corporate personality of Adam and of Christ. This seems an appropriate use of Paul, insofar as for Paul Christ's grace must abound more powerfully than Adam's sin, and insofar as Paul insists upon incorporation into Christ's grace by baptism.

QUESTION 69: THE EFFECTS OF BAPTISM

In the ten articles of question sixty-nine, on baptism's effects, Pauline citations appear twenty-six times. Sixteen of these are from Romans. Paul frequently describes baptism's effects, and arguably this question, along with question sixty-six, shows the most influence of Paul among the four questions of the treatise on baptism.

The first article asks whether baptism takes away all sins; Aquinas answers in the affirmative. The *respondeo* relies upon Romans 6:3 and 6:11. As we have seen, Romans 6:3 states that we are baptized into Christ's death. Romans 6:11 then sums up what baptism accomplishes: "So you also must consider yourselves dead to sin and alive to God in Christ Jesus." By dying, Christ conquered sin and destroyed death. When we share in Christ's death through baptism, we share in his conquest of sin, so that baptism takes away our sins and ushers us into the new life of grace. In his reply to the first objection of article one, Aquinas amplifies his argument that baptism takes away *all* sins. The first objection had argued that baptism only forgives original sin. In reply, Aquinas quotes Romans 5:15–16, which states that "the judgment following one trespass brought condemnation, but the free gift following many trespasses brings justification." Romans 5:16 shows that the "free gift" forgives not only the "one trespass" (original sin) but also "many trespasses" (all of our sins). Paul also appears in response to the second objection's claim that all our sins, other than original sin, are already forgiven simply by our repentance prior to baptism. In his reply to this objection, Aquinas focuses on the fact that the source of all forgiveness is Christ's passion, whose saving power we appropriate by faith and the sacraments. With regard to Christ's passion, he quotes Hebrews 9:22, "Without the shedding of blood there is no forgiveness of sins"—a point that Hebrews makes in order to explain how the sacrifices of the Mosaic law prefigure Christ's once-and-for-all sacrifice. Aquinas concludes that although the intention to repent and be baptized does indeed bring about the forgiveness of sins, nonetheless this forgiveness is received more perfectly in baptism.

The second article, regarding whether baptism frees us from all debt of punishment, quotes Romans three times: once in the first objection, once in the *sed contra*, and once in the *respondeo*. The citation of Romans in the first objection is not particularly significant. The objection quotes Romans 13:1, which in Aquinas's version (different from the RSV) reads: "Those things that are of God are well ordered [*Quae a Deo sunt, ecundat sunt*]." According to the objection, a well-ordered plan would require punishment even after baptism for the sins that people committed before baptism. This position, however, misunderstands what baptism is. In the *sed contra*, we find once more Ambrose's remarks on Romans 11:29, "For the gifts and call of God are irrevocable." Ambrose emphasizes that baptismal grace freely remits all punishment. The *respondeo* relies upon Paul's insistence that "if we have died with Christ, we believe that we shall also live with him" (Rom 6:8). Baptism enables us to share fully in the redemptive power of Christ's passion, so that we owe no debt of punishment for sins committed prior to baptism. In a reply to an objection, Aquinas adds that this has to do with the debt of punishment owed to God, not with a debt of punishment owed to society; baptism does not free sinners from the latter kind of penalty.

The third article presses this topic further: why is it that after baptism, if Christ's passion frees us from our entire debt of punishment, we still have to endure penalties of sin such as concupiscence and (especially) death? In this article we find eight citations of Paul, six from Romans and two from 1 Corinthians 15. The first objection quotes Romans 5:15, which compares the trespass of Adam with the "free gift" in Christ and argues that the latter is more powerful. Yet, as the objection points out, it seems as though Romans 5:15 is undermined by Paul's own argument in Romans 5:12, where Paul states that "sin came into the world through one man and death through sin." If the free gift in Christ is so powerful, then why is the penalty of death still operative among those who have received baptismal grace?

Aquinas begins to answer this question in the *sed contra*, which relies on the gloss to Romans 6:6, "We know that our old self was crucified with him so that the sinful body might be destroyed." The gloss comments that Christ's passion takes away the *sting* of concupiscence and death, so that these can no longer permanently harm those who are incorporated into Christ by baptism. In the *respondeo*, Aquinas adds that baptism could have taken away such penalties as concupiscence and death, but Christ willed that baptism do this for us when our bodies are raised from the dead at the end of time rather than in the present life. It is at the end of time that, as 1 Corinthians 15:54 says, "The perishable puts on the imperishable, and the mortal puts on immortality." The delay enables the members of Christ's body to be fully conformed to Christ, not least by sharing in his suffering. In this regard Aquinas quotes Romans 8:17, where Paul teaches that we are "heirs of God and fellow heirs with Christ, provided we suffer with him in order that we may also be glorified with him." Again citing the gloss on Romans 6:6, Aquinas observes that the trials of concupiscence and death serve as a spiritual training that prepares us to be crowned with Christ in glory. Lest the trials seem overwhelming, Aquinas recalls Paul's promise in Romans 8:11, "If the Spirit of him who raised Jesus from the dead dwells in you, he who raised Christ Jesus from the dead will give life to your mortal bodies also through his Spirit who dwells in you."

Aquinas also points out that if Christ had willed for baptism to remove these trials, people would have flocked to baptism solely for bodily immortality rather than for the true glory of eternal life. Here Aquinas quotes Paul's remark, "If for this life only we have hoped in Christ, we are of all men most to be pitied" (1 Cor 15:19). In its context, Paul's remark has to do with some Corinthians' denial of the resurrection of the dead, but nonetheless Aquinas's application of this text to the foolishness of seeking Christ solely for earthly rewards is a reasonable extension of Paul's intended meaning. In his reply to the first objection, Aquinas returns to Romans 6:6, focusing on Paul's statement that "we might no longer be enslaved to sin" and again quoting the gloss on this verse. The gloss compares the fact that baptism does not immediately destroy concupiscence and death to the fact that a captured enemy might be permitted to live for a little while in order to magnify the victory.

In the fourth article, which explains that baptism causes grace and the virtues to be present in us with a new fullness, Aquinas cites Paul only once, but in the pivotal position of the *sed contra*. He quotes Titus 3:5–6, which says that God "saved us, not because of deeds done by us in righteousness, but in virtue of his own mercy, by the washing of regeneration and renewal in the Holy Spirit, which he poured out upon us richly through Jesus Christ our Savior." Aquinas takes this as something of a definition of baptism. As a "washing" that unites us to God's mercy in Christ, baptism causes "regeneration and renewal in the Holy Spirit." This assures Aquinas that baptism must indeed interiorly bestow grace and the virtues, a point with which Paul would certainly agree.

Article five, containing four references to Paul, asks whether baptism causes three virtuous acts in particular: incorporation into Christ, enlightenment (*illuminatio*), and fruitfulness (*fecundatio*). Aquinas grounds his *respondeo* upon Paul's description of the spiritual life in Galatians 2:20: "I have been crucified with Christ; it is no longer I who live, but Christ who lives in me; and the life I now live in the flesh I live by faith in the Son of God, who loved me and gave himself for me." Paul here beautifully conveys the intensity and intimacy of our incorporation into the crucified and risen Christ. Yet, as the first objection points out, it hardly seems that baptism causes this incorporation. Rather, faith would seem to be the cause of incorporation into Christ. In support of this position, the objection quotes Ephesians 3:17, where Paul urges "that Christ may dwell in your hearts through faith." The second objection then adds the concern that enlightenment or *illuminatio* does not actually arise from baptism; if it did, then we would not need catechesis. On this view, Christians are enlightened not by baptism, but by the catechetical instruction that they receive before baptism (Aquinas's defense of infant baptism does not keep him from preserving the primacy of adult baptism). The objection appeals to the evidence of another passage from Ephesians 3, where Paul speaks of his evangelizing mission: "To me, though I am the very least of all the saints, this grace was given, to preach to the Gentiles the unsearchable riches of Christ, and to make all men see [*illuminare*] what is the plan of the mystery hidden for ages in God who created all things" (Eph 3:8–9). If baptism enlightened people, then Paul's preaching and teaching, by which he illumines the saving plan of God, would seem to be redundant and unnecessary.

How does Aquinas reply to these objections? He grants that spiritual incorporation occurs by faith prior to the baptism of adults. But he notes that baptism adds corporeal incorporation by means of the visible sacrament, and he insists that desire for the sacrament of baptism belongs to right faith itself. Spiritual incorporation prior to baptism, in other words, leads one to desire baptism. Similarly, external preaching and teaching are necessary, even though God's interior enlightenment of our minds does indeed enable us to affirm the truth of the realities of faith. Baptism causes an interior enlightenment or *illuminatio* that increases our understanding of the truths of faith.

The third objection of article five has to do with fruitfulness or *fecundatio*. The objection argues that baptism is fruitful by generating sons and daughters of Christ, and so therefore fruitfulness should be applied to baptism itself rather than being considered an effect of baptism. In his reply to this objection, Aquinas again has recourse to Paul. He quotes 1 Corinthians 4:15, "I became your father in Christ Jesus through the gospel," in order to differentiate between spiritual begetting, which is not an effect of baptism, and fruitfulness in doing good works, which is an effect of baptism. The fruitfulness or *fecundatio* that is an effect of baptism consists not in adoptive filiation but in a new power of doing good works. Although Aquinas's investigation of baptism's effects is much more speculative or analytical than are Paul's rhetorically powerful exhortations, one can see how important Paul is for Aquinas's insistence on baptism's causality, by the power of Christ's cross and the Holy Spirit, of new life in us. Aquinas is not wrong in thinking that Paul teaches that baptism causes the effects identified by Aquinas.

The sixth article, on whether infants receive grace and the virtues from baptism, quotes Romans in the third objection and in the *respondeo*. The third objection makes the problem clear by means of Romans 4:5, "And to one who does not work but trusts him who justifies the ungodly, his faith is reckoned as righteousness." As the objection says, how can an infant, who does not have the use of intelligence, believe or trust in "him who justifies the ungodly"? If trusting in "him who justifies the ungodly" is the standard, then it would seem that an infant could not be reckoned righteous, and thus could not receive sanctifying grace and the virtues in baptism. Baptism might still imprint a "character" that enables the infant to receive sanctifying grace and the virtues when he or she reaches the age of reason. Yet the problem with this is that absent sanctifying grace and the virtues, one is still enslaved by original sin and not truly incorporated into Christ. If this were the case, then it would mean that the baptized infant, were he or she to die before reaching the age of reason, would die in a state of alienation from God despite having received baptism.

Can this problem be solved? In his reply to the objection, Aquinas recalls what he has already said about infant baptism, namely that just as infants depend for life upon their mothers, so infants depend for new life upon mother church: "Children believe, not by their own act, but by the faith of the Church, which is applied to them." In the *respondeo* Aquinas deals with the question of how infants, having no use of reason, can be said truly to have virtues such as faith and charity through baptismal grace. Does a baptized infant really have faith in "him who justifies the ungodly"? In response, he emphasizes first that if baptized infants do not receive grace and the virtues, then baptism would be of no use to infants who die after baptism, since they would have not received the grace of eternal life. In this regard he quotes Romans 6:23, "For the wages of sin is death, but the free gift [*gratia*] of God is eternal life in Christ Jesus our Lord." Given the truth that baptized infants receive grace, do they receive real virtues such as faith? Aquinas explains that although infants, lacking the use of reason, cannot undertake acts of faith and charity, they nonetheless can have the *habitus* of these virtues. When God transforms the infant's soul by the gift of sanctifying grace, the infant receives the virtues as real habits, even without being able to perform the acts of these habits. This truth of this distinction between act and habit can be seen in the case of adults: adults do not lose the virtue of faith every time they go to sleep and cannot undertake acts of faith.

The seventh article is about whether baptism opens the gates of heaven for the baptized person, but this article does not refer to Paul. By contrast, the eighth article on whether baptism has the same effect in all persons possesses two references to Paul. The *sed contra* is taken from Ephesians 4:5, "One faith, one baptism." Paul certainly did not have in view the question of whether baptism has the same effect in all persons when he was writing the letter to the Ephesians. Yet his principle of baptism's unity, when combined with his acceptance of a diversity of gifts of grace, renders him an important source for answering the question that the later church posed. If baptism does not have the same effect in all persons, then the unity of baptism would be threatened. Yet would not baptism have a greater effect upon those who have a larger number of sins? Likewise, would not adults who approach baptism with more devotion receive a greater grace and more perfect virtues from baptism?

In his *respondeo*, Aquinas distinguishes between baptism's "essential effect" and its "accidental effect." In order to preserve the unity of baptism, he argues that all who intentionally receive baptism are completely freed of all their sins. In this sense, baptism's effect is equal in all persons. This is true even if, as Aquinas believes, the devotion with which we approach baptism does in fact influence the degree of grace and the virtues that we receive. What then of the "accidental effect" of baptism? Aquinas considers that God sometimes miraculously adds effects to the sacrament of baptism that add something to the "essential effect" of the remission of sins. The accidental effects of baptism can include such things as the utter abolition of concupiscence in the person or the restoration of bodily health. In support of this view, Aquinas cites Romans 6:6, "We know that our old self was crucified with him so that the sinful body might be destroyed, and we might no longer be enslaved to sin" (in his version this reads "that we may serve sin no longer [*ut ultra non serviamus peccato*]"). Although Paul hardly seems to have in view the meaning that Aquinas derives from this passage, nonetheless Aquinas is right that to be utterly freed from slavery to sin, so that we serve sin no longer, would require the removal of concupiscence. Aquinas takes this interpretation of Romans 6:6 from the gloss, which he also quotes in his *respondeo*. The gloss adds a comment so that its readers would not make the mistake of thinking that the complete removal of concupiscence is a normal effect of baptism.

The last appearance of Paul in Aquinas's treatise on baptism occurs in the first objection of article nine of question sixty-nine, since the tenth article has no Pauline citations. Article nine inquires into whether insincerity—due to lack of faith, rejection of the necessity of the sacrament, or lack of devotion—hinders the effect of baptism. Aquinas argues that insincerity does hinder the effect, although he also thinks that whoever intentionally receives baptism thereby receives the baptismal "character." What insincerity obstructs is the baptismal grace, which will not take effect until the person's heart changes. The first objection, however, quotes Galatians 3:27, "For as many of you as were baptized into Christ have put on Christ." Taken literally, this passage from Paul seems to mean that all baptized persons, even those who received baptism while interiorly scorning it, have been incorporated into Christ by grace and the virtues. Aquinas replies that "all put on Christ, through being configured to Him by the character, but not through being conformed to Him by grace." Is this something that Paul could have recognized as being in accord with his perspective? Although Paul obviously does not differentiate baptismal "character" from baptismal grace, I think that he was aware that baptism requires a good intention in order to make its full difference in the baptized person.

How should we evaluate the role that Paul plays in question sixty-nine? First, Aquinas here introduces two Pauline passages that would have been sorely missed had they been entirely lacking from the four questions on baptism—that is, Titus 3:5–6, which states that God "saved us ... by the washing of regeneration and renewal in the Holy Spirit, which he poured out upon us richly through Jesus Christ our Savior," and Galatians 2:20, "I have been crucified with Christ; it is no longer I who live, but Christ who lives in me; and the life I now live in the flesh I live by faith in the Son of God, who loved me and gave himself for me." Both of these passages parallel other passages that have more significance in the treatise. The one from Titus is most significant, since unlike Galatians 2:20 it would appear to be an explicit allusion—even if only an allusion—to baptism. Titus's description of "the washing of regeneration" fits with Ephesians 5:26's reference to Christ's cleansing the church "by the washing of water with the word." For its part, Galatians's emphasis on our incorporation into the crucified and risen Christ fits not only with Galatians 3:27 but also with Romans 6:3–11.

Second, Aquinas's presentation of the effects of baptism relies heavily upon Romans 6. In question sixty-nine, Romans 6 appears in five of the eight articles in which Paul is quoted. This preponderance of Romans 6 accomplishes two purposes. It grounds Aquinas's theology of baptism's effects in Christ crucified and risen, and it contrasts the "wages of sin" with the "free gift of God." To receive baptism's effects is to die to sin and to rise to newness of life. Our "old self" was enslaved to sin, but our new self has been truly configured to Christ's charity: we no longer owe the penalty of sin, since we have been forgiven in Christ. Our previous destiny was bodily and spiritual death, but our new destiny is bodily resurrection and eternal life. This raises the question: why we do not now possess this new life in its fullness? Why does baptism not transport us directly into eternal life? It also raises the question of whether the effects of baptism are really as all-encompassing as Paul suggests, since it certainly appears that many more people are weighed down by Adam's fall ("the wages of sin") than are uplifted by Christ's grace. By means of Romans 6, Aquinas also shows that faith and evangelization are not sufficient of themselves but instead point to the sacrament of baptism. Romans 6 thus helps Aquinas to identify, contextualize, and respond to the central issues regarding baptism's effects.

Third, insofar as the topic of the effects of baptism touches upon infant baptism, Paul proves to be of help, despite the fact that Paul himself does not discuss the issue. Romans 4:5 assists Aquinas in framing the crucial issue: how can anyone be justified without personal faith? Aquinas argues that since infants possess the disease of original sin, the medicinal effects of baptism must be fully applicable to infants, as to all people. It would not suffice for baptism solely to impress a "character" rather than to sanctify infants. Infants too must be able to be fully incorporated into the body of Christ so as to receive eternal life through baptism, rather than remaining captive to the "wages of sin."

CONCLUSION

Because Paul devoted most of his writing about baptism to describing its effects, Paul's most significant role in Aquinas's four questions on baptism comes in question sixty-nine. For Paul, baptism is a dying to sin and a rising to new life. Baptism has its pattern in Christ's pasch, and it gives us eternal life by incorporating us fully into Christ. Baptism is thus intimately linked with faith as the mode by which we receive God's free gift of salvation. In question sixty-nine, Paul can often be found at the heart of not only Aquinas's responses but also the formulation of the questions. For example, whether baptism takes away all sins and all debt of punishment, whether baptism infuses grace and the virtues, whether spiritual enlightenment and incorporation into Christ flow from baptism, and whether baptism is one sacrament as regards its effect are all topics that can be shown to have their source in Pauline theology, even if not exclusively so.

This is not the case for questions 66–68. The articles in question sixty-six, on the nature of baptism, do not have a particularly Pauline resonance to them: whether baptism is the washing with water, when baptism was instituted, whether water is necessary for baptism, whether the baptismal formula of the Latin Church is accurate, whether immersion is necessary, and whether re-baptism is possible all involve clarifications made by the later church. Even here, however, the most important Pauline baptismal texts are present. Ephesians 4:5 ("one faith, one baptism") appears in five of the twelve articles of question sixty-six, and Romans 6 appears in four of the twelve articles. The crucial typological text from 1 Corinthians 10, about the baptism of the Israelites, makes an appearance, as does Paul's emphasis in 1 Corinthians 1 that baptism unites us to Christ rather than to a particular apostle. Three important baptismal texts from Hebrews—6:2, 6:6, and 10:22—also receive a place. Ephesians 5:26 helps to show that the sacrament of baptism involves both washing with water, and the word or baptismal formula. When question sixty-six treats the central aspects of baptism, therefore, Paul has a significant role in Aquinas's presentation. Paul makes clear that Christian faith includes baptism as a necessary sacrament, that this sacrament involves a participation in Christ's pasch, that this sacrament was prepared for among the people of Israel, that this sacrament is characterized by a washing with water, and that this sacrament unites us in Christ.

In question sixty-seven, on the ministers of baptism, the distance from Paul is more pronounced. As we saw, Aquinas draws heavily on Isidore and on papal teaching for his account of who should baptize. Paul certainly does not address whether deacons, priests, bishops, women, unbaptized persons, or several persons at one time can validly baptize. Nor does Paul talk about the responsibilities of godparents. Nonetheless, certain important baptismal texts that we saw in question sixty-six have significant roles in question sixty-seven, especially Ephesians 5:26, Ephesians 4:5, and 1 Corinthians 1:17. Aquinas's quotation of 1 Corinthians 10:17, which refers to the eucharist, also serves a crucial purpose in locating baptism within an ecclesial rather than individualistic context. As Aquinas writes: "By baptism a man becomes a participator in ecclesiastical unity, wherefore also he receives the right to approach our Lord's Table."[4]

In question sixty-eight, on the recipients of baptism, we find the fa-

---

4. *ST* III, q. 67, a. 2.

miliar texts of Ephesians 5:26 and Romans 6:4. More importantly, we find Galatians 3:27 ("For as many of you as were baptized into Christ have put on Christ") and Romans 5:12–18, where Paul draws the typological connection between Adam and Christ. In light of Romans 5, Romans 6:3–4 makes sense; we are baptized into Christ's death so as to share in his payment of the "wages of sin" that are due to Adam. We are incorporated into Christ's body so that we receive eternal life with him. Again, the topics here are often technical or draw on parts of the New Testament (especially the Gospel of John) outside the Pauline epistles: whether all must receive baptism, whether anyone can be saved without baptism, whether baptism should be deferred, whether unrepentant sinners should be baptized, whether baptized persons should make satisfaction for the sins they committed prior to baptism, whether confession of sins is necessary before baptism, whether faith and intention are required for baptism (and if so how infants can be baptized), whether an infant in the womb can be baptized, and so forth. Yet Aquinas situates these questions within a strongly Pauline framework, with Romans—quoted in eight of the twelve articles of question sixty-eight—as the central voice, especially Romans 5–6's praise of Christ's victory over sin and our baptismal participation in this victory.

Would Aquinas's treatment of baptism be recognizable to Paul? Paul does not ask many of the questions that Aquinas, guided by later debates in the church, asks about the sacrament of baptism. Yet Aquinas's inclusion of eighty-nine quotations of Paul in the forty-two articles of his "treatise" on baptism has a decisive impact. With Paul, Aquinas insists on "one baptism" (Eph 4:5); insists that in baptism we "put on Christ" (Gal 3:27) and are "baptized into his death" so that we are "dead to sin and alive to God in Christ Jesus" (Rom 6:3, 11); draws together baptism with faith and eternal life; identifies baptism as a "washing of water with the word" (Eph 5:26) and as the "washing of regeneration and renewal in the Holy Spirit" (Tit 3:5); envisions baptism as the enlightening and renewing of our minds; and compares baptism with circumcision and with the Israelites' exodus journey. Even so, the baptism that Aquinas has in view is more of an institutional reality insofar as he addresses a number of issues regarding the proper form and minister of the sacrament. Likewise, Aquinas seeks answers to various problems that arose after Paul's time, such as rebaptism, infant baptism, the relationship of baptism and martyrdom, and the distinction between the baptismal "character" and grace. But the way in which Aquinas addresses these issues and problems is deeply indebted to the Pauline framework that he lays out. Indeed, if we had only the gospels, there would be no possibility of the kind of theology of baptism that we find in Aquinas. Its fundamentally Pauline character indicates that, in Aquinas and Paul, we indeed find "one faith, one baptism" (Eph 4:5).

PART 2

THE ORDER OF THE PAULINE LETTERS

CHAPTER 4

THE MOSAIC LAW

IN A RECENT ESSAY on Moses in the *Summa theologiae*, Franklin Harkins observes that "a number of times throughout the *Summa* and in widely divergent contexts, Thomas grapples with the reality that Moses had a very special knowledge of God by virtue of the fact that God spoke to him face to face (Exod 33:11; Num 12:8; Deut 34:10)."[1] This special knowledge relates to the fact that Moses is the one through whom God gives the people of Israel the law at Mount Sinai. As Harkins makes clear, when Aquinas thinks of the Mosaic law, he does not imagine simply a legal code for an ancient near-Eastern people. Rather, he thinks of divine pedagogy that prepares the people of God in various ways for the person and work of the messiah. It is also important to note that he does not think of the Mosaic law as being of theological interest only in the past. For Aquinas, Christians continue to need to reflect upon the Mosaic law. The divine wisdom that Moses conveys remains necessary for understanding the pattern of life in Christ.[2]

---

1. Franklin T. Harkins, "*Primus Doctor Iudaeorum*: Moses as Theological Master in the *Summa Theologiae* of Thomas Aquinas," *The Thomist* 75 (2011): 70.

2. For further discussion of Aquinas on the Mosaic law, see Matthew Levering, *Christ's Fulfillment of Torah and Temple: Salvation according to Thomas Aquinas* (Notre Dame, Ind.: University of Notre Dame Press, 2002) and "Ordering Wisdom: Aquinas, the Old Testament, and *Sacra Doctrina*," in *Ressourcement Thomism: Sacred Doctrine, the Sacraments, and the Moral Life*, ed. Reinhard Hütter and Matthew Levering (Washington, D.C.: The Catholic University of America Press, 2010), 80–91; Douglas Kries, "Thomas Aquinas and the Politics of Moses,"

Paul has a wide array of things to say about the Mosaic law. Indeed, recent biblical scholarship has witnessed a burst of energy regarding Paul's use of the Mosaic law. Richard Hays's *Echoes of Scripture in the Letters of Paul* focuses entirely on the question: "How did Paul interpret Israel's Scriptures?"[3] Hays's book has stimulated a number of more specialized investigations, such as Ross Wagner's treatment of Paul's use of Isaiah. It has also stimulated studies that further investigate Paul's quotations from the Torah, most notably Francis Watson's *Paul and the Hermeneutics of Faith*.[4] A central question for the present chapter is how Paul's insights should instruct Christian theological reflection on the Mosaic law.

In Thomas Aquinas's treatise on the old law in questions 98–104 of *pars prima-secundae* of the *Summa theologiae*, quotations from Paul (including Hebrews) occur 116 times. The dominant Pauline voice in these seven questions is Hebrews, with thirty-five citations. Romans is next with twenty-six citations, followed by Galatians with sixteen and 1 Corinthians with thirteen. A much smaller number of citations come from Colossians (seven), 1 Timothy (seven), 2 Corinthians (five), Ephesians (five), Philippians (one), and 2 Timothy (one). Titus, 1 and 2 Thessalonians, and Philemon are not present in the treatise. Hebrews is by far the leading Pauline source for questions 101–4, which have to do with the ceremonial and judicial precepts of the old law. The leading Pauline source with regard to questions 98–100, on the old law in itself, the distinction of precepts, and the moral precepts, is Romans. Twenty-one of the twenty-six citations of Romans appear in these first three questions, whereas twenty-seven of the

---

Review of Politics 52 (1990): 84–104; Beryl Smalley, "William of Auvergne, John of La Rochelle and St. Thomas Aquinas on the Old Law," in *St. Thomas Aquinas 1274–1974: Commemorative Studies*, vol. 2, ed. Armand Maurer (Toronto: Pontifical Institute of Mediaeval Studies, 1974), 11–71; A. Paretzky, "The Influence of Thomas the Exegete on Thomas the Theologian: The Tract on Law (Ia-IIae, qq. 90–108) as a Test Case," *Angelicum* 71 (1994): 549–78; Ulrich Kühn, *Via caritatis: Theologie des Gesetzes bei Thomas von Aquin* (Göttingen: Vandenhoeck and Ruprecht, 1965); John Y. B. Hood, *Aquinas and the Jews* (Philadelphia: University of Pennsylvania Press, 1995).

3. Richard B. Hays, *Echoes of the Scripture in the Letters of Paul* (New Haven, Conn.: Yale University Press, 1989), x.

4. See Francis Watson, *Paul and the Hermeneutics of Faith* (London: T. and T. Clark International, 2004) and J. Ross Wagner, *Heralds of the Good News: Isaiah and Paul in Concert in the Letter to the Romans* (Leiden: Brill, 2003).

thirty-five citations of Hebrews appear in the last four questions. Twelve of the sixteen citations of Galatians appear in question ninety-eight, on the old law in itself, and in question 103, on the duration of the ceremonial precepts (where we would certainly expect to find Galatians). Eight of the thirteen citations of 1 Corinthians appear in question 102, on the reasons or causes for the ceremonial precepts. This also might have been expected given 1 Corinthians's discussion of the sacraments, especially the eucharist.

Of the letters other than Hebrews, then, we can say the following: Romans and Galatians play the dominant role (twenty out of twenty-five citations) in question ninety-eight, the inaugural question of the treatise and the only question that concerns the old law in its entirety. Romans also is the leading voice in question one hundred, on the moral precepts. First Corinthians and Romans are highly significant in question 102, and Galatians is important in question 103. Even excluding Hebrews, therefore, Paul's voice resounds throughout much of the treatise. With Hebrews included, Aquinas's dependence on the Pauline letters for his understanding of the Torah (in itself and in relation to the new law inaugurated by Jesus Christ through the sending of the Holy Spirit at Pentecost) is even more evident.

This chapter offers a detailed inquiry into the role of the Pauline citations in Aquinas's treatise on the old law. The first and most important section of the chapter focuses on the citations of Romans, 1 Corinthians, and Galatians. Second, I inquire into the significance of the letters that appear only occasionally, namely 2 Corinthians, 1 and 2 Timothy, Ephesians, Philippians, and Colossians. Last, I explore the contributions of Hebrews. The place of this epistle within the Pauline corpus is unclear at best but which nevertheless plays a significant role here. I aim to uncover how Paul's voice—or the voices that Aquinas thought to be Paul's—informs Aquinas's approach to the Mosaic law.

ROMANS, 1 CORINTHIANS, AND GALATIANS IN AQUINAS'S TREATISE ON THE OLD LAW

Romans

The first article of the treatise contains more than one third of the references to Romans found in the whole treatise (nine out of twenty-six). This article asks whether the old law was good. Clearly a lot hinges on the answer to this issue. The Gnostics of the second century, the Manichees of the later patristic period, and the Albigensians and Cathars of the medieval period all considered the old law to be evil. Martin Luther argued that God stuffed the Mosaic law full of impossible precepts so as to teach us that we cannot attain salvation by works and to punish those who tried. For Friedrich Schleiermacher, the Old Testament should not be a source for Christian theology, and for G. W. F. Hegel it was a phase in religious history that has been superseded, in accord with the gradual triumph of the spiritual over the carnal.[5] It is worth noting that even the Old Testament itself has passages that seem to express a strong critique of the Mosaic law, especially a passage found in Ezekiel 20:24–26:

> I [God] swore to them in the wilderness that I would scatter them among the nations and disperse them through the countries, because they had not executed my ordinances, but had rejected my statutes and profaned my Sabbaths, and their eyes were set on their fathers' idols. Moreover I gave them statutes that were not good and ordinances by which they could not have life; and I defiled them through their very gifts in making them offer by fire all their firstborn, that I might horrify them; I did it that they might know that I am the Lord.[6]

As the first objection in his article on whether the Mosaic law was good, Aquinas quotes part of this passage from Ezekiel, namely verse 25: "I gave them statutes that were not good and ordinances by which they could not have life." In reply to the difficulties posed by this text, Aquinas points out

---

5. See Friedrich Schleiermacher, *The Christian Faith*, trans. D. M. Baillie et al., ed. H. R. Mackintosh and J. S. Stewart (Edinburgh: T. and T. Clark, 1989); Georg W. F. Hegel, *The Philosophy of History*, trans. J. Sibree (Buffalo, N.Y.: Prometheus Books, 1991).

6. For discussion see Jon D. Levenson, *The Death and Resurrection of the Beloved Son: The Transformation of Child Sacrifice in Judaism and Christianity* (New Haven, Conn.: Yale University Press, 1993), 5–8.

that in a certain sense the ceremonial precepts—namely the laws governing Israel's sacrificial worship—were not fully good, because Israel's animal sacrifices did not make the people holy, although the ceremonies did assist the people to confess their sinfulness. Nothing that they could offer, even their greatest possible goods (namely, their firstborn children), could provide satisfaction for this injustice. This disposed them, Aquinas thinks, to look for a messiah who would redeem them. In this way, the ceremonial precepts could inspire (implicit) faith.

How does Romans function in Aquinas's exploration of the topic? First, Aquinas quotes Romans to suggest that the old law was "not salutary" but instead was "deadly and hurtful."[7] This is the view that Aquinas opposes, but he grants that Romans contains some passages that seem to favor this view. In particular, he quotes Romans 5:20, "law came in, to increase the trespass," and Romans 7:8–9, "but sin, finding opportunity in the commandment, wrought in me all kinds of covetousness. Apart from the law sin lies dead. I was once alive apart from the law, but when the commandment came, sin revived and I died." It would seem that the Mosaic law here plays a fundamentally negative role: the law increases Paul's sin and proves deadly to Paul.

Second, however, Romans also contains passages that show the goodness of the Mosaic law. Aquinas thinks that these passages are decisive. In the *sed contra*, which brings to bear the authority that Aquinas deems most favorable to his own position, he cites Romans 7:12: "So the law is holy, and the commandment is holy and just and good." This verse gives the hermeneutic for interpreting the apparently negative comments about the Mosaic law found in Romans 7:8–9 (whose perspective is continued by verses 10–11). In his *respondeo* Aquinas notes that the goodness of a law depends on whether it is in accord with reason. He argues that by repressing concupiscence and forbidding numerous sins, the Mosaic law was certainly in accord with reason.

He also differentiates between imperfect goodness and perfect goodness with respect to law. A perfectly good law must be sufficient in itself for leading human persons to the ultimate end for which we were created.

---

7. *ST* I-II, q. 98, a. 1, obj. 2.

An imperfectly good law is one that "is of some assistance in attaining the end, but is not sufficient for the realization thereof."[8] Aquinas thinks that the passages in Romans that appear to be negative about the law are manifesting its imperfectly good status, whereas other passages in Romans speak about the perfectly good law, namely the grace of the Holy Spirit through Jesus Christ, which fulfills rather than negates the precepts of the Mosaic law.

Along these lines, Aquinas in his *respondeo* sets forth two further passages from Romans 7 that confirm Paul's view that the Mosaic law is good and that militate against interpreting Romans 7:7–11 as a rejection of the Mosaic law. One of these passages is Romans 7:16, where Paul discusses the rebellion of the flesh against the spirit—that is, even though we know what is good for us, we do the opposite. In Romans 7:16, Paul points out that this tension itself shows the goodness of the law: "Now if I do what I do not want, I agree that the law is good." The other such passage comes from Romans 7:22, again in the midst of Paul's discussion of concupiscence. As he says in Romans 7:21, concupiscence itself is a kind of law, to the extent that "I find it to be a law that when I want to do right, evil lies close at hand." Romans 7:22, which Aquinas quotes, underscores Paul's awareness of the goodness of the law. Here Paul states that "I delight in the law of God, in my inmost self." Paul goes on to distinguish this law, which Aquinas links with the Mosaic law (especially its moral precepts), from the "law of sin which dwells in my members" (Rom 7:23). It is this law of concupiscence, and emphatically not the Mosaic law, that is the bad law which leads to death. The problem with the Mosaic law, then, is that it is an imperfectly good law. It is good, but since it does not overcome our concupiscence, we are unable to follow it and therefore we are unable to be in holy fellowship with God. Holy fellowship with God comes through the grace of the Holy Spirit, which enables us to fulfill the Mosaic law in and with the messiah of Israel.

In Aquinas's view, Romans speaks of this perfectly good law when Paul writes about charity and the grace of the Holy Spirit. Aquinas quotes Romans 5:5, "God's love [or the love of God] has been poured into our

---

8. *ST* I-II, q. 98, a. 1.

hearts through the Holy Spirit who has been given to us." It is love that enables us to fulfill the law of God. We are enabled to love, and thus to fulfill God's law, "through the Holy Spirit who has been given to us." In the same context Aquinas also quotes Romans 6:23, "For the wages of sin is death, but the free gift [or grace] of God is eternal life in Christ Jesus our Lord." God's grace enables us to fulfill God's law, and so the grace of the Holy Spirit, which is conferred by Christ Jesus, perfects and fulfills the Mosaic law. The important point is that the Mosaic law, although imperfect, is not opposed to the perfect "law" that is the grace of the Holy Spirit. Rather, both are good, and the perfect "law" enables us in Christ to fulfill the imperfect law.

Returning to Romans 7:9–11 in his answers to the objections, Aquinas states again that the Mosaic law "is said to be deadly, as being not the cause, but the occasion of death, on account of its imperfection: in so far as it did not confer grace enabling man to fulfil what it prescribed, and to avoid what it forbade."[9] Thus Paul is not blaming the law itself for causing spiritual death. The law does not cause humans to sin against the law. Instead, we are the cause of our own sins. Does this fit with what Paul says in Romans 7:11, "For sin, finding opportunity in the commandment, deceived me and by it killed me"? According to Aquinas, Paul means that because the law did not itself give the grace needed to obey it, the precepts of the law did not stop the Israelites from sinning. Instead they found an opportunity even in the law, and due to their reception of the law, their sins became even more grievous because the law explicitly forbade such sins and also "because concupiscence increased, since we desire a thing the more from its being forbidden."[10] But how does Aquinas know that the Mosaic law did not confer the grace of the Holy Spirit? In answer, Aquinas quotes Romans 9:16, "So it depends not upon man's will or exertion, but upon God's mercy." God's mercy comes to us in Christ Jesus. We receive the mercy of God, the forgiveness of sins and the indwelling of the Holy Spirit, through Jesus. Does this mean, then, that no Israelite had the grace of the Holy Spirit prior to Christ's coming? On the contrary,

---

9. *ST* I-II, q. 98, a. 1, ad 2.
10. Ibid.

Aquinas interprets Psalm 119:32 as indicative of the psalmist's awareness that God has given him, an Israelite, the grace to "run in the way of your commandments."

We have reviewed the nine references to Romans in the first article of question ninety-eight. Aquinas uses Romans to establish both the goodness and the imperfection of the Mosaic law. He also uses Romans to relate the Mosaic law to the grace of the Holy Spirit that comes through Jesus Christ. Romans appears four more times in question ninety-eight: twice in article four, and twice in article six. Article four asks whether God should have given the Mosaic law to the entire human race rather than to the Jews alone. In his *sed contra*, Aquinas cites Romans 3:1–2 in order to confirm God's special election of the Jews. In this passage, Paul asks and answers two rhetorical questions: "Then what advantage has the Jew? Or what is the value of circumcision? Much in every way. To begin with, the Jews are entrusted with the oracles of God." These "oracles" are the sacred writings of scripture, preeminently the Torah or Mosaic law. Paul has argued that the Jews, like the Gentiles, have failed to be holy, since that the Mosaic law was not sufficient by itself to make the people of Israel holy. Like the Gentiles, the people of Israel need the messiah who fulfills the Mosaic law and pours forth the grace of the Holy Spirit, by which we are enabled to love God and neighbor in a holy fellowship. But Paul does not wish to undermine God's unique election of the people of Israel, an election that, as Aquinas says, is confirmed most evidently by the fact that God's revelation, "the oracles of God," was given to the Jewish people.

Why should God elect a people in this way? Aquinas argues that the primary reason is that the messiah—the redeemer and mediator—must come from a particular people, and must be prepared for within that people. This messiah saves not only the people of Israel but all peoples. Even so, he accomplishes the redemption of all peoples in a particular way that can be fully understood only by reading the scriptures of Israel and understanding how Christ has brought God's promises and covenants to fulfillment, so as to establish in Christ a holy nation composed of Jews and Gentiles. For his argument that God elected the people of Israel above all for the purpose of bringing forth the Messiah, Aquinas quotes Romans 9:4–5, where Paul says of his beloved kinsmen: "They are Israelites, and to them belong the sonship, the glory, the covenants, the giving of the law, the worship, and the promises; to them belong the patriarchs, and of their race, according to the flesh, is the Christ, who is God over all, blessed for ever."

The sixth article asks whether the Mosaic law should have been given earlier or later—for example, immediately after the fall, or at the time of Abraham, or at the time of David. Romans assists Aquinas in showing why the time of Moses was fitting for the giving of the law. Aquinas argues that the purpose of God's law is to restrain the proud and instruct the good. Beginning around the time of Abraham, Aquinas thinks, humans began to be tremendously proud of human knowledge and power, due to the development of civilizations. Because of the weakness of human knowledge and power, however, this period was also the time in which the foolish worship of various gods took root and proliferated, and in which humans entered into "the most shameful vices." Thus, among humans who considered themselves to be wise, the natural law itself "began to be obscured on account of the exuberance of sin." Human ignorance was such that the Mosaic law arrived just in time.

Quoting Romans 3:20, where Paul remarks that "through the law comes knowledge of sin," Aquinas concludes that when God allowed humans, in their pride, to live under the natural law alone, the result was the obscuration of natural law. God gave the Mosaic law to restore in the people of Israel a clear knowledge of what constitutes sin. Instructed about sin by the Mosaic law, the people of Israel then came to realize that they could not obey this law by their own power—they could not do what they knew to be right. Once the people of Israel had fully realized this, then they began to await a messiah who would redeem them and make them holy. In the respect Aquinas quotes Romans 8:3–4, where Paul proclaims: "For God has done what the law, weakened by the flesh, could not do: sending his own Son in the likeness of sinful flesh and for sin, he condemned sin in the flesh, in order that the just requirement of the law might be fulfilled in us, who walk not according to the flesh but according to the Spirit."

In summary, Aquinas employs Romans in question ninety-eight (on the old law as a whole) to underscore the goodness and imperfection of the Mosaic law, to gain an appreciation for the election of Israel, and to reflect on how the Mosaic law restored to the people of Israel the knowledge about sin that had been lost due to the obscuring of the natural law as a result of human pride. In every way, Romans serves to affirm the goodness of the Mosaic law without undermining the significance of the coming of Christ to pour forth the grace of the Holy Spirit.

In question ninety-nine, Aquinas refers twice to Romans, once in the first article, and once in the fourth. Question ninety-nine is on the precepts of the old law, and the first article asks whether the old law contains only one precept. The basis for this question is Romans 13:9, which Aquinas quotes in an objection: "The commandments, 'You shall not commit adultery, You shall not kill, You shall not steal, You shall not covet,' and any other commandment, are summed up in this sentence, 'You shall love your neighbor as yourself.'" Recall that in the next verse Paul adds that because love always does the good, "love is the fulfilling of the law" (Rom 13:10). In answer to the question of whether there is really only one precept, Aquinas notes that although all the precepts are ordered to one end—friendship with God and neighbor in love—nonetheless there are various precepts because to attain this end we need to do (and to avoid doing) various kinds of things.

The role of Romans in article one of question ninety-nine is therefore pivotal. What about article four? This article asks whether there are judicial precepts in the old law. Given the general principles of the natural law, judicial precepts are applications of these principles with respect to particular cases involving justice toward our fellow human beings. In this regard, Aquinas interprets Romans 7:12 to sanction the threefold division of the Mosaic law into moral, ceremonial, and judicial precepts. Romans 7:12 says that "the commandment is holy and just and good." The ceremonial precepts are holy, the moral precepts are good, and the judicial precepts are just. This seems like a stretch as far as Paul's meaning is concerned. But nonetheless one can easily suppose that Paul recognizes these three dimensions of the Mosaic law, namely the general principles of justice (the moral precepts) and the particular applications of these general principles, given Israel's time and place, with respect to God (the ceremonial precepts) and to our fellow human beings (the judicial precepts).

In question one hundred, on the moral precepts, Romans figures in articles one, four, six, and twelve. The first article asks whether the moral precepts of the Mosaic law all belong to the natural law. Aquinas answers affirmatively and employs Romans 2:14 in the *sed contra*: "When Gentiles who have not the law do by nature what the law requires, they are a law to themselves, even though they do not have the law." In pointing here to "what the law requires," Paul seems to have in view the moral precepts of the law, since the Gentiles could not be expected to be able to obey "by nature" the specific prescriptions of the ceremonial and judicial laws of Israel. If the moral precepts ("what the law requires") can be fulfilled "by nature," then the Mosaic law's moral precepts must pertain to the natural law. Yet Aquinas observes that not all the moral precepts belong to the natural law in the same way. Some are evident precepts of the natural law, whereas others require much more complex reflection in order for human reason to recognize their truth. Others are in accord with reason but also exceed reason in a certain sense, because they have to do with how to relate to the creator God.

In the fourth article Romans plays only a small role. The article inquires into whether the precepts of the Decalogue are suitably distinguished from each other. An objection quotes Romans 7:7, where Paul writes, "I should not have known what it is to covet if the law had not said, 'You shall not covet.'" In Exodus 20, however, God issues not one commandment about coveting (as Paul can be read to suggest), but two commandments: "You shall not covet your neighbor's house; you shall not covet your neighbor's wife" (Exod 20:17; cf. Deuteronomy 5:21). As Aquinas notes in his reply, Augustine's list of the ten commandments divides Exodus 20:17 into two commandments on the grounds that covetousness differs in kind due to its different objects.

Article six has to do with the order of the ten commandments. The role of Romans is again small, even though Aquinas quotes Romans 13:1 in the *sed contra*. Aquinas's text of this passage reads: "The things that are of God, are well ordered [*Quae a Deo sunt, ordinata sunt*]." Paul is speaking of authorities as having been ordained by God. Although Aquinas does not use this text according to its literal sense (even had he known its correction translation), still one can see that the basic principle—namely that God is in charge, and his governance is wise—certainly must apply to the Decalogue if it applies to anything. Aquinas also cites Romans in his answer to the second objection. The objection argues that in the precepts that pertain to how we should treat each other, the negative precepts (such as "Do not kill") should have preceded the affirmative precepts (such as "Honor your father and mother"). Aquinas argues that in the order of knowledge, as opposed to the order of execution, virtue precedes vice, and he defends this claim by means of quotations from Aristotle's *De Anima* and from Romans 3:20, "Through the law comes knowledge of sin." Knowing what is good precedes knowing what is evil. This is not the point that Paul is trying to make in this passage, of course.

Lastly, in article twelve, on whether the moral precepts of the old law justified humans, Romans appears twice. It has a major role in setting the terms of the question. As Aquinas notes in his first objection, it would seem that the moral precepts do indeed justify humans, because Paul says in Romans 2:13 (to which I add verse 14), "For it is not the hearers of the law who are righteous before God, but the doers of the law who will be justified. When Gentiles who have not the law do by nature what the law requires, they are a law to themselves." From this it follows both that there are Gentiles who do "what the law requires," and that there are "doers of the law who will be justified." It would therefore seem that doing the moral precepts is sufficient to justify human beings. In Aquinas's *respondeo*, Romans again has a major place. He quotes Romans 4:2, "For if Abraham was justified by works, he has something to boast about, but not before God." Aquinas makes a distinction between acquired and infused justice. Only the latter, which is a gift of grace, justifies us "before God." This is so because only Christ, by his passion and death, can take away original sin and make us truly just. Nonetheless, the moral precepts do indeed contain the requirements of acting justly, and so those who obey them do exercise the acquired virtue of justice. Although this is not justification in its full sense, it is a valid secondary way of understanding justification. Aquinas explains Romans 2:13–14 as a description of this secondary sense of justification.

In question one hundred, then, Romans has a major role in the first and last articles, but not in between. In the first and last articles, the key text is Romans 2:13–14. Aquinas uses this text both to argue that the moral precepts all have to do with the natural law and to argue that obeying the moral precepts justifies a person in one sense (as the acquired virtue of justice) but not in another sense (as the holiness required for salvation by God, inclusive of the forgiveness of original sin).

Of the remaining four questions of Aquinas's treatise on the old law, only one contains any citations of Romans. In question 102, on the reasons or causes of the ceremonial precepts, Aquinas cites Romans five times—once in the first article, once in the third article, twice in the fifth article, and once in the sixth and final article. Are any of these citations significant?

The first article raises the question of whether the ceremonial precepts are rational or simply arbitrary determinations on God's part. The *respondeo* includes the passage from Romans 13:1 that, as we have seen, Aquinas's version mistranslated. Aquinas goes on to argue, indebted to Maimonides, that the reason for particular ceremonial precepts (for example, why a garment should not be made of wool and linen) can be found in what God was signifying or excluding. Romans's place in this article, then, is minimal.

The third article takes up the topic of whether there is a fitting cause for the Mosaic law's sacrifices. The fifth objection argues that since God is the author of life, it would have been more fitting to offer him live animals than dead ones. This is especially so, says the objector, given Paul's exhortation that we should present our "bodies as a living sacrifice, holy and acceptable to God" (Rom 12:1). Why then did the Mosaic law command that the Israelites slay the sacrificial animals in offering them to God? This is an intriguing and important question, and the citation from Romans greatly contributes to sharpening it. In his answer to the objection, Aquinas offers three reasons for the fittingness of slaying the sacrificial animals. First, slain animals are useful to us as food and for this purpose their flesh is cooked by fire; second, the slaying of the animals signifies both the destruction of sins and the fact that our sins condemn us to death; third, the slaying of the animals prefigures the death of Christ for the expiation of our sins.

Article five, on whether the sacraments of the old law have a fitting reason, quotes Romans 4:9 in the reply to the first objection and Romans

8:3 in the reply to the sixth objection. The first objection argued that circumcision was unfitting because God elsewhere warned the Israelites not to cut themselves, as pagans sometimes did in worship ceremonies. Aquinas replies that circumcision is appropriate to the worship of the one God, on the grounds that it is a sign of what Abraham (to whom God first commanded circumcision) did when in faith he obeyed God and cut himself off from his pagan family. To support this view, Aquinas makes use of Romans 4:11, where Paul writes that Abraham "received circumcision as a sign or seal of the righteousness which he had by faith while he was still uncircumcised." It seems a stretch to argue from Paul's words that Abraham's righteousness comes from cutting himself off from his pagan family and worshipping the one God. Nonetheless, one can agree with Aquinas that, if circumcision is a sign of the righteousness that Abraham had before he was circumcised, then this righteousness is manifested by Abraham's obedience to God's command: "Go from your country and your kindred and your father's house to the land that I will show you" (Gen 12:1). The sixth objection has to do with apparent absurdities in Leviticus 16, including the notion that sins can be carried away by a goat. In his reply, Aquinas quotes Romans 8:3, where Paul describes Christ as being "in the likeness of sinful flesh," and he argues that the goat figuratively signified Christ's flesh.

Lastly, Aquinas again quotes Romans 8:3 in article six, on whether the ceremonial observances (such as the food laws) had a reasonable cause. This citation from Romans occurs in the reply to the fourth objection, about the commandment not to boil a kid in its mother's milk. Aquinas suggests that there may be a figurative reason here: the kid signifies Christ's human flesh, and Christ was not allowed to be killed in his infancy. It is safe to say, then, that Romans plays a very marginal role in question 102, as opposed to its crucial role in question ninety-eight and significant role in question one hundred (namely in the first and last articles, through Romans 2:13–14). The role of Romans in question ninety-nine is not significant, but it is arguably not as minor as Romans's role in question 102. Looking at these five questions in which Romans appears, we can conclude that Romans is truly central only in question ninety-eight, where Romans helps Aquinas to confirm the goodness of the Mosaic law, and in question 102, especially in the third article, where Romans adds force to a difficult problem that arises from the Mosaic law's animal sacrifices—namely, why so many animals had to be killed in service to the God who gives life to all creatures, including to these very animals.

1 Corinthians

In his treatise on the old law, Aquinas cites 1 Corinthians thirteen times; eight of these citations are in question 102, on the reasons for the ceremonial precepts. I will first treat the five citations of 1 Corinthians that appear in the other questions in the treatise before turning to question 102.

Article ten of question one hundred includes two references to 1 Corinthians. The topic of the article is whether the Mosaic law commands the "mode" of charity, that is, commands that its precepts must be observed with love. Aquinas answers no, on the grounds that this would mean that whoever, without love, obeyed a commandment—for example, by taking care of his or her needy parents—would be sinning mortally even by the very act of taking care of his or her needy parents, which is in fact a just act. The two references to 1 Corinthians are both in the objections to Aquinas's position. The first objection notes that good works do not in themselves suffice for eternal life, and quotes 1 Corinthians 13:3: "If I give away all I have, and if I deliver my body to be burned, but have not love, I gain nothing." The second objection observes that there is a precept identified by Paul that commands that good works be done in charity: "So, whether you eat or drink, or whatever you do, do all to the glory of God" (1 Cor 10:31). Only charity enables us to "do all to the glory of God." In answer, Aquinas explains that one can obey one precept of the Mosaic law without obeying another one. To fulfill all the precepts of the Mosaic law does indeed require obeying God's commandment, "You shall love the Lord your God with all your heart, and with all your soul, and with all your might" (Deut 6:5). But one can obey the commandment to honor one's parents, and not commit a mortal sin in so honoring them, even if one does not honor them from charity. One would thereby break the commandment regarding loving God and would merit punishment, but the punishment would not be for breaking the commandment to honor one's parents.

First Corinthians also appears in an objection in article three of question 101. This article asks whether there should have been fewer ceremonial precepts. In the first objection Aquinas quotes 1 Corinthians 8:6: "There is one God, the Father, from whom are all things and for whom we exist, and one Lord, Jesus Christ, through whom are all things and through whom we exist." Since the ceremonial precepts were intended to focus the people of Israel on the worship of the one God, and also to signify the coming messiah, it seems that the oneness of God and Christ would be better served by fewer ceremonial precepts. Aquinas answers that the difficulty of forming people in the worship of the one God, and the difficulty of preparing people for a mystery as sublime as that of Jesus Christ, made it appropriate that there be many ceremonial precepts, just as many medicines are sometimes used to address one significant malady.

Already we can note that although these passages from 1 Corinthians have little importance in the articles in which they appear, nonetheless the passages themselves are important. It makes sense that a Christian discussion of the Mosaic law should be illumined by such passages as 1 Corinthians 13:3: "If I give away all I have, and if I deliver my body to be burned, but have not love, I gain nothing"; 1 Corinthians 10:31, "So, whether you eat or drink, or whatever you do, do all to the glory of God; and 1 Corinthians 8:6, "There is one God, the Father, from whom are all things and for whom we exist, and one Lord, Jesus Christ, through whom are all things and through whom we exist." These passages are indeed central for Paul's understanding of Christ's relationship (and ours) to the Mosaic law. They show that the practices of the Mosaic law have been re-ordered around Christ and the grace of the Holy Spirit.

The next place that 1 Corinthians appears (excluding question 102 for now) is article one of question 103. This article asks whether the ceremonies of the Mosaic law predated the actual Mosaic law. For example, sacrifices, burnt offerings, altars, priesthood, and circumcision all preceded the giving of the law to Moses; one must also consider the distinction between clean and unclean animals, which God employed when speaking to Noah about the animals that should enter the ark (see Genesis 7:2–3). Aquinas explains that there were certainly many religious ceremonies that humans had established prior to the giving of the Mosaic law. He also thinks that some humans were given prophetic wisdom prior to the giving of the Mosaic law, and that these persons were enabled to worship the one God in a manner that prefigured Christ. Perhaps with Melchizedek in mind, he remarks that these persons also were enabled to prefigure Christ by what they did. In this regard he quotes a portion of 1 Corinthians 10:11, "These things happened to them as a figure [τυπικῶς, RSV "warning"], but they were written down for our instruction, upon whom the end of the ages has come." The last citation of 1 Corinthians apart from question 102 is found in the second article of question 104. This article asks whether the judicial precepts were not only literal but also figurative. Aquinas answers in the affirmative by again quoting 1 Corinthians 10:11, this time as evidence that everything that happened to the people of Israel had an aspect that prefigured Christ and the church.

These two citations of 1 Corinthians 10:11 have importance for Aquinas's treatise. We would expect to find this verse in Aquinas's treatise on the Mosaic law. In question 103 on the ceremonial precepts, it is interesting to find the verse as the linchpin of an argument that even prior to the Mosaic law, some ceremonies and deeds already prefigured Christ due to God's dispensation. In question 104 on the judicial precepts, the verse helps Aquinas to insist that nothing that pertains to Israel (and thus ultimately nothing of the Old Testament) lacked a role in prefiguring and preparing for Christ and the church. By quoting this verse, Aquinas emphasizes God's figuration in Israel and the nations.

Among the eight citations of 1 Corinthians in question 102 are two more of 1 Corinthians 10:11. Article two asks whether the ceremonial precepts have a solely figurative purpose. The *sed contra* quotes 1 Corinthians 10:11 to make the point that we have seen above, namely that the whole Old Testament prefigured Christ. Aquinas draws the conclusion that the possession of a figurative sense does not militate against also possessing a literal sense. Article six applies this point specifically to the ceremonial observances such as the food laws. Quoting 1 Corinthians 10:11, Aquinas states that these observances certainly prefigured Christ, and he adds that they also had a rational cause (rather than being arbitrary).

The third article asks whether the ceremonies pertaining to animal sacrifices had a rational cause. In an objection, Aquinas quotes 1 Corinthians 10:18, "Consider the practice of Israel; are not those who eat the sacrifices partners in the altar?" It seems reasonable that "those who eat the sacrifices" be "partners in the altar," but as Aquinas points out, the offerers of certain sacrifices were in fact excluded from eating certain parts of the animals. The ceremonial precepts that command this exclusion thus appear to be unreasonable. In his reply, Aquinas gives reasons for why certain parts of the sacrificial animals were not eaten or were eaten only by the priests. Thus, 1 Corinthians 10:18 helps Aquinas to raise a question, but not a major one. As with the other verses from 1 Corinthians, however, this verse is one that we would expect to find in a Christian treatise on the Mosaic law.

Article five has two citations of 1 Corinthians 5:7 and one of 5:8. The topic of the article is whether there is a reason for the sacraments of the old law, such as the paschal lamb. Objection three observes that since the paschal lamb prefigured the sacrament of eucharist, there should be sacraments of the Mosaic law that prefigure the other six sacraments. Aquinas takes 1 Corinthians 5:7, "Christ, our paschal lamb, has been sacrificed," as evidence that the paschal lamb prefigured the eucharist. The same verse appears in Aquinas's reply to the second objection. The objection involves the commandment to eat in haste the paschal lamb and the unleavened bread; it seems unfitting to eat in haste. In his reply, Aquinas quotes 1 Corinthians 5:7 and 5:8 in order to show the figurative value of the paschal meal. In his view, 1 Corinthians 5:7 indicates that the paschal lamb prefigured Christ's sacrifice, while 1 Corinthians 5:8 ("Let us, therefore, celebrate the festival, not with the old leaven, the leaven of malice and evil, but with the unleavened bread of sincerity and truth") indicates that the unleavened bread prefigured the holy church's partaking of the eucharist. Surely Paul does have some such symbolism in mind. The figuration to which these citations attest is highly important for Aquinas, and we can also note, once again, that a Christian treatise on the Mosaic law should be expected to refer to these verses.

The last two citations of 1 Corinthians in question 102 are found in article six. Here Aquinas quotes 1 Corinthians 9:4 and 9:9. In the eighth objection Aquinas suggests that the ceremonial observances are not all reasonable, since Paul asks rhetorically, "Is it for oxen that God is concerned?" (1 Cor 9:9), whereas the Mosaic law does indeed contain precepts regarding the proper care of animals. In the reply to this objection, he argues that the precepts regarding the care of animals have both a literal and a figurative reason. The literal reason is to regulate human behavior, including proper behavior toward animals. The figurative reason is, just as Paul says, to show that the apostles "have the right to our food and drink" (1 Cor 9:4) just as oxen, too, should not be muzzled while working in the grain field. Paul's point is that the law given in Deuteronomy 25:4 appears to be about oxen but actually was intended by God to be read in a figurative sense and applied to humans. This fits well with Aquinas's understanding of how to read the precepts of the Mosaic law. For Aquinas as for Paul, the figurative sense of the Mosaic law is crucial, even though Aquinas goes out of his way to make clear that the ceremonial precepts are not solely figurative.

Galatians

Galatians has a prominent role in questions ninety-eight and 103. In question ninety-eight, Aquinas cites Galatians 3 seven times. In this chapter of Galatians, Paul is remonstrating with his congregation for turning to observance of the Mosaic law. He repeatedly contrasts depending on "works of the law" (Gal 3:2) for salvation and depending on faith for salvation. The "curse" (Gal 3:10) of the law is that we cannot fulfill it and so we must suffer its penalty, but Christ by his death has borne the curse for us, and through faith in him we can receive the Spirit of righteousness. Aquinas's quotations of Galatians 3 address the issue of why, if we cannot fulfill the law outside Christ, God gave the law in the first place. Put another way, why does Moses have a place between Abraham and Christ?

The second article asks whether God gave the Mosaic law. If the Mosaic law was imperfect and in certain ways intensified sin, then it would seem that the good God would not give his people such a law. The *respondeo* assures us that God did indeed give the Mosaic law, because it prepared his people for Christ by prefiguring him and by directing human worship toward the one God. Aquinas thinks that this preparation is what Paul has in view in Galatians 3:23: "Now before faith came, we were confined under the law, kept under restraint under faith should be revealed."

This restraint is not that of a prison or of something evil, but rather it is the restraint of a pedagogue who disciplines and prepares a child in view of the child's attainment of full maturity. The same point is made in the responses to the first and second objections. The response to the first objection explains that "precepts that are given to children are perfect in comparison with the condition of those to whom they are given, although they are not perfect simply," something that Aquinas confirms by quoting Galatians 3:24: "The law was our custodian [pedagogue] until Christ came." The response to the second objection explains why God would give the Mosaic law even though it was not intended to last forever (that is, outside its fulfillment in Christ). Here Aquinas refers to Galatians 3:25, "Now that faith has come, we are no longer under a custodian."

The third article asks whether the Mosaic law was given directly by God or by God through the angels. The *sed contra* comes from Galatians 3:19 and makes clear that the answer is the angels. Paul states that the Mosaic law "was ordained by angels through an intermediary." Aquinas's version of this text reads: "The law was given by angels in the hand of a Mediator [*Lex data est per angelos in manu mediatoris*]." The fourth article asks why the Jews alone received the Mosaic law. In his *respondeo*, Aquinas answers that the reason was because of God's promises to Abraham, Isaac, and Jacob. In other words, the reason had to do with God's election of the people of Israel rather than with a particular goodness that, prior to the giving of the law, separated this people from other peoples. In identifying the content of God's promises, Aquinas quotes Galatians 3:16, "Now the promises were made to Abraham and to his offspring. It does not say, 'And to offsprings,' referring to many; but, referring to one, 'And to your offspring,' which is Christ."

The last article of question ninety-eight contains references to both Galatians 3:16 and 3:19. As we noted above, this article treats whether the Mosaic law should have been given earlier (or later). The second objection states that since God gave the promises to Abraham, God should have given the law at this time as well. With regard to the messianic referent of God's promises, Aquinas here quotes Galatians 3:16. The *sed contra* cites Galatians 3:19 as a theology of history. The Mosaic law, Paul says, "was added because of trangressions, till the offspring should come to whom the promise had been made" (Gal 3:19). This explains why the Mosaic law was given after Abraham and prior to Christ.

Question 103, on the duration of the ceremonial precepts, refers to Galatians 2 three times, to Galatians 4 once, and to Galatians 5 once. The three citations of Galatians 2 come in articles two and four, respectively. The *sed contra* of article two quotes (apparently mistakenly) an amalgam of Galatians 2:21 and 3:21. The key text, however, is Galatians 2:21: "For if justification were through the law, then Christ died to no purpose." This provides the answer to article two, which asks whether the ceremonies of the Mosaic law were able to justify the Israelites. Aquinas comments that these ceremonies did not cause grace, and so they did not in themselves justify anyone. Yet, as he goes on to say, since these ceremonies prepared for and prefigured Christ, they were able to inspire implicit (or even explicit) faith in Christ in the Israelites who observed them. In this way, the ceremonies certainly did conduce to justification and holiness among the people of Israel.

Article four asks whether the ceremonies of the Mosaic law can be observed without mortal sin after Christ's passion. Like Augustine, Aquinas allows for a transitional time period during which the apostles observed the ceremonies without supposing them to be binding for salvation upon either Jews or Gentiles. Aquinas does not here directly answer whether Jews today act in mortal sin by observing the commandments. His two quotations from Galatians 2 have to do with the controversy between Jerome and Augustine about the disagreement between Peter and Paul. In the second objection and in his response to this objection, Aquinas quotes Galatians 2:11–12, "But when Cephas came to Antioch I opposed him to his face, because he stood condemned. For before certain men came from James, he ate with the Gentiles; but when they came he drew back and separated himself, fearing the circumcision party." In his reply to the objection, Aquinas argues that Peter "did not sin, by observing the legal ceremonial for the time being [i.e., in this transitional period]; because this was lawful for him who was a converted Jew. But he did sin by excessive minuteness in the observance of the legal rites lest he should scandalize the Jews, the result being that he gave scandal to the Gentiles." In the *sed contra* of this same article Aquinas quotes Galatians 5:2, where

Paul makes clear that salvation comes from Christ rather than from also observing the Mosaic law: "I, Paul, say to you that if you receive circumcision, Christ will be of no advantage to you."

The last reference to Galatians in question 103 occurs in article two, which we have already discussed. Arguing that the ceremonies of the Mosaic law did not have in themselves the power to justify, Aquinas quotes Galatians 4:9, where Paul warns the Galatians against turning once more "to the weak and beggarly elemental spirits" (Aquinas's version reads "*egena et infirma elementa*"). Aquinas associates these *elementa* with the weakness of the flesh and blood of sacrificial animals as compared to the power of Jesus Christ. Paul, however, seems to have in mind the return of the Galatians to pagan "bondage to beings that by nature are no gods" (Gal 4:8).

Galatians appears once in question ninety-nine, namely in article six, which asks whether the Mosaic law should have induced people to obedience by means of temporal promises and threats. Why did the Mosaic law not instead make promises and threats regarding eternal life? Aquinas notes in his *respondeo* that the imperfect disposes to the perfect. Spiritual perfection consists in "despising temporal things and cleaving to things spiritual," whereas "those who are yet imperfect desire temporal goods, albeit in subordination to God" and those who are sinful "place their end in temporalities." The Mosaic law was a pedagogue for the imperfect, leading them toward perfection. In this regard Aquinas quotes his favorite passage from Galatians, namely 3:24: "The law was our custodian until Christ came."

In the twelve articles of question one hundred, on the moral precepts, Aquinas twice refers to Galatians. The third objection of article one cites Galatians 5:6, "For in Christ Jesus neither circumcision nor uncircumcision is of any avail, but faith working through love." The point of the objection is that if faith is truly so important for the moral life, then the moral precepts of the Mosaic law cannot all pertain to natural law, since faith is a supernatural gift. In reply, Aquinas allows that some of the moral precepts must be taught to us by God, namely the precepts about how to worship God. The twelfth article, on whether the moral precepts had the power to justify, includes Galatians 3:12 in Aquinas's reply to the second objection. Leviticus 18:5 promises that if a person keeps God's law, that person will live. This text is quoted by Paul in Galatians 3:12, where Paul makes the point that because we are unable by our own power to keep the whole law, we are doomed to incur its penalty unless, through faith in Christ, we are united to the one who has fulfilled the law and borne the penalty for us.

The last citation of Galatians in Aquinas's treatise on the old law occurs in the third article of question 104. This article asks whether the judicial precepts of the Mosaic law are binding forever. Aquinas explains in his *respondeo* that "the judicial precepts were not instituted that they might be figures, but that they might shape the state of that people who were directed to Christ. Consequently, when the state of that people changed with the coming of Christ, the judicial precepts lost their binding force." He confirms this understanding of the law by once again quoting Galatians 3:24, "The law was our custodian until Christ came."

As we would anticipate given the importance of Galatians 3 for Christian understanding of the relationship of the Mosaic law to Christ, therefore, ten of sixteen references to Galatians in Aquinas's treatise on the old law come from Galatians 3. Galatians has a crucial function in Aquinas's treatise, by helping him to account for the Mosaic law's work of preparation for and prefiguration of the messiah.

To sum up this section: Aquinas's treatise on the Mosaic law relies in particular upon Romans 7:8–8:4 (ten out of twenty-six citations), 1 Corinthians 9–10 (seven out of thirteen citations), and Galatians 3 (ten out of sixteen citations). These texts are particularly helpful for Aquinas's task of reading the Mosaic law in light of Christ. Romans 7:8–8:4 insists upon the goodness of the Mosaic law, while at the same time underscoring that it does not suffice for salvation because it cannot overcome the "law" of concupiscence. First Corinthians 9–10 shows that the Mosaic law should often be read typologically or figuratively. It makes this point especially in light of the sacraments of baptism and the eucharist—one might also mention at this juncture 1 Corinthians 5:7–8, cited three times, which depicts Christ as our paschal lamb. Galatians 3 distinguishes between faith and "works of the law." Since it is impossible for us to obey the whole law in our fallen condition, we are bound to the "curse" of the law (death) unless we embrace the promised messiah, Jesus Christ, by faith. The Mosaic law served as a "custodian" or pedagogue to prepare for and prefigure the Messiah, who makes all people "Abraham's offspring, heirs according to the promise" (Gal 3:29).

2 CORINTHIANS, EPHESIANS, PHILIPPIANS, COLOSSIANS, 1 & 2 TIMOTHY

These letters have a relatively minor role in Aquinas's treatise on the old law. None of them is cited more than seven times total, and the most any of them is cited in any particular question is three times. Yet Aquinas introduces passages from these letters that do indeed contribute significantly to a Christian understanding of the Mosaic law.

Aquinas's treatise contains five citations of 2 Corinthians. The first appears in the second article of question ninety-nine. This article asks whether the Mosaic law has moral precepts. It would seem obvious that moral precepts are found in the Mosaic law, but an objection suggests that it would be unfitting for moral precepts to be found in the Mosaic law, because as Paul says in 2 Corinthians 3:6, "The written code kills, but the Spirit gives life." Since the moral precepts, such as the commandment to honor one's parents, can hardly be said to "kill," it seems that somehow there must not be moral precepts in the Mosaic law. Following Augustine, Aquinas replies that "even the letter of the law is said to be the occasion of death, as to the moral precepts; in so far as, to wit, it prescribes what is good, without furnishing the aid of grace for its fulfilment."[11] He has made this point earlier in the treatise when discussing, with the aid of Romans, whether the Mosaic law was good. Yet here he adds a controversial and important passage from 2 Corinthians, one that needs to be interpreted in any Christian theology of the Mosaic law.

Articles eight, nine, and twelve of question one hundred each possess one reference to 2 Corinthians. The eighth article inquires into whether the commandments of the Decalogue are always binding. In the second objection of article eight, Aquinas grants that it would seem that humans cannot dispense other humans from a God-given law. But it seems that

---

11. *ST* I-II, q. 99, a. 2, ad 3.

God, as the giver of the law, can make dispensations from it. Furthermore, since the apostles receive God-given authority in the Christian community, it seems that the pope and bishops ought to be able to dispense others from the commandments of the Decalogue. In support of the authority of the apostles to act *in persona Christi*, Aquinas quotes 2 Corinthians 2:10, where Paul says: "What I have forgiven, if I have forgiven anything, has been for your sake in the presence of Christ [Aquinas's version reads "*in persona Christi*"]." I will discuss Aquinas's reply below, because he builds his reply around 2 Timothy 2:13, "If we are faithless, he [God] remains faithful—for he cannot deny himself." The reference to 2 Corinthians in this case does not seem to be a particularly significant text, not least because Paul has in view forgiveness rather than dispensation from the Decalogue.

The ninth article again employs 2 Corinthians in one of the objections. This article asks whether the commandments of the Mosaic law include the "mode" of the virtuous act that they command (for example, honoring parents would have to be done out of filial piety). Aquinas answers that in order to obey the commandment to honor one's parents (for example), one has to perform an act that truly honors them, but one does not necessarily have to possess the virtue of filial piety. In objection three, however, Aquinas quotes 2 Corinthians 9:7, which seems to suggest the opposite: "Each one must do as he has made up his mind, not reluctantly or under compulsion, for God loves a cheerful giver." It would appear that it is not enough to give alms, but rather one must also give them cheerfully in order to perform a good act of almsgiving. To be cheerful in almsgiving requires possessing the virtues of charity and benevolence. Aquinas argues that in one sense the Mosaic law does command such charity, but in another sense the commandment to give alms commands simply that such alms be given freely. Again the use of 2 Corinthians does not play a major role.

In article twelve, on whether the moral precepts justified human beings, the *sed contra* comes from 2 Corinthians 3:6: "The written code kills [Aquinas's version reads "*Littera occidit*"]." This passage from 2 Corinthians, so important for Augustine's *De spiritu et littera*, is again interpreted by Aquinas to mean that the Mosaic law itself did not infuse the grace of the Holy Spirit (the "new law") needed for obedience to the moral precepts of the Mosaic law. The messiah was necessary.

The final reference to 2 Corinthians appears in article five of question 102, an article that contains a profusion of Pauline references. The article explores whether there are fitting reasons for the sacraments commanded by the Mosaic law. In the response to the fourth objection, Aquinas quotes 2 Corinthians 6:17, which itself is a direct quotation from Isaiah 52:11: "Therefore come out from them, and be separate from them, says the Lord, and touch nothing unclean; then I will welcome you." His argument is that Paul here provides a hermeneutic for reading many of the laws about ritual uncleanness, since in 2 Corinthians 6 Paul is talking about the difference between Christian worship and pagan worship. Aquinas understands Paul to mean that generally speaking "the uncleanness contracted by touching an unclean thing denotes the uncleanness arising from consent in another's sin."[12] Aquinas thereby aims to ground a figurative sense of the Mosaic law's precepts about ritual uncleanness. I am not sure, however, that Paul's use of Isaiah 52 warrants this, although it does seem to me that Paul would accept a figurative sense of the Mosaic law's precepts about ritual uncleanness.

The most important passage from 2 Corinthians, then, is the observation in 3:6 that "the written code kills, but the Spirit gives life." It stands to reason that at some point in his treatise, Aquinas would need to cite and interpret this passage. As we have seen, he does so twice, and one of these citations comes in a *sed contra*, as befits a Pauline text as significant as this one.

Ephesians appears five times in Aquinas's treatise. In question ninety-nine, article one, the *sed contra* comes from Ephesians 2:15 (to which I add verse 14), "For he [Christ] is our peace, who has made us both one, and has broken down the dividing wall of hostility, by abolishing in his flesh the law of commandments and ordinances, that he might create in himself one new man in place of the two." This passage is obviously of central significance for Pauline (and thus Christian) interpretation of the Mosaic law in relation to Christ. Aquinas surely includes it for precisely this rea-

---

12. *ST* I-II, q. 102, a. 5, ad 4.

son. Interestingly, however, the article is actually about whether the law has more than one precept (that is, charity) and, in the *sed contra*, Aquinas employs Ephesians 2:15 because it speaks of "the law of commandments and ordinances" and thereby makes clear that the law has many precepts. He uses an important passage for a rather unimportant purpose.

Article four of question 101 quotes Ephesians 5:2 in the first objection. The article inquires into whether we can suitably divide the ceremonies of the Mosaic law into sacrifices, sacred things, sacraments, and observances. The first objection notes that the ceremonies of the Mosaic law were ordained partly in order to prefigure Christ. It would seem that only the Mosaic law's sacrifices, however, prefigured Christ, and so only the sacrifices are properly called ceremonies. To buttress this claim about the unique significance of the sacrifices, the objection quotes Ephesians 5:2, where Paul uses sacrificial language drawn from the Mosaic law in order to depict Christ's cross: "Christ loved us and gave himself up for us, a fragrant offering and sacrifice to God." Aquinas replies by insisting that not only the Mosaic law's sacrifices, but also its sacred things, sacraments, and observances prefigured Christ and the church. This text from Ephesians is similar to 1 Corinthians 5:7, "Christ, our paschal lamb, has been sacrificed." These are important texts for understanding how Paul conceives of Christ's cross as fulfilling the Mosaic law. Yet Aquinas's use of Ephesians 5:2 here simply helps him to formulate an objection regarding the classification of the "ceremonial" precepts.

The final citations to Ephesians in this treatise occur in question 102, on the reasons for the ceremonial precepts. Ephesians 2:15 appears in article one, Ephesians 5:2 in article three, and Ephesians 3:5 in article four. The first objection of article one quotes Ephesians 2:15, "abolishing in his flesh the law of commandments and ordinances," because the gloss on this verse states that the new law replaced the Mosaic law's observances with decrees based on reason. The implication seems to be that the Mosaic law's ceremonies did not have a reasonable basis, but instead only had a figurative basis. Aquinas grants in reply that in themselves, the details of the Mosaic law's ceremonies did not have a reason (for example, why "a garment should not be made of wool and linen"). But he adds that "there could be a reason for them in relation to something else: namely, in so far as something was signified or excluded thereby."[13] The argument that God framed the ceremonies so as to exclude certain idolatrous or unhealthful practices comes from Maimonides.

In article three, Aquinas employs Ephesians 5:2 in his *respondeo*. He argues that all the Mosaic law's sacrifices prefigure the perfect sacrifice of Christ. On the cross, Christ freely gives his life for our sins out of his supreme charity; and this offering is God's gift to us because he sent his Son for our redemption. Aquinas combines Ephesians 5:2 with John 3:16 and Hebrews 10:11 (which I will discuss below), and in this way presents a full portrait of the gift by which "Christ loved us and gave himself up for us, a fragrant offering and sacrifice to God."

Lastly, Ephesians 3:5 is referenced, without being fully quoted, in the reply to the fourth objection in article four. The objection argues that the temple (and tabernacle) should not have been divided by veils, because God is undivided. Aquinas gives various reasons for the value of the veils. For one, he thinks that these veils signified the different degrees to which the Israelites knew about the coming messiah. He supposes that those closer to the heart of Israel's worship, namely the priests, would have had a better understanding of the prophetic meaning of the rites. In the new covenant, by contrast, the veils are not needed because the mystery of Christ has been fully made known. As evidence for the theology of history that he is presenting here, he directs the reader to Ephesians 3:5, where Paul remarks that "the mystery of Christ ... was not made known to the sons of men in other generations as it has now been revealed to his holy apostles and prophets by the Spirit."

To sum up Aquinas's use of Ephesians, it seems clear that Ephesians 2:15 and 5:2 are texts that should find a place in any Christian treatise on the Mosaic law. Paul's point that Christ "[abolishes] in his flesh the law of commandments and ordinances" seems quite negative about the Mosaic law, but Paul also references the Mosaic law in a more positive way by describing the crucified Christ as a "fragrant offering and sacrifice to God." These texts both pertain to the fulfillment of the Mosaic law by the messiah. While strongly affirming this fulfillment, Aquinas uses these texts

---

13. *ST* I-II, q. 102, a. 1, ad 1.

(along with Ephesians 3:5) to defend the goodness and rationality of the Mosaic law, including its multiplicity of ritual ceremonies, its animal sacrifices, its commandments and ordinances, and its temple and tabernacle with their interior arrangements.

Philippians appears only once in the treatise. In the sixth article of question ninety-nine, as we have seen, Aquinas asks whether the Mosaic law should have employed temporal promises and threats as the means of encouraging the Israelites to obey it. In his *respondeo* Aquinas argues that the Mosaic law serves as a pedagogue for those who love God but are not yet spiritually perfect. As he understands it, spiritual perfection requires freely renouncing material goods. This view of spiritual perfection calls to mind the counsels that pertain to vowed religious. Aquinas defends this view by quoting Philippians 3:13 and 15 (I add verse 14), where Paul says, "I do not consider that I have made it [spiritual perfection in Christ] my own; but one thing I do, forgetting what lies behind and straining forward to what lies ahead, I press on toward the goal for the prize of the upward call of God in Christ Jesus. Let those of us who are mature be thus minded." Most importantly perhaps, Aquinas makes clear that the Mosaic law describes temporal rewards and punishments not because the Israelites are unspiritual (or alienated from God), but simply because they are not perfectly spiritual.

Colossians appears seven times in all, twice in question 101, three times in question 102, and twice in question 103. Articles two and four of question 101 both quote Colossians 2:16–17. In article two, the passage serves as the *sed contra*: "Let no one pass judgment on you in questions of food and drink or with regard to a festival or new moon or a sabbath. These are only a shadow of what is to come; but the substance belongs to Christ." This article asks whether the ceremonial precepts are figurative. It is very important to Aquinas, therefore, that Paul says that not only festivals (such as Passover) foreshadow Christ, but also even food laws and sabbath practices are "a shadow of what is to come." Colossians 2:16–17 helps him to account for the value of all the ritual elements of the Mosaic law in preparing for the coming of the messiah.

In the fourth article of question 101, Colossians 2:16–17 serves to formulate an objection to Aquinas's position that the Mosaic law's ceremonies can be divided into sacrifices, sacred things, sacraments, and observances. It seems that the festivals mentioned by Colossians do not find a place among these four categories. In his reply to this objection, he explains that he includes the festivals in what he means by "sacred things." Although Colossians 2:16–17 is about the fulfillment brought by Christ, Aquinas uses it to take seriously the various kinds of ritual ceremonies commanded by the Mosaic law.

In question 102, article four, Aquinas discusses the ceremonies pertaining to "holy things," such as the tabernacle, altar, and festival days. The sixth objection inquires into whether the things contained in the tabernacle were appropriate, especially in light of God's commandment at Sinai, "You shall not make for yourself a graven image, or any likeness of anything that is in heaven above, or that is in the earth beneath, or that is in the water under the earth" (Exod 20:4). Aquinas argues that there are both rational and figurative causes for each thing that is in the tabernacle. For example, according to Hebrews 9:4 (which we will discuss below), the ark that was in the tabernacle contained an urn made of gold, in which the manna was kept. Aquinas considers that this golden urn prefigures Christ's soul, and the manna here prefigures "the whole fullness of deity" (Col 2:9) that dwells in Christ. This typological interpretation has eucharistic resonances. It also connects broadly with the New Testament's depiction of Christ as the new temple. It is insightful with respect to the Mosaic law only given the supposition of Colossians 2 that the things of the Mosaic law are "a shadow" whose "substance belongs to Christ."

The fifth article twice quotes Colossians 2:11: "In him [Christ] also you were circumcised with a circumcision made without hands, by putting off the body of the flesh in the circumcision of Christ" (a reference to baptism). In his response to the first objection, Aquinas uses this text from Colossians to explain the figurative reason for circumcision. Circumcision prefigures "the removal of corruption."[14] The same text from Colossians appears later in the article, in his response to the third objection. Here Aquinas also cites verse twelve, where Paul adds that "you were buried with him in baptism." The point that Aquinas wishes to make is that some

---

14. *ST* I-II, q. 102, a. 5, ad 1.

sacraments of the new law, including baptism, were directly prefigured by a specific sacrament of the Mosaic law. Colossians, then, helps Aquinas to read the Mosaic law in light of Christ and the church.

Lastly, the same passages from Colossians appear once more in question 103, article three. This article discusses whether the Mosaic law's ceremonies ceased at Christ's coming. In the *sed contra*, Aquinas first quotes Colossians 2:16–17. As we have seen, this passage makes clear that followers of Christ do not need to observe the Mosaic law's ceremonies, because Christ is the fulfillment or the "substance" of these ceremonies. Indeed, were a Christian to observe the Mosaic law's ceremonies in any serious fashion, this would be tantamount to suggesting that Christ had not yet come. The fourth objection argues that circumcision should be an enduring ceremony, since everyone is called to remember and imitate Abraham's faith. In his reply to this objection, Aquinas quotes Colossians 2:11–12, which states that circumcision finds its fulfillment in baptism. Aquinas explains that Abraham's faith pointed to his promised offspring in whom all nations would be blessed. Now that this offspring, Jesus Christ, has come, it is appropriate to signify Abraham's faith by means of a new sign instituted by Christ.

Five of the seven questions in Aquinas's treatise on the old law contain a quotation of 1 Timothy, but three of these questions have only one such quotation, and the other two questions each have only two quotations of 1 Timothy. Article two of question ninety-eight refers in the fourth objection to 1 Timothy 2:4, where Paul says that God "desires all men to be saved and to come to the knowledge of the truth." If God wants all humans to be saved, says the objector, then God would only give a law that can save them. Since the Mosaic law does not suffice by itself to save humankind from sin, it would seem that God did not give it. In his response, Aquinas notes that the Mosaic law prepared for the mediator, Christ, who saved humankind. Aquinas also points out that people from every time and place could be united salvifically to this mediator by implicit faith. Thus 1 Timothy 2:4 enables Aquinas to raise a challenging question regarding the particularity and apparent limits of the Mosaic law.

The next three references to 1 Timothy—once in question ninety-nine and twice in question one hundred—all cite 1 Timothy 1:5. In the RSV, this verse reads, "The aim of our charge is love that issues from a pure heart and a good conscience and sincere faith." The version that Aquinas used, however, translates the first part of this sentence as "the end of the commandment is charity [*finis praecepti caritas est*]." As Aquinas reads it, then, 1 Timothy 1:5 is parallel to Romans 13:10, "love is the fulfilling of the law," and to Jesus's teaching about the commandments regarding love of God and neighbor that "on these two commandments depend all the law and the prophets" (Mt 22:40). Yet Aquinas's understanding of 1 Timothy 1:5 may not be as far off as it appears, since his point is simply that the goal of law, including the commandments of Moses and the injunctions of Paul, is to establish true fellowship between humans and between humans and God.

In the first article of question ninety-nine, Aquinas cites 1 Timothy 1:5 in his response to the second objection. The second objection argued that the Mosaic law can really be said to have only one commandment. Aquinas replies that the whole Mosaic law has only one end or goal—namely love—but that the Mosaic law has many precepts. In the fifth article of question one hundred, 1 Timothy 1:5 again appears in an objection. Citing 1 Timothy 1:5, the objector observes that all the precepts of the Decalogue have to do with love. It seems then that God should have commanded that we love our children and other neighbors, rather than simply commanding that we love our parents. Aquinas replies that the Decalogue is speaking about the unique debt of gratitude that we owe to our parents for bringing us into the world. Last, in the tenth article of the same question, Aquinas explains that the Mosaic law does not command that all other virtues be formed by charity, as in fact they must be in order to lead to salvation. He quotes 1 Timothy 1:5 to show that the act of every virtue has love as its ultimate goal.

First Timothy 4:4 appears twice in question 102 and once in question 103. Speaking of those "who forbid marriage and enjoin abstinence from foods" (1 Tim 4:3), Paul remarks that "everything created by God is good, and nothing is to be rejected if it is received with thanksgiving" (1 Tim 4:4). In article five of question 102, Aquinas draws upon Paul's insistence that "everything created by God is good" in order to formulate an objection to the Mosaic law's teaching about ritual impurity caused by touching a corpse. Since a corpse is created by God and is therefore good, it does not seem that it should cause ritual impurity. In his response to this objection, Aquinas observes that the purity laws relate to our spiritual and bodily integrity before God. Death corrupts our bodily integrity, and so the Mosaic law reasonably connected ritual impurity with touching a corpse. Figuratively, touching a corpse symbolizes spiritual death, and so again the connection with ritual impurity is fitting. Article six of the same question again employs 1 Timothy 4:4 to formulate an objection, this time with respect to the laws forbidding certain foods as unclean. Although Paul probably does not have in mind the Mosaic law's precepts about unclean foods, the objection still fits—if God creates everything good, then there seems no reason for any food to be unclean. Aquinas replies that with regard to its nature, no food can make anyone unclean or defiled, but nonetheless some foods are connected with corruption, such as the flesh of pigs who feed on rotting slops and wallow in mud. The final citation of 1 Timothy 4:4 comes in article four of question 103. Here Aquinas emphasizes the last part of the verse: "Nothing is to be rejected if it is received with thanksgiving." His concern is the council of the apostles in Jerusalem, at which, according to Acts, gentile believers were commanded to "abstain from what has been sacrificed to idols and from blood and from what is strangled" (Acts 15:29). Aquinas quotes 1 Timothy 4:4 in his argument that this prohibition was only for the transitional period during which the new law was taking hold. Under the new law, no food is prohibited as unclean.

Among the Pauline letters that appear infrequently in Aquinas's treatise, only 2 Timothy remains for our study. The lone citation of 2 Timothy occurs in question one hundred, article eight, regarding whether God (or anyone else) can dispense the precepts of the Decalogue. In his reply to the second objection, Aquinas quotes 2 Timothy 2:13: "If we are faithless, he remains faithful—for he cannot deny himself." God cannot deny the order of his own justice; thus he cannot dispense from the Decalogue, although he can accomplish his just will directly through human beings, as for example when he punished the Egyptians by commanding some of their goods to be taken by the Israelites (an act that, as the execution of God's punishment, cannot be considered to be stealing).

In these six letters, what are the most significant passages employed by Aquinas in his treatise on the old law? The answer seems to be: 2 Corinthians 3:6, Ephesians 2:15 and 5:2, Colossians 2:11 and 2:16–17, and 1 Timothy 4:4. Here we learn that "the written code kills, but the Spirit gives life"; that Christ abolishes "in his flesh the law of the commandments and ordinances," that Christ's cross can be rightly depicted in sacrificial language, that we have been "circumcised with a circumcision made without hands, by putting off the body of flesh in the circumcision of Christ," that the Mosaic law's ceremonies "are only a shadow of what is to come; but the substance belongs to Christ," and that "everything created by God is good, and nothing is to be rejected if it is received with thanksgiving." Not surprisingly, these passages emphasize the fulfillment of the Mosaic law in Christ. This fulfillment is significant for any Christian account of the Mosaic law, and so we can safely say that Aquinas's treatise would be impoverished by the lack of them. They help us to understand why we as Christians do not practice circumcision, dietary laws, and many other ceremonies and ordinances found in the Mosaic law. Aquinas interprets them, however, in a way that also points to the value of the Mosaic law in itself. Christians can easily read the Torah without paying attention to the particular laws. Aquinas succeeds in presenting both the fulfillment of the Mosaic laws and their value (including prophetic value) for the people to whom God gave them.

HEBREWS

At the outset of this chapter, I promised to pay attention to Hebrews, although at less length because in certain respects it stands outside the set of Pauline epistles. Each of the seven questions in Aquinas's treatise has at least one citation of Hebrews. Hebrews is quoted twelve times in question 102, six times each in questions 101 and 103, five times in question ninety-eight, three times in question 104, twice in question one hundred, and once in question ninety-nine. Of these quotations, seven come from Hebrews 7; eight from Hebrews 9; six from Hebrews 13; four from Hebrews 1; three from Hebrews 10; two each from Hebrews 6 and 8; and one each from Hebrews 11 and 12. Perhaps the best approach, then, is first to survey

Aquinas's use of Hebrews 7, 9, and 13. Why are these chapters of Hebrews so important in Aquinas's treatise?

Hebrews 7, 9, 13

Article one of question ninety-eight quotes Hebrews 7:19, and article two of the same question quotes Hebrews 7:18. Question 101, article three quotes Hebrews 7:18–19. Question 102, article five quotes Hebrews 7:19 and 7:28. Question 104, article three quotes Hebrews 7:12 and 7:18. In short, we find five citations of Hebrews 7:18–19, one citation of Hebrews 7:12, and one of Hebrews 7:28. What makes Hebrews 7:18–19 preeminent? In this passage, Paul (or the author of Hebrews) says concerning Christ's priesthood after the order of Melchizedek: "On the one hand, a former commandment is set aside because of its weakness and uselessness (for the law made nothing perfect); on the other hand, a better hope is introduced through which we draw near to God." One can see already that this passage is much like the other fulfillment passages that we have discussed above, especially those from Galatians 3, Ephesians 2:15, and Colossians 2:11 and 16–17.

In his *respondeo* in question ninety-eight, article one, Aquinas uses Hebrews 7:19 to confirm that the Mosaic law was imperfect. In the next article of question ninety-eight, Hebrews 7:18 appears in an objection, to the effect that because the Mosaic law does not continue forever (although it does continue forever as fulfilled in Christ), it cannot be a work of God. The *respondeo* of the third article of question 101 employs Hebrews 7:18–19 to underscore the imperfect character of the Mosaic law's ceremonies, and therefore the need to have many such ceremonies. The reply to the third objection of question 102, article five quotes Hebrews 7:19 to help explain why the sacrament of confirmation does not have a typological parallel in the Mosaic law, since the sacrament of confirmation perfects the grace of baptism whereas the Mosaic law is imperfect. In question 104, article three, Hebrews 7:18 appears in the third objection, which argues that the ceremonial precepts are indeed set aside now that Christ has come but the judicial precepts should be retained.

Hebrews 7:18–19 serves Aquinas's reflection not only regarding why Christians no longer observe the Mosaic law as a whole, but also regarding why the Mosaic law has so many ceremonies, the significance of the different kinds of laws (ceremonial, judicial, moral) that are contained in the Mosaic law, and what it means to say that the Mosaic law is imperfect. In this way, Hebrews 7:18–19 helps Aquinas to study the Mosaic law appreciatively—as divine law—and to study it from the perspective of a Christian who does not observe many of the Mosaic law's commandments.

Hebrews 7:12 only appears once, in the *sed contra* of the third article of question 104. It is less significant for Aquinas's treatise than one might expect. Paul states that "when there is a change in the priesthood, there is necessarily a change in the law as well." The messiah has come, and as the high priest of all creation he reconfigures the law around himself, so that we observe its substance in him through the grace of the Holy Spirit. Aquinas uses this verse to show simply that, given the change in the law, the judicial precepts are no longer in force for the messianic people of God. Hebrews 7:28, which states that "the law appointed men in their weakness as high priests" (by contrast to the high priest Jesus Christ), appears in the reply to the sixth objection in question 102, article five. Aquinas uses it to explain why the Mosaic law commanded that on the day of atonement the high priest should first sacrifice a calf in atonement for his own sins.

Hebrews 9:6–14 can be read as a unit. Paul first describes the structure and regulations of the temple, particularly with regard to the Holy of Holies. Only the high priest was allowed to enter the Holy of Holies, and then only once a year, on the day of atonement. In Paul's view, this signified that the way into the heavenly sanctuary had not yet been opened by Christ. He goes on to say that the ceremonies that pertain to the temple service "cannot perfect the conscience of the worshiper, but deal only with food and drink and various ablutions, regulations for the body imposed until the time of reformation" (Heb 9:9–10). Christ, however, "entered once for all into the Holy Place, taking not the blood of goats and calves but his own blood, thus securing an eternal redemption" (Heb 9:12). Through Christ's priestly offering, we are made holy.

Aquinas quotes Hebrews 9:9–10 three times, Hebrews 9:13 twice, and Hebrews 9:4, 9:6, and 9:8 once each. The fourth article of question 101 refers to Hebrews 9:9 in formulating the fifth objection, to the effect that the division of the ceremonial precepts into those pertaining to sacrifices, sacred things, sacraments, and observances is insufficient because Paul also mentions "gifts and sacrifices." In article two of question 103, on whether the ceremonies of the Mosaic law caused the forgiveness of sins, Aquinas in his *respondeo* quotes Hebrews 9:10, where Paul calls the ceremonies "regulations for the body" and makes clear that they could not make people holy. The third objection of question 104, article three refers along the same lines to Hebrews 9:9–10—the ceremonies of the Mosaic law could not make people holy. The two references to Hebrews 9:13, where Paul says that the animal sacrifices sufficed "for the purification of the flesh," occur in article two of question 103 (which also quotes Hebrews 9:10). In the *respondeo* Aquinas quotes Hebrews 9:13 to confirm that the ceremonies did not in themselves cleanse from sin. In the reply to the first objection, Aquinas quotes Hebrews 9:13 to show that when the priests were purified by the blood of sacrificial animals, this served to appoint them to the divine service and removed bodily impediments, but did not purify them from sins.

Aquinas's five quotations of Hebrews 9:9–13, therefore, focus on the point that the Mosaic law's ceremonies did not cause the forgiveness of sins, which comes only through the messiah. What about his references to Hebrews 9:4, 9:6, and 9:8? He cites Hebrews 9:4 and 9:6 in question 102, article four. The response to the fourth objection discusses the separation of the holy place and the Holy of Holies in the temple. Aquinas quotes Hebrews 9:6 to show that the priests (with the exception of the high priest on the day of atonement) only entered into the holy place, and he argues that this fact symbolized the imperfection of the Mosaic law and its orientation toward the new law. The response to the sixth objection refers to Hebrews 9:4, which describes the contents of the Holy of Holies. Aquinas considers that these contents, such as the ark of the covenant, symbolized the contents of the heavenly realm: God, the divine ideas, and angels. Article two of question 101 cites Hebrews 9:8 in the *respondeo*. Aquinas says that the ceremonial precepts were figurative because, as Hebrews 9:8 says, the way to our heavenly country had not yet been fully revealed by Christ. These three citations (Hebrews 9:4, 9:6, 9:8) help Aquinas display the dynamic orientation of the Mosaic law toward eternal life.

Aquinas quotes Hebrews 13:12 four times, Hebrews 13:15 once, and Hebrews 13:8 once. Hebrews 13:12 states: "So Jesus also suffered outside the gate in order to sanctify the people through his own blood." In the treatise on the old law, Aquinas first cites this verse in question 101, article four. Responding to the second objection, he states that the eucharist contains Christ precisely as the one who sanctifies us, and he quotes Hebrews 13:12 as confirmation that Christ sanctifies us. In article five of question 102, Aquinas cites Hebrews 13:12 twice, first in his response to the fifth objection and then in his response to the sixth objection. In the former case, he is making a link between Christ suffering "outside the gate" and the red cow that the Mosaic law commanded to be sacrificed outside of the camp (Numbers 19). In the latter case, he links Christ suffering "outside the gate" and the Mosaic law's command that a scapegoat suffer outside the camp on the day of atonement (Leviticus 16). Lastly, Aquinas quotes Hebrews 13:12 in the second article of question 103. In his reply to the first objection, he notes that the cleansing of the priests by the blood of sacrificial animals prefigured Jesus's sanctifying "the people through his own blood."

Hebrews 13:8 and 13:15 both appear in article four of question 102. In his response to the sixth objection of this article, Aquinas seeks figurative reasons for the two altars (one for burnt offerings and one for incense), and suggests that the altar of incense prefigures Christ, in accord with Hebrews 13:15: "Through him then let us continually offer up a sacrifice of praise to God." In his response to the tenth objection of this article, Aquinas says that the Mosaic law's daily sacrifice of a lamb prefigured the perpetual saving efficacy of Christ as the lamb of God, and in this regard he quotes Hebrews 13:8, "Jesus Christ is the same yesterday and today and for ever." In short, the citations of Hebrews 13 in Aquinas's treatise have to do with sanctification, which comes from Christ but is prefigured in various ways by the Mosaic law.

Hebrews 1, 5, 6, 8, 10–12

In addition to his multiple citations of Hebrews 7, 9, and 13, Aquinas refers a total of fourteen times to other passages from Hebrews. In article three of question ninety-eight, he quotes Hebrews 1:2, 1:14, and 2:2. Argu-

The Mosaic Law

ing that God gave the Mosaic law directly rather than through the angels, the third objection cites Hebrews 1:14, where Paul calls the angels "ministering spirits." The *respondeo* then quotes Hebrews 1:2, which makes clear that the new law was given by the Son of God, and 2:2, which states plainly that the Mosaic law was "the message declared by angels." One further citation of Hebrews 1 occurs in the treatise. In article four of question 102, the reply to the sixth objection argues that the mercy seat prefigures Christ, and that it was fittingly supported by images of cherubim because of Christ it is written, "Let all God's angels worship him" (Heb 1:6). The treatise's use of Hebrews 1, then, focuses on the role of the angels.

Aquinas cites Hebrews 5 once in the treatise, in the reply to the fifth objection of question 101, article four. Here he is arguing that the ceremonies are fittingly divided into sacrifices, sacred things, sacraments, and observances. He states that oblations and gifts are not a separate category, but belong in the category of sacrifices. As support for this position, he quotes Hebrews 5:1, "For every priest chosen from among men is appointed to act on behalf of men in relation to God, to offer gifts and sacrifices for sins." This is a passage that one might have expected to find more frequently in Aquinas's treatise.

Hebrews 6 appears in question one hundred, article five and in question 102, article four. In the fifth article of question one hundred, Aquinas quotes Hebrews 6:16 with regard to the Decalogue's prohibition of taking the Lord's name in vain. Hebrews 6:16 notes that humans regularly "swear by a greater than themselves, and in all their disputes an oath is final for confirmation." In the fourth article of question 102, Aquinas observes in response to the sixth objection that the rod in the ark of the covenant figuratively signified the priestly power of Christ, in which regard he quotes Hebrews 6:20, which states that Jesus has "become a high priest for ever after the order of Melchizedek." These citations of Hebrews do not seem particularly significant, though they help Aquinas to relate Christ (and the fulfillment he brings) to the Mosaic law.

Hebrews 8 also appears twice. In article four of question 102, the *sed contra* quotes Hebrews 8:4–5, "Now if he [Christ] were on earth, he would not be a priest at all, since there are priests who offer gifts according to the law. They serve a copy and shadow of the heavenly sanctuary; for when Moses was about to erect the tent, he was instructed by God, saying, 'See that you make everything according to the pattern which was shown you on the mountain.'" Aquinas concludes from this that the Mosaic law's "holy things," such as the tabernacle, reflected the divine wisdom both in themselves and in their prefiguring of Christ and the church. This passage of Hebrews is one that a reader might expect to find more frequently in Aquinas's treatise, since it helps draw the connection between the state of the Mosaic law, on the one hand, and the states of the new law and of heavenly glory, on the other. Hebrews 8:13 is found in the *sed contra* of question 103, article three. Like Colossians 2:16–17, which also appears in this *sed contra*, Hebrews 8:13 teaches the fulfillment of the Mosaic law. Interpreting Jeremiah 31, Hebrews 8:13 states: "In speaking of a new covenant, he [the Lord] treats the first as obsolete. And what is becoming obsolete and growing old is ready to vanish away." Perhaps the reason why Aquinas's treatise only cites this verse once is that Aquinas draws upon a repertoire of similar Pauline fulfillment texts.

Aquinas cites Hebrews 10 three times in the treatise. Question 101, article two includes Hebrews 10:1 in its *respondeo*. This verse is another fulfillment text that Aquinas might have been expected to use more often: "For since the law has but a shadow of the good things to come instead of the true form of these realities, it can never, by the same sacrifices which are continually offered year after year, make perfect those who draw near." The ceremonial precepts of the Mosaic law prefigure the new law, which itself is merely an image of the heavenly glory to come. In question 102, article three, Aquinas quotes Hebrews 10:11 in the *respondeo*: "Every priest stands daily at his service, offering repeatedly the same sacrifices, which can never take away sins." Here he is showing the figural relationship of the Mosaic law's sacrifices to the cross of Jesus Christ. Lastly, Hebrews 10:4, quoted by Aquinas in the *respondeo* of article two of question 103, has a similar import: "For it is impossible that the blood of bulls and goats should take away sins." Aquinas employs this verse to underscore that the sacrifices of the Mosaic law did not in themselves cleanse from sin. The presence of these verses from Hebrews 10 in the *respondeo* of the articles indicates their value for Aquinas's theology of the relationship of the Mosaic law's animal sacrifices to Christ's cross.

Hebrews 11:6 appears in article four of question one hundred. The first objection treats the Decalogue's commands that "you shall have no other gods before me" and that "you shall not make for yourself a graven image." Augustine counts these two commandments as one, but the objector considers that they are in fact two, because one has to do with faith and the other with worship. In his response to this objection, Aquinas quotes Hebrews 11:6, "whoever would draw near to God must believe that he exists," and argues that belief in God is self-evident to anyone who possesses faith. He therefore defends Augustine's position that the Decalogue here gives us one commandment (about worship, presupposing faith) rather than two.

Finally, we find one quotation from Hebrews 12. In the *sed contra* of article two of question ninety-nine, Aquinas quotes Hebrews 12:11: "For the moment all discipline seems painful rather than pleasant; later it yields the peaceful fruit of righteousness to those who have been trained by it." Aided by the gloss, he is making an argument that "discipline" here means moral precepts. This argument is something of a stretch, even though one can certainly see that moral precepts discipline us, especially when we do not fully have the appropriate virtues.

In sum, the main task of Hebrews in Aquinas's treatise is to strengthen his presentation of the fulfillment of the Mosaic law by Christ. Certain verses of Hebrews have a particularly significant role in the treatise, as can be seen from their repeated citation. These passages include Hebrews 7:19, "the law made nothing perfect"; Hebrews 9:9–10, which states that the Mosaic law's ceremonies "cannot perfect the conscience of the worshiper, but deal only with food and drink and various ablutions, regulations for the body imposed until the time of reformation"; and Hebrews 13:12, "So Jesus also suffered outside the gate in order to sanctify the people through his own blood." Other passages only occur once in the treatise, but the treatise would nonetheless be quite weakened by their absence. For example, Hebrews states that "when there is a change in the priesthood, there is necessarily a change in the law as well" (Heb 7:12), and Hebrews comments that "since the law has but a shadow of the good things to come instead of the true form of these realities, it can never, by the same sacrifices which are continually offered year after year, make perfect those who draw near" (Heb 10:1). These verses have an important place in any Christian theology of the Mosaic law, since Christians consider that the messiah's fulfillment and reconfiguration of the law around himself means that we do not need to practice the ceremonies of the Mosaic law.

CONCLUSION

How does Paul's voice inform Aquinas's reception of the Mosaic law? The most important texts come from Romans 7:8–8:4. This is Paul's defense of the law, a defense undertaken in light of the messiah's salvific work. Paul insists both on the goodness of the Mosaic law and on its awakening him to sin and condemning him to spiritual death. He insists that "the law is holy, and the commandment is holy and just and good" (Rom 7:12). But because he could not obey the whole law due to his own sinfulness, the law by itself cannot bring him to holiness. He would still be in his sins had it not been for the messiah, Jesus, who fulfills the law for us: "For God has done what the law, weakened by the flesh, could not do: sending his own Son in the likeness of sinful flesh and for sin, he condemned sin in the flesh, in order that the just requirement of the law might be fulfilled in us, who walk not according to the flesh but according to the Spirit" (Rom 8:3–4; cf. Galatians 3). Paul's approach is exactly that of Aquinas. Since Paul considers the law to be good and holy, Aquinas is eager to understand the law, including even the smaller details of its various precepts. Since Paul considers sinners to be unable to fulfill the law, and therefore rejoices in the coming of Christ who fulfills the law for us and pours forth the Holy Spirit upon us, Aquinas reads the Mosaic law consistently in light of Christ and the church.

A central way in which Paul reads the Mosaic law in light of Christ and the church is by reading typologically. For this reason, 1 Corinthians 9–10, Colossians 2, and Hebrews 10 are highly significant in Paul's (or in Pauline) theology of the Mosaic law. In light of these passages, Aquinas freely employs typology in his theology of the Mosaic law, without thereby reducing the Mosaic law to solely typological status. A proper reading of the Mosaic law will be attentive to its modes of prefiguring the messiah and the messianic community. Paul makes this clear when he says of Deuteronomy 25:4, which records a precept about how to treat oxen, that "it was written for our sake" (1 Cor 9:10) so as to instruct the community on how to care for those who are called to preach the gospel. Paul likewise argues that many of the events described in Exodus happened to the Israelites as a typological prefiguring of situations that the messianic people now face, and as a typological prefiguring of the sacraments of baptism and the eucharist. Paul's interpretation of circumcision in Colossians runs along these lines: "In him [Christ] also you were circumcised with a circumcision made without hands, by putting off the body of flesh in the circumcision of Christ; and you were buried with him in baptism, in which you were also raised with him through faith in the working of God, who raised him from the dead" (Col 2:11–12). Indeed, according to Paul, the food laws and holy days of Israel "are only a shadow of what is to come; but the substance belongs to Christ" (Col 2:17). Aquinas agrees with him. The "substance" does not however destroy the significance of the figure or "shadow." Aquinas often points out that the sacraments of the new law are themselves typological figurations of eschatological glory. The Mosaic law teaches us to understand reality typologically and thus sacramentally.

In accord with this typological perspective, Paul makes clear that the Mosaic law is good but imperfect. It leads God's people toward holiness, but it cannot make us holy. This is why we need the messiah. Hebrews 10:1 speaks in this way: "For since the law has but a shadow of the good things to come instead of the true form of these realities, it can never, by the same sacrifices which are continually offered year after year, make perfect those who draw near." Christ is the "high priest" who makes atonement for all sins and who, from the right hand of the Father, pours forth God's gifts upon us through the Holy Spirit. The imperfection of the law—"the law made nothing perfect" (Heb 7:19)—means that, in a certain sense, the law has become "obsolete" (Heb 8:13) now that the messiah has perfected it. Paul elsewhere refers to the law as a pedagogue or "custodian until Christ came" (Gal 3:24). This pairing of imperfect-perfect, however, should not be construed as a negation. If it were a negation, then study of the Mosaic law would no longer be necessary, and Aquinas studies the Mosaic law at great length and with real appreciation.

At times Paul speaks in ways that seem dismissive of the Mosaic law, and Aquinas has to show how to interpret these passages on the basis of other Pauline passages. For example, Paul speaks of the Decalogue graven on the two tablets as "the dispensation of death" and "the dispensation of righteousness" (2 Cor 3:7, 9). In a passage that Aquinas quotes twice, Paul states that "the written code kills, but the Spirit gives life" (2 Cor 3:6). Ephesians 2:15 proclaims that Christ united Jews and Gentiles in his Messianic community "by abolishing in his flesh the law of commandments and ordinances, that he might create in himself one new man in place of the two." If the law can simply be abolished, then it hardly seems to have been particularly good in the first place. Similarly, in Romans 7:11 Paul appears to blame the Mosaic law for the spiritual death of those who seek to obey it: "For sin, finding opportunity in the commandment, deceived me and by it killed me."

Aquinas addresses each of these passages and shows how they can be interpreted positively in light of the view that the Mosaic law, while not perfect, is certainly good and holy. The imperfection of the Mosaic law consists in its inability to make humans holy; only Christ and the Holy Spirit can do this. The Mosaic law teaches about holiness and prepares a people for the coming of Christ and the outpouring of his Spirit. For both these reasons, it requires the ongoing attention of Christians. Compared with Paul, Aquinas devotes much more attention to the particular laws contained in the Torah. Paul certainly knew these laws, but his letters have another purpose. As we have seen, Aquinas's interpretation of the particular laws of the Torah is thoroughly Pauline.

CHAPTER 5

GRACE

ROMANUS CESSARIO has remarked, "It is impossible to underestimate how much the human creature requires the gift of divine grace."[1] As the Gospel of John says, grace comes to us through Jesus Christ, who pours out the Holy Spirit upon all who are united to him by faith and love: "And from his fullness have we all received, grace upon grace" (Jn 1:16). Humans are created for communion with God but are cast down by sin. We need healing and we desire to share in God's life, but these gifts can come only from God. Consider Moses's warning that the people of Israel not forget what God has done for them. Moses tells the people, "Beware lest you say in your heart, 'My power and the might of my hand have gotten me this wealth.' You shall remember the Lord your God, for it is he who gives you power to get wealth; that he may confirm his covenant which he swore to your fathers, as at this day" (Deut

---

1. Romanus Cessario, OP, *Introduction to Moral Theology* (Washington, D.C.: The Catholic University of America Press, 2001), 224–25. This insight motivates his warnings against conflating nature and grace. See, for example, his "Is Aquinas's *Summa* Only about Grace?" in *Ordo Sapientiae et Amoris*, ed. C.-J. Pinto de Oliveira, OP (Fribourg: Éditions universitaires, 1993), 197–209. For Aquinas on grace see also Reinhard Hütter, "St. Thomas on Grace and Free Will in the *Initium Fidei*: The Surpassing Augustinian Synthesis," *Nova et Vetera* 5 (2007): 521–53; Joseph Wawrykow, *God's Grace and Human Action: 'Merit' in the Theology of Thomas Aquinas* (Notre Dame, Ind.: University of Notre Dame Press, 1995); Bernard Lonergan, SJ, *Grace and Freedom: Operative Grace in the Thought of St. Thomas Aquinas*, ed. Frederick E. Crowe and Robert M. Doran (Toronto: University of Toronto Press, 2000); and A. N. Williams, *The Ground of Union: Deification in Aquinas and Palamas* (Oxford: Oxford University Press, 1999).

8:17–18).² Moses has to remind the people continually that it is not their power or righteousness that earned them God's favor. But Moses himself is no exception; he revels ever so slightly in his own power, and his punishment consists in not being able to enter the promised land. God says to him that "you broke faith with me in the midst of the people of Israel at the waters of Meribath-kadesh, in the wilderness of Zin; because you did not revere me as holy in the midst of the people of Israel" (Deut 32:51).³

The Old Testament themes of divine grace, mercy, and election lead, in the Old Testament itself, to the expectation that God will restore his people and make them holy through the righteousness of the messiah, who will fulfill God's covenants.⁴ God promises through the prophet Jeremiah: "This is the covenant which I will make with the house of Israel after those days, says the Lord: I will put my law within them, and I will write it upon their hearts; and I will be their God, and they shall be my people .... [F]or they shall all know me, from the least of them to the greatest, says the Lord; for I will forgive their iniquity, and I will remember their sin no more" (Jer 31:33–34). The people had received the grace of a covenantal or spousal relationship with God, but they had not been able to live up to it in holiness. Instead, they turned away from God. Through the prophet Zechariah, God promises to "bring my servant the Branch" and "remove the guilt of this land in a single day" (Zech 3:9). He will do this through the suffering servant, who, as Isaiah prophesies, "was wounded for our transgressions," so that "upon him was the chastisement that made us whole, and with his stripes we are healed. All we like sheep have gone astray; we have turned every one to his own way; and the Lord has laid upon him the iniquity of us all" (Is 53:5–6).⁵

---

2. On Deuteronomy's doctrine of election, see Joel S. Kaminsky, *Yet I Loved Jacob: Reclaiming the Biblical Concept of Election* (Nashville, Tenn.: Abingdon Press, 2007), 99–105.

3. For further discussion of sin and grace in Deuteronomy, see Mark J. Boda, *A Severe Mercy: Sin and Its Remedy in the Old Testament* (Winona Lake, Ind.: Eisenbrauns, 2009), 97–114.

4. On the role of the Messiah according to Old Testament texts as interpreted in the Second Temple period, see Michael F. Bird, *Are You the One Who Is to Come? The Historical Jesus and the Messianic Question* (Grand Rapids, Mich.: Baker Academic, 2009). Bird's work is in part a response to Joseph A. Fitzmyer, SJ, *The One Who Is to Come* (Grand Rapids, Mich.: Eerdmans, 2007).

5. The interpretation of prophetic texts is endlessly contested, but see especially *The Suffer-*

Having seen the risen Lord, Paul envisions God's plan for salvation as reaching its culmination in Jesus Christ: "God, who is rich in mercy, out of the great love with which he loved us, even when we were dead through our trespasses, made us alive together with Christ (by grace you have been saved)" (Eph 2:4–5).[6] Aquinas's treatise on grace in the *Summa theologiae* is therefore a place where we would expect Paul to be amply represented. In fact, in the forty-four articles found in questions 109–14 of the *prima-secundae pars*, Pauline citations occur seventy times—a significant number but somewhat less than one might have guessed. A glance at the articles suggests a possible reason: Aquinas relies heavily on Augustine. Since Augustine's theology of grace is profoundly Pauline, this might explain why Paul is not directly quoted more often. With that said, seventy citations is still a large number, and we can be sure that we will gain insight into Aquinas's treatise by exploring his citations of Paul. My goal is to understand where and how Paul's voice shapes Aquinas's theology of grace in the *Summa theologiae*.

The six questions in Aquinas's treatise examine the necessity of grace (question 109); grace in itself (question 110); the division of grace, as for example into sanctifying grace and gratuitous grace (question 111); the cause of grace (question 112); the effects of grace (question 113); and the effect of co-operating grace, namely merit (question 114). In these questions, Romans appears thirty-four times, 1 Corinthians twelve times, 2 Corinthians four times, Galatians four times, Ephesians nine times, Philippians once, Colossians once, 1 Timothy once, 2 Timothy twice, and Hebrews twice. Ten of the fourteen letters that Aquinas considered Pauline are present, the exceptions being Titus, 1 and 2 Thessalonians, and Philemon. Yet fifty-five of the seventy quotations come from three letters: Romans, 1 Corinthians, and Ephesians. Romans is especially strong in question 109 (ten of sixteen) and question 113 (seven of nine). In question

---

ing Servant: Isaiah 53 in Jewish and Christian Sources, trans. Daniel P. Bailey, ed. Bernd Janowski and Peter Stuhlmacher (Grand Rapids, Mich.: Eerdmans, 2004).

6. See N. T. Wright, *Justification: God's Plan and Paul's Vision* (Downers Grove, Ill.: IVP Academic, 2009). The authorship of Ephesians is, of course, disputed: for the arguments against Pauline authorship, see Rudolf Schnackenburg, *The Epistle to the Ephesians: A Commentary*, trans. Helen Heron (Edinburgh: T. and T. Clark, 1991), 24–29, and Margaret Y. MacDonald, *Colossians and Ephesians* (Collegeville, Minn.: Liturgical Press, 2000), 15–17.

111 Romans provides five of the eleven Pauline quotations, and in question 114 nine of seventeen. Romans is weakest in question 110 (one of five) and question 112 (two of twelve). Since questions 110 and 112 are particularly important—on grace in itself and on the cause of grace—the minor role of Romans in these questions is perhaps surprising.

The generally privileged place of Romans in the treatise fits with Aquinas's statement, in his commentary on Romans, that the subject matter of the whole epistle is the grace of the church. The inclusion of merit in his theology of grace might seem to be an anomaly, but recall that Aquinas defines merit as an effect of cooperating grace. When God moves the will (by causing its free motion) from sinful to righteous, this is an act of operating grace because God is the principle of the change. When a graced person performs a good act, the principles of this action are both God and free will, and so this is called cooperating grace. The same distinction applies to habitual grace: inasmuch as habitual grace justifies the soul, it is called operating grace, but inasmuch as habitual grace serves along with the will as the principle of good works, it is called cooperating grace. Merit, then, has an appropriate place in a theology of grace.

Given the complexity of the theological points that Aquinas seeks to make in these six questions on grace and their significance for his theology as a whole, I will examine in detail the function of Romans and the other Pauline letters in these questions. Following the order of the Pauline letters, I note each place that a particular Pauline passage appears in the treatise on grace and then reflect upon the way in which Aquinas's various appeals to particular Pauline passages are connected.

ROMANS

Romans 1–5

We begin with Aquinas's fifteen citations of Romans 1–5. Nine of these citations are of Romans 3:24 and 4:4–5, but it may well be that the most important citation comes from the first chapter of Romans. This is so because in Aquinas's crucial discussion of whether grace implies anything (*ponat aliquid*) in the soul (question 110, article one), the first objection quotes Romans 1:7, "Grace to you and peace from God our Father and the Lord Jesus Christ," as well as the gloss on this verse. The Gloss defines "grace" as the forgiveness of sins. In this light the objection quotes Psalm 32:2: "Blessed is the man to whom the Lord imputes no iniquity." The objection concludes that the forgiveness of sins does not do anything to the soul, but instead simply consists in God not imputing the sin, so that the person is not punished. The issue of whether forgiveness of sin is merely forensic is here on display.[7] What is the "grace and peace" that comes to us "from God our Father and the Lord Jesus Christ"? In his reply to this objection, Aquinas argues that when God forgives our sins, his love causes there to be in our soul something pleasing to him. Grace does indeed imply a change in the condition of the soul.

Romans 1–2 is well known for its account of the gentiles. In his theology of grace, Aquinas references this account for the purpose of imagining whether created rational powers would have sufficed before the fall for obeying the moral precepts of divine law (question 109, article four). Aquinas's task here consists in seeking to articulate what "grace" is in relation to created human nature, and vice-versa. He observes that in one sense our created powers would have been sufficient for obeying the moral precepts, for otherwise sin would be natural. Given our ordination to supernatural beatitude, however, our created powers would not have been sufficient because God wills for us to obey his commandments out of charity and this is impossible without grace. The citation of Paul in this article occurs in the first objection. Quoting Romans 2:14, "when Gentiles who have not the law do by nature what the law requires, they are a law to themselves," the objection states that if gentiles can "do by nature what the law requires," this must mean that we can obey the law without grace. Following Augustine, Aquinas replies that these gentiles who "do by nature what the law requires" must have received grace and thereby had their fallen nature healed and elevated.

The three citations of Romans 3:24 highlight the superabundance of God's grace and its powerful effects. Question 109, article nine addresses

---

7. For a beautifully nuanced discussion, see Bruce D. Marshall, "*Beatus vir*: Aquinas, Romans 4, and the Role of 'Reckoning' in Justification," in *Reading Romans with St. Thomas Aquinas*, ed. Matthew Levering and Michael Dauphinais (Washington, D.C.: The Catholic University of America Press, 2012), 216–37.

whether those in a state of grace need further grace to do good and avoid evil. In the *sed contra*, Aquinas quotes Augustine to the effect that just as a healthy eye needs light in order to see, so as a spiritually healthy person, who has been "justified by his grace as a gift" (Rom 3:24), continues to need God's help in order to act rightly. In question 111, article one, on the distinction between sanctifying grace (*gratia gratum faciens*) and gratuitous grace (*gratia gratis data*), the third objection points out that sanctifying grace comes to us gratuitously. The distinction between sanctifying grace and gratuitous grace thus seems to be a superficial one, since all grace is gratuitous. Here Aquinas quotes Paul's remark that all "are justified by his grace as a gift, through the redemption which is in Christ Jesus" (Rom 3:24). In his reply to this objection, Aquinas observes that sanctifying grace makes us pleasing to God, whereas other graces are freely given by God but do not make us pleasing to God. Lastly, the second article of question 113 takes up the topic of whether the forgiveness of sins (justification) requires an infusion of grace. In the pivotal *sed contra*, Aquinas cites Romans 3:24, where Paul directly links the infusion of grace with justification. The *respondeo* expands further upon what grace is and does. Grace is an effect of God's eternal love in us. God's love makes us worthy of union with him by freeing us from the guilt of sin and enabling us to cleave to God. The infusion of grace not only ensures that God does not impute the guilt of our sins to us, but also renews our soul so that we are filled with charity.

The six references to Romans 4:4–5 underscore the priority of God, the utter gratuity of grace, the connection of grace and faith, and the power of grace. The gratuitous character of grace is the subject of Aquinas's reply to the second objection in question 111, article one. Aquinas emphasizes that God does not owe grace to us. God is not our debtor, even with respect to our meritorious works or with respect to what is due to our created nature. Quoting Romans 4:4, "now to one who works, his wages are not reckoned as a gift but as his due," Aquinas makes clear that since grace is freely given, the fact that meritorious works arise from grace does not mean that God owes us grace.

The second article of question 112 asks whether humans must prepare themselves to receive grace. The first objection states that if we prepared ourselves for grace, this preparation would be a good act, and therefore in some sense God would owe us the reward of grace. If so, then grace would not be grace, as the objection observes by quoting Romans 4:4. Aquinas emphasizes that all our preparation flows from God's grace: without giving us yet the gift of sanctifying grace, God moves our wills to draw closer to him. For this reason, we can and do prepare ourselves to receive habitual grace, which as a new accidental form does indeed require preparation on the part of the recipient. The fifth article of question 114 asks whether we can merit for ourselves the first grace that we receive. To underscore the utter gratuity of grace, the *sed contra* cites Romans 4:4. To merit something means to receive it as one's due, but grace by definition is not received as our due. Therefore we cannot merit the first grace.

The first article of question 113 examines whether justification is the forgiveness of sins. In the *respondeo*, Aquinas argues in favor of an affirmative answer with help from one of the many Pauline texts he could have chosen, namely Romans 4:5: "And to one who does not work but trusts him who justifies the ungodly, his faith is reckoned as righteousness." Romans 4 is an important chapter for this topic, since Romans 4 focuses on how Abraham was made righteous. The third article of question 113 discusses whether justification occurs without our free will, or requires a movement of our free will. In the *respondeo*, Aquinas quotes Romans 4:5: God "justifies the ungodly." The point is that God, not our free will, has priority in our justification. But God moves our will in a manner that accords with the freedom of our will. As Aquinas puts it, God "so infuses the gift of justifying grace that at the same time he moves the free will to accept the gift of grace." We freely accept the gift of grace by our free will, but not by our free will alone, since it is God who frees our free will so that it might rise from sin and embrace his good gifts. Lastly, article four of question 113 is about whether justification requires a movement of faith. The third objection argues that since faith involves a large number of articles proposed for our belief, justification would be delayed while the person thought about each article in turn. To this objection, Aquinas replies that in the act of faith as pertaining to justification, it is necessary is to believe (either explicitly or implicitly) in Christ, through whom God justifies us. We must "trust him who justifies the ungodly" (Rom 4:5), just as Abraham trusted.

The wide-ranging influence of Romans 4 on the *Summa*'s theology of grace should by now be evident. Romans 5 is less significant, but influential nonetheless. Aquinas quotes three different verses from Romans 5, including Romans 5:1 twice. Three of the four quotations of Romans 5 appear in objections, and one appears in the *sed contra*. Even those that appear in objections, however, have a role in shaping Aquinas's arguments for our continual dependence upon further grace, and for the link between grace, faith, and charity. The third article of question 112 cites Romans 5:1 in the first objection. Taking up the issue of whether grace is necessarily given to all those who prepare themselves and do what they can, the objection argues that grace is necessarily given to such a person. This seems to be implied by Romans 5:1, "since we are justified by faith, we have peace with God through our Lord Jesus Christ," or at least by the gloss on this verse, which states that God welcomes those who seek him. In the *respondeo* and in the reply to the first objection, Aquinas observes that our sincere preparation for sanctifying grace is itself caused by God's grace, and so in this sense our preparation necessarily receives its reward. But considered solely as an act of our free will, God would not owe grace to it. For its part, article four of question 113 asks whether justification requires on our part a movement of faith. In the *sed contra*, Aquinas quotes Romans 5:1 to argue that if we are "justified by faith," then not only an infusion of grace and a movement of our free will are necessary for justification; the act of faith is also necessary. Faith consists in an act of the intellect, moved by the will.

In question 109, article three, on whether by nature (without grace) we can love God above all things, Aquinas cites Romans 5:5 in the first objection. This objection argues that only supernatural charity enables us to love God above all things. Quoting Romans 5:5, "God's love has been poured into our hearts through the Holy Spirit who has been given to us [*caritas Dei diffusa est in cordibus nostris per Spiritum Sanctum, qui datus est nobis*]," the objection notes that we can only possess charity through the indwelling Holy Spirit. If only charity allows us to love God above all things, and if charity only comes through the Holy Spirit, then grace is necessary to love God above all things. Aquinas replies that had we not corrupted our nature by sin, it would have been within the scope of our created rational powers to love God above all things, because God is indeed most lovable of all things. Yet, without grace one cannot love God in the way that supernatural charity does, because charity involves a real fellowship with God, a joyful sharing in his life.

In the tenth article of question 109, Aquinas takes up the topic of whether perseverance in grace requires further grace. He notes that insofar as perseverance is a virtuous habit, the infusion of grace includes the infusion of the virtue of perseverance. But if we are talking about perseverance in grace throughout a lifetime so as to attain to eternal life, then we do indeed need not merely habitual grace but also further grace for such perseverance. This is so because we continually need God's help (even beyond habitual grace) in guiding us toward our proper good and in fending off concupiscence. The one quotation of Paul in this article occurs in the third objection, where Aquinas cites Paul's contention in Romans 5:20 that grace abounds more than sin. The objection argues that Adam "received what enabled him to persevere," and therefore further grace is not necessary.

The first five chapters of Romans serve Aquinas's theology of grace, therefore, in a variety of ways. Often citing Romans in the objections, Aquinas draws upon these chapters to discuss imputation, the capacities of human nature in light of our supernatural ordination, our constant dependence upon further grace, the superabundance of grace, the gratuity of grace, God's movement of our free will, the forgiveness of sins, preparation for grace, faith, charity, and perseverance unto eternal life. Almost all of these discussions clearly reflect theological debates that Paul himself engaged in. In his use of Romans 1–5, Aquinas hews quite close to Paul's own concerns while developing a number of refined speculative conclusions, such as regarding the need for further grace in order to persevere in a state of grace.

Romans 6–8

We find twelve citations of Romans 6–8 in Aquinas's six questions on grace, and five of these are of Romans 6:23. The citations of Romans 6:23 shed light on the fact that eternal life is purely God's gift, even when we merit it condignly. The fifth article of question 109 twice quotes Romans 6:23, once in the *sed contra* and again in the reply to the second objection.

The topic of the article is whether anyone can merit eternal life without grace. Aquinas answers no, because eternal life in union with God is a sheer gift, beyond our created powers. Only by doing works of supernatural virtue, insofar as the principle of such works is the Holy Spirit, can we merit the reward of eternal life in union with God. In the *sed contra*, Aquinas employs Romans 6:23 to underscore the point that eternal life is the fruit of God's grace rather than of our natural powers: "the free gift of God is eternal life [*gratia Dei vita aeterna*]." In the reply to the second objection, Aquinas cites Romans 6:23 in order to employ the gloss's commentary on this verse. As the gloss says, we do indeed merit eternal life by good works, but these works are made possible by God's grace.

The second article of question 114 asks whether we can merit eternal life by our works, without grace. Clearly the answer is no, and the *sed contra* shows this by quoting Paul's linkage of grace and eternal life in Romans 6:23: "The free gift of God is eternal life in Christ Jesus our Lord." In the *respondeo*, Aquinas cites the other part of this verse in order to show that without grace, our works merit simply death: "For the wages of sin is death" (Rom 6:23). Intimate communion in the divine life, adoptive sonship, is something that we cannot deserve by means of merely human works, a point that is especially obvious with respect to fallen human nature.

Question 114, article three addresses the condign meriting of eternal life. The second objection cites Romans 6:23, "the free gift of God is eternal life," in order to cite the gloss on this verse. The gloss notes that Paul, having just said that "the wages of sin is death," could have paired this with "the wages of justice is eternal life," but Paul instead emphasized that eternal life is God's merciful free gift. Congruent merit is consistent with mercy on the part of the one who gives the reward, whereas in condign merit the reward is owed in a strict sense of justice. In reply, Aquinas distinguishes between God's merciful grace as the "first cause" of our eternal life, and the condign merit that God's grace makes possible for our actions.

The eight and ninth articles of question 109 both cite Romans 7:25, which Aquinas employs to show our ongoing need for further grace even when we are in a state of grace. The eighth article of question 109 examines whether we can avoid sin without grace. Aquinas points out that to sin means to violate our nature, to do something that goes against what is truly good for us. In this sense, it would have been within the scope of our natural powers, before the fall, to do the good and to avoid sin. Yet Aquinas emphasizes that this does not imply that we would then not have needed God, who is the source of our being and action. After the fall, however, we cannot entirely avoid sin without grace, although people in a state of sin can avoid particular sins (otherwise those outside the state of grace would immediately fall into every sin). When grace heals us, says Aquinas, we experience this healing primarily in our soul, whereas our bodies continue to bear the disorder of concupiscence. To support this view, Aquinas in the *respondeo* quotes Romans 7:25, "I of myself serve the law of God with my mind, but with my flesh I serve the law of sin." Aquinas takes Romans 7:25 to be speaking in the voice of one who, although restored by grace, still suffers from concupiscence.

Article nine of question 109 pertains to whether, once we have received God's grace, we need further grace in order to do good and avoid sin. In the *respondeo*, Aquinas answers this problem by distinguishing between habitual grace and other graces. We do not need further habitual grace, because the habit of grace—the qualification of the soul by grace—suffices for acts of supernatural virtue. But we do need further gracious help from God. This is so not only because we need God's help for every action, but also because we are weakened by concupiscence and therefore we continue to be subject to "the law of sin" (Rom 7:25).

Aquinas cites Romans 8, which is a paean to God's grace, five times in the treatise. He first employs Romans 8:17–18 to show both that our human works cannot be compared to the reward of eternal glory, and that our works nonetheless condignly merit such a reward because of our adoptive sonship. The third article of question 114 is about whether in a state of grace we can condignly merit eternal life. To merit condignly means to perform works that merit a particular reward in a strict sense, as their exact recompense. By contrast, to merit congruently means to perform works that can be given a particular reward that is not strictly owed, but is nonetheless fitting. It seems that nothing that we do in this life could be great enough to merit condignly an eternal share in the trinitarian communion. In the first objection, Aquinas quotes Romans 8:18 to underscore the difference of this life from eternal glory: "I consider that the sufferings of this present time are not worth comparing with the glory that is to be revealed to us." Aquinas points out that the sufferings of Paul and other saints are the greatest works that can be performed. If such works are not worthy of comparison with the glory of eternal life, then it does not seem that we can condignly merit eternal life.

Nonetheless, Aquinas holds that we do indeed merit eternal life condignly. He explains that in the state of grace, our good works have two principles: the Holy Spirit and our free will. When viewed simply as coming from our free will, our good works merit eternal life only congruently: it is fitting, but certainly not necessary in justice, that God amply reward our striving. When viewed as coming from the grace of the Holy Spirit, however, the same works can be said to merit eternal life condignly, because of the dignity of our adoptive sonship. Insofar the Holy Spirit makes us sons and daughters in the Son, our works truly deserve the inheritance that God gives us, namely our eternal sharing in his life. In this respect, Aquinas quotes Romans 8:17, "If children, then heirs, heirs of God and fellow heirs with Christ, provided we also suffer with him in order that we may also be glorified with him." Even if Paul does not have in view this distinction between what is owed to works that proceed solely from free will and what is owed to works that proceed from free will and the grace of the Holy Spirit, Paul's discussion of our suffering with Christ as adoptive sons and daughters portrays the reality that Aquinas is describing.

In article nine of question 109, Aquinas addresses the question of whether in order to do good and avoid evil, we need further grace even when we are in a state of grace. As we have seen, he answers in the affirmative. Among other things, he notes that we suffer from ignorance caused by sin, so that we lack full knowledge of ourselves and our true good, and "we do not know how to pray as we ought" (Rom 8:26). In order actually to do the good in particular circumstances, therefore, we need not simply habitual grace, but also God's further grace that helps us to know and do what is right.

In question 113, article one, on whether justification consists in the forgiveness of sins, Aquinas twice quotes Romans 8:30, where Paul is praising God's saving work in his elect. Aquinas quotes Romans 8:30 first in objection three, which proposes that the remission of sins consists not in justification but in being called. Citing the priority of God's call in Paul's statement that "those whom he called he also justified," the objection argues that when God calls us, the movement back to God (and away from sin) commences. In reply to this objection, Aquinas interprets God's call as his grace by which he moves us to give up sin, and he notes that this grace causes the remission of sins but is not yet the remission of sins. The remission of sins takes place not when we are called but when we are justified, although of course temporally these may be simultaneous. Thus the *sed contra* quotes Romans 8:30 and the gloss on this verse, which interprets "he also justified" as meaning "by the remission of sins."

The role that Romans 6–8 plays in the treatise, therefore, consists in significant part in helping Aquinas to address the question of merit. Insofar as we are adopted sons and daughters in the Son, the Holy Spirit works in our actions and enables us to merit the inheritance of Christ, even though this meriting must always be understood as a gift of grace. Aquinas also finds in Romans 7:25 an indication of our concupiscence and thus of our continual dependence upon God for the further graces that will enable us to attain salvation. He emphasizes once more the forgiveness of sins by God's grace.

Romans 9–13

The six questions that Aquinas devotes to grace contain seven citations from Romans 9–13, including two of Romans 9:16, two of Romans 11:6, and two of Romans 11:35. The two citations of Romans 9:16 have to do with our radical dependence on God's grace and our cooperation with this grace. The second article of question 109 asks whether we can will or accomplish any good if we are not in a state of grace. In the *respondeo*, Aquinas first points out that we cannot will or accomplish any good without the help of God, since all our created acts require the transcendent action of God. This does not mean, however, that we cannot will or accomplish any good unless we are in a state of grace. Yet he goes on to observe that our natural powers have been corrupted by sin and its consequences. We can accomplish certain good works in a state of sin, but in this condition we cannot do all the good that pertains to human flourishing, and neither can we do the works of supernatural virtue by which we are intended to attain the ultimate end that God has given us. Absent grace, in other words, our works will be frustrated, since no matter what we do, we will come no closer to the fulfillment that God intends for us. In this sense, our works in a state of sin will not be good, because they fail to serve our union with God. To confirm this point, Aquinas in the *sed contra* quotes Romans 9:16: "So it depends not upon man's will or exertion, but upon God's mercy." We require God's merciful grace in order to do works that are good in the sense of meriting the reward that fulfills us.

The second article of question 111 sets forth the distinction between operative and co-operative grace. The third objection of this article quotes Romans 9:16 in support of the view that works of grace depend solely on God, so that grace should always be called operative rather than co-operative. In reply to this objection, Aquinas notes that God directs us toward our true end by means of his operative grace. This is dependent solely upon "God's mercy" and "not upon man's will." By contrast, once we have been ordered by God's mercy toward this supernatural end, then God's grace co-operates with our will in our accomplishment of good works. God's grace is the same whether it is operative or cooperative; the difference consists in the role of our will.

The two citations of Romans 11:6 underscore the gratuity of grace. In question 111, article one, which examines the distinction between sanctifying grace and gratuitous grace, Aquinas quotes Romans 11:6 in the *sed contra*: "If it is by grace, it is no longer on the basis of works; otherwise grace would no longer be grace." This passage makes clear that all grace is gratuitously (or freely) given. Aquinas adds that every grace is freely given, but not every grace is sanctifying. The second citation of Romans 11:6 occurs in question 114, article five, which asks whether merit can apply to the first grace. In the *respondeo* Aquinas notes that this would be impossible, not only because of our sinfulness (which grace reverses) but also because of grace's utter disproportion to our natural powers. He notes that Romans 11:6 completely rules out the notion that without grace, we could merit to receive grace. Only God can elevate us to the status of his adopted children.

Both of Aquinas's two quotations of Romans 11:35 pertain to merit. The first article of question 114 asks whether we can merit anything from

God. In the third objection, Aquinas uses Paul to formulate the key problem, namely that no creature can make God a debtor, because every good of creation and salvation is God's sheer gift from eternity. The objection quotes Romans 11:35, "Who has given a gift to him [God] that he might be repaid?" Since we have nothing that is not from God, and since God is not our fellow creature, we cannot put God in our debt in this way. Merit, however, arises from good actions that claim a well-deserved reward from God. In his *respondeo*, Aquinas emphasizes that humans and God "are infinitely apart, and all man's good is from God." But God ordains from eternity that humans, by their good works, should merit a reward from God. In the reply to the third objection, therefore, Aquinas points out that we can indeed merit a reward from God because this is part of God's plan for our salvation. God wills that he become our debtor by means of our good works, which he makes possible.

In question 114, article two Aquinas shows that we cannot merit eternal life by our works, apart from grace. In the reply to the third objection, which compared our meriting from God to the way in which our good works merit reward from other humans, Aquinas quotes Romans 11:35 so as to make clear that meriting something from other human beings is utterly different from meriting something from God, who is the source of all our good.

Lastly, Aquinas employs Romans 13:1 to depict God as wisely arranging for diverse graces. In the *respondeo* of question 111, article one, on the distinction between sanctifying and gratuitous grace, Aquinas begins with Romans 13:1, which in his version reads "those things that are of God are well ordered." God's grace accomplishes different things in us in accord with the different ways that God moves humans to eternal life. Sanctifying grace unites us to God, whereas gratuitous grace enables us to cooperate with God in leading others to union with God.

Much of Aquinas's use of Romans 9–13 in his questions on grace, then, again involves the issue of merit. This is not surprising given the need to combat the tendency to place grace and merit in opposition. At the same time, he explores our radical dependence on God, the role of cooperative grace, the gratuity of all grace, and the diverse kinds of grace. Indeed, the role of Romans 9–13 is quite similar to the role that we identified for Romans 1–8. Aquinas's use of Romans shows conclusively that his theology of grace, for all its speculative refinement, is a commentary on Paul.

1 & 2 CORINTHIANS, GALATIANS, EPHESIANS

1 Corinthians 2–4, 12–13

Since Aquinas's theology of grace does not limit itself to Romans, how do other Pauline letters contribute to his exposition? Aquinas cites 1 Corinthians 2–4 seven times in his questions on grace. Four of these citations address the issue of whether it is possible for us to know that we are in a state of grace; two other citations have to do with merit. In the *respondeo* of question 114, article two, Aquinas argues that we cannot merit eternal life without grace because "everlasting life is a good exceeding the proportion of created nature; since it exceeds its knowledge and desire." In this regard he quotes 1 Corinthians 2:9, where Paul praises "what no eye has seen, nor ear heard, nor the heart of man conceived, what God has prepared for those who love him." Aquinas goes on to emphasize that our meritorious works are themselves God's gifts.

The fourth objection of question 112, article five cites 1 Corinthians 2:12, "Now we have received not the spirit of the world, but the Spirit which is from God, that we might understand the gifts bestowed on us by God." This passage seems to require that we be able to know when we have received the gift of sanctifying grace. If we receive the Holy Spirit not least in order to understand what God has given us, then surely the Holy Spirit will enable us to know his gift of sanctifying grace. In reply, Aquinas suggests that either Paul is speaking about our knowledge in faith of the gifts of glory, or Paul has in view the knowledge of grace that comes from a special revelation. Such a special revelation, says Aquinas, could be the meaning of 1 Corinthians 2:10, "God has revealed to us through the Spirit." But the former interpretation is much more likely given the context: Paul seems to be speaking about faith's knowledge of the gifts of glory.

In article four of question 114, Aquinas asks whether in our meritorious actions, grace works through charity rather than through the other virtues. At issue is the centrality of charity. In the second objection, Aquinas quotes a Pauline passage that stresses that our reward matches our labor: "He who plants and he who waters are equal, and each shall receive his wages according to his labor" (1 Cor 3:8). Since charity makes it easier for us to do good works, says the objection, charity decreases our labor and thus should not be given the central place in our meriting. This objection is rather specious, and it gives Aquinas the opportunity to observe in reply that "charity does not lessen the toil—rather, it makes us undertake the greatest toils."

Arguing against the view that a person in a state of grace needs further grace to do good and avoid sin, the second objection of question 109, article nine quotes 1 Corinthians 3:16: "Do you not know that you are God's temple and that God's Spirit dwells in you?" If the Holy Spirit dwells in us, then it would certainly seem that we do not need further grace, because the Holy Spirit is powerful enough to ensure that we do good and avoid evil. Aquinas replies that the work of the Holy Spirit "is not circumscribed by the effect of habitual grace which it causes in us; but beyond this effect He, together with the Father and the Son, moves and protects us."

Question 112, article five is devoted to showing that by means of our own reflection we cannot know with certitude that we possess sanctifying grace, because the cause of grace (God) exceeds our knowledge. In his *respondeo* Aquinas cites 1 Corinthians 4:3–4, where Paul observes that he cannot know by his own powers whether or not he is in a state of grace: "I do not even judge myself. I am not aware of anything against myself, but I am not thereby acquitted. It is the Lord who judges me." Aquinas explains that Paul can only surmise that he is in a state of grace. Paul knows that he delights in God and has no mortal sin on his conscience, but his knowledge of his sins is imperfect, as is made clear by 1 Corinthians 4:4.

These texts from 1 Corinthians 2–4 personalize the teachings on grace that Aquinas gains from Romans. The main issue is the condition of the person who has been caught up by God's powerful grace. It might seem that the indwelling Holy Spirit would make himself known clearly to us and would make things easy for us. Using 1 Corinthians 2–4, Aquinas makes clear that grace does not work this way, since it prepares us for eternal glory.

In addition to his seven citations of 1 Corinthians 2–4, Aquinas quotes 1 Corinthians 12–13 five times in his questions on grace. Two of these citations have to do with the various manifestations of the Holy Spirit in the church, and a further two with the primacy of charity. The first article of question 109 inquires into whether grace is required to know any truth. The first objection quotes 1 Corinthians 12:3, "No one can say 'Jesus is Lord' except by the Holy Spirit." The gloss on this verse states that all truth comes from the Holy Spirit, which would seem to imply that grace is needed to know any truth whatsoever. In reply, Aquinas says that all truth comes from the Holy Spirit in a twofold way, namely "as bestowing the natural light, and moving us to understand and speak the truth." Thus not all truth requires the *grace* of the Holy Spirit.

The *respondeo* of question 111, article one treats the distinction between sanctifying and gratuitous grace. Aquinas defines gratuitous grace as enabling us to cooperate with God in drawing others to union with God, and he finds a description of such grace in 1 Corinthians 12:7, "To each is given the manifestation of the Spirit for the common good." In the fourth article of question 111, the *sed contra* comes from 1 Corinthians 12:8–10, and indeed the whole article has to do with the suitability of Paul's division of gratuitous grace in that passage. First Corinthians 12:8–10 reads, "To one is given through the Spirit the utterance of wisdom, and to another the utterance of knowledge according to the same Spirit, to another faith by the same Spirit, to another gifts of healing by the one Spirit, to another the working of miracles, to another prophecy, to another the ability to distinguish between spirits, to another various kinds of tongues, to another the interpretation of tongues." Paul does clearly make a distinction between the grace that heals and unites us to God, and the other gracious gifts of the Holy Spirit such as the ones that he speaks about in 1 Corinthians 12. In his *respondeo*, Aquinas explains that gratuitous grace encompasses all the gifts of God that enable us to guide others toward the supernatural end that God has ordained for humans. Along these lines, he shows that Paul's list in 1 Corinthians 12 is particularly suitable, because in order to guide others toward the supernatural end, we need wisdom, knowledge, healing, miracles, prophecy, discerning of spirits, and speaking and interpreting in diverse languages.

In article five of question 111, Aquinas discusses whether gratuitous grace is superior to sanctifying grace, since all members of the church have the latter but not all have the former. Aquinas draws his *sed contra* from 1 Corinthians 12:31: "I will show you a still more excellent way." This way turns out to be charity, and it is "more excellent" than all the kinds of gratuitous grace. Since the virtue of charity flows from sanctifying grace, it follows that sanctifying grace is superior to gratuitous grace. The key is that sanctifying grace unites us to our supernatural end, whereas gratuitous grace does not unite us to the end but instead enables us to help others attain to the end. The superior grace is that which immediately connects the human person with God.

The purpose of question 114, article four is to show that the grace of the Holy Spirit works primarily through charity. In response to the third objection, which argues that the martyrs worked primarily through other virtues, Aquinas quotes Paul's insistence that "if I give away all I have, and if I deliver my body to be burned, but have not love, I gain nothing" (1 Cor 13:3). This passage demonstrates the primacy of charity in our meritorious action.

To sum up Aquinas's use of 1 Corinthians in his theology of grace, he focuses on whether we can know that we possess sanctifying grace, on the diverse graces that sustain the church, and on the primacy of charity. Again, the main role of 1 Corinthians seems to be applying the doctrine of grace—grace's radical gratuity and our utter dependence upon it for meritorious action—to our personal and ecclesial life. The relationship of sanctifying grace and gratuitous grace is a prime example of this. Although Paul does not spell out theoretically this distinction of graces, he presents it clearly in 1 Corinthians 12–13. Aquinas makes much of the centrality of charity here, just as he did for 1 Corinthians 2–4's discussion of the spiritual gifts that we receive through the apostolic ministry.

2 Corinthians and Galatians

A total of eight quotations of 2 Corinthians and Galatians appear in Aquinas's treatise; two of these are of 2 Corinthians 12:9, and two are of Galatians 6:15. These citations have to do with a variety of themes, most of which are familiar by now: merit, whether preparation for grace is necessary, whether knowing truth requires grace, justification, charity, our knowledge of grace, and grace as a new quality of the soul.

Aquinas holds that in the state of grace we can condignly merit eternal life. Taking up this issue, the third objection of article three of question 114 points out that "no act of the present life can equal everlasting life." It would seem, then, that condign merit is impossible. In reply, Aquinas quotes 2 Corinthians 1:22, "He has put his seal upon us and given us his Spirit in our hearts as a guarantee." The indwelling Holy Spirit is the principle of our condign meriting. Certainly this point is far from Paul's own intended meaning in the passage, but even so, Paul does strongly affirm the presence of the indwelling Spirit at work in Paul's charitable works. Therefore, Aquinas's use of Paul in the context of the speculative analysis of merit is appropriate.

In question 109, article one, Aquinas explores whether grace is required to know truth. The third objection quotes 2 Corinthians 3:5: "Not that we are sufficient of ourselves to claim anything as coming from us; our sufficiency is from God." If nothing comes from us, then it certainly seems that we cannot know any truth without grace. Again, this is far from Paul's contextual meaning, but one can see how Paul's emphasis on grace leads to such speculative queries. Given that our minds are obscured by sin and that we not sufficient to claim anything as coming from us, how can we gain any truth about reality without crediting grace for this knowledge? In reply, Aquinas notes that Paul's statement corresponds to the fact that we need God's help in order to know any truth, since the intellect cannot move from potency to act by itself; human autonomy is a mirage. But although we always need God's help for any act, we do not need the *grace* of the Holy Spirit in order to know truths that belong to the realm of what our intellects can know by their created abilities.

In article three of question 111, Paul appears in the second objection. The topic is whether grace can be divided into prevenient and subsequent, based upon its relation to a particular effect (for example, the healing of the soul). This is another speculative issue that Paul did not take up but that flows inevitably from the grace-saturated vision of human life in Christ. The second objection argues that God's sanctifying grace is not divisible, because as God tells Paul, "My grace is sufficient for you" (2 Cor 12:9). If we received this grace both before and after a particular effect, we would seem to be receiving a divided and insufficient grace. In answer to this objection, Aquinas states, "The division into prevenient and subsequent grace does not divide grace in its essence, but only in its effects, as was already said of operating and co-operating grace." The same grace can be active in us both before and after a certain effect, just as the same grace can first rectify our will and then cooperate with our will. As in Paul's portrait of grace, therefore, grace is not divided: the speculative divisions of grace are intended to aid our understanding of grace's diverse effects, not to press us to imagine divisions within the grace of the Holy Spirit itself. This important clarification enables us to further appreciate the closeness of Aquinas's vision to Paul's.

In the *respondeo* of question 112, article five, Aquinas discusses whether we can know that we are in a state of sanctifying grace. He argues that we can know something in three ways: by revelation, by means of our own reflection, and by conjecture through signs. Only in the first of these ways, by revelation, can we know with certitude that we are in a state of grace. God sometimes reveals to certain persons that they possess sanctifying grace, in order to sustain them in difficult missions. Aquinas thinks that this was likely the case for Paul, to whom God revealed, "My grace is sufficient for you" (2 Cor 12:9). Recall that Paul, beset by a thorn in the flesh, begged God to relieve him but received instead this promise that God's grace would preserve Paul from harm. Aquinas here takes care to point out that God thereby gave Paul a special revelation, one that we should not all expect to receive with regard to our state of grace. Aquinas's point fits broadly with the context of 2 Corinthians 12, in which Paul is describing "the abundance of revelations" (2 Cor 12:7) that he has been receiving from God, an abundance that Paul does not suggest is standard for all Christians.

The seventh article of question 109 quotes Galatians 2:21 in the *sed contra*. The topic of this article is whether we can rise from sin without the help of grace. Aquinas defines rising from sin as being restored in a threefold way: regaining grace, regaining our natural good, and paying the debt of punishment (namely damnation). In all three ways, only God can enable us to rise from sin. In the *sed contra*, Galatians 2:21—"I do not nullify the grace of God; for if justification were through the law, then Christ died to no purpose"—serves to confirm that Christ came to save us because we could not restore ourselves. If we could rise from sin without the help of grace, then we would not need Christ's help and he would have "died to no purpose." The work that Galatians does here is similar to what we observed in Aquinas's use of Romans.

In question 114, article four, Aquinas argues that the grace of the Holy Spirit works primarily through charity, and secondarily through the other virtues as commanded by charity. The third objection argues that the martyrs' faith, patience, and bravery shows that grace works more through other virtues than it does through charity. Aquinas replies by citing Paul's praise of "faith working through love" (Gal 5:6). Paul makes clear that grace works primarily through charity. In accord with Paul's own practice, Aquinas's inquiry ensures that the primacy of charity is affirmed without the other virtues being reduced to a negligible status.

In question 110, article two, on whether grace should be described as a "quality" of the soul, the third objection quotes Galatians 6:15, "For neither circumcision counts for anything, nor uncircumcision, but a new creation." This "new creation" consists in grace, which renews the human person in a manner that goes far beyond anything that circumcision could accomplish. The objection argues that if grace is a "new creation," then it has a subsistence of its own or at least does not rely entirely on its subject. On this view, grace cannot be a quality, since quality is an accident. Certainly Paul would not have known this philosophical terminology, drawn from Aristotle's categories, but he could obviously have appreciated the point: does the "new creation" qualify the existing human being or are we changed into something entirely new? In his reply to the objection, Aquinas observes that "properly speaking no accident comes into being or is corrupted, but is said to come into being and to be corrupted inasmuch as its subject begins or ceases to be in act with this accident." The point is that grace is not a new creature, but rather it is a new mode of being on the part of the soul. Surely this is what Paul thought as well; the philosophical clarification illumines rather than distorts his meaning.

Question 112, article two treats preparation for grace. The third objection points out that God, who is infinitely powerful, does not need us to prepare ourselves for his gift. In the act of creation, for example, God does not need well-disposed matter; in fact he does not need matter at all, since he creates from nothing. The objection argues that since grace is a "new creation" (Gal 6:15), then no more than in the original creation does God's grace require the preparation of creatures. In reply to this objection, Aquinas observes that the infinitely powerful God has the ability to bring about the preparation in us needed for the reception of sanctifying grace. Here Paul's point about the "new creation" is again being maintained against a potential misunderstanding of what the phrase entails for the life of grace.

Aquinas's use of 2 Corinthians and Galatians generally takes up notable insights about the life of grace—such as "my grace is sufficient for you" and "for neither circumcision counts for anything, nor uncircumcision, but a new creation"—and employs them in a speculative manner either to comprehend more fully the reality of grace or to preserve it against possible distortions. Certainly Aquinas's use of Paul often proceeds in this manner, but it is particularly noticeable in the treatise on grace in the case of 2 Corinthians and Galatians, where Aquinas's use of the Pauline text does not relate much to the meaning of Paul's words in their context. By contrast, as we saw, Aquinas employs Romans and 1 Corinthians within his speculative questions on grace in a manner that broadly fits with Paul's meaning in context. Nonetheless, Aquinas's quotations of 2 Corinthians and Galatians accomplish two valuable purposes: they introduce into his treatise crucial ways in which Paul understands grace and the life of grace, and they assist Aquinas in warding off certain serious misunderstandings of the life of grace.

Ephesians

The nine quotations from Ephesians have a widely diverse application; Aquinas treats predestination, new creation, the diversity of vocations in the church, and various elements drawn loosely from Ephesians' use of "light." In the *respondeo* of question 110, article one, which considers whether grace implies something in the soul, Aquinas first distinguishes three ways in which the word "grace" is understood in common parlance: someone's love or favor toward another; a freely given gift; or our gratitude for the gift. God's love or favor toward us is not a response to goodness in us; rather, God's love or favor causes our goodness. Grace is in us to the extent that God heals and elevates us so that we share in him in a supernatural manner. Aquinas adds, however, that grace in us differs from God's plan of grace (or predestination), which is in God rather than in us. Aquinas finds predestination in Ephesians 1:5 (to which I add verse six): "He destined us in love to be his sons through Jesus Christ, according to the purpose of his will, to the praise of his glorious grace which he freely bestowed on us in the Beloved." The relationship of grace to predestination is certainly present in Ephesians and worth considering with regard to how grace affects the soul of the graced person.

In question 111, article one, which distinguishes between sanctifying grace and gratuitous grace, Aquinas in the *sed contra* quotes Ephesians 1:6, "His glorious grace which he freely bestowed on us in the Beloved." He considers that this passage refers in particular to the power of grace to sanctify. This seems quite right in the Pauline context. In the second article of question 110, Aquinas argues that grace qualifies the soul. In this regard Aquinas cites Ephesians 2:10, where Paul states that we have been "created in Christ Jesus for good works." To be created anew in this way is to have our souls given a new quality or accidental form by grace, so that it becomes easy or (supernaturally) natural for us to move toward our supernatural good, eternal life. This fits with Galatians' description of the graced person as a "new creation."

In the fourth article of question 112, Aquinas cites Ephesians 4:7 in the *sed contra* and Ephesians 4:12 (building upon 4:7) in the *respondeo*. The article's topic is whether God causes some persons to have more grace than others. Ephesians 4:7 states that "grace was given to each of us according to the measure of Christ's gift." Aquinas interprets this to mean that we do not all receive the same degree of grace, because if we did, then "the measure of Christ's gift" would be the same measure for each recipient (and thus hardly a measure at all). As Ephesians goes on to say, Christ gives different gifts: some are "apostles, some prophets, some evangelists, some pastors and teachers" (Eph 4:11). Arguably, the grace that Christ gives is differentiated, just as these gifts, too, are different. Aquinas notes in the *respondeo* that sanctifying grace, with respect to its end (union with God), cannot be greater or lesser, because it always accomplishes precisely this end. However, with respect to the subject who possesses it, sanctifying grace can be greater or lesser insofar as it can be possessed more or less intensely and perfectly. God wills that this be so, in order that the church possess the beauty of diversity. Here Aquinas quotes Ephesians 4:12, where Paul explains the diversity of Christ's gifts as being "for the equipment of the saints, for the work of ministry, for building up the body of Christ."

The third article of question 110 asks whether grace is the same as virtue. Aquinas answers negatively; rather, grace gives the soul a higher participation in God or a higher nature, so that the powers of the soul then possess supernatural virtues such as charity. The powers of the soul can also possess the acquired virtues by means of created human nature without the aid of grace. In the *respondeo*, Aquinas quotes Ephesians 5:8, "For once you were darkness, but now you are light in the Lord; walk as children of light." The "light" here is grace, both for Aquinas and for Paul. By the light of grace, we can walk suitably toward our supernatural end by doing deeds of love. A similar discussion occurs in the first article of question 109, where Aquinas argues that the knowledge of truth does not generally require grace. To know truth requires the use of an "intellectual light," says Aquinas, because "when anything is exposed by the light it becomes visible, for anything that becomes visible is light" (Eph 5:13). Paul, of course, does not here intend to develop a theory of knowledge. Instead, Paul is describing the life of grace and the need to avoid shameful deeds. Using for his own purposes Paul's reference to light, Aquinas argues that our power of knowing is a created light that participates in God (as every creature does) and that needs the action of God in order to act. This dependence on God for our act of knowing means that every truth is from the Holy Spirit, not insofar as he dwells in us by sanctifying grace, but insofar as he gives us the created gift of the natural light of the intellect. Whereas the reference to Ephesians 5:8 in question 110 sticks closely to Paul's meaning, this reference to Ephesians 5:13 uses the text to make a philosophical point. Nonetheless, Paul's contrast between light and darkness certainly has an epistemological significance.

The fifth article of question 112 treats whether we can know that we are in a state of sanctifying grace. The third objection cites Ephesians 5:13, "anything that becomes visible is light," in order to argue that since we can know with certitude when we are in the darkness of sin, we are much more able to know when we are in the light of grace. Aquinas replies that since sin involves "commutable good, which is known to us," it is easily knowable, whereas the divine "object or end of grace is unknown to us on account of the greatness of its light." This is an intriguing solution to a problem that does indeed arise from Ephesians 5's contrast between light and darkness. Namely, if the light is so powerful, it would seem that we should always know when we are in a state of grace.

In question 109, article seven, the issue is whether we need grace in order to rise from sin. The first objection argues that in order to prepare for the coming of grace, we must rise from sin by choosing to sin no more. The objection presents this view as a plausible interpretation of Ephesians 5:14, "Awake, O sleeper, and arise from the dead, and Christ shall give you light." In other words, Christ will enlighten us by his grace once we choose to stop sinning. Aquinas has already replied to something like this perspective in the sixth article, where he held that even our preparation for sanctifying grace is enabled by God's grace. In his reply to the first objection of article seven, Aquinas notes that our struggle, moved by God, to free ourselves from the shackles of sin cannot accomplish its goal without the infusion of sanctifying grace (justification). Paul would certainly agree.

In short, Ephesians provides Aquinas with some significant insights into the reality of grace, including Paul's emphasis on God's "glorious grace which he freely bestowed on us in the Beloved," Paul's insistence that "grace was given to each of us according to the measure of Christ's gift," and Paul's exhortation that we "walk as children of light." As with Romans and Galatians, Aquinas's use of these passages from Ephesians generally fits at least broadly with their context in the letter. This is not to suggest that it is illegitimate to use a Pauline text to reflect speculatively on a question that arises from Pauline theology of grace, as Aquinas does when he reflects on whether the strong association of "light" with the life of grace means that we must be able to know with certitude that we are in a state of grace. In my view, Ephesians' most irreplaceable contribution to the *Summa*'s questions on grace consists in the connection between the theology of grace and the Church's diverse vocations "according to the measure of Christ's gift."

PHILIPPIANS, COLOSSIANS, 1 & 2 TIMOTHY, HEBREWS

Lastly, five letters appear a total of seven times: Philippians, Colossians, 1 and 2 Timothy, and Hebrews. There are some significant new themes here, including our meriting of an increase in grace, Christ's condign meriting of the first grace for other humans, and the necessity of hating our past sins. These new themes are rather loosely drawn from Paul's meaning in the actual letters. Question 113, article five asks whether justification requires a movement of the free will not only with respect to loving God, but also with respect to hating sin. Arguing that the person being justified should solely look forward toward a new life with God, rather than backward in hatred of past sin, the second objection quotes Paul's words in Philippians 3:13–14: "Forgetting what lies behind and straining forward to what lies ahead, I press on toward the goal for the prize of the upward call of God in Christ Jesus." In replying to this objection, Aquinas explains that Paul speaks of "forgetting what lies behind" because Paul knows that recollecting our sins might renew our desire to live as we did before we accepted Christ. Whether or not this is what Paul actually means, it seems clear that Aquinas is right that Paul is not denying that justification includes freely rejecting sin. When accepting Christ, we should at the same time actively reject the sins of our past life, and for this purpose we must recollect our sins. In Philippians 3, after all, Paul himself reflects on his life prior to his conversion, including his persecution of the church.

The reply to the first objection in question 111, article one describes the way in which grace sanctifies us or makes us pleasing to God. As noted above, grace does so by giving our souls a new quality or accidental form. As Paul observes (quoted by Aquinas), God "has qualified us to share in the inheritance of the saints in light" (Col 1:12). Aquinas's philosophical language about a new "quality" of the soul aims to express the extraordinary reality of becoming adopted children of God. The fifth article of question 112 is about our knowledge of the state of sanctifying grace, and includes a quotation of 1 Timothy in the reply to the third objection. Aquinas emphasizes that grace involves a cleaving to the infinite creator whose light is so powerful that we are blinded. Since God is so great, we cannot be entirely sure that we are united to God, although we can conjecture that we are so on the basis of signs such as whether we delight in God. To convey God's greatness, Aquinas quotes 1 Timothy 6:16, where Paul describes God as the one "who alone has immortality and dwells in unapproachable light, whom no man has ever seen or can see."

In the eighth article of question 114, on whether once we are in a state of grace we can merit an increase in grace, the third objection contains a quotation of 2 Timothy. The objection argues that if we can merit an increase in grace, this would mean that *every* charitable act efficaciously merits an increase in grace and charity. Here Aquinas quotes 2 Timothy 1:12, an important text for the doctrine of merit: "I know whom I have believed, and I am sure that he is able to guard until that Day what has been entrusted to me." However, as our charitable actions are often not particularly fervent and in such cases do not seem to change us, it appears that we must not be able to merit an increase in grace or charity. Aquinas replies that God rewards every charitable action but does not do so immediately; instead God increases our grace and charity when we are ready for this increase. In the third article of question 114, the *sed contra* quotes another crucial text for Aquinas's theology of merit, 2 Timothy 4:8: "Henceforth there is laid up for me the crown of righteousness, which the Lord, the righteous judge, will award to me on that Day." A just judge awards what is owed in justice. If the Lord, precisely as a just judge, will reward Paul with an eternal "crown," then Paul has truly merited such a crown.

The sixth article of question 114 inquires into whether one person can merit the first grace for another person. It might seem that when charitable persons pray for others, they merit to have their prayers answered. Aquinas explains that God can ordain that one person receive the first grace because of the prayers of another person, but this is never a condign meriting. The prayers of one person can never make it so that God in strict justice owes the first grace to any person. God might fittingly reward a just person's prayers by giving grace to a sinner, but God certainly does not owe this reward. There is one exception to this rule: Jesus Christ. Since the grace of the Holy Spirit fills Christ not only for himself but also as head of the church, his prayers for his members condignly merit the first grace for us. Here Aquinas cites Hebrews 2:10, "For it was fitting that he, for whom and by whom all things exist, in bringing many sons to glory, should make the pioneer of their salvation perfect through suffering." Christ's mission is to lead "many sons to glory," and so his works of love (above all his suffering, but also his prayers) merit the first grace for us. Although Hebrews 2:10 seems quite far from Aquinas's technical language about meriting the first grace for another person, Paul certainly thinks that Christ condignly merits the first grace for all his members; otherwise God could not be said to bring "many sons to glory" in Christ.

Finally, in the *respondeo* of question 113, article four, Aquinas notes that our turning toward God occurs not only by our will, but indeed first and foremost by a turning of our intellect to God so as to know his existence and love for us. Here he quotes Hebrews 11:6, "Without faith it is impossible to please him. For whoever would draw near to God must believe that he exists and that he rewards those who seek him." In this way, God's grace unites the whole soul, both intellect and will, to himself. Since the act of faith is moved by the will, Aquinas adds that faith's movement toward God is made "living" or salvific by charity, which God infuses along with faith in the moment of justification.

Aquinas's inclusion of Hebrews among the Pauline letters enables him to extend his reflection on grace to how Christ is the source of the grace of the Holy Spirit for us, and to the impact of grace not only upon will but also upon the intellect. Yet Hebrews' own concerns are not really present in the *Summa*'s questions on grace. The same can be said for 1 Timothy, although 1 Timothy's depiction of God's inapproachable glory helps to underscore that we cannot know with certitude when we are sharing in the divine life by sanctifying grace. Second Timothy provides concrete support, in the form of Paul's anticipation of his "crown of righteousness," for Aquinas's theology of merit. Philippians and Colossians offer inspiring rhetorical descriptions of the goal of the life of grace, even if Aquinas's focus in quoting from these two letters has in each case a smaller theoretical problem in view; namely, what the movement of justification involves and what it means to call grace a new quality of the soul. Even if the central concerns of these letters are not present in the *Summa*'s questions on grace, they nonetheless clearly strengthen the theological portrait of grace that Aquinas derives especially from Romans, 1 Corinthians, and Ephesians.

CONCLUSION

In accord with the method I have chosen for Part II of this book, the present chapter focused on the place and function of each Pauline letter in Aquinas's six questions on grace. We are now in a position to look back and reflect on each question in turn. In question 109, Aquinas's theoretical or speculative investigation of the necessity of grace may seem quite different from Paul's epistolary arguments. After all, Paul typically does not explore whether people outside the state of grace can know some truth and do some good; Paul does not ask whether a human being prior to the fall could, by his created powers, have loved God above all things; nor does Paul inquire into the sufficiency of created powers prior to the fall as regards obeying the moral precepts of God's law. These questions are hypotheticals designed to tease out the specific contribution of grace to human life. Paul certainly would reject even the thought that we could merit eternal life without grace, or prepare ourselves (without grace) to receive grace, or rise from sin without grace. Paul also does not have in view the distinction between habitual grace and other graces that enables Aquinas to ask questions about persons who possess habitual grace but need God's help in other ways.

Nonetheless, Aquinas's answers consistently show his indebtedness to Paul's theology of grace. Thus, in treating the broad issue of whether grace is necessary for salvation, one could not quote better Pauline texts than the ones quoted by Aquinas, including 2 Corinthians 3:5 ("our sufficiency is from God"), Romans 9:16 ("it depends not upon man's will or exertion"), Romans 5:5 on charity and the Holy Spirit, Romans 2:14 on gentiles who do the law, Romans 6:23 on God's free gift of eternal life, Galatians 2:21 on Christ having not died in vain, Romans 7:25 on concupiscence, 1 Corinthians 3:16 on the indwelling Holy Spirit, and Romans 3:24 on justification by God's grace. These texts treat the necessity of God's grace from a variety of angles. The causal power of God (Father, Son, and Holy Spirit) in lifting up the sinner unto eternal life is the main theme, along with human neediness. Like Paul, Aquinas insists upon the necessity of superabundant grace if we are to attain salvation. At the same time, Aquinas attempts to clarify what pertains to grace in distinction from created nature, as well as to clarify what pertains to grace as a habit rather than to superadded graces. These are not Paul's concerns, but the omnipresence and necessity of grace certainly is Paul's concern. Aquinas confirms this omnipresence and necessity of grace in his use of Paul.

Similarly, Aquinas's insistence that grace puts something in our souls (question 110)—so that we are truly made just rather than simply imputed to be just—helps to interpret Paul's insistence that God makes us a new creation (see Galatians 6:15 and Ephesians 2:10). Without addressing the technical point of whether grace is a new "quality" or accidental form added to the soul, Paul makes clear what it means to say that grace is such a quality: namely, we are changed into a new creation without becoming a new species. Grace in us enables us to act virtuously, as Ephesians 5:8 shows. These Pauline passages thus have much to teach about the nature of grace, even if Paul himself does not ask Aquinas's technical questions.

Even more clearly, the distinction between sanctifying grace and gratuitous grace (question 111) is rooted in Paul. Here the guiding Pauline texts are 1 Corinthians 12:7–10 and 1 Corinthians 12:31 with regard to gratuitous grace, and Ephesians 1:6, Romans 11:6, and Colossians 1:12 with regard to sanctifying grace (which, like gratuitous grace, is freely given). Romans 9:16 and 2 Corinthians 12:9 also play a valuable role in showing the priority of God's grace. The portrait of grace that Aquinas provides—freely given by God, bestowed upon us in Christ, manifesting the Holy Spirit, rooted in God's mercy rather than our good works, providing us with the ability to build up Christ's body the church, displaying itself through love—constitutes a marvelous commentary on Paul's theology of grace.

When Aquinas raises Pelagian problems (question 112), he turns especially to Romans 4–5 to contextualize and answer these problems. Paul himself does not speak of preparation for grace, but Paul's insistence that grace remain grace (rather than becoming something that God owes us) provides the framework for Aquinas's discussion. Aquinas asks questions that have to do with our perception of grace in ourselves and in others: do some people receive more grace, and can we know if we have grace? He roots the former question in Ephesians 4:7–12, where Paul defends the diversity of graces—if not necessarily a diversity of degrees of sanctity—on the grounds that they assist in the upbuilding of the church. It would be absurd to suppose that Paul, pastor that he was, did not recognize degrees of sanctity. With respect to the latter question, the central Pauline text is 1 Corinthians 4:3–4, where Paul states that he does not know himself well enough to be certain that he will pass through the judgment, even though he is not conscious of any sin. Aquinas also recognizes the difficulties posed by 1 Corinthians 2:12 and 2 Corinthians 12:9, which seem to suggest that Paul knows he has grace. With regard to justification or the forgiveness of sins (question 113), Aquinas relies in particular on Romans 3:24, 4:5, 5:1, and 8:30. He discusses the various elements that appear in Paul's presentation, including the infusion of grace, the movement of the free will toward God, the act of faith, and the rejection of sin.

Paul's voice also guides the major lines of Aquinas's thought about merit (question 114). In accord with Romans 4:4, 6:23, 11:6, and 11:35, Aquinas rules out the notion that we can put God in our debt; rather, we receive eternal life as God's gift in Christ (see also Hebrews 2:10). We cannot earn the grace that enables us to attain eternal life. Yet other Pauline passages speak about earning eternal life as a reward; 2 Timothy 4:8, for example, describes the "crown" that Paul expects to receive from the just judge on the day of the Lord. Likewise, 1 Corinthians 3:8 comments on the reward that each servant of the Lord will receive. Even more importantly, Paul depicts the inheritance that is indeed due to us as adopted children of God and "fellow heirs of Christ, provided we suffer with him in order that we may also be glorified with him" (Rom 8:17). We will receive this eternal inheritance if we suffer with Christ through works of love. It is the "Spirit in our hearts" (2 Cor 1:22) that enables us to do these works so as to receive eternal life. Love makes our good works to be life-giving (see 1 Corinthians 13:3, Galatians 5:6). Paul's various statements could be interpreted as inconsistent, but Aquinas shows how they fit together in an account of God enabling us to perform meritorious works due to the grace of the Holy Spirit dwelling within us.

Lastly, one might ask whether Aquinas preserves the true voice of Paul even in the piecemeal fashion that he presents Paul, and even in the various theoretical or speculative questions that arise not directly from Paul but instead from controversies in the later church or from a theological desire to clarify difficult matters. What does Paul have to do with questions such as whether by our natural powers alone we could love God above all things, whether grace is a quality of the soul, whether grace can rightly be divided into operating and cooperating grace, and whether we must prepare for the reception of grace? The answer, once more, is that Paul's perspective shapes Aquinas's answers to post-Pauline debates. The question about our natural ability to love God, for example, gives Aquinas a chance to reflect upon the consequences of original sin. The question about grace as a quality of the soul gives rise to reflection on what it means for us to be a "new creation." The question about operating and cooperating grace helps to distinguish the aspect according to which God's justifying work is sheer mercy, from the aspect according to which grace enables our free will to cooperate with God. Aquinas's treatise does not, of course, aim to function as a biblical commentary. But it does allow Paul's voice to guide a speculative or sapiential probing into the mystery of God's work of grace in our lives.

CHAPTER 6

THE VIRTUE OF RELIGION

THOMAS AQUINAS treats the virtue of religion (*religio*), including its interior and exterior acts, in questions 81–89 of the *secunda-secundae pars* of the *Summa theologiae*. These questions are important because they establish what Aquinas thinks all humans owe in justice to God. Jean Porter summarizes Aquinas's position: "Since we are embodied creatures whose thought processes are grounded in sense data, it is necessary for us to express our devotion and love for God by means of exterior signs. These signs provide the sphere of operation proper to the virtue of religion.... The inclination to show honor to a divine creator through cultic acts is grounded in human nature."[1] As Porter goes on to say, acts of religion thus belong to the natural law, although the specific forms that these acts should take are governed by the divine law given to Israel and the church.

---

1. Jean Porter, "The Virtue of Justice (IIa IIae, qq. 58–122)," in *The Ethics of Aquinas*, ed. Stephen J. Pope (Washington, D.C.: Georgetown University Press, 2002), 279. For further discussion of Aquinas on the virtue of religion, see Odon Lottin, OSB, *L'âme du culture. La vertu de religion d'après s. Thomas d'Aquin* (Louvain: Bureau des oeuvres liturgiques, 1920); Georges Cottier, OP, "La vertu de religion," *Revue Thomiste* 106 (2006): 335–52; John W. Curran, OP, "The Thomistic Concept of Devotion," *The Thomist* 2 (1940): 410–43, 546–80; R. Jared Staudt, "Sin as an Offense against God: Aquinas on the Relation of Sin and Religion," *Nova et Vetera* 9 (2011): 195–207; and Rodolfo Vázquez, "La religión según Santo Tomás de Aquino," *Revista de Filosofía* 16 (1983): 245–84.

Scripture makes clear that human history is filled with sins against the virtue of religion. Just to name one example, the northern ten tribes of Israel went into exile in Assyria around 722 BC because, according to 2 Kings 17:15, "They went after false idols, and became false, and they followed the nations that were round about them, concerning whom the Lord had commanded them that they should not do like them." Specifically, their idolatrous actions consisted in the following: they "made for themselves molten images of two calves; and they made an Asherah, and worshipped all the host of heaven, and served Baal. And they burned their sons and their daughters as offerings, and used divination and sorcery" (2 Kgs 17:16–17).[2] The rulers and people of Judah did somewhat better, but they too eventually went into exile because of the actions of King Manasseh in the mid-seventh century—actions that were apparently all too popular. Manasseh "erected altars for Baal, and made an Asherah, as Ahab king of Israel had done, and worshiped all the host of heaven, and served them.... And he built altars for all the host of heaven in the two courts of the house of the Lord. And he burned his son as an offering, and practiced soothsaying and augury, and dealt with mediums and wizards" (2 Kgs 21:3, 5–6).

Prior to the giving of the Mosaic law, some acts of religion are described that meet with God's favor. Consider what happened after the birth of Seth's child (the grandson of Adam and Eve): "At that time men began to call upon the name of the Lord" (Gen 4:26). The same point holds for God's covenant with Noah and Noah's act of worship: "Noah built an altar to the Lord, and took of every clean animal and of every clean bird, and offered burnt offerings on the altar. And when the Lord smelled the pleasing odor, the Lord said in his heart, 'I will never again curse the ground because of man'" (Gen 8:20–21). Noah worshipped God by means of sacrificial offerings that embodied Noah's interior devotion, and God approved of this worship.

Perhaps the best known instance in the Old Testament of acceptable worship outside of God's covenantal relationships is the act of religious

---

2. For historical-critical background, see Mark S. Smith, *The Early History of God: Yahweh and Other Deities in Ancient Israel*, 2nd ed. (Grand Rapids, Mich.: Eerdmans, 2002) and Richard Elliott Friedman, *Who Wrote the Bible?* 2nd ed. (New York: HarperCollins, 1997).

devotion performed by Melchizedek, king of Salem. Melchizedek, we read, "brought out bread and wine; he was priest of God Most High. And he blessed him and said, 'Blessed be Abram by God Most High, maker of heaven and earth; and blessed be God Most High, who has delivered your enemies into your hand!'" (Gen 14:19–20). This worship before God by means of a meal of bread and wine, consecrated by words of blessing, identifies Melchizedek as a devout priest who knows how to worship God rightly.[3] This is the place to mention, too, Abraham's near-sacrifice of his son Isaac. In Genesis 22, God commands Abraham to take Isaac to the land of Moriah and to offer Isaac as a burnt offering. Does this mean that God approves of child sacrifice as an acceptable mode of worshiping God?[4] God prevents Abraham from following through with the deed: "Do not lay your hand on the lad or do anything to him; for now I know that you fear God, seeing you have not withheld your son, your only son, from me" (Gen 22:12). God sees to it that Isaac is replaced by a ram, which Abraham offers to God in sacrificial worship. By replacing Isaac with a ram, God shows the pattern of acceptable worship (and prefigures Christ).[5]

When Aquinas turns to the virtue of religion, he draws heavily upon the biblical testimony to what counts as acceptable worship and what

---

3. Leon Kass comments: "In Hebrew, *El Elyon* means God-the-Most-High. But El is the name of the Canaanite sky god, and Elyon is perhaps the name of another local deity, or, perhaps, an attribute like 'lofty,' one that befits the sky god. Perhaps the text means to suggest that Melchizedek worships the highest or loftiest of the gods and in that respect is on his way toward monotheism. But there is no suggestion that Melchizedek knows the Lord who called Abram. However, when Melchizedek invokes *El Elyon*, Abram thinks of the God-Most-High that he knows. Melchizedek, without meaning to, reminds Abram of the Lord." See Leon R. Kass, *The Beginning of Wisdom: Reading Genesis* (New York: Free Press, 2003), 303n7. For the connection made by Hebrews 7:1–10 between the priest Melchizedek and the perfect priest Jesus, see R. R. Reno, *Genesis* (Grand Rapids, Mich.: Brazos Press, 2010), 154.

4. See Jon D. Levenson, *The Death and Resurrection of the Beloved Son: The Transformation of Child Sacrifice in Judaism and Christianity* (New Haven, Conn.: Yale University Press, 1993) and Leroy A. Huizenga, *The New Isaac: Tradition and Intertextuality in the Gospel of Matthew* (Leiden: Brill, 2009).

5. For discussion of Christ's death in relation to the Aqedah, see Isabelle Mandrella, *Das Isaac-Opfer. Historisch-systematische Untersuchung zu Rationalität und Wandelbarkeit des Naturrechts in der mittelalterlichen Lehre vom natürlichen Gesetz* (Münster: Aschendorff Verlag, 2002); Matthew Levering, *Sacrifice and Community: Jewish Offering and Christian Eucharist* (Oxford: Blackwell, 2005), chapter 2; Huizenga, *The New Isaac*, chapters 6–11.

counts as idolatry and false worship. In this sense, his account of the virtue of religion is not drawn strictly from philosophical reasoning, although he does employ philosophers such as Aristotle and Cicero. In this inquiry into the positive elements of the virtue of religion, Aquinas cites Paul fifty-six times over the course of nine questions (questions 81–89). In what follows, therefore, I will explore the role of Romans, 1 and 2 Corinthians, Galatians, Ephesians, 1 Thessalonians, 1 and 2 Timothy, and Hebrews in Aquinas's treatise. The bulk of Aquinas's quotations—thirty-six of fifty-six—come from Romans and the Corinthians correspondence. Quotations from Paul are present in eight of the nine questions, the exception being question eighty-two on devotion as an act of religion. What do Paul's letters have to do with a virtue of religion that, according to Aquinas, expresses what all humans owe to God simply by the fact of having been created? Paul himself obviously does not investigate the "virtue" of religion, though he does presume that certain elements should be present in any worship of God. Does Aquinas's use of Paul in discussing the virtue of religion do justice to Paul's Israel- and Christ-centered view of worship? Let us begin by considering the role of Romans in Aquinas's theology of religion.

ROMANS IN AQUINAS'S THEOLOGY OF RELIGION

Question eighty-one treats religion in itself, while questions 82–89 treat the interior and external acts of religion. The first mention of Romans in Aquinas's treatise occurs in question eighty-one, article seven. The topic of the article is whether religion possesses an external act, since after all religion—as the virtue of offering what is due to God—is primarily an interior reality. In the *respondeo*, Aquinas observes that the perfection of our soul consists in honoring and reverencing God, and our body has a rightful share in these spiritual actions. In worshiping God, we use sensible things as signs that guide our minds and hearts toward God and that express our interior worship. This interaction of spiritual and bodily components in our worship fits, Aquinas thinks, with Paul's statement that "ever since the creation of the world his invisible nature, namely, his eternal power and deity, has been clearly perceived in the things that have been made" (Rom 1:20). As Aquinas points out, Paul here connects interior worship with our contemplation of created things. The visible world serves as a sign of God's existence, and the very existence of created things should move us to worship their creator. In Romans 1, of course, the problem is that instead of worshiping the creator, humans became stuck on creatures, so that we worshipped things like the sun or even images of humans or bulls. The use of created things in worship is thus both necessary and, in our fallen condition, somewhat dangerous.

Whereas Aquinas quotes Romans 1:20 near the beginning of his treatise on the virtue of religion, he cites Romans 1:25 near the end of his treatise, in question eighty-nine, article six. This article asks whether one can rightly swear by creatures, for instance by the gospel. Jesus's words in Matthew 5:34–36 seem to make clear that the answer is no. Objection three, furthermore, reminds us that an oath is an act of religion and concludes on this basis that to swear by the gospel would be to worship a created thing, which Paul warns against in Romans 1:25: "They exchanged the truth about God for a lie and worshiped and served the creature rather than the Creator." Aquinas replies that a good oath can invoke either God or something that reflects God. To swear by the gospel is to swear by God who makes known his truth through the gospel, just as to swear by the saints is to swear by those who believed and kept God's truth. The use of Paul here seems marginal, since he simply helps Aquinas to formulate an objection. Yet this verse of Romans does indeed stand among the most important Pauline verses pertaining to what we owe God.

Aquinas quotes Romans 3:19 in question eighty-five, article four, on whether we are all bound to offer sacrifice. In the *respondeo*, Aquinas explains that all are bound to offer interior sacrifice (devotion). As for external sacrifice, Aquinas makes a threefold distinction: the Christian sacrifice of the mass enables believers to participate in the sacrificial death of Jesus Christ; the Jewish sacrifices were prescribed by God to enable the Jewish people to worship God and to prefigure Christ; and those outside the Mosaic law, prior to the coming of Christ, "were bound to perform certain outward actions in God's honor, as became those among whom they dwelt." But Aquinas's quotation of Romans 3:19 comes in the first objection. The objection argues that the Mosaic law's commandment to offer sacrifice is binding only for the people of Israel, so that no other nations are bound to offer sacrifice. In the course of his argument that the people of Israel failed to obey the Mosaic law, Paul states that "whatever the law says it speaks to those who are under the law" (Rom 3:19). Aquinas makes clear in reply that the other nations were not bound to offer the precise sacrifices prescribed in the Mosaic law, but they were bound to offer sacrifices.

Romans 8:26 appears twice, both times in question eighty-three, which treats prayer. The RSV reads, "we do not know how to pray as we ought," whereas Aquinas's version has "what we should pray for as we ought, we know not [*Nam quid oremus sicut oportet, nescimus*]." Question eighty-three, article five asks whether, when we pray, we should ask for anything definite or simply ask that God's will be done. The first objection cites Romans 8:26 and concludes that since we do not know for what we rightly should pray, we should not ask for anything definite. Aquinas replies that the Holy Spirit helps us to know what we should pray for, and so we can ask for definite things in prayer. The first objection of question eighty-three, article ten cites another part of Romans 8:26, one with respect to which the RSV and Aquinas's version agree: "The Spirit himself intercedes for us." This causes another problem, namely, does the divine person pray? Aquinas replies that Paul describes the Holy Spirit as interceding for us, not in the sense that the Holy Spirit (who is God) needs to pray for anything, but in the sense that the Holy Spirit moves us to ask for certain things in prayer. The Holy Spirit's intercession consists in moving our wills so that, in union with God's will, we pray for certain things. In this way the Holy Spirit acts on our behalf but does not approach the Father in the beseeching mode proper to a creature.

Romans 8:38–39 appears in the *respondeo* of question eighty-one, article eight, on whether religion is the same as sanctity. Aquinas defines sanctity (*sanctitas*) as having a twofold meaning: purity (*munditia*) and firmness (*firmitas*). The person who possesses sanctity will be firm or immoveable in the application of his or her mind to God by knowledge and by love. In this regard, Aquinas quotes Romans 8:38–39, "For I am sure that neither death, nor life, nor angels, nor principalities, nor things present, nor things to come, nor powers, nor height, nor depth, nor anything else in all creation, will be able to separate us from the love of God in Christ Jesus our Lord." This firm attachment to God characterizes sanctity. Sanctity is the same thing as the virtue of religion, because the virtue of religion consists in applying ourselves interiorly and externally to the worship of God, and sanctity enables us to apply *all* our actions toward the end of the worship of God. The holy person, in this sense, prays without ceasing and does everything out of devotion to God. This use of Romans 8:38–39 interprets it in a direction different from its meaning in context, which has to do with God's fidelity rather than with ours; on the other hand, the interpretation that Aquinas gives does in fact illumine Paul's portrait of the believer.

In the second objection of article three of question eighty-five, Aquinas quotes Romans 12:1, "I appeal to you therefore, brethren, by the mercies of God, to present your bodies as a living sacrifice, holy and acceptable to God, which is your spiritual worship [*rationabile obsequium vestrum*]." The topic of the article is whether offering sacrifice is a special act of virtue. The objection's quotation of Romans 12:1 supports the contrary view that sacrifice is included in the acts of many virtues: when we present our bodies "as a living sacrifice," this means mainly that we are to live temperately rather than living for pleasure. In reply, Aquinas grants that the acts of other virtues, such as almsgiving or ascetic practices, can be called sacrifices. But he adds that the offering of sacrifice is a special act of the virtue of religion, when one offers something to God in a way that is praiseworthy only for the reverence through which the offering is made, rather than being an act of some other virtue.

Aquinas again quotes Romans 12:1 in question eighty-eight, article two. Here he is exploring whether a vow should always be about a better good (*de meliori bono*). It would seem that a vow could be about an indifferent matter, or even about something that tends to be harmful to a person (for example, lengthy fasting). In his reply to the third objection, Aquinas points out that bodily mortification is only virtuous when it does not harm our bodily health. Vows should have to do only with virtuous acts, and thus with better goods. In this regard Aquinas relies upon his version of Romans 12:1, which has "reasonable service [*rationabile obse-*

quium vestrum]" rather than the RSV's "spiritual worship." We should present our bodies "as a living sacrifice" but only within the bounds of reason. Aquinas's rejection of vows that require us to do things harmful to our health is an appropriate application of Paul's exhortation that our presentation of our "bodies as a living sacrifice" to God be done in accord with reason as an expression of our interior service to God.

Finally, Romans 15 is cited twice in question eighty-three. The first objection of the eighth article argues that we should not pray for our enemies, because there are many psalms that curse enemies (such as Psalm 6:10). The objection holds that since "whatever was written in former days was written for our instruction" (Rom 15:4), we should be instructed by these psalms not to pray for our enemies. Aquinas replies that prayer is an act of charity, and so just as we must love our enemies, we must also pray for them. He gives four ways of interpreting the imprecatory psalms, each of which removes the sting of lack of charity. Romans 15:30 assists Aquinas in article seven, which inquires into whether we should pray for others. The third objection proposes that we do not need to pray for the good, because they can pray for themselves. In his reply, Aquinas quotes Paul, who certainly was among the good. Paul asks that his fellow Christians pray for him: "I appeal to you, brethren, by our Lord Jesus Christ and by the love of the Spirit, to strive together with me in your prayers to God on my behalf."

What then is the impact of Romans on Aquinas's treatise on the virtue of religion? From one angle, the impact is a very small one. Of the ten references, six appear in the objections. They formulate objections that are typically somewhat tangential to the main point. He does not rely on Romans to sketch what the virtue of religion involves, or to show that there is such a thing as the virtue of religion. This lack of a central place for Romans is what we might have anticipated, since Paul certainly does not devote the letter to the Romans to sketching the lineaments of what all humans, by virtue of creation, owe to their creator.

On the other hand, gathering these quotations from Romans can help us to see how and why Aquinas argues that there is a virtue of religion. Of the ten verses that Aquinas quotes, the following four stand out: "they exchanged the truth about God for a lie and worshiped and served the creature rather than the Creator" (Rom 1:25); "we do not know how to pray as we ought, but the Spirit himself intercedes for us" (Rom 8:26); "I appeal to you ... to present your bodies as a living sacrifice, holy and acceptable to God, which is your spiritual worship" (Rom 12:1); "I appeal to you ... to strive together with me in your prayers to God on my behalf" (Rom 15:30). Romans 1:25 shows that there is something that all humans owe to God: all must worship him, and all must worship him rather than worshiping creatures. This by itself justifies Aquinas's view that there must be a virtue of religion that belongs to justice. Romans 8:26 and Romans 15:30 show that, among the acts of religion, prayer has a central position. Not surprisingly, the prayer offered by those who enjoy supernatural life in Christ differs from the prayer that humans could otherwise offer to God. In the former, the darkness of prayer is illumined, if only partly, by the presence of the Holy Spirit guiding one's prayer. Even so, Paul does not present prayer as something that originates, simply speaking, with the supernatural indwelling of the Holy Spirit. As rational creatures, we are created to pray to God. Prayer belongs to what we owe God, to the acts proper to the virtue of religion. Prayer forms the communal and not solely the individual lives of believers.

Romans 12:1, about presenting one's body as a living sacrifice, indicates the degree of devotion that is constitutive of the Christian practice of the virtue of religion. Paul considers that devotion to God should constitute the lives of all of God's rational creatures. The lack of devotion to God plagued those who "worshiped and served the creature rather than the Creator" and who thereby fell into intemperate living, among other sins. The grace of the Holy Spirit enables us to regain the virtue of religion and to be truly devout. In this narrative of redemption (implicit in the treatise on the virtue of religion), Aquinas does not fail to include the people of Israel, and if anything he does so more positively than Paul does. Whereas Paul in Romans 3:19 means to show that Israel is condemned by its failure to obey the Mosaic law, for instance, Aquinas quotes this text—"whatever the law says it speaks to those who are under the law"—as a way of differentiating the sacrifices commanded by God to Israel from those of any other people. Aquinas also takes seriously Romans 15:4, "Whatever was written in former days was written for our instruction." The prayers and sacrifices that were offered by the people of Israel should instruct us in what a virtuous life requires. Finally, he recognizes that the virtue of religion cannot be solely an interior affair, and in this regard his appreciation for "the things that have been made" is noteworthy, even if his understanding of these things as signs that we should employ in worship goes beyond what Paul says in Romans 1.

1 & 2 CORINTHIANS

The eighteen citations of 1 Corinthians in the *Summa theologiae*'s questions on the virtue of religion span the fourth to the sixteenth chapter of the epistle. In terms of the letter's order (rather than the order of the treatise), the first verse cited is 1 Corinthians 4:5: "Therefore do not pronounce judgment before the time, before the Lord comes, who will bring to light the things now hidden in darkness and will disclose the purposes of the heart." This verse appears in the reply to the third objection of question eighty-nine, article two. The topic of the article is whether swearing an oath is lawful. Oaths have to do with the virtue of religion, in Aquinas's view, because they invoke the name of God in order to call God to witness. The third objection, however, argues that to call God to witness is a form of tempting God, because it is like asking God to show a sign of his providence. Aquinas replies that calling God to witness does not presume to put God on a timetable. God will bear witness at the end of time, when God brings "to light the things now hidden in darkness." The citation of 1 Corinthians 4:5 thus serves to support Aquinas's view that calling God to witness is not a presumptuous way of testing God, because (as Paul makes clear) God is indeed the true witness and judge of all things.

First Corinthians 4:16 appears in the third objection of question eighty-eight, article four, on whether it is expedient to take vows. The objection points out that we do not read of Christ or the apostles taking a vow (although Paul, according to Acts 18:18, took a vow). The apostles imitated Christ, and we should imitate the apostles in their imitation of Christ. The Latin text of 1 Corinthians 4:16 differs from the RSV, but the meaning is similar enough. As Aquinas quotes the verse, it reads: "Be imitators of me, as I am of Christ," whereas the RSV has simply, "I urge you, then, be imitators of me." The objection concludes from this verse that we should imitate Christ and the apostles in not taking vows. In reply, Aquinas remarks that Christ did not need vows, not only because he was God, but also because his human will was firmly united to his divine will. But the members of the church should take vows, Aquinas thinks, because the prerogatives of Christ do not pertain to them. That the apostles took the equivalent of vows can be shown by their leaving everything to follow Christ.

Aquinas quotes 1 Corinthians 6:9–10 in question eighty-three, article nine. Here he asks whether the seven petitions in the Lord's prayer are appropriate. He explains the seven petitions in terms of God as our end or goal. The first petition has to do with willing God's glory; the second with willing to share in his glory; the third with how we merit beatitude; the fourth with how we are helped to merit; the fifth with the removal of sin; the sixth with the removal of temptation; and the seventh with the penal condition under which we labor in this life. Regarding the fourth petition, "forgive us our trespasses," Aquinas notes that those persons who die in a state of sin will not receive beatitude. This is confirmed, he thinks, by 1 Corinthians 6:9–10: "Do not be deceived; neither the immoral, nor idolaters, nor adulterers, nor homosexuals, nor thieves, nor the greedy, nor drunkards, nor revilers, nor robbers will inherit the kingdom of God."

First Corinthians 7:33–34 appears in the *respondeo* of question eighty-eight, article eleven, on whether one who has taken a solemn vow of perpetual chastity can be dispensed from this vow. Aquinas explains that there are three aspects to such a vow: its solemnity; its perpetuity and universality; and its content (perpetual chastity). The solemnity of the vow entails the person's perpetual consecration to God. Aquinas examines the relationship between the solemn purpose of the vow and perpetual chastity. In the case of orders, he notes, perpetual chastity is not inextricably linked with orders, but rather this link is instituted by the church. With regard to religious life, however, perpetual chastity belongs at the heart of the solemn consecration, because in the religious state "a man renounces the world and binds himself wholly to God's service." Therefore the vow of chastity cannot be dispensed by the church as regards the religious life. The role of 1 Corinthians 7:33–34 in this argument is twofold. Aquinas first quotes Paul's statement that "the unmarried woman or girl is anxious about the affairs of the Lord, how to be holy in body and spirit" (1 Cor 7:34). In Aquinas's view, this exhortation aims to encourage believers to embrace chastity so as to be able to focus on contemplation. Since a vow of contemplation can be dispensed, there is nothing intrinsic to chastity that makes it impossible also to dispense a vow of chastity. In making his case that chastity is intrinsic to the religious state and therefore cannot be dispensed (just as the religious state cannot be dispensed), however, Aquinas discusses Paul's comparison of the unmarried person and the married person. The duties of the married person are opposed to the duties of the person who remains unmarried for the sake of the Lord. Chastity is intrinsic to taking on the duties of the religious state, as Paul shows when he says that "the married man is anxious about worldly affairs, how to please his wife, and his interests are divided" (1 Cor 7:33–34). Surely Paul does not have in view the religious state as Aquinas knew it, but I do think that Aquinas's fundamental insight into the purpose of chastity is fully Pauline and appropriately informs his understanding of the vows taken by members of religious orders.

The first article of question eighty-seven, on whether God commands the people of God to tithe, refers twice to 1 Corinthians 9 (in the *respondeo* and in the reply to the second objection) and once to 1 Corinthians 10 (in the *respondeo*). In the *respondeo* Aquinas explains that just as it is the duty of a people to provide for its rulers and soldiers, so also is it the duty of a people to provide for those who administer the divine worship. Here Aquinas refers to Paul's words in 1 Corinthians 9:7, "Who serves as a soldier at his own expense? Who plants a vineyard without eating any of its fruit?" The requirement to give a one-tenth share of one's income, however, comes not from natural law but from God's command to Israel, and from the church's command. The church requires a one-tenth share not least in order to show that the church's ministers are of as much value as Israel's. But the tithe also has its roots, says Aquinas, in the fact that ten is a perfect number: the one-tenth share given to God signifies that perfection will come from God. Along these lines Aquinas quotes 1 Corinthians 10:11: "These things happened to them as a figure [RSV, "warning"]." The second objection argues that under the new law, believers are required to obey only the commands of Christ and the apostles, who do not mention tithing. In the reply to this objection, Aquinas points out that although the fixing of the proportion is the duty of the church, both Christ and the apostles insist that the ministers of divine worship must be supported by the people of God. Aquinas quotes Jesus's comments in Matthew 10:10 and Paul's remark, "Do we not have the right to our food and drink?" (1 Cor 9:4).

Further quotations of 1 Corinthians 9 occur in questions eighty-one, eighty-six, and eighty-seven. In question eighty-one, article six, Aquinas inquires into whether the virtue of religion has preference over all other moral virtues. The second objection argues that the virtue of religion does not have preference, because the greater the obligation to do something, the less praiseworthy it is. For this principle Aquinas relies on 1 Corinthians 9:16, "For if I preach the gospel, that gives me no ground for boasting. For necessity is laid upon me." In reply, Aquinas states that the fact that we have an obligation to do something does not make our action less meritorious, but instead only means that we are not doing more than our duty. The point is not that Paul's preaching belongs to the virtue of religion, except in the sense that religion commands all actions done to God's glory. Rather, Aquinas's point here is that the obligation intrinsic to religion does not lessen the merit associated with religion. It seems likely that Paul, too, would insist upon the privileged status of the acts by which he directly reveres God.

In question eighty-six, article two, Aquinas refers in the *respondeo* to 1 Corinthians 9:13, "Do you not know that those who are employed in the temple service get their food from the temple, and those who serve at the altar share in the sacrificial offerings?" Paul's obvious conclusion is that the ministers of Christ should be able to earn their living by their ministry. Aquinas's topic in this article is whether the oblations or offerings given to the church should go to priests alone. He answers that although the oblations should indeed go solely to priests, the priests should divide these oblations in a threefold manner: for their own living, for things that pertain to the divine worship, and for the care of the poor. His quotation of 1 Corinthians 9:13 comes in support of the priests' use of oblations to sustain their own living and not simply for the divine worship and for the care of the poor. This accords completely with Paul's view.

Aquinas quotes 1 Corinthians 9:11 in the *respondeo* of question eighty-seven, article two. This article asks whether believers have to pay a tithe on all their income. The objections propose that believers need only pay a tithe on some portion of their income. Aquinas answers by observing that the rationale for tithing is that we owe a portion of our worldly goods to those who minister spiritual goods to us. Paul articulates this rationale: "If we have sown spiritual good among you, is it too much if we reap your material benefits?" (1 Cor 9:11). Since none of our income is excluded from our "material benefits," Aquinas concludes that we owe a tithe on all our income and not solely on a portion of it.

Aquinas twice cites 1 Corinthians 10:31, "So, whether you eat or drink, or whatever you do, do all to the glory of God." The first time occurs in question eighty-one, article four, which has to do with whether religion is a distinct or special virtue. The second objection of this article argues that religion is not a distinct virtue, on the grounds of 1 Corinthians 10:31. On this view, doing "all to the glory of God" would mean that we do *everything* in order to honor and revere God, which would imply that religion has no particular action of its own. In reply, Aquinas notes that religion commands that we do acts of other virtues out of reverence for God, but religion elicits certain actions of its own that make it a distinct virtue. The second occurrence of 1 Corinthians 10:31 appears in the *respondeo* of question eighty-three, article fourteen. Insofar as prayer arises from the desire of charity, says Aquinas, prayer should be continual, just as all our works should be done charitably and "to the glory of God." But as a distinct action, prayer cannot be continual because we have other things that we must do, and because we cannot focus our minds for very long without becoming tired.

We find 1 Corinthians 11:29 in the *respondeo* of question eighty-nine, article two. We have already discussed this article because in the reply to the third objection, Aquinas cites 1 Corinthians 4:5. The issue is whether we can lawfully swear oaths. Aquinas emphasizes that one can make bad use of even good things, and in this regard he quotes Paul's remark about the eucharist that "any one who eats and drinks without discerning the body eats and drinks judgment upon himself" (1 Cor 11:29). Many people make bad use of oaths because of habitual swearing, but that does not rule out their good use.

First Corinthians 14:14 appears in question eighty-three, article thirteen, and 1 Corinthians 14:15 appears in question eighty-three, article four and question eighty-four, article two. The two verses read as follows: "For if I pray in a tongue, my spirit prays but my mind is unfruitful. What am I to do? I will pray with the spirit and I will pray with the mind also; I will sing with the spirit and I will sing with the mind also." The thirteenth article of question eighty-three asks whether we need to be attentive in prayer. In vocal prayer, our mind sometimes wanders; does this destroy the value of prayer? In his *respondeo*, Aquinas answers that, on the one hand, when we set out with a good intention to pray, the merit of this good effort and its impetration with God does not disappear even if we at times find ourselves inattentive in prayer. On the other hand, prayer should also produce a spiritual refreshment in us, and this is impossible when our attention wanders. He considers that this is what Paul means when he says, "if I pray in a tongue, my spirit prays but my mind is unfruitful," because when one prays in a tongue whose meaning one does not know, one's mind necessarily wanders because one cannot be attentive to the words or to their meaning.

In the second objection of question eighty-three, article four, Aquinas quotes 1 Corinthians 14:15 without including its Pauline context regarding the practice of speaking in tongues. The topic of the article is whether we should pray to God alone. Aquinas responds that we should pray to God alone because only God can fulfill our prayer, but we should also pray through the saints so that our prayers might be heard through the intercession of the saints (see Revelation 8:4). The objection argues that the dead, as dead, do not know what the living are doing or thinking. It quotes 1 Corinthians 14:15 to show that prayer is often an interior act that God alone knows: "I will pray with the spirit and I will pray with the mind also." This is not the point that Paul has in view. Aquinas replies that the objection underestimates what God does for the dead: it is fitting that the blessed dead know in the Word our condition and our petitions.

Aquinas uses 1 Corinthians 14:15 in a similar way in the second article of question eighty-four, regarding whether adoration is an action of the body. He answers that our adoration of God is twofold, spiritual and bodily, the latter being ordered to the former. The second objection, however, argues that adoration is solely spiritual, because adoration arises from prayer. To show that prayer consists in a spiritual rather than a bodily action, the objection quotes 1 Corinthians 14:15, "I will pray with the spirit and I will pray with the mind also." In reply, Aquinas points out that just as prayer is chiefly in the mind but can and should be expressed in vocal words, so also adoration is primarily spiritual reverence of God but should also include bodily signs of devotion and humility.

The final quotation of 1 Corinthians in this treatise comes in question eighty-nine, article seven. At issue is whether an oath has binding force. In 1 Corinthians 16:5, Paul tells the Corinthians that "I will visit you after passing through Macedonia." But in 2 Corinthians 1:16–17, Paul observes that in fact he had not been able to visit the Corinthians, and he defends himself against the charge of "vacillating" and of making "my plans like a worldly man, ready to say Yes and No at once." The first objection quotes these passages in order to argue that assertions about the future—such as Paul's promise to visit the Corinthians—can be true whether or not one is able to do what one promises; Paul did not lie. Since one swears an oath in order to confirm the truth of an assertion, it follows that oaths can be true even if what one promises to do turns out not to be possible. If so, then an oath would not have binding force. Aquinas replies that one should not swear an oath about merely any assertion about one's plans. Rather, one should only swear an oath when one intends to do everything possible in order to accomplish one's plans.

Following the order of 2 Corinthians rather than the order of treatise, we can begin with 2 Corinthians 1:11 in question eighty-three, article seven. This article has to do with whether we should pray for others, including (as we saw earlier with regard to Romans 15:30), whether we should pray for the just. In his reply to the third objection, Aquinas reasons that we should pray for the just as a way of thanking God for the graces that God has bestowed on the just, graces that redound to the benefit of many. In this regard he quotes 2 Corinthians 1:11, where Paul says, "You also must help us by prayer, so that many will give thanks on our behalf for the blessing granted us in answer to many prayers."

Aquinas cites 2 Corinthians 1:15 in the first objection of question eighty-nine, article seven, about whether an oath has binding force. I have already commented on this objection in connection with 1 Corinthians 16:5, and so I do not need to repeat here how Aquinas employs 2 Corinthians 1:15. In the sixth article of question eighty-nine, Aquinas asks whether one can lawfully swear by creatures (for instance, by the gospel). I discussed this article in connection with Romans 1:25. In his *respondeo*, Aquinas gives an example of Paul swearing by his soul: "I call God to witness upon my soul [*ego autem testem Deum invoco in animam meam*]" (2 Cor 1:23). The RSV, however, reads "I call God to witness against me." But Aquinas's point is that in calling God to witness, it is lawful to swear that if one is speaking falsely, God's righteous judgment may stand against the creature (such as one's soul) by which one swears. Paul certainly would agree with this.

Second Corinthians 2:10 appears in the twelfth article of question eighty-eight. This article treats whether only a prelate of the church can dispense a person from a solemn vow made to God. Aquinas argues that the answer is yes, because a prelate of the church has the authority to speak on behalf of God and therefore can dispense in certain cases from solemn vows. For this account of the church's prelates, Aquinas draws in the *respondeo* on 2 Corinthians 2:10, which in his version reads: "*Nam et ego quod donavi si quid donavi propter vos in persona Christi.*" In the RSV, the translation is: "What I have forgiven, if I have forgiven anything, has been for your sake in the presence of Christ." The difference between "in persona Christi" and "in the presence of Christ" is significant here, because the former gives the sense of the manner in which the apostles and bishops exercise authority in the church, whereas the latter may simply indicate Christ's presence in the church in general. Even so, it seems likely that the interpretation given by Aquinas can still hold in the sense that Paul does see his apostolic authority as mediating the authority of Christ. But Aquinas's discussion of solemn vows and the authority of prelates also goes beyond Paul in the sense that bishops dispensing from religious vows is obviously not something that Paul has in view.

The first article of question eighty-seven treats whether Christians are required to tithe. I have already discussed this article with regard to 1 Corinthians 9–10. In his *respondeo*, Aquinas also cites 2 Corinthians 3:7–8: "Now if the dispensation of death, carved in letters of stone, came with such splendor that the Israelites could not look at Moses' face because of its brightness, fading as this was, will not the dispensation of the Spirit be attended with greater splendor?" Aquinas here is not trying to enter into Paul's full argument, which has to do with the relationship of the "dispensation of the Spirit" (now that the messiah has come) to the Torah. Instead, Aquinas simply seeks to defend the point that the church's ministers deserve to be materially supported no less fully than were the ministers of the Mosaic law.

Aquinas quotes 2 Corinthians 4:18 in article six of question eighty-three. This article investigates whether in prayer we should ask God for temporal things. The first two objections are taken from Jesus's words in the sermon on the mount, which urge his followers to seek eternal things. The third objection turns to Paul's proclamation that "we look not to the things that are seen but to the things that are unseen; for the things that are seen are transient, but the things that are unseen are eternal" (2 Cor 4:18). If we are supposed to look to unseen, eternal things, then surely we are not supposed to ask for temporal things in prayer. Aquinas replies that Paul warns us against seeking temporal things so as to rest in them, which is quite different from seeking temporal things so as to assist our progress (and others' progress) toward beatitude. The latter constitutes the good purpose of temporal things.

In this treatise, Aquinas does not quote from chapters 5–8 of 2 Corinthians. When he turns again to 2 Corinthians, it is to refer to 2 Corinthians 9:7, "Each one must do as he has made up his mind, not reluctantly or under compulsion, for God loves a cheerful giver." In question eighty-eight, article six, this verse helps Aquinas to formulate an objection to the view that it is more praiseworthy to do something in fulfillment of a vow than without a vow. It seems that vowing to do something means that when we do it, we do it "under compulsion" and therefore less meritoriously. In reply, Aquinas differentiates the necessity that comes from compulsion from the necessity that comes from a vow. A vow, when freely taken, strengthens the will toward what the will already wishes to do. At the same time, Aquinas recognizes that something that we have vowed to do might become, by the time when have to do it, repugnant to our will—for example, fasting. But to do such a good thing in fulfillment of a vow would still be more meritorious than to do it without a vow, since fulfilling a good vow is itself a highly virtuous act of religion.

Lastly, in the twelfth article of question eighty-eight, we find a further discussion of the role of prelates in dispensing vows. Aquinas refers to 2 Corinthians in his reply to the second objection. In this reply, Aquinas denies that a prelate can dispense a person from any vow, which would mean that people could break their vows without sin whenever permitted to do so by their prelate. Against this view, Aquinas cites Paul's statement about his own apostolic authority: "For even if I boast a little too much of our authority, which the Lord gave for building you up and not for destroying you, I shall not be put to shame" (2 Cor 10:8). To destroy a person, Aquinas reasons, would be to lead them into sin; whereas to build them up would be to unite them more closely to God's wisdom and will. Therefore a prelate does not have absolute power: he cannot command sin or forbid virtue. In some cases, vows simply cannot be dispensed. This is an extension of Paul's view of apostolic authority, rather than something that Paul himself would have envisioned.

What then is the role of the Corinthian correspondence in Aquinas's treatise on the virtue of religion in the *Summa theologiae*? Of the twenty-six times that Aquinas quotes 1 or 2 Corinthians in this treatise, his quotation of Paul with regard to supporting ministers of divine worship stands out as particularly noteworthy. Recall Paul's insistence to the Corinthians that they must support materially those who devote themselves to the gospel: "Do we not have the right to our food and drink?" (1 Cor 9:4); "Who serves as a soldier at his own expense? Who plants a vineyard without eating any of its fruits?" (1 Cor 9:7); "If we have sown spiritual good among you, is it too much if we reap your material benefits?" (1 Cor 9:11); "Do you not know that those who are employed in the temple service get their food from the temple, and those who serve at the altar share in the sacrificial offerings?" (1 Cor 9:13). Aquinas connects these passages with tithing and with oblations. Although Paul does not have the later church's teachings on tithing and oblations in mind, nonetheless Aquinas's connection of these verses with tithing and oblations is hardly a stretch.

Aquinas also employs certain Pauline passages to evoke the various elements of the virtue of religion. Paul, for example, urges believers to "help us by prayer, so that many will give thanks on our behalf for the blessing granted us in answer to many prayers" (2 Cor 1:11). Prayer, like supporting ministers, belongs to what we owe God. Admittedly, Paul in 1 Corinthians devotes significant attention to praying in tongues, a topic that Aquinas does not treat in this treatise. Instead he uses for his own purposes the passages where Paul is speaking about praying in tongues: he directs these texts of Paul to issues such as finding spiritual refreshment in prayer, praying to saints, and the relationship of bodily and spiritual adoration of God.

When Aquinas treats vows and oaths, he makes good use of Paul's account of an unmarried life devoted entirely to God: "The married man is anxious about worldly affairs, how to please his wife, and his interests are divided. And the unmarried woman or girl is anxious about the affairs of the Lord, how to be holy in body and spirit; but the married woman is anxious about worldly affairs, how to please her husband" (1 Cor 7:33–34). Clearly Paul does not envision what Aquinas knows as the religious state of life, but the basic principles regarding the vow of chastity are present. Aquinas is aware, of course, that Jesus Christ and the apostles did not practice the religious life. He holds that the apostles, in leaving everything to follow Christ, laid down the foundations of religious life even if they did not practice it in the precise way of later generations. Aquinas also draws his theology of oaths partly from Paul. Paul's calling God to witness provides the paradigm for Aquinas's understanding of a solemn oath.

It might seem obvious that religious practice is praiseworthy, but in a sense religious practice is simply doing our duty. In the context of his apostolic vocation, Paul speaks of this duty when he says that "necessity is laid upon me. Woe to me if I do not preach the gospel!" (1 Cor 9:16). As Aquinas shows, this does not mean that the duties of religion fail to be meritorious. Aquinas also considers Paul's remark, with regard to almsgiving, that "each one must do as he has made up his mind, not reluctantly or under compulsion, for God loves a cheerful giver" (2 Cor 9:7). Aquinas applies this statement to his theology of vows, but one can also consider it in light of the "necessity" that Paul has earlier spoken of. With regard to dispensations from solemn vows, Aquinas creatively extends Paul's reflections on his apostolic authority, "which the Lord gave for building you up and not for destroying you" (2 Cor 10:8).

In addition, Aquinas employs Paul to press a central issue: whether there is a distinct virtue of religion at all. After all, Paul says (in the context of the question of eating food that has been sacrificially offered to idols) that "whether you eat or drink, do all to the glory of God" (1 Cor 10:31). In this case, Aquinas ignores the context of Paul's words but nonetheless employs the passage to answer a question related to Paul's emphasis on glorifying God. If we are supposed to glorify God in *all* that we do, how can there be special practices—such as prayer, oblations, tithes, vows, oaths and so forth—that pertain particularly to the virtue of honoring and reverencing God? Aquinas grants that our entire lives should, in a sense, be a prayer. Yet prayer should still be a distinct practice, as Paul likewise recognizes.

Aquinas's use of the Corinthian correspondence in his treatise on the virtue of religion makes particularly clear that Aquinas is not trying to imagine what religion—that is to say, honoring and reverencing God—would look like if humans had not sinned and if God had not revealed himself. Rather than trying to sketch a natural religion, Aquinas takes up his various topics in a manner that has the church always in view. He wants to know, for example, whether prelates can dispense from vows and whether we should pray to the saints. He does not claim that these topics arise from Paul, even though he makes use of Paul to help illuminate the issues involved. Although he leaves to the side many of the concerns that were central to the controversies of Paul's day, Aquinas's citations of the Corinthian correspondence recall much of Paul's religious culture: his emphasis on prayer, his insistence that ministers of the gospel should be supported materially, his insistence upon apostolic authority, and his occasional use of an oath. Furthermore, Aquinas's citations of the Corinthian correspondence in these questions on religion help us to see that within revealed Christian faith, there are practices that belong to any honoring and reverencing of God: for example, prayer, tithing, and vows, although all of these will take various forms depending on historical context.

GALATIANS, EPHESIANS, 1 THESSALONIANS, 1 & 2 TIMOTHY, HEBREWS

There are twenty further references to the Pauline epistles (or at least to epistles considered to be Pauline by Aquinas) in the treatise on the virtue of religion. Twelve of these come from Hebrews. Following the order of Paul's letters, I will begin with the two references to Galatians, both of which occur in the first article of question eighty-one—the very first article of the treatise. The topic of this article is whether religion, as a virtue, directs human beings to God alone. Charity directs us to both God and our neighbor, and so the objections ask whether this also holds for the virtue of religion. Along these lines, the third objection cites Galatians 5:13, "Through love be servants of one another." In Galatians itself, this verse belongs to Paul's urging the Galatians not to resume the rites of the Mosaic law, but the objection uses this portion of the verse as a means of drawing a connection between charity and service. The virtue of religion, too, involves service. If charity means service to God and neighbor, then, says the objection, so too religion means service to God and neighbor rather than solely to God. Aquinas replies that God, as creator of all, is Lord of all and therefore requires a unique kind of service, which consists in the virtue of religion.

The second reference to Galatians occurs in the reply to the fifth objection of the same article. The fifth objection pointed out that although all who worship God are "religious," nonetheless in a particular way the name "religious" is given to those who devote their entire selves to God by renouncing the world and living a life of obedience to human superiors in community. In this way, it might seem that religion involves not only an ordering to God, but also an ordering toward fellow humans in the practice of religious obedience. In reply, Aquinas recalls how Paul reminds the Galatians that they had originally "received me [Paul] as an angel of God, as Christ Jesus" (Gal 4:14). In consecrated religious life, Aquinas observes, obedience is given to superiors as to Christ not in order to honor the human superiors, but in order to be able better to honor God through renouncing one's own will. In other words, the virtue of religion, even when it involves religious obedience to superiors, relates us solely to God rather than also to humans.

The one quotation of Ephesians in the treatise occurs in the *sed contra* of question eighty-one, article three, on whether religion is one virtue. Here we see particularly clearly the overlap between Aquinas's understanding of the virtue of religion and his understanding of Christian faith and practice, which supernaturally instantiate and elevate the virtue of religion. The *sed contra* quotes Ephesians 4:5, "One Lord, one faith." With this as his biblical authority, Aquinas observes that the virtue of religion directs us to have faith in one God, notwithstanding the fact that God is three persons. Since the virtue of religion has one object, religion is one virtue.

In the fourteenth article of question eighty-three, Aquinas quotes 1 Thessalonians for the first and only time in the treatise. The topic of this article is the duration of prayer. In 1 Thessalonians 5:17, Paul exhorts the Thessalonians to "pray constantly [*sine intermissione orate*]." Aquinas quotes this verse in his *sed contra*, which also functions as the fourth objection. He wishes to affirm that in a certain sense we must "pray constantly," but also to make clear that we cannot spend our entire lives in prayer. Not only are there other things that we must attend to, but also if we tried literally to pray without ceasing, we would soon become too tired to pray attentively.

Aquinas twice quotes 1 Timothy. The first appearance of 1 Timothy is found in question eighty-three, article seventeen, on the different kinds of prayer. In Aquinas's view, as made clear in the *sed contra*, 1 Timothy 2:1 provides a nice division of the kinds of prayer: "I urge that supplications, prayers, intercessions, and thanksgivings be made for all men." In the *respondeo*, Aquinas explains this division as follows. The term "prayers" indicates the rising of the mind to God; the term "intercession" indicates our desire to be helped by God, whether generally or concretely; the term "supplication" indicates our pleading to God, in which we know that we will be heard because of his holiness and love; and finally the term "thanksgiving" indicates our gratitude for God's gifts, a gratitude which makes our prayer pleasing to God.

First Timothy is also cited in question eighty-nine, article three, on the conditions that suitably accompany an oath. These conditions, says Aquinas, are justice, judgment, and truth. The third objection, however, argues that these three conditions should characterize all our actions rather than having a particular application to oaths. In this regard the objection quotes 1 Timothy 5:21, which in Aquinas's version reads "Do nothing without pre-judgment [*Nihil facias sine praeiudicio*]," and which in the RSV reads "keep these rules without favor, doing nothing from partiality." The objection interprets "praeiudicio" to mean that we should only act when we have judged the matter beforehand, and of course we should only act justly and truthfully. It therefore seems that justice, judgment, and truth should accompany all actions and not solely oaths. In reply, Aquinas states that swearing oaths involves a greater risk, because one is calling God to witness to the truth of what one says. This greater risk means that oaths, even more than other actions, need the conditions of justice, judgment, and truth.

Like 1 Timothy, 2 Timothy also appears twice in the treatise. In question eighty-seven, article two, at issue is whether we have to pay tithes on all things, or whether instead we need only pay tithes on inherited property or on livestock or produce. In his reply to the first objection, Aquinas explains why we have to pay tithes on property that we have acquired by our own work (such as commerce) rather than solely paying tithes on the fruits of our farms, orchards, and livestock, as the Mosaic law commands. Aquinas accounts for this in terms of the shift from the Mosaic law to the new law. The Levites held no land or livestock, but they were allowed to earn income by other work. By contrast, the ministers of the church are not generally allowed to engage in other income-earning work. In support of this prohibition of clergy from engaging in commerce or soldiering, Aquinas quotes Paul's words to Timothy: "No soldier on service gets entangled in civilian pursuits, since his aim is to satisfy the one who enlisted him" (2 Tim 2:4). Taking this statement somewhat differently from its contextual meaning, Aquinas considers that it applies to priests in the sense that they have "enlisted" in service to Christ, and so they should not become "entangled in civilian pursuits." Aquinas adds that many Christians no longer live on inherited land but instead make their income from trade. In order to obtain the material support they need, therefore, the ministers of the new law need us to tithe not only produce, fruit, and livestock but also monetary income.

In question eighty-three, article sixteen, Aquinas quotes 2 Timothy 3:5 in the second objection. This article treats whether sinners gain anything by prayer. Aquinas offers a twofold answer: when the prayer of sinners expresses a sinful desire, God does not hear this prayer except to punish; when the prayer of sinners expresses a good desire, God hears this prayer out of pure mercy. The second objection, however, argues that our prayers are efficacious insofar as we possess grace and charity. The objection concludes that the prayer of sinners is impious and gains nothing. In this regard, the objection appeals to the gloss on Paul's remarks in 2 Timothy 3:5, where Paul describes sinners as, among other things, "holding the form of religion but denying the power of it." On this view, since sinners lack the power of holiness, their prayers cannot be efficacious. Aquinas replies that if a sinner prays for something that pertains to holiness, God mercifully answers this prayer.

Turning now to Hebrews, I observe that Aquinas does not quote in his questions on religion from the first four chapters of Hebrews. Of his twelve citations of Hebrews, two are of Hebrews 5:1 and six are of Hebrews 6:16 and 6:17. He quotes Hebrews 5:1 in articles two and four of question eighty-six. I have already commented on article two with respect to 1 Corinthians 9:13. As we saw, the topic of this article is whether priests alone are in charge of using and dispensing the oblations that people offer to God. In his *respondeo*, Aquinas answers in the affirmative on the grounds that a priest, as a mediator between God and humans, has the twofold responsibility of conveying divine things (teachings and sacraments) to the people and of offering the people's prayers, sacrifices, and oblations to God. The latter role means that priests alone have responsibility for using and dispensing the oblations given to God by the people. In support of this view of the priesthood, Aquinas cites Hebrews 5:1, "For every high priest chosen from among men is appointed to act on behalf of men in relation to God, to offer gifts and sacrifices for sins." Although Christ fulfills the role of high priest, he enables men to share in his priesthood in a ministerial fashion.

The fourth article of question eighty-six asks whether we all owe firstfruits. In Aquinas's view, the answer varies according to the custom of the country and the needs of the church in particular times and places. He quotes Hebrews 5:1 in the *respondeo*, in the context of his explanation of why the first-fruits offered to God under the Mosaic law were placed under the charge of the priests.

The six references to Hebrews 6:16 and 6:17 occur in question eighty-nine, on oaths. This is not surprising, as Hebrews 6:16–17 reads: "Men indeed swear by a greater than themselves, and in all their disputes an oath is final for confirmation. So when God desired to show more convincingly to the heirs of the promise the unchangeable character of his purpose, he interposed with an oath." The first article of question eighty-nine treats whether to swear an oath is to call God to witness, and Aquinas's *respondeo* begins by observing—with reference to Hebrews 6:16—that the purpose of an oath is to confirm a contingent fact whose truth cannot be assumed solely on the basis of human testimony. The second article of question eighty-nine asks whether it is lawful to swear oaths, and Aquinas again quotes Hebrews 6:16 in the *respondeo*, this time to explain that oaths help to resolve disputes. The fourth article of question eighty-nine refers twice to Hebrews 6:16, once in the first objection and again in the *respondeo*. The topic of the article is whether an oath is an act of religion (*latria*). Thus the first objection argues that oaths have to do not with God but with human "disputes" (Heb 6:16), while the *respondeo* corrects this picture by quoting the first part of the verse: "Men indeed swear by a greater than themselves." Lastly, the tenth article of question eighty-nine cites Hebrews 6:16 in the first objection and Hebrews 6:17 in the reply to the fourth objection. This article has to do with when an oath is void. The first objection holds that anyone is competent to employ an oath for the "confirmation" (Heb 6:16) of his or her statements. In reply, Aquinas points out that children and some others cannot validly swear oaths. The fourth objection argues that since even angels swear oaths (see Revelation 10:6), no mere human has so much dignity as to be excused from swearing oaths. Aquinas's reply explains that the context of Revelation 10:6 shows that the angel is not being asked to confirm his word, but rather the oath simply shows God's unchangeable word. In this sense, even God, whose word must obviously be trusted, can be said to validate his promise "with an oath" (Heb 6:17).

Hebrews 7:25 appears in question eighty-three, article eleven, on whether the saints in heaven pray for us. After giving various objections, Aquinas in his *respondeo* argues that the saints in heaven do pray for us. His argument draws upon his version of Hebrews 7:25, which reads: "Going to God by His own power to make intercession for us [*Accedens per semetipsum ad Deum ad interpellandum pro nobis*]." If the glorified Christ makes intercession for us, then certainly the saints in heaven, who are joined to him by charity, also make intercession for us.

Aquinas refers to Hebrews 11:32 in question eighty-eight, article two, regarding whether a vow always regards a better good. I have already discussed this article in connection with Romans 12:1. The second objection raises the case of Jephthah, whose vow led him to kill his own daughter. As the objection points out, Jephthah is listed among the great men and women of faith in Hebrews 11:32. Certainly his vow did not involve a better good. In his reply, Aquinas notes that a vow might be good in itself even if, when one attempts to keep the vow, one produces an evil result. He explains that in such cases one must not keep the vow. Regarding the list in Hebrews 11:32, Aquinas speculates that Jephthah repented of his evil deed.

Lastly, Hebrews 13:16 appears twice in the treatise. This verse states, "Do not neglect to do good and to share what you have, for such sacrifices are pleasing to God." In the third article of question eighty-five, Aquinas examines whether offering sacrifice is a special (or particular) act of virtue. The second objection employs both Romans 12:1 and Hebrews 13:16 to argue that it is not a special act of virtue, because doing good and sharing possessions belong to charity, mercy, and liberality rather than marking out the contours of a distinct virtue. Aquinas answers that devotion and prayer are interior acts of sacrifice or self-gift that pertain to the virtue of religion, even though they are motivated by charity. Likewise the sacrificial offering of external things can also belong to the virtue of religion, although it can also pertain to mercy and liberality (as with almsgiving).

The first objection of question eighty-six, article two relies upon Hebrews 13:16. I have already addressed this article with respect to 1 Corinthians 9:13 and Hebrews 5:1. The first objection argues that oblations offered to God should be given not only to priests but also to the poor. The objection's argument relies upon Hebrews 13:16's injunction to "share what you have." Aquinas replies that an oblation, properly speaking, consists in an offering to God rather than an act of almsgiving. As such, oblations must be used and dispensed by priests, who certainly should give a portion of the oblations to the poor.

How might we sum up the ways in which Aquinas uses these six Pauline letters—Galatians, Ephesians, 1 Thessalonians, 1 and 2 Timothy, and Hebrews—in the treatise on the virtue of religion? He employs Galatians when he treats the virtue of religion in itself (question eighty-one). Against the view that "religion" is directed to both God and humans, he explains that religious life includes obedience to human superiors as a means of obeying God's will. He emphasizes that the virtue of religion, unlike the virtue of charity, does not involve serving both God and neighbor, but instead has to do properly with honoring and reverencing God. He makes use of Ephesians when he observes that since the virtue of religion has one object, God, it is one virtue. In treating prayer, he interprets 1 Thessalonians 5:17, "pray constantly." First Timothy 2:1 provides him with a definition of the various kinds of prayer. He uses 2 Timothy to reflect on tithing and prayer, in both cases going beyond the contextual meaning of Paul. Hebrews 5:1 serves as a definition of priesthood that makes sense of why priests have charge over oblations and first-fruits, while Hebrews 13:16 seems to depict every good act as a sacrifice (or oblation). Hebrews 6:16–17 offers a crucial definition of oaths that is particularly important given Jesus's seeming rejection of swearing oaths. Hebrews 11:32 stimulates Aquinas's consideration of the vow of Jephthah.

Most of these citations either do not have much importance or go well beyond the Pauline context. For example, the two citations of Galatians clarify Aquinas's concerns, but these citations have little or nothing to do with Paul's own concerns. Aquinas uses Galatians to raise an interesting problem, namely whether religion, like charity, should be directed to both God and neighbor. Paul however would never have thought of this problem. The citation of 1 Thessalonians on praying constantly has more connection to Paul's own conception of the Christian life, although of course Paul would never have intended this to be taken in the sense of literally never ceasing to pray (a sense that Aquinas considers but rules out). Although the passage from 1 Timothy 2:1 does not function in Paul as a definition of kinds of prayer, one can see how it may be legitimately used as such. It does seem, then, that 1 Thessalonians and 1 Timothy are of some use for Aquinas in engaging Paul's own conception of prayer. The texts from 2 Timothy, however, veer quite far from Paul's concerns, even though they make interesting points regarding why priests should not engage in commerce or soldiering and about whether sinners can have their prayers heard. Finally, Hebrews is obviously significant for giving a "Pauline" basis to Aquinas's theology of oaths and priesthood.

CONCLUSION

Has Aquinas truly identified a virtue of religion, part of the virtue of justice? Or has he simply replicated certain aspects of Christian faith and practice, rooted in Jewish faith and practice, and then deemed these aspects to be normative in justice even apart from Christian revelation? It seems to me that Aquinas is on strong ground when he proposes that there must be a virtue of religion, of honoring and reverencing God. Surely honoring God is a profoundly reasonable thing to do. For a human being to be just necessarily includes gratitude and praise to the creator.

It also seems plausible to me to approach the virtue of religion by identifying practices within Israel and the church that enact reverence to God. Such practices include prayer, adoration, sacrifice, oblations and firstfruits, tithes, vows, and oaths. By naming these practices, of course, one does not name an existing "natural religion." On the contrary, as Aquinas was aware, religious practice outside cultures not influenced by Abrahamic revelation generally involves either a variety of gods or nothing "divine" at all. Prayer to a variety of gods is something quite different from honoring and reverencing God. The same holds for sacrifice, vows, and all the rest. Yet it remains the case that people in polytheistic cultures do pray, adore, sacrifice, and so forth. They support the ministers of their worship financially, if not by tithing then in other ways. In so doing, they often understand themselves to be performing a duty owed in justice by behaving toward the divine realm in a grateful manner.

But why introduce Paul into all of this, since after all Paul is a known scourge of idolatrous religious practice? As Romans 1 shows, Paul thinks that people were able to perceive God clearly from the things that God made, and when people turned away from the God whom they perceived, God abandoned them in the sense of permitting them to fall into all sorts of morally degraded practices, including idolatrous worship, which is the height of proud absurdity. Indeed, as we recall, Aquinas quotes Romans 1:25 in the treatise: "They exchanged the truth about God for a lie and worshiped and served the creature rather than the Creator, who is blessed for ever!"

Aquinas introduces Paul most importantly because Paul gives him a context for thinking about prayer. Even Christian prayer, he recognizes, must be deficient: "We do not know how to pray as we ought, but the Spirit himself intercedes for us" (Rom 8:26). The culture of Christian prayer is rooted in mutual prayer to God for each other. In passages quoted by Aquinas, Paul says, "I appeal to you ... to strive together with me in your prayers to God on my behalf" (Rom 15:30) and "You also must help us by prayer, so that many will give thanks on our behalf for the blessing granted us in answer to many prayers" (2 Cor 1:11). Paul urges us to "pray constantly" (1 Thess 5:17). Paul helps Aquinas to think about the various kinds of prayer, that is, "supplications, prayers, intercessions, thanksgivings" (1 Tim 2:1). Paul warns against false prayer, rooted in a morally degraded life, which operates by "holding the form of religion but denying the power of it" (2 Tim 3:5). Jesus is our model of prayer and the one who intercedes for us at the right hand of the Father (Hebrews 7:25). Aquinas even weaves in Paul's comments on praying in tongues (1 Corinthians 14:15). For Aquinas, these comments help to underscore the necessity of praying with an attentive mind. Prayer helps to raise the mind to the unseen eternal God (2 Corinthians 4:18).

Second, Paul's insistence on the necessity of supporting the ministers of divine worship has a particularly important role in Aquinas's treatise. Paul's defense in 1 Corinthians 9 of the right of the apostles to receive food and drink from the community stands out because Aquinas cites it four times, in three distinct articles. The authority of the ministers of divine worship is also an issue for Aquinas in this treatise, especially as concerns dispensation from vows (see 2 Corinthians 2:10 and 10:8) and having charge of oblations and first-fruits (see Hebrews 5:1). These issues of authority go beyond Paul's concerns; instead Aquinas's discussion here pertains particularly clearly to the church of his own day. Aquinas also employs Paul in describing the reasons for vows of chastity (1 Corinthians 7:34).

Lastly, Aquinas uses Hebrews 6:16–17 as the foundation for his theology of oaths. Hebrews 6:16 makes a claim that intentionally pertains to religious practice in diverse cultures and that shows how integral religious practice is to everyday affairs: "Men indeed swear by a greater than themselves, and in all their disputes an oath is final for confirmation." Aquinas quotes this verse five times, more than any other "Pauline" verse in the treatise. By contrast, Hebrews 6:17, which Aquinas quotes once, has a specifically covenantal and Judeo-Christian meaning: "So when God desired to show more convincingly to the heirs of the promise the unchangeable character of his purpose, he interposed with an oath." Aquinas refers to this verse in order to make clear that God's oath does not mean that we must require an oath even from God in order to be sure of his truthfulness. Rather God's oath simply underscores the unchangeable character of his promise.

Paul is therefore a significant presence in the treatise on the virtue of religion. It would be a mistake to exaggerate this presence, because much of Aquinas's treatise comes from elsewhere. Yet Aquinas's approach to prayer, tithes, and oaths, in particular, has strong Pauline resonances. Reading Aquinas's treatise, one can certainly see the church of his own day. Aquinas presumed that devout Christians of his own day practiced, within the church, the virtue of religion as healed and elevated by faith and charity. Equally, his treatise makes room for non-Christian religious practice, without thereby minimizing the deleterious effects of idolatry or ignoring the transformative power of Christian revelation.

PART 3

TRACING
PAULINE TEXTS
IN THE
Summa Theologiae

CHAPTER 7

ROMANS 1:20 IN THE
Summa Theologiae

CAN WE know God's existence and attributes by reflection upon the good things that we see around us? If so, what is the relationship between knowing God through reflection on created things and knowing God in Jesus Christ? According to St. Paul, who here draws heavily upon the Wisdom of Solomon, "Ever since the creation of the world his [God's] invisible nature, namely, his eternal power and deity, has been clearly perceived in the things that have been made" (Rom 1:20).[1]

---

1. Paul's condemnation of the gentiles in Romans 1:18–32 is rooted in the claim that they knew God or at least were culpable for not knowing God. Just as Wisdom of Solomon teaches that "from the greatness and beauty of created things comes a corresponding perception of their Creator" (Wis 13:5), Paul teaches that "what can be known about God is plain to them, because God has shown it to them. Ever since the creation of the world his invisible nature, namely, his eternal power and deity, has been clearly perceived in the things that have been made" (Rom 1:20). On the other hand, Paul differs from Wisdom of Solomon in that the latter distinguishes between the philosophers and those who worship images. According to Wisdom of Solomon, the philosophers are the ones who "failed to find sooner the Lord of these things" (Wis 13:9) but who at least receive credit for "seeking God and desiring to find him" (Wis 13:6). In addition to giving some credit to the philosophers, Wisdom of Solomon holds that while "all men who were ignorant of God were foolish by nature" (Wis 13:1), nonetheless some humans—the worshippers of images—were much more ignorant and foolish than others. Paul argues that certain humans knew the truth about God and suppressed this truth. He emphasizes that all gentiles now culpably and foolishly worship creatures rather than the creator: "Claiming to be wise, they became fools, and exchanged the glory of the immortal God for images resembling

Paul means what he says. As N. T. Wright observes, "Paul clearly does believe that when humans look at creation they are aware, at some level, of the power and divinity of the creator," so that there is a "divine self-revelation in creation."[2] Nevertheless, Wright expresses concern that Romans 1:19–21 has "had to bear the weight of debates about 'natural theology.'"[3] After all, Paul's main point in this section of Romans is not about whether fallen humans can know God without supernatural revelation. Rather, as Wright observes, Paul's main point is that "this knowledge does not save those who possess it, but only renders them guilty."[4] The gentiles are made guilty by this knowledge because rather than praising and wor-

---

mortal man or birds or animals or reptiles" (Rom 1:22–23). The positive note about the philosophers that we observed in Wisdom of Solomon is thus not present in Paul. Lest we exaggerate the difference between Paul and Wisdom of Solomon, however, we should recall that the latter says of the philosophers that "not even they are to be excused" (Wis 13:8). For the significance of Paul's debt to Wisdom of Solomon, as well as the argument that from Paul's side "this relationship is at times mischievous, and even subversive," see Douglas A. Campbell, *The Deliverance of God: An Apocalyptic Rereading of Justification in Paul* (Grand Rapids, Mich.: Eerdmans, 2009), 360–62 (quotation at 362).

2. N. T. Wright, *The Letter to the Romans: Introduction, Commentary, and Reflections*, in *The New Interpreter's Bible*, vol. X: *Acts, Romans, 1 Corinthians* (Nashville, Tenn.: Abingdon Press, 2002), 432. By contrast, Douglas A. Campbell argues that in Romans 1:18–32, Paul is describing a position held by an anonymous opponent of Paul's in Rome, a position that the entire letter to the Romans aims to repudiate. For Campbell, "the speaker [of Romans 1:18–32] is a recognizable 'Teacher' of some sort, whose influence at Rome Paul is seeking to neutralize throughout Romans. And Romans 1:18–32 is in fact the fullest presentation of the Teacher's position that we receive from the hand of Paul" (Campbell, *The Deliverance of God*, 542). This interpretation strikes me as implausible, despite Campbell's obvious erudition. For a similar position to Campbell's, see Walter Schmithals, *Der Römerbrief* (Gütersloh: Gerd Mohn, 1988). Largely because he misunderstands what natural knowledge of God would entail (he thinks it would cripple the proclamation of the gospel in various ways), it is crucial for Campbell that the real Paul repudiate "any fundamental or foundationalist role for natural theology," although Campbell allows that "the repudiation of a *foundationalist* theological role for natural theology does *not* exclude the *rhetorical* (i.e. persuasive) manipulation of an audience's presuppositions that might create an *Anknüpfungspunkt*, or 'point-of-contact,' for the gospel's announcement. At stake here is not the epistemological grounding of the gospel's truth in human assumptions and arguments, but the creation of a communicative situation of intelligibility if not of curiosity—precisely the dynamic that seems to underlie Paul's speeches in Acts 13 and 17. These two rhetorics can look very similar, but the underlying epistemological differences are worlds apart, and so must be carefully identified and distinguished" (Campbell, *The Deliverance of God*, 162).

3. Wright, *The Letter to the Romans*, 432.
4. Ibid.

shiping the God they know, they have rebelled against God. Thus knowledge of God through created things, no matter how feasible such knowledge may be, cannot give humans a place to stand outside of Christ.[5]

Anna Moreland points out that there is a "strictly limited but still legitimate place of natural knowledge of God in Thomas' theology."[6] Valuable studies of this aspect of Aquinas's thought have proliferated in recent years.[7] Since Aquinas considers it necessary to affirm the ability of human reasoning to attain to knowledge of God, it might seem, then, that Aquinas would be a likely candidate for employing Romans 1:20 in a manner that would disturb Wright's sensibility.[8] In this light, the present chapter

---

5. Regarding the interpretation of Romans 1:19–21 as teaching a natural knowledge of God, Wright observes: "As with some other doctrines that have wandered to and fro seeking biblical support, this one has fastened upon certain brief passages" (ibid.). As Wright goes on to say, none of these passages (including Acts 17:22–31) offers more than "an allusion on the way to making some other point" (ibid.). He does not deny that these passages affirm that we can know God through created things, but he urges us to attend primarily to the larger point about sin and salvation in Christ.

6. Anna Bonta Moreland, *Known by Nature: Thomas Aquinas on Natural Knowledge of God* (New York: Crossroad, 2010), 156.

7. See especially Edward Feser, *Aquinas: A Beginner's Guide* (Oxford: Oneworld, 2009); Thomas Joseph White, OP, *Wisdom in the Face of Modernity: A Study in Thomistic Natural Theology* (Ave Maria, Fla.: Sapientia Press, 2009) and "Engaging the Thomistic Tradition and Contemporary Culture Simultaneously: A Response to Burrell, Healy, and Schindler," *Nova et Vetera* 10 (2012): 605–23; Francesca Aran Murphy, *God Is Not a Story* (Oxford: Oxford University Press, 2007); Ralph McInerny, *Praeambula Fidei: Thomism and the God of the Philosophers* (Washington, D.C.: The Catholic University of America Press, 2006); Denys Turner, *Faith, Reason and the Existence of God* (Cambridge: Cambridge University Press, 2004); Gregory Rocca, *Speaking the Incomprehensible God: Thomas Aquinas on the Interplay of Positive and Negative Theology* (Washington, D.C.: The Catholic University of America Press, 2004). See also for patristic background A. N. Williams, *The Divine Sense: The Intellect in Patristic Theology* (Cambridge: Cambridge University Press, 2007).

8. For Aquinas's reading of Romans 1:20 in his *Commentary on Romans*, see especially Leo J. Elders, SVD, "Saint Paul et la connaissance naturelle de Dieu par l'homme (Rom 1, 18–32) selon le commentaire de saint Thomas d'Aquin," in Elders, *Sur les traces de saint Thomas d'Aquin théologien. Étude de ses commentaires bibliques. Thèmes théologiques*, trans. Véronique Pommeret (Paris: Parole et Silence, 2009), 141–66. See also the treatment of Aquinas's commentary on Romans 1 in Eugene F. Rogers, Jr., *Thomas Aquinas and Karl Barth: Sacred Doctrine and the Natural Knowledge of God* (Notre Dame, Ind.: University of Notre Dame Press, 1995), 112–65. Rogers suggests that for Aquinas, one cannot have proper knowledge of God without the grace of the Holy Spirit changing the will so that we love God. On this view, any knowledge of God to which the wicked arrive without faith in Jesus Christ is only a lifeless set of propositions that

examines the sixteen explicit references that St. Thomas Aquinas makes to Romans 1:20 in the *Summa theologiae*.[9] These references make clear that the teaching that we can know God by reflection on material things has a wide-ranging impact within Aquinas's theology. This impact extends from confirming the goodness of material creatures and the goodness of the human mode of knowing (rather than supposing that materiality impedes our knowledge of God), all the way to defending the fittingness and intelligibility of the incarnation and the sacraments. I conclude that precisely within the context of Paul's broader argument in Romans 1 about sin and salvation, Aquinas's use of Romans 1:20 in the *Summa* exhibits the theological value of affirming with Paul (and with the church fathers and Vatican I) that natural reason can know God by reflecting on "the things that have been made."

ROMANS 1:20 IN THE *PRIMA PARS*: AGAINST AGNOSTICISM AND ANGELISM

Aquinas quotes Romans 1:20 seven times in the *prima pars*. Although in what follows I discuss each of these seven references, I should say at the outset that the main function of Romans 1:20 in the *prima pars* is to confirm that we can know God by natural reason and that our materiality is not the reason that we have trouble knowing God. Our minds are made

---

cannot really awaken the mind to their truth. This seems to me to be a mistaken view of Aquinas's position, but it nonetheless does indicate the importance of the relationship of intellect and will in Aquinas's theology. On the latter point see also Adam G. Cooper, "Degrading the Body, Suppressing the Truth: Aquinas on Romans 1:18–25," in *Reading Romans with St. Thomas Aquinas*, ed. Matthew Levering and Michael Dauphinais (Washington, D.C.: The Catholic University of America Press, 2012), 113–26.

9. In the *Summa theologiae* Aquinas also quotes Romans 1:19 five times: *ST* I, q. 1, a. 6; *ST* I, q. 12, a. 12; *ST* I, q. 56, a. 3; *ST* I, q. 111, a. 1; *ST* II-II, q. 167, a. 1. Romans 1:19 is quite similar to 1:20: "For what can be known about God is plain to them, because God has shown it to them." For our purposes, the most interesting use of Romans 1:19 comes in the *sed contra* of *ST* I, q. 12, a. 12, which asks whether we can know God by natural reason in this life. In the *respondeo* Aquinas explains that we can know God from his effects, and so we can know that he exists and "what must necessarily belong to Him, as the first cause of all things, exceeding all things caused by Him." The answer to the third objection states that while only the good can know God by grace, even those who are not in a state of grace can know God by natural reason, because (as Augustine says) even the wicked can know many truths.

to know God by means of reflection that begins with particular material things.

We now turn to the seven references. The second article of question two of the *prima pars* asks whether it can be demonstrated that God exists. In this article, Romans 1:20 plays the decisive role: in the *sed contra*, where Aquinas provides the authority for his response, he names Romans 1:20. According to Aquinas, St. Paul could not have claimed that God's invisible nature could be seen from created things unless the existence of God were philosophically demonstrable—that is, demonstrable by natural reason through reflection on created things. Since Aquinas presumes Paul's words to be true, it follows that human reason must be capable of knowing, with demonstrative certitude, that God exists. Aquinas observes, however, that the existence of God is not self-evident. We must reason to this knowledge, and such reasoning can easily falter. Aquinas also makes clear that knowing that God exists is not the gift of supernatural faith, although it removes an obstacle to faith and thus can be described as a "preamble" to faith. Only supernatural faith is salvific knowledge. Faith obviously includes rather than contradicts the truth that God exists, and so Aquinas can say that "faith presupposes natural knowledge, even as grace presupposes nature."[10] He also notes that most humans, who will not be able to apprehend the philosophical demonstration of God's existence, can simply affirm God's existence within the act of faith.

Romans 1:20 appears in question thirteen, article five in favor of the view that names such as being and good are applied to God and creatures analogously rather than equivocally. Aquinas points out that Maimonides considered that because God is utterly transcendent, the meaning of a perfection that we recognize in creatures cannot be anything like what that perfection might mean in God. Aquinas agrees that God is utterly transcendent and unlike creatures, yet if the names by which we describe God signify God equivocally, this would mean that they do not signify God truly at all. If names about God and creatures signified equivocally, Aquinas points out, then Paul could not have said that God's "invisible nature, namely his eternal power and deity, has been clearly perceived

---

10. *ST* I, q. 2, a. 2.

in the things that have been made." Paul's statement is true only if we can gain true conceptual knowledge about God by reasoning from created things. We could not gain such true knowledge if any concept by which we named God applied to him equivocally. Nor, of course, can any concept apply to God and creatures univocally, because the infinite God transcends creatures: God is not the greatest being among beings. Names instead apply to God and creatures analogously, based on the relationship of effect to cause.

Question fifty-six, article three uses Romans 1:20 to speculate on how the angels, who are incorporeal rational creatures, know God. Humans do not know God directly on earth; rather, as Romans 1:20 and 1 Corinthians 13:12 make clear, we know God as "in a mirror" by knowing him through created things. Aquinas reasons that an angel, who like us is in the image of God, knows God by knowing its own angelic nature. To know the nature of pure created spirit is to know God as in a mirror, because God's image is expressed in pure created spirit. The angel knows God in knowing itself, rather than knowing God directly. By contrast, we do not have direct knowledge of either God or ourselves. We know our own mind, which is in the image of God, only by knowing material things and reflecting upon this knowledge. All our acts of knowing require a material image from which we abstract a universal concept.

In the first article of question sixty-five of the *prima pars*, Aquinas observes: "Certain heretics maintain that visible things are not created by the good God, but by an evil principle, and allege in proof of their error the words of the Apostle (2 Cor. 4:4), *The god of this world has blinded the minds of unbelievers*." Against this view, Aquinas insists that material things are good. Materiality cannot be blamed for human lack of knowledge of God. He quotes Romans 1:20 in this context, in answer to an objection drawn from another Pauline passage. The objection cites 2 Corinthians 4:18, "We look not to the things that are seen but to the things that are unseen; for the things that are seen are transient, but the things that are unseen are eternal."[11] It might seem, then, that "the things that are seen"—material things—get in the way of our knowing God

---

11. See *ST* I, q. 65, a. 1, obj. 3.

and therefore are blameworthy. Quoting Romans 1:20, Aquinas replies that "creatures of themselves do not withdraw us from God, but lead us to Him."[12] Created things lead us to God because by reflecting on them, we can perceive their creator—God's "invisible nature, namely, his eternal power and deity." On the other hand, in our present fallen condition, we are often entranced by created things and fail to attend to their creator. This is not the fault of created things, but rather is the fault of our fallen will: "If, then, they withdraw men from God, it is the fault of those who use them foolishly. Thus it is said (Wis. 14:11): *Creatures are turned into a snare at the feet of the unwise.*"[13] Indeed, Aquinas turns on its head the argument that material things block us from perceiving God. He points out that material things could only ensnare and allure us if they had some goodness, a goodness that in fact can only come from God. In this vein he comments that "the very fact that they can thus withdraw us from God proves that they came from Him, for they cannot lead the foolish away from God except by the allurements of some good that they have from Him."[14] The goodness and beauty of material things should lead us to the source of this goodness and beauty.

Aquinas next cites Romans 1:20 in question seventy-nine, article nine of the *prima pars*. Reflecting on Augustine's distinction between the higher and lower reason—the former having to do with eternal realities (*sapientia*) and the latter with temporal ones (*scientia*)—Aquinas emphasizes that the intellective faculty of the human soul is not thereby divided into two. Instead, we rise to knowledge of God's "invisible nature, namely his eternal power and deity," through our knowledge of the temporal "things that have been made." The reason's "lower" operations lead to its "higher" ones. The opposite view would be that material creatures prevent us from knowing God by distracting our mind. Aquinas here again insists that the way our minds work cannot be blamed for the fact that we struggle to know God. Quoting Romans 1:20, he states that "by way of discovery, we come through knowledge of temporal things to that of things eternal." Once we come to know eternal realities, we can then judge temporal things on the basis of our knowledge of eternal realities. At least, this is

---

12. *ST* I, q. 65, a. 1, ad 3.   13. Ibid.
14. Ibid.

what we should do; but we can also rebel against the God whom we have come to know. In this rebellion, we "are without excuse" (Rom 1:20) because we cannot blame our idolatry on the weakness of our human minds. The key point is that the way God created our human minds is good; we cannot blame our darkness upon the fact that we are merely human and cannot directly perceive God.

Aquinas also takes up Romans 1:20 in setting forth his position on the relationship of the "divine ideas" or "eternal types" to our knowledge of material things. In question eighty-four, article five of the *prima pars*, Aquinas addresses the obvious indebtedness of Augustine's theory of knowledge to that of Plato. Aquinas comments that "whenever Augustine, who was imbued with the doctrines of the Platonists, found in their teaching anything consistent with faith, he adopted it: and those things which he found contrary to faith he amended." Plato's theory of the eternal ideas or forms of things was confused because Plato envisioned each idea as existing separately in a realm of divine ideas. Augustine changed Plato's theory for the better by arguing that the divine ideas exist solely in the supremely simple God. Aquinas advances a similar account, according to which "the intellectual light itself which is in us, is nothing else than a participated likeness of the uncreated light, in which are contained the eternal types."[15] But Aquinas adds that this participated intellectual light does not mean that we directly know the eternal types. Rather, "intelligible species, which are derived from things, are required in order for us to have knowledge of material things."[16] The role of Romans 1:20 in this discussion consists in prompting us to consider what is at stake: do we know God's "invisible nature" (and thus the divine ideas) by knowing creatures, or do we know creatures by knowing the divine ideas? Aquinas wants to insist that the divine ideas (as God's knowledge) have priority, since our intellectual light is "a participated likeness of the uncreated light." However, he also wants to say that in the act of knowing, we do not directly know the eternal ideas. Instead, we gain knowledge by abstracting from particular material things.

15. *ST* I, q. 84, a. 5.
16. Ibid.

Aquinas next quotes Romans 1:20 in question eighty-eight, article three of the *prima pars*, which takes up the question of how the human soul knows immaterial things. Aquinas argues against those who hold that "God is the first object known by the human mind." On this view, the first thing that we know is our intellectual light, which reveals eternal truth (God) to us. Aquinas again responds that the first thing we know is not our intellectual light, but rather is the essence of a particular material creature. He explains that "the light itself of our intellect is not the object it understands, but the medium whereby it understands."[17] He quotes Romans 1:20 to secure his argument about the human soul. If we knew God directly as the mind's first object, he points out, then there would be no need to discover God through "the things that have been made." In this way, Aquinas continues his opposition to what might be called angelism. We should indeed have the clear knowledge of God that Paul describes in Romans 1:20, but we have this knowledge in an embodied manner rather than as a direct perception of God.

ROMANS 1:20 IN THE *SECUNDA PARS*: KNOWING, LOVING, WORSHIPPING, AND CONTEMPLATING GOD

In the *prima pars* Aquinas employs Romans 1:20 to reflect on how we know God and on the fact that our bodiliness is not the cause of the difficulty we have in knowing God. In the *secunda pars* he again quotes Romans 1:20 seven times, using it to show that our knowledge of God in faith relies upon knowing his effects (such as the humanity of Jesus Christ), and that worship and contemplation also require knowing God through his effects. In short, in the *secunda pars* he goes further along the lines set forth in the *prima pars*: not only does he insist upon the important contribution that knowing God's material effects makes to knowing God, but he also shows how our worship of God and ecstatic experiences such as rapture reflect the pattern of ascending to God through creatures.

The sole citation of Romans 1:20 in the *prima-secundae pars* occurs

---

17. *ST* I, q. 88, q. 3, ad 1.

in question ninety-three, article two, where Aquinas discusses the eternal law and the natural law. The eternal law, says Aquinas, is the divine idea of the ordering of all things to God. Article two asks whether all humans know the eternal law. Following Augustine, Aquinas answers that all humans do. On its face, this seems a strange reply because it suggests that all humans somehow know the mind of God. To clarify his answer, therefore, Aquinas points out that one can know something either in itself or in its effects. In this life, we do not know God (or the mind of God) in himself. Outside the beatific vision, we cannot see the divine essence. Yet we can know God through his effects. With respect to the ordering of all things to God, we can know God's eternal law because God has created us with a rational participation in the eternal law, his wisdom for the ordering of humans to himself. This participation enables us to know the eternal law not in full (as we will know it in the beatific vision) but in part and to varying degrees. This participation in the eternal law is called natural law, and the basic principles of natural law—the basic principles of human flourishing, rooted in the natural inclinations toward the human good—cannot be effaced from our minds. As Aquinas observes, quoting Romans 1:20, our knowledge of God's eternal law (i.e., our possession of "natural law") constitutes one way in which God's "invisible nature" is made known to us "in the things that have been made."[18]

In II-II, question two, article three, Aquinas addresses our need for faith. Opposing the view that it is "unnecessary for salvation to believe anything above natural reason," he argues that given the subordination of our nature to God, the perfection of our nature occurs through two movements: the first belongs to our nature itself, and the second comes from God. The latter movement consists in God's elevation of our nature so that we participate in God supernaturally through the beatific vision.[19] Our reason has the natural power to know God in a limited way, but to know the extent of God's gifting toward us in Christ requires the "light of faith," which is itself God's gift.[20] Aquinas points out that if by means of visible things we can "clearly" perceive invisible things—God's "eternal

---

18. See *ST* I-II, q. 93, a. 2, ad 1. 19. *ST* II-II, q. 2, a. 3.
20. Ibid.

power and deity" (Rom 1:20)—then it might seem that we do not need faith, because we can already clearly apprehend the eternal power of God. In reply, he observes that faith perceives God's invisible nature "in a higher way," namely one that enables us to believe in the work of the Son and Holy Spirit for our salvation. Natural knowledge of God can tell us that God is all-powerful, but only faith unites us to the triune God's saving action, from which our perfection flows.

Two gifts of the Holy Spirit, namely understanding and knowledge (see Isaiah 11:2), strengthen our apprehension and judgment regarding the truths of faith. With regard to the gift of knowledge, Aquinas addresses in II-II, question nine, article two the Augustinian distinction between wisdom (*sapientia*) and knowledge (*scientia*). Recall that wisdom has to do with eternal realities, knowledge with temporal ones. It might seem, Aquinas observes, that Paul in Romans 1:20 makes this distinction untenable, since Paul suggests that knowledge of "the things that have been made" enables us to perceive God's "invisible nature."[21] If this is so, it would seem that knowledge (*scientia*) has as much to do with eternal realities as it does with temporal ones. But Aquinas argues that the distinction remains of value. The gift of knowledge, he observes, assists faith by strengthening the judgments that we have "formed through created things."[22] Faith requires such judgments because faith works through the human mode of knowing: we come to faith not by a direct vision of the divine essence, but by learning of the words and deeds of Jesus Christ in the flesh. The point is that although faith is greater than the knowledge of God described in Romans 1:20, faith nonetheless adheres to the mode of human knowing about God that Romans 1:20 portrays. We know God through creatures. This is as much the case for faith's supernatural knowledge of God as it is for reason's natural apprehension of God's "invisible nature."

In II-II, question twenty-seven, article three, Aquinas discusses a challenge to Romans 1:20's claim that we know God through creatures. The challenge runs as follows. Romans 1:20 teaches that we are able to know God's "invisible nature" through "the things that have been made." When

---

21. See *ST* II-II, q. 9, a. 2, obj. 2.
22. *ST* II-II, q. 9, a. 2, ad 2.

we know God in this way, we do so by knowing creatures: that is to say, we do so indirectly. It might seem that this indirection would also pertain to loving God, since love follows upon knowledge. If we know God by knowing creatures, we might also love God by focusing on creatures. However, we would then be loving God not for his own sake or in himself, but rather on account of what he has done in creatures. In reply, Aquinas observes that when we come to know God by indirect means, we thereby attain to a real knowledge of God, not merely of our concept of God.[23] Once we know God in this way, we can love him in himself, that is to say, directly rather than indirectly.

In II-II, question eighty-one, article seven, on the external act of the virtue of religion, Aquinas emphasizes anew that material things do not obstruct our path to God. On the contrary, the path to God that Romans 1:20 sketches—a path that involves material things—befits our embodied nature. Thus, against the claim that Jesus's command to "worship in spirit and truth" (Jn 4:24) requires that we worship God in a purely spiritual manner (rather than including bodily movements and sacraments in our acts of worship), Aquinas argues that Jesus's command has in view simply that our mind be subjected and conformed to God. Jesus does not thereby rule out bodily movements and sacraments. Indeed, our mind would be at a loss without bodily signs. Quoting Romans 1:20, Aquinas states that "the human mind [*mens*], in order to be united to God, needs to be guided by the sensible world.... Wherefore in the divine worship it is necessary to make use of corporeal things, that man's mind may be aroused thereby, as by signs, to the spiritual acts by means of which he is united to God." Aquinas is not saying that these bodily movements and sacraments are the central aspect of worship. That would make of worship a mere outward form. The central aspect of worship is our interior reverence and adoration of God. But this interior act of worship requires, for rational animals such as ourselves, the assistance of external acts and signs.

In II-II, question 175, article one, on rapture, Aquinas connects Romans 1:20 with 2 Corinthians 12:2, "I know a man in Christ who fourteen years ago was caught up to the third heaven—whether in the body or out of the

---

23. Ibid., ad 2.

body I do not know, God knows." He does so by first arguing that it is natural, "in accordance with man's nature," to "be uplifted to things divine."[24] The question, then, is whether it was natural for Paul to be rapt up to the "third heaven," or whether this was the work of grace in Paul. Was the cause of his experience the interior dynamisms of his soul (dynamisms that God gives in creation) or was the cause a special, supernatural action on the part of God? Romans 1:20 helps Aquinas to formulate his answer. Paul's ascent (rapture) did not take place on the basis of his senses. Paul did not know whether he was in the body or out of it. Such an ascent differs from the kind of ascent that is already possible for humans simply by reflecting on "the things that have been made." In this way, rapture constitutes not a "natural" ascent but an instance of God's gracious action in the life of the Christian. Yet by quoting Romans 1:20 in this way, Aquinas shows that the dynamism of ascent is already built into the human capacity for knowing.[25] Sensible things are not our real problem in the ascent to God.

In II-II, question 180, article four, Aquinas argues that contemplation pertains properly to the truth about God, but he quotes Romans 1:20 in order to make clear that this does not reduce contemplation to a purely spiritual or angelic enterprise. Romans 1:20 shows that by reflecting upon the things that God has made, we can rise to knowledge of God's "invisible nature." Indeed, Romans 1:20 suggests that we should all be contemplatives in this sense. All people are called to reflect upon the beauty, goodness, being, and finitude of created things so as to ascend in contemplation toward the invisible, all-powerful, eternal God. To do this, however, we must not be tied down to creatures by the vices. Aquinas grants that the consideration of sensible things is merely the first step on the path toward perfect contemplation of God—the highest step of which involves going beyond, by grace, what reason can grasp (that is to say, entering into a mystical darkness). But his understanding of contemplation retains its rootedness in the portrait that Paul gives in Romans 1:20 of the value of sensible things, as well as in Paul's awareness of human sinfulness. Aquinas

---

24. *ST* II-II, q. 175, a. 1, obj. 1. Aquinas cites Augustine's *Confessions*: "You have made us for yourself, and our heart is restless until it rests in you." See Augustine, *Confessions*, I.i.1, trans. Henry Chadwick (Oxford: Oxford University Press, 1991), 3.

25. See *ST* II-II, q. 175, a. 1, ad 1.

states in this regard that "four things pertain, in a certain order, to the contemplative life; first, the moral virtues; secondly, other acts exclusive of contemplation; thirdly, contemplation of the divine effects; fourthly, the complement of all which is the contemplation of the divine truth itself."[26]

ROMANS 1:20 IN THE *TERTIA PARS*: INCARNATION AND SACRAMENTS

In the *tertia pars*, Aquinas quotes Romans 1:20 only twice, but at crucial junctures of his reflection: on the fittingness of the incarnation and on the rationale of the sacraments. In the earlier parts of the *Summa*, he has shown how important Romans 1:20 is for understanding how we know, worship, and contemplate God. In this final part of the *Summa*, he makes clear that Romans 1:20 sheds irreplaceable light on how God comes to meet us in Jesus Christ and the sacraments.

In III, question one, article one, on the fittingness of the incarnation, Aquinas quotes Romans 1:20 at the most prominent juncture, the *sed contra*, in order to underscore that God consistently reveals himself to rational animals through sensible things. God made the material world not to obstruct us from knowing him, but to help us know him. The purpose of the material world is theophany. Aquinas states that "it would seem most fitting that by visible things the invisible things of God should be made known; for to this end was the whole world made, as is clear from the word of the Apostle (Rom. i. 20)."[27] Although God freely wills to become incarnate, nonetheless the incarnation fits with what we might have expected of God's self-revelation. Just as "ever since the creation of the world" created things have revealed God's "invisible nature, namely his eternal power and deity," so also God chose to reveal his goodness, wisdom, justice, and power by taking flesh in Jesus Christ. Put another way, because God is good, God wills to communicate himself in the most perfect way to his rational creature. Humans learn about God by reflecting on sensible things. What better way, then, for us to learn about the invisible God than by encountering the incarnate Son?

26. *ST* II-II, q. 180, a. 4.
27. *ST* III, q. 1, a. 1.

This discussion of the fittingness of the incarnation emphasizes the positive side of material creatures, namely that God reveals his invisible nature through them. As Aquinas has repeatedly emphasized, material creatures serve rather than impede our knowledge of God. Yet after the fall, there is also a negative side to material creatures. Specifically, fallen humans tend to cleave to material creatures instead of worshipping the creator of such beautiful creatures. The sacraments, which are an extension of the incarnation, help to cure this idolatry. In III, question sixty-one, article one, on whether sacraments are necessary for salvation, Aquinas points out that not only does God thereby provide for human nature, "which is such that it has to be led by things corporeal and sensible to things spiritual and intelligible," but also by means of sacramental medicine God redirects our love for sensible creatures. He enables us to find him in material things, and he heals our disordered love by encountering us powerfully in these things. Aquinas observes that God graciously comes to us in this way because "if man were offered spiritual things without a veil, his mind being taken up with the material world would be unable to apply itself to them." Our pride, too, is healed by this means: we can easily consider ourselves too spiritual to encounter God through material things. God humbles us by encountering us as the rational animals that we are.

However, in the first objection of III, question sixty, article two, Aquinas quotes Romans 1:20 in order to express a problem that confronts this understanding of sacraments. If we can perceive God "in the things that have been made," then all creatures are signs of God; but "all sensible things cannot be called sacraments." As the objection makes clear, Romans 1:20 encourages a sacramental view of the world; when understood properly, the whole world reveals God. To speak about particular sacraments, then, requires some way of identifying which material things signify God in a way that, properly speaking, makes them "sacraments." Aquinas responds that "sacraments" are those material things that signify not simply God per se, but God as the cause of making us holy. Specifically, the sacraments signify Christ and his body (the church).[28] In this way Aquinas again affirms Paul's crucial distinction between perceiving God through created

---

28. See *ST* III, q. 60, a. 3, *sed contra*.

things and coming to know "the power of God for salvation to every one who has faith" (Rom 1:16).

CONCLUSION

Discussing the vision of Pierre Teilhard de Chardin, Annie Dillard states: "The material world for Teilhard dissolves at the edges and grows translucent. The world is a Solutrean blade. It thins to an atom. As a young scientist, he held the usual view that the world is all material; from it spirit cannot derive. Soon he inverted the terms: The world is all spirit, from which matter cannot derive save through Christ."[29] By contrast, Aquinas can allow matter to remain matter. He is able to affirm fully the goodness of matter and its distinction from spirit. Material things do not have to be spirit in order to make manifest God, who "is spirit" (Jn 4:24). Reflection about material things leads us to the immaterial creator. Even our fallen love for material things helps to explain why God became incarnate and why we now receive the incarnate Lord through visible sacraments. Aquinas also emphasizes that the dynamism toward God possessed by our natural knowing is fulfilled when faith and the gifts of the Holy Spirit elevate this dynamism. Faith is not "blind," but rather moves the mind more deeply into the relationship with God for which the mind was made. We do not need to envy the spiritual knowledge of the angels, because we too can know God by means of our created nature.

Aquinas employs Romans 1:20 to assist his discussions of analogy, angelic and human knowing, the goodness of material things, the divine ideas, natural and eternal law, faith, the gift of knowledge, charity, religion, rapture, contemplation, the incarnation, and the sacraments. Without doubt, then, Aquinas's use of Romans 1:20 goes well beyond the themes of Paul's letter to the Romans. Yet the basic theses that Aquinas advances are profoundly related to those of Paul. First, human knowing of God takes place through reflection on material things, so that God is "clearly perceived in the things that have been made." Second, this natural knowing is insufficient in itself and is fulfilled in faith—and ultimately in

---

29. Annie Dillard, *For the Time Being* (New York: Alfred A. Knopf, 1999), 194–95.

heavenly union with God. Third, worship of God properly has a bodily component. Fourth, fallen humans need to be healed from the cleaving to creatures that is the root of so many sins. Fifth, this healing comes from Jesus Christ, who fulfills in an extraordinary manner our natural mode of knowing God through creatures. As Paul concludes his letter, therefore, "to the only wise God be glory for evermore through Jesus Christ! Amen" (Rom 16:27).

CHAPTER 8

1 CORINTHIANS 13 IN THE
Summa Theologiae

Arguing that Thomas Aquinas's theology of charity accords with scripture rather than with modern theories that reduce charity simply to a good motivation, Michael Sherwin comments: "That the New Testament authors eschew formalism in their treatment of charity is evident in the works of St. Paul. When St. Paul wishes to describe charity and the Christian life, he presents them in terms of characteristic types of actions. Paul acknowledges that not everyone who exhibits apparently virtuous actions is necessarily doing them from the love of charity [cf. 1 Cor 13:1–7]."[1] Just as 1 Corinthians 13 plays a significant role in Aquinas's theology of charity, so it does in Aquinas's theology of faith. Thus Romanus Cessario presents 1 Corinthians 13:13 as capturing

---

1. Michael S. Sherwin, OP, *By Knowledge and By Love: Charity and Knowledge in the Moral Theology of St. Thomas Aquinas* (Washington, D.C.: The Catholic University of America Press, 2005), 224–25. For further studies of Aquinas on charity, see Michael S. Sherwin, OP, "Aquinas, Augustine, and the Medieval Scholastic Crisis concerning Charity," in *Aquinas the Augustinian*, ed. Michael Dauphinais, Barry David, and Matthew Levering (Washington, D.C.: The Catholic University of America Press, 2007), 181–204; Josef Pieper, *Faith, Hope, Love*, trans. Richard and Clara Winston (San Francisco: Ignatius Press, 1997); Christopher J. Malloy, "Thomas on the Order of Love and Desire: A Development of Doctrine," *The Thomist* 71 (2007): 65–87; Thomas M. Osborne, Jr., *Love of Self and Love of God in Thirteenth-Century Ethics* (Notre Dame, Ind.: University of Notre Dame Press, 2005); and Matthew Levering, *The Betrayal of Charity: The Sins that Sabotage Divine Love* (Waco, Tex.: Baylor University Press, 2011).

the meaning of "theological virtue."[2] Cessario concludes that "knowledge in faith unites us to 'God, the Father of Our Lord Jesus Christ' (Col 1:3), for through faith we come to see the Truth, though for now we see it, as St. Paul says, 'in a mirror, dimly' (1 Cor 13:12)."[3]

Chapter thirteen of 1 Corinthians comprises a mere thirteen brief verses. One of the shortest chapters in the New Testament, it is nonetheless cited sixty-nine times by Aquinas in the *Summa theologiae*, more than any other chapter from a Pauline epistle, with the sole exceptions of Romans 5 and 8, which are cited seventy-four and one hundred times, respectively. In what follows, then, my goal is to provide a sense of how 1 Corinthians 13 functions in the *Summa*. Aquinas cites 1 Corinthians 13 nine times in the *prima pars*, seventeen times in the *prima-secundae pars*, thirty-seven times in the *secunda-secundae pars*, and six times in the *tertia pars*. Of the thirteen verses, Aquinas cites twelve of them; rather surprisingly, he does not cite verse seven: "Love bears all things, believes all things, hopes all things, endures all things." Twenty-four of the sixty-nine citations come from verses 9–12, which have to do primarily with faith, whereas forty-five of the citations come from the eight verses of 1 Corinthians 13 in which love is particularly prominent. Given the large number of citations of 1 Corinthians 13 in the *Summa* and the theological importance of the themes it treats, it seems worthwhile here to explore in detail Aquinas's use of chapter 13.[4]

---

2. Romanus Cessario, OP, *Christian Faith and the Theological Life* (Washington, D.C.: The Catholic University of America Press, 1996), 8.

3. Ibid., 50; see also 76–77.

4. Richard Hays remarks: "Love is sometimes singled out as the great imperative at the center of the New Testament's witness. This proposal can, of course, claim the precedent of Mark 12:28–34 and 1 Corinthians 13. Nevertheless, for reasons that will emerge in the course of this investigation, I want to argue that the concept of love is insufficient as a ground of coherence for the New Testament's moral vision" (Hays, *The Moral Vision of the New Testament: Community, Cross, New Creation; A Contemporary Introduction to New Testament Ethics* [New York: HarperCollins, 1996], 5). This view is worth challenging, but Hays is right that love—especially when separated from faith and hope—can easily lose its integral connection to the three themes of "community, Cross, and new creation" that Hays presents as the heart of the New Testament's moral theology.

1 CORINTHIANS 13 IN THE *PRIMA PARS*

The first appearance of 1 Corinthians 13 occurs in question twelve, article eleven. Here Aquinas is discussing whether, even in this life, a person could experience a vision of God (the divine essence). He answers that this is not possible. The first objection, however, argues the contrary on the basis of Genesis 32:30 and 1 Corinthians 13:12. In Genesis 32:30, Jacob, having wrestled all night with the mysterious visitor, proclaims: "I have seen God face to face." The objection combines this with the promise in 1 Corinthians 13:12 that we shall see "face to face," so that our faith will be perfected by vision. Although Aquinas does not think so, the juxtaposition might be taken to mean that Jacob has already experienced what 1 Corinthians 13:12 is describing. The purpose of 1 Corinthians 13 here, then, is to invite us to reflect upon the extent of our knowledge of God.

The next passage from 1 Corinthians 13 in the *prima pars* is found in the fifth article of question forty-three, on the invisible mission of the Son. The invisible mission has to do with the indwelling of the whole Trinity, including the Son, in humans by sanctifying grace. The Son dwells invisibly in our soul, and he does so as begotten by the Father (and thus as "sent"). Again Aquinas employs 1 Corinthians 13 to formulate an objection. The objection argues that since the Son proceeds as Word, it seems that the Son is sent invisibly when our intellects are elevated by grace. But faith, which elevates our intellect, can be possessed without grace, because faith can exist in persons who lack charity. To make this point, the objection quotes 1 Corinthians 13:2: "If I have prophetic powers, and understand all mysteries and all knowledge, and if I have all faith, so as to remove mountains, but have not love, I am nothing." If faith and love can be separated in this way, then it seems that faith is not a gift of sanctifying grace—and thus that the Son does not proceed invisibly. Aquinas's answer clarifies the unity of knowledge and love that signals the presence of the invisible mission of the Son. The purpose of the quotation of 1 Corinthians 13 is here to reflect upon the relationship of faith and love, insofar as this relationship has to do with sanctifying grace and the invisible missions of the Son and Holy Spirit.

The first reference has to do with our (perfect) knowledge of God; the second with the relationship of faith's knowledge to the love that comes from the grace of the Holy Spirit. The next reference, in the third article of question fifty-six, moves from the treatise on the triune God to the treatise on the angels. Could it be, asks Aquinas, that the angels have a natural knowledge of God? He answers that although the angels cannot know the divine essence by their natural powers, nonetheless they do have a natural knowledge of God, just as humans do in a more limited way. Once again 1 Corinthians 13 appears in an objection. The objection quotes verse 12, "For now we see in a mirror dimly, but then face to face." This might seem to imply that there are two ways of knowing God: the vision of the divine essence ("face to face"), which cannot be accomplished by the natural powers even of the angels; and knowing God indirectly by reasoning from sensible things ("in a mirror"), which is impossible for angels since their knowledge does not depend on sensible things. First Corinthians 13 here serves Aquinas's reflection on how creatures, in this case angels, can know God.

Aquinas employs 1 Corinthians 13 twice more in his treatise on the angels, both times in formulating objections: in question fifty-eight, article seven and in question sixty-two, article seven. In article six of question fifty-eight, he distinguishes between two kinds of angelic knowledge of created things: "morning" and "evening" knowledge. The "morning" knowledge of angels is their knowledge of how things exist in the divine Word. The "evening" knowledge of angels is their knowledge of how things exist in themselves. The question that Aquinas treats in article seven, then, is whether these two kinds of knowledge are in fact one. The objections argue in the affirmative. In this vein, the third objection quotes 1 Corinthians 13:10, "When the perfect comes, the imperfect will pass away." It would seem that the perfect knowledge of things consists in how they exist in the Word. If so, then the evening knowledge would "pass away" because of its imperfection; it could not exist with the perfect "morning knowledge." On this view, supposing that the angels have both morning and evening knowledge (without the latter passing away) would require that the two knowledges be one and the same. Aquinas, however, wishes to preserve a real distinction between these two kinds of angelic knowledge of created things. He does so in his reply to the objection by pointing out that knowing a thing in its cause (that is, in the Word) is not opposed to knowing a thing in itself; one can know a thing perfectly or imperfectly in its cause, and perfectly or imperfectly in itself. This use of 1 Corinthians 13 provides Aquinas with a principle regarding the relationship of perfect and imperfect knowledge.

In question sixty-two, article seven Aquinas asks whether in the angels, natural knowledge and love continue alongside beatified knowledge and love. Angels have a natural knowledge and love, since they can know and love God by their natural powers. As beatified rational creatures, they know and love God by seeing the divine essence directly. Does beatification overwhelm or displace the lesser form of knowing and loving? The first objection appeals to 1 Corinthians 13:10, "When the perfect comes, the imperfect will pass away." Aquinas answers this objection by pointing out that nature is not the opposite of grace: imperfection in nature is opposed to perfection in nature, just as imperfection in grace is opposed to perfection in grace. What passes away, then, is any imperfection in nature, rather than the natural powers themselves.

The next place that 1 Corinthians 13 is found has to do with the human soul. In question eighty-two, article three, Aquinas asks whether the will, which has the good as its object, is superior to the intellect, which has the true as its object. In the third objection, he brings in 1 Corinthians 13:2, which he quoted above in relation to the missions of the Son and Spirit, to argue that since charity is nobler than faith, the will is superior to the intellect. In his reply, he answers that sometimes the will is superior to the intellect, namely when the will's object is higher than the soul itself, since the intellect draws the object into the soul, whereas the will reaches out to embrace the object in itself. But he observes that with respect to the order of the soul to its object, we must first know something in order to will it, and in this respect the intellect is superior.

In question eighty-nine, article five we again find 1 Corinthians 13 in an objection. Aquinas discusses the separated human soul, that is, the soul as it exists after death but before the resurrection. A major problem for this discussion consists in how the separated soul can know anything, because human knowledge in this life always relies upon sensible things. Since the separated soul lacks a body, it has no way of knowing in a properly human mode. The fifth article asks whether the habit of knowledge that we acquire in this life remains in the soul after death, so that the separated soul can remember and engage what it knows. In the first objection, Aquinas quotes 1 Corinthians 13:8 to argue that death puts an end to the knowledge that we acquired in this life: "As for knowledge, it will pass away." In reply, Aquinas suggests that the imperfection of the act of knowing will pass away, but the knowledge that we acquired will not pass away. The function of 1 Corinthians 13:8 here is to inquire into what knowledge we can hope for after death.

The last two references in the *prima pars* to 1 Corinthians 13 occur in the first two articles of question 107, which, in the context of the divine government of all things, asks how angels communicate or "speak." This time 1 Corinthians 13 finally appears somewhere besides the objections. In the first article, the *sed contra* cites 1 Corinthians 13:1, "If I speak in the tongues of men and of angels, but have not love, I am a noisy gong or a clanging cymbal." This passage provides a warrant for discussion of the angelic "speech," which is obviously analogous since angels do not have tongues. The second article returns to the pattern of including 1 Corinthians 13 in the objections. This article asks whether an inferior angel is able to speak to a superior one. The concern that motivates the article comes from the gloss on 1 Corinthians 13:1, where the gloss says that angelic "speech" is the intellectual enlightenment that a superior angel can offer to an inferior one. In the first objection, Aquinas quotes 1 Corinthians 13:1 in order to introduce the concern raised by the gloss on this verse.

In sum, the nine references in the *prima pars* to 1 Corinthians 13 have to do, not surprisingly, with knowing and loving. Two of the references are about human knowledge of God. Three of the references involve angelic knowledge. Two more references have to do with the human soul: the relationship of intellect and will, and the knowledge that a separated soul possesses after death. Lastly, two references involve what "speech" means for angels. All but one of the references appear in the objections. Aquinas pays particular attention to verse ten—"when the perfect comes, the imperfect will pass away"—so as to avoid the conclusion that natural powers pass away when we are beatified. In this way Aquinas is faithful to Paul, whose meaning is that our knowledge will be perfect rather than imperfect as it is now. The first verse, "if I speak in the tongues of men and of angels," provides a foundation for the argument that angels can indeed communicate with each other by some analogous form of "speech." Paul clearly does not have this in mind, because he seems merely to take for granted that angels can speak in some sense. Aquinas inquires into how this might be, since angels do not have bodies. The twelfth verse, "for now we see through a mirror dimly, but then face to face," enables Aquinas to ask questions about whether we can even now see "face to face" and about whether angels, who do not "see through a mirror dimly" in the way that we do, have a knowledge of God by means of their natural powers. Aquinas uses the second verse, "if I have all faith, so as to remove mountains, but have not love, I am nothing," to reflect upon the relationship of faith and charity, intellect and will. Since faith and charity are linked to the missions of the indwelling Son and Holy Spirit, Aquinas inquires into what it might mean for faith to be present without charity. He also wonders whether Paul's exaltation of charity requires a parallel exaltation of the will over the intellect in Christian anthropology. Lastly, verse eight—specifically the portion where Paul says that "as for knowledge, it will pass away"—helps Aquinas to consider whether, after death, we will remember the knowledge that we acquired in our earthly lives. These functions of 1 Corinthians 13 (mainly in the objections) differ significantly from each other and from Paul's own purposes, but they all serve to enrich Christian reflection on natural and graced knowing and loving—which is a central task of the *prima pars*'s contemplation of God and the created order.

1 CORINTHIANS 13 IN THE *PRIMA-SECUNDAE PARS*

The *prima-secundae pars* has sixteen references to 1 Corinthians 13. Seven of these occur in questions 62–68, where Aquinas discusses the virtues and the gifts of the Holy Spirit. Three others are found in question 106, where Aquinas treats the new law. How does 1 Corinthians 13 contribute to these and other themes of the *prima secundae*?

The first reference in the *prima secundae* to 1 Corinthians 13 occurs in question four, article two. As usual, we find 1 Corinthians 13 in an objection. The topic of article two is whether intellectual vision or charitable delight is primarily constitutive of human happiness. Aquinas argues that it is the intellectual vision of the divine goodness that causes the human will to rest in delight. The vision of God, therefore, has a certain priority to the will's delight in what the intellect perceives. The third objection employs 1 Corinthians 13:13, "the greatest of these is love," to argue that the will's delight (linked to charity) must have priority to the intellect's vision. Aquinas replies that charity seeks God himself and finds God in what the intellect perceives.

The next reference to 1 Corinthians occurs in the treatise on the passions. Aquinas has defined true pleasure as being caused by obtaining one's proper good and knowing that one has obtained it. The fifth article of question thirty-two raises the issue of whether we can gain pleasure from others' actions. In his *respondeo*, Aquinas answers yes, for three reasons. The third of these reasons is that "another's actions, if they be good, are reckoned as one's own good, by reason of the power of love, which makes a man to regard his friend as one with himself." In this context Aquinas quotes 1 Corinthians 13:6, where Paul says that love "does not rejoice at wrong, but rejoices in the right." Thus, we receive pleasure from rejoicing in the good actions of others.

Question sixty-two treats the theological virtues, that is, those virtues that God bestows upon us by grace and that unite us with him in a supernatural manner. In the third article, the issue is whether the theological virtues are three in number: faith, hope, and love. The *sed contra* answers in the affirmative, on the basis of 1 Corinthians 13:13, "So faith, hope, love abide, these three; but the greatest of these is love." It seems unlikely that Paul intends to define the three theological virtues in this passage, but he does identify the central elements of our relationship to God in Christ and the Holy Spirit. Aquinas shows how these three virtues surpass what is possible for our natural capacities and thereby merit the name "theological virtues."

In the fourth article of the same question, 1 Corinthians 13:13 again appears as the *sed contra*. This time the issue is whether faith precedes hope and hope precedes charity, or whether a different order is correct. Aquinas presents 1 Corinthians 13:13, "faith, hope, love," as evidence that this is indeed the right order. Paul does not seem here to be making a statement about their order, but on the other hand, it does seem that for Paul—as for Aquinas—we must first know God in faith before we can hope to be united to him, and our hope in God fosters our love for God.

The next citation of 1 Corinthians 13 is found in question sixty-five, article three. The first objection quotes the fourth verse of 1 Corinthians 13: "Love is patient and kind; love is not jealous or boastful." The objection is arguing that love alone suffices for the Christian moral life, since according to 1 Corinthians 13:4, love includes within itself the moral virtues. Aquinas replies that the moral virtues are needed by the Christian in addition to the virtue of charity. However, he notes that God infuses these virtues along with charity, so that the charitable person need not fear being without them. Good works are those that lead us to our goal, which is eternal life. Charity orders all our actions toward this goal. When God infuses charity as the principle of good works, God also infuses the virtues that make doing good works easy for our will and our passions—just as when God gives the human animal a rational soul, he also gives the human animal the necessary bodily organs to carry out the works proper to the rational soul.

First Corinthians 13 occupies the *sed contra* in article six of question sixty-six. Here Aquinas asks whether charity is the greatest of the theological virtues, and not surprisingly he finds his answer in 1 Corinthians 13:13, "The greatest of these is love." He explains that charity is more united to God than is either faith or hope, because neither faith nor hope possesses its object, whereas charity already (even if incompletely) possesses its object, "since the beloved is, in a manner, in the lover, and, again, the lover is drawn by desire to union with the beloved."

The second article of question sixty-seven presents 1 Corinthians 13 in the first objection. The concern here is whether the intellectual virtues remain in eternal life. The first objection argues that they do not, and for this view the objection appeals to Paul's remark, "as for knowledge, it will pass away," because "our knowledge is imperfect" (1 Cor 13:8–9). Since the intellectual virtues are imperfect, it would seem that they will not be needed after this life, with the result that we will remember nothing that we learned in this life. Aquinas replies that so long as we hold that memory is an intellective rather than bodily power, there is no reason to suppose that the truths that we acquire in this life will disappear from our minds in eternal life. In his view, Paul is simply speaking about our mode of our understanding, since it is right to say that death obliterates the sense images and bodily powers that are required in this life for the act of understanding. I doubt that Paul is actually making this rather complex Aristotelian point. Instead it seems to me that Paul is saying that the limited knowledge which we now have will be replaced by the perfect fullness of knowledge. Yet Aquinas's conclusion that death does not obliterate our memory of the truths we learned on earth seems to accord with Paul's perspective.

In the sixth article of question sixty-seven, Aquinas quotes both 1 Corinthians 13:10 and 13:8. The issue in this article is whether charity remains in glory. The first objection argues that the answer is no because of the principle that "when the perfect comes, the imperfect will pass away" (1 Cor 13:10). Our charity now is imperfect, at least in certain ways. In his reply, Aquinas again observes that the same thing can move from being imperfect to being perfect, and so the something need not "pass away" even when its imperfection passes away. The *sed contra* comes from 1 Corinthians 13:8, "Love never ends." This expresses Paul's view, and Aquinas's.

In question sixty-eight, article eight Aquinas asks whether the virtues are superior to the gifts of the Holy Spirit. He wants to say that the opposite is the case. First Corinthians 13:4 plays a minor role in the reply to the third objection, which has to do with whether the gifts (such as wisdom and understanding) can be misused. If the gifts of the Holy Spirit could be misused, then they would necessarily be inferior to the virtues, which cannot be used for an evil intention. Aquinas observes that since the gifts are quickened by charity and cease to exist without it, they cannot be misused. In 1 Corinthians 13:4, he finds evidence that love cannot motivate harmful acts. His version of the relevant portion of 1 Corinthians 13:4 contains a clause that is not found in the RSV (but is found in the Vulgate): "*caritas ... non agit perperam.*" The text that one finds in the RSV, however, includes the basic point that Aquinas is trying to make.

In question seventy-three, article four Aquinas has in view the gravity of various sins, and in particular he asks whether their degree of gravity depends upon the degree of excellence of the virtues that they oppose. The answer is yes: when one deviates from a greater virtue, one commits a greater sin. But the third objection quotes 1 Corinthians 13:13 in an effort to argue that this is not the case. According to the objection, charity is greater than faith or hope, but unbelief is worse than hatred, which is opposed to charity. If this is so, then a greater sin comes from opposing a lesser virtue. Aquinas answers that unbelief is certainly worse than hating humans, but it is not worse than hating God.

The next appearance of 1 Corinthians 13 occurs fourteen questions later, in question eighty-seven, article four. The topic of this article is whether the debt of punishment incurred by sin is an infinite debt. In his *respondeo*, Aquinas makes a distinction: sin turns away from an infinite good (God), and so the pain of loss that sin incurs is infinite, but sin turns toward a finite good, and in this respect the pain that sin incurs is finite. Aquinas quotes 1 Corinthians 13:2 in replying to the first objection, which suggested that God punishes sin by annihilating the sinner. He argues that God punishes sinners not by literally reducing them to nothingness, but rather by depriving them of spiritual goods, which expresses a certain kind of nothingness, as Paul indicates when he says that "if I have all faith, so as to remove mountains, but have not love, I am nothing" (1 Cor 13:2).

Thirteen questions separate this citation of 1 Corinthians 13 from the next one, which is found in question one hundred, article ten. The topic here is whether the Mosaic law, in commanding various actions (such as honoring one's parents), commands that these actions be done in charity. If so, then someone could break the Mosaic law by honoring one's parents but without doing it with a charitable intention. The first objection argues that the commandments do indeed include the prescription that they be obeyed in charity. Certainly 1 Corinthians 13:3 contains this prescription: "If I give away all I have, and if I deliver my body to be burned, but have not love, I gain nothing." Aquinas replies by noting that two of the precepts of the Mosaic law specifically command charity, but that the Mosaic law does not command the mode of charity when it commands, for instance, that we honor our parents. Yet by honoring our parents without charity, we break the precept commanding charity and therefore fail to fulfill the law.

The fourth article of question 106 quotes 1 Corinthians 13 three times. This article asks whether the new law will last until the end of the world or give way to something better, in a manner similar to how the Mosaic law was fulfilled by Jesus Christ. The first objection quotes the principle that we have already seen in a number of previous objections: "When the perfect comes, the imperfect will pass away" (1 Cor 13:8). To this principle, the objection adds the observation that the new law is imperfect, because as Paul says, "our knowledge is imperfect" (1 Cor 13:9). It seems to follow that the new law will pass away rather than lasting until the end of the world. In his reply to this objection, Aquinas observes that the state of the new law is imperfect by comparison not with any further earthly condition, but by comparison with heavenly glory. Our present condition will indeed pass away when the state of glory commences at the end of the world. As evidence for this future transition from earthly life to glory, Aquinas quotes 1 Corinthians 13:12, "For now we see in a mirror dimly, but then face to face."

The final reference in the *prima secundae* to 1 Corinthians 13 occurs in question 114, article four. Question 114 has to do with merit, and the fourth article asks whether grace is the principle of merit through charity. It might seem that grace works equally through every virtue in enabling us to merit. Aquinas replies that charity orders all our actions toward the goal of enjoying God forever. The acts of the other virtues, when they are ordered toward eternal life, are commanded by charity, and so it is evident that grace causes meritorious actions in us through charity. In his reply to the third objection, Aquinas draws an example from 1 Corinthians 13:3 so as to show that the acts of patience and fortitude are not meritorious unless commanded by charity: "If I give away all I have, and if I deliver my body to be burned, but have not love, I gain nothing."

The main role of 1 Corinthians 13 in the *prima secundae*, therefore, is to explore the virtue of charity. Often this is done in relation to faith. Thus Aquinas asks whether charity has priority over vision in eternal life, whether charity prompts us to rejoice in others' good actions, whether charity (and faith and hope) are theological virtues, whether they are the only three theological virtues, whether charity alone suffices without the moral virtues, whether charity is the greatest theological virtue, whether charity remains in eternal life, whether charity can motivate an evil act, whether the sin that directly opposes charity is the greatest sin, whether God brings the sinner to "nothing" when he punishes the sinner by removing spiritual goods (such as charity), whether the commandments of the Mosaic law can only be observed in charity, and whether grace works through charity to makes the acts of the other virtues meritorious. Since the *prima secundae* has to do with human free will and action, whose ultimate purpose is union with God, it is no wonder that charity is so important. When we fail to possess charity, the entire purpose of our free will and action is frustrated.

In the *prima secundae*, the dimension of 1 Corinthians 13 that pertains to knowledge is also under discussion, even if not so much as it is in the *prima pars*. This is especially the case in the question on the new law, where Aquinas applies 1 Corinthians 13:9–12 to the way in which the new law is going to pass away: not by being fulfilled through a further earthly state, as the Mosaic law was fulfilled, but rather by being fulfilled through the gift of perfect knowledge at God in eternal life. It is also the case in the question that asks whether the intellectual virtues that we acquire in our earthly lives remain in heaven. In addition, 1 Corinthians 13's discussion of knowledge has a role when the *prima secundae* compares faith and charity. The best example of this is where Aquinas uses 1 Corinthians 13:13 in his discussion of the priority of the vision of God over charitable delight in that vision. It also is exemplified in his presentation of the theological virtues and their ordering, as well as in his account of God's punishment of sin by the deprivation of spiritual goods—not only charity but also the good of the beatific vision.

1 CORINTHIANS 13 IN THE *SECUNDA-SECUNDAE PARS*

First Corinthians 13 is quoted thirty-seven times in the *secunda secundae*, thirteen instances of which are in the treatise on charity. The *secunda secundae* treats the theological and moral virtues at length, and then concludes with the gratuitous graces (such as prophecy) and the states of life. Other than the thirteen references in the treatise on charity, most of

Aquinas's references to 1 Corinthians 13 in the *secunda secundae* appear in questions 1–6 on faith (eight references) and in questions 171–86 on the gratuitous graces and the states of life (twelve references). The remaining four references appear in Aquinas's questions on prudence and fortitude.

We begin with the citations of 1 Corinthians 13 in the treatise on faith. The second article of question one inquires into whether the object of faith is complex so as to be known propositionally. It would seem that the answer is no, because God is simple. The third objection argues in this vein that because in the beatific vision we know God as supremely simple, so also in faith we must know God as supremely simple. To demonstrate the link between faith and vision, the objection quotes 1 Corinthians 13:12, "For now we see in a mirror dimly, but then face to face. Now I know in part; then I shall understand fully, even as I have been fully understood." Aquinas replies that in the beatific vision we see God as he is and thus by a simple understanding, whereas in faith we do not see God as he is and therefore need a variety of propositions to describe him.

The same verse appears, again in the objections, in article four of question one. This time the question is whether, in faith, we see God through intellectual vision. If "now we see in a mirror dimly" (1 Cor 13:12), then it seems that even now, in faith, we see God. Aquinas answers that in this life we cannot have intellectual vision of God, because otherwise faith would be a demonstrative knowledge. Instead faith knows God through seeing his revealed effects, preeminently the holy humanity of Jesus Christ.

The next article (the fifth) also cites 1 Corinthians 13:12, now in the *respondeo*. At issue is whether the realities that we know by faith can also be the object of science, which is based upon demonstrative reasoning. Aquinas answers that faith's knowledge cannot be proven by reason, even though there are some truths that are included in faith (for example, that God exists) that can be known by reason. Nonetheless, in eternal life we will indeed see the realities of faith and have true knowledge of them; this is what Paul means by saying, "For now we see in a mirror dimly, but then face to face."

Question four, article two contains yet another citation of 1 Corinthians 13:12. Here the verse appears as the *sed contra*, in support of Aquinas's claim that faith is in the intellect (rather than in the will). The next article contains 1 Corinthians 13:13 in the first objection. The topic is whether charity is the form of faith, in the sense that charity directs faith to its proper goal of union with God. The first objection reasons that since faith and charity are different virtues, one cannot be the form of another. In his reply, Aquinas explains that one act can be quickened by different habits, and so the act of faith can be informed by charity. The next article (the fourth) also includes 1 Corinthians 13 in the first objection. The topic here has to do with the relationship of faith formed by charity (living faith) to faith uninformed by charity (dead faith). Are these two kinds of faith distinct habits, or are they the same habit, with dead faith being the disordered form of the one habit of faith? Aquinas thinks that they are the same habit, so that dead faith can become living faith without God having to infuse a new habit of faith. But he uses 1 Corinthians 13:10—"when the perfect comes, the imperfect will pass away"—to argue that when living faith comes, dead faith passes away, so that living faith is an entirely new habit.

The second objection of question five, article one contains another quotation of 1 Corinthians 13:12. Aquinas wishes to argue that in their original state, the first humans and angels possessed faith. But the objection uses 1 Corinthians 13:12 to suggest the opposite. According to the objection, the first humans and angels had a clear knowledge of God, whereas faith involves a dark knowledge, because as Paul says, "now we see in a mirror dimly." Aquinas replies that faith would have a certain darkness even without the obscuring effect of sin upon our intellects: "Every creature is darkness in comparison with the immensity of the divine light."[5]

Question six, article two asks whether faith, if lifeless (that is, unformed by charity), is still a gift infused by God. The *sed contra* cites 1 Corinthians 13:2 in order to cite the gloss on this verse, because the gloss states that even faith that lacks charity is God's gift. Recall that Paul says that "if I have all faith, so as to remove mountains, but have not love, I am nothing." Paul is speaking here of lifeless faith—faith without charity—but he obviously does not think it is entirely worthless, because it has power "to remove mountains." Therefore even this faith is still God's gift, despite the

---

5. *ST* II-II, q. 5, a. 1, ad 2.

lack of charity that prevents us from attaining union with the God whom we know in faith.

Aquinas's treatise on charity begins with question twenty-three. In the fourth article of this question, Aquinas quotes 1 Corinthians 13 twice, in the second objection and in the *sed contra*. The topic of the article is whether charity is a general virtue—so that we are to do all things in a loving way—or a special (particular) virtue. The second objection argues that charity is a general virtue by quoting 1 Corinthians 13:4, "Love is patient and kind." On this view, charity should be found in all human actions, just as all actions should be marked by kindness. In reply, Aquinas states that charity is the form of the virtues by commanding them rather than by eliciting them immediately. The *sed contra* adds to this by pointing out that Paul enumerates charity, along with faith and hope, as a special virtue: "So faith, hope, love abide, these three" (1 Cor 13:13). Charity is a particular kind of love because it is love of the divine good as the object of human happiness.

First Corinthians 13 appears again in the *sed contra* of articles six and seven of question twenty-three. In article six the topic is whether charity is the greatest virtue, and the *sed contra* quotes Paul's remark that "the greatest of these is love" (1 Cor 13:13). Charity is the greatest because it attains God most profoundly, so as to rest in him. Article seven asks whether without charity, one can possess any true virtue, and the *sed contra* quotes Paul's statement, "If I give away all I have, and if I deliver my body to be burned, but have not love, I gain nothing" (1 Cor 13:3). On this basis Aquinas answers that there cannot be true virtue without charity, but he goes on to make an important distinction. Insofar as every true virtue is directed toward our ultimate end, which is union with God, there can be no true virtue without charity; but insofar as virtues are also ordered to a particular good, there can be a true virtue without charity, even though it remains imperfect unless directed to the ultimate end by charity.

The next three appearances of 1 Corinthians 13 occur in the objections. In question twenty-five, article four, the topic is whether each person should love himself or herself out of charity. Aquinas answers yes, not least because if we do not love ourselves, we cannot love our neighbor as ourselves (see Leviticus 19:18; Luke 10:27). The third objection, however, quotes 1 Corinthians 13:4 (in Aquinas's version) as evidence that charity does not do evil, and then argues that self-love is in fact evil: "In the last days there will come times of stress. For men will be lovers of self, lovers of money, proud, arrogant, abusive" (2 Tim 3:2). In reply, Aquinas points out that true love of self means loving not only one's body but also one's soul, so as to desire union with God. The eighth article of question twenty-five addresses whether we should love our enemies, and the third objection argues on the basis of Aquinas's version of 1 Corinthians 13:4 that since charity does not do anything wrongly, charity should follow the normal course by loving friends and not loving enemies. Otherwise, the charitable person would be vulnerable to Joab's charge against King David, "You love those who hate you and hate those who love you" (2 Sam 19:6). In reply, Aquinas points out that while we do not love the enmity of our enemies, we do need to love our enemies insofar as we share human nature and share the ultimate end of union with God. Lastly, in question twenty-six, article four, Aquinas asks whether we should love ourselves more than our neighbors. The third objection quotes 1 Corinthians 13:5 to the effect that love does not seek its own (Aquinas's version of this text differs from the RSV and reads "*non quaerit quae sua sunt*"). Aquinas replies that this means that love seeks the common good above one's own private good. A charitable person always prioritizes the common good. We must love ourselves more than our neighbors, however, in the sense that we should not sin (and thereby harm our own soul) even in order to free our neighbor from sin.

Question twenty-seven, article four discusses whether in charity we are able to love God immediately, even though in this life we can only know God through creatures rather than knowing him immediately. The first objection quotes 1 Corinthians 13:12, "now we see in a mirror dimly," and on this basis the objection concludes that just as in this life we know God indirectly, so also we can only love him indirectly. But the *sed contra* observes that in 1 Corinthians 13:12 Paul states that in eternal life our indirect knowledge of God will be replaced by "face to face" knowledge; whereas in 1 Corinthians 13:8 Paul makes clear that love, by contrast, "never ends." Love differs from knowledge because once we know God indirectly, we have a real communion with him and can love him directly.

The next three references to 1 Corinthians 13 are contained in objections. In question twenty-eight, article two, on whether the spiritual joy that results from charity can be mixed with sorrow, the first objection cites 1 Corinthians 13:6, where Paul says that charity "does not rejoice at wrong, but rejoices in the right." The objection then argues that rejoicing in the right is perfectly compatible with sorrow, since Paul elsewhere instructs believers, "Rejoice with those who rejoice, weep with those who weep" (Rom 12:15). Aquinas replies, however, that spiritual joy in the God whom we love is a pure joy, without sorrow. When we love God we love him with pure joy, because he is perfect good; whereas when we weep with our neighbor, we weep because something is hindering our neighbor from full bodily and spiritual participation in good.

The third objection of question thirty-one, article two argues that we should not try to do good to all. In support of this position, the objection remarks that doing good to an enemy of the common good is wrong. In this regard, the objection cites the clause of 1 Corinthians 13:4 that is found in the Vulgate but not in the RSV: charity "does not deal perversely." In reply, Aquinas notes that we must not help people to do evil, but on the other hand we must help all people, including evildoers, when they are in distress, so long as we do not directly help them to do evil.

The first objection of question thirty-two, article one quotes 1 Corinthians 13:3 in order to show that one can give alms without having charity: "If I give away all I have, and if I deliver my body to be burned, but have not love, I gain nothing." The objection concludes that almsgiving should not be categorized as an act of charity. In his *respondeo*, Aquinas states that almsgiving is an act of mercy, and since mercy is an interior effect of charity, almsgiving constitutes an act of charity. In reply to the first objection, Aquinas grants that one can give alms without charity, but only in charity can one give alms for God's sake and with delight.

The final reference to 1 Corinthians 13 in the treatise on charity appears in the tenth article of question thirty-two. In the *respondeo*, Aquinas argues that we should give abundant alms. To be abundant, alms need to be great in comparison with our means. Alms should also be sufficient to meet the needs of the recipient, but they should not be more than sufficient, because there are many who are in need. Regarding this latter point,

Aquinas quotes 1 Corinthians 13:3, "if I give away all I have," and the gloss's commentary on this verse. The gloss urges that in giving alms, we give to many persons rather than solely to one. In this case, Aquinas cites Paul mainly in order to cite the gloss.

I turn now to 1 Corinthians 13's role—admittedly a small one—in Aquinas's treatise on the moral virtues, beginning with prudence. The *respondeo* of question forty-seven, article ten quotes 1 Corinthians 13:5 in favor of the view that prudence extends to the common good, rather than being limited only to one's own good. Aquinas's version of the relevant portion of 1 Corinthians 13:5 states that love "does not seek her own," rather than saying (as the RSV does) that love "does not insist on its own way." Even in the RSV, however, it is clear that Paul is talking about the kind of selflessness that Aquinas thinks belongs to prudence.

First Corinthians 13 does not appear again in the questions on prudence, and it is also missing from Aquinas's lengthy treatises on justice and temperance. In Aquinas's treatise on fortitude, however, 1 Corinthians 13 is cited three times. Let me review these citations, none of which is overly important for Aquinas's argument, but all of which make a certain contribution nonetheless.

In the second article of question 124, Aquinas asks whether martyrdom is an act of fortitude. The second objection argues that martyrdom is an act of charity, not an act of fortitude. In favor of this view, the objection cites 1 Corinthians 13:3, "If I give away all I have, and if I deliver my body to be burned, but have not love, I am nothing." Charity, not fortitude, is what makes the act of martyrdom to be the virtuous and meritorious act that it is. In reply, Aquinas grants that charity is the virtue that commands martyrdom, but he explains that the virtue that elicits martyrdom is fortitude. In other words, to give up one's life under the promptings of charity requires that one be brave enough to actually go through with it.

Fortitude includes the virtue of magnanimity, which inclines one toward great deeds. One of the vices opposed to magnanimity is ambition. Aquinas treats this vice in question 131, article one. In the *sed contra* he quotes 1 Corinthians 13:5 in his version: "Charity is not ambitious, it does not seek her own [*caritas non est ambitiosa, non quaerit quae sua sunt*]." As we noted above, the RSV is different. It rules out being "arrogant" (1

Cor 13:5), but it does not mention ambition. Still, the difference does not undo Aquinas's interpretation, because Paul is here ruling out the arrogance and boasting that characterize ambition.

Still under the rubric of fortitude, Aquinas treats patience in question 136. In article three, he argues that it is not possible to have patience without grace. In the *respondeo* he explains that patient endurance of suffering can only be accomplished when we seek a good higher than the natural goods of which suffering deprives us. Seeking a higher good comes about through charity, which loves God above created things. In confirmation of his conclusion that charity (and thus grace) causes patience, he quotes Paul's remark that "love is patient" (1 Cor 13:4).

The remainder of Aquinas's references in the *secunda secundae* to 1 Corinthians 13 occur in his discussion of the gratuitous graces and the states of life. Seven of these citations appear in questions 171–78 on the gratuitous graces (or gifts) such as prophecy, rapture, and miracle-working. In article four of question 171, Aquinas asks whether God reveals all matters of prophecy—all that can be known prophetically—to each prophet. Unsurprisingly, he answers no. The reply to the second objection explains that a prophet does not need to have knowledge of all that can be known prophetically, because prophecy is imperfect of its nature. God's perfect or full revelation will come to us only in eternal life. In support of this position, Aquinas cites 1 Corinthians 13:8–10.[6] Here Paul states that "our prophecy is imperfect" (1 Cor 13:9) and observes that "as for prophecies, they will pass away" (1 Cor 13:8) and that "when the perfect comes, the imperfect will pass away" (1 Cor 13:10). In this case, the "perfect" consists in the fullness of revelation that will be manifested only in the beatific vision. When the beatific vision arrives, there will be no further need for prophetic knowledge.

Question 172, article four poses the problem of whether to be a prophet requires that one live a good life. Can only holy people receive the gift of prophecy? On the basis of Matthew 7:22–23, Aquinas answers that a good life is not a prerequisite for receiving the gift of prophecy. God can

---

6. Since Aquinas cites these three verses with his own comments interspersed, they could be counted as three citations. I count them here as one citation because of their proximity in the reply to the second objection.

make even an unrepentant sinner the bearer of prophetic knowledge. In the *respondeo* Aquinas cites 1 Corinthians 13:2 as evidence that prophetic knowledge is not necessarily paired with charity. Recall that in this verse Paul states, "If I have prophetic powers, and understand all mysteries and all knowledge, and if I have all faith so as to remove mountains, but have not love, I am nothing." It seems to Aquinas that Paul here entertains the real possibility of having "prophetic powers" without having love. I think that this is a plausible interpretation, even if Paul is speaking hyperbolically here or even if he is speaking of a case that in reality is unlikely to occur.

Two quotations of 1 Corinthians 13 occur in question 173, article one, on whether prophets obtain their knowledge by seeing the divine essence. Aquinas answers, as we would expect, that prophetic knowledge does not come in this way. The *sed contra* reasons on the basis of 1 Corinthians 13:8, "as for prophecies, they will pass away." Prophecies would not pass away if they were based on seeing the divine essence, since the vision of God does not pass away in eternal life. In the *respondeo* Aquinas distinguishes prophetic knowledge, which is imperfect, from the perfect knowledge that is beatific vision. He refers here to Paul's statement that "when the perfect comes, the imperfect will pass away" (1 Cor 13:10).

Question 175, article three examines whether Paul, in the rapture that he describes in 2 Corinthians 12, saw the divine essence. Like Augustine, Aquinas thinks that this is probable. But against this view he cites 1 Corinthians 13:10–12 in the third objection. This objection observes that according to verses 10–12, the face-to-face vision of God will enable us to understand God fully, and thus to move from the imperfection of faith to the perfection of vision. Yet Paul continued to have faith, even while he was in rapture. The objection concludes that Paul, in his experience of rapture, must have not seen the divine essence. Aquinas replies that Paul could have retained the habit of faith, even while for a short time his act of faith was replaced by an act of vision.

The two articles of question 178, on the gift of working miracles, each contain one reference to 1 Corinthians 13:2. The first article asks whether the power of working miracles requires a grace from God. On the basis of 1 Corinthians 12, where Paul lists miracle-working among the gifts that God gives to believers, Aquinas argues that miracle-working is indeed a grace or divine gift. The fifth objection makes the opposite case by observing the connection between miracle-working and faith. In this vein, the objection quotes 1 Corinthians 13:2, which explicitly links having "all faith" with the ability to miraculously "remove mountains." The logic here is that faith should suffice by itself for miracle-working, rather than requiring another divine gift. In reply, Aquinas points out that the grace of faith is also combined by God with the gift of preaching, so that people can come to faith. In the same way, the gift of miracle-working is combined with the gift of faith, rather than being simply the same gift.

The second article of this question probes whether the wicked, who are alienated from God, can work miracles. It seems that they cannot, not least because of the connection between miracle-working and faith that we have noted above. In the *sed contra*, however, Aquinas quotes 1 Corinthians 13:2, now as evidence that the wicked can indeed work miracles if God gives them the grace of doing so. After all, if a person who lacks charity is nonetheless still able to miraculously move mountains, then it is clear that the wicked can do miracles when God gives them the grace. The question, I suppose, is whether Paul intends his example of the mountain-mover who lacks charity simply as a hyperbolic statement rather than an actual possibility. As I commented above, I think that Paul's statement is certainly hyperbolic, but nonetheless the passage does confirm the possibility of the wicked performing miracles.

The last five references in the *secunda secundae* to 1 Corinthians 13 come in Aquinas's questions on the contemplative life, the state of perfection, and the religious state. Question 180, on the contemplative life, has three references to 1 Corinthians 13. The fourth article examines whether the contemplative life consists solely in the contemplation of God, or consists in the contemplation of any truth. In his *respondeo* Aquinas answers this by means of a distinction: on the one hand, the contemplative life principally consists in contemplating God (as Aristotle, Augustine, and Gregory the Great make clear); on the other hand, since we come to know God through his effects, the contemplative life secondarily includes contemplating God's effects insofar as they lead us to the knowledge of God. In this life, our contemplation of God is imperfect, whereas in eternal life will be perfect. With regard to the imperfection of our present contemplation, Aquinas quotes 1 Corinthians 13:12, "For now we see in a mirror dimly."

In the seventh article, Aquinas asks whether contemplation produces delight, so that not only the intellect but also the will is involved. The answer certainly is yes, but 1 Corinthians 13:12 provides the grounds for an objection, namely there can be no delight in an imperfect operation. Aquinas replies that we have imperfect delight in imperfect contemplation, but nonetheless the delight is real and, because we are contemplating God, it is greater than the delight that can be obtained from any other kind of earthly contemplation.

The eighth article inquires into whether the contemplative life is continuous (*diuturna*). Aquinas grants that the height of contemplation cannot be achieved in a continuous fashion in this life, but he argues that in other ways the contemplative life should be thought of as continuous. Yet the first objection denies this on the grounds that the intellectual perfections that we experience now will pass away when we die, as Paul seems to say when he comments, "Love never ends; as for prophecies they will pass away; as for tongues, they will cease; as for knowledge, it will pass away" (1 Cor 13:8). If our earthly love continues but our earthly knowledge ceases, then it seems that our contemplation is discontinuous from this life to the next. In reply, Aquinas admits that our contemplation in this life is quite different in mode from our contemplation in the next. He notes, however, that what we contemplate and love in this life is the same divine reality that we contemplate and love in the next. Since our love for the reality that we contemplate remains the same, the contemplative life can be said to be continuous between this life and the next.

In question 184, article two, the issue is whether anyone can be perfect in this life. Aquinas holds that one can be perfect, although not in an absolute sense. Perfection consists in charity. It is impossible, however, for a creature to love God perfectly if by that is meant loving God as much as he is lovable. In this life, it is also impossible to love God fully at every moment because we are not always contemplating and love God with our fullest concentration. But it is possible to have perfect love in this life in a more limited sense, namely by ceasing to love anything that is contrary to charity and by ridding oneself of all that hinders our love from tending fully to God. Not surprisingly, 1 Corinthians 13:10 appears in the first objection: "When the perfect comes, the imperfect will pass away." Our love will be perfect in eternal life, and thus it would seem that it is imperfect now. Aquinas replies that Paul is speaking about heavenly perfection, as opposed to the limited perfection of charity that is possible in this life.

In question 186, article seven—which contains the final reference in the *secunda secundae* to 1 Corinthians—Aquinas asks whether religious perfection consists in the observance of poverty, chastity, and obedience. This is a complex question, as shown by Aquinas's answering it through considering the religious state in terms of three goals: seeking the perfection of charity, relieving the mind from temporal business, and offering one's whole life (and possessions) fully to God. First Corinthians 13 plays a small role in the answer to the first objection, which had argued that religious perfection consists more properly in inward acts such as contemplation and charity. In his answer to this objection, Aquinas argues that the goal of the religious vows is the perfection of charity. The vows are the means to the interior end; the perfection of the religious state consists in the suitability of these three vows to the attainment of this interior end. In order to show that the other virtues come under charity, he quotes 1 Corinthians 13:4, "Love is patient and kind; love is not jealous or boastful."

Is there a way of summing up the contributions of 1 Corinthians 13 to the *secunda secundae*? It is clear that 1 Corinthians 13 shapes in important ways Aquinas's treatise on faith, just as it does his treatise on charity. First Corinthians 13 is generally absent from his theology of the moral virtues, but on the other hand it is present in significant places: helping to show that prudence extends to the common good; helping to define the quintessential Christian act of martyrdom; helping to differentiate between the virtue of magnanimity and the sin of ambition; and helping to show that patient endurance of suffering requires charity and grace. Since prudence governs all our actions, the fact that it extends to the common good and not solely to our individual good is crucial not only for the government of merely human societies but also for Christian communion in the body of Christ. Charity calls believers to great acts of love, which require magnanimity and include the willingness to be martyred in imitation of Christ's giving up of his life. This life will therefore involve hardships, and so patient endurance of suffering belongs at the center of the life of faith and charity.

The whole Christian life, therefore, can be shown to be shaped by charity, and 1 Corinthians 13 has a significant (though quantitatively small) role even in Aquinas's discussion of the moral virtues. As we might expect, we find 1 Corinthians 13 playing a major role in Aquinas's discussion of the gratuitous graces or gifts, such as prophecy, rapture, and miracle-working. The basic question is whether these gifts require that the prophet or miracle-worker possess charity. Aquinas thinks that this is not the case, and he uses the second verse as evidence. He uses verses 8–10 to show that prophetic knowledge is imperfect and that prophets do not gain their knowledge from seeing God's essence. The imperfection of prophetic knowledge is an important point because Aquinas holds, with Paul, that all prophecy and all faith will be perfected only in eternal life when we see God face to face. Yet Aquinas does not thereby exclude experiences of rapture in which believers may for a short period of time enjoy beatific vision. Such experiences are not opposed to the habit of faith; they do not remove faith because they are not the permanent infusion of beatific vision. In this way Aquinas uses 1 Corinthians 13 both to account for the imperfection of all our faith-knowledge, and to allow for mystical experiences that go beyond the bounds of what faith can perceive.

With regard to charity, 1 Corinthians 13 helps Aquinas to show that charity is a particular or special virtue. He employs 1 Corinthians 13 prominently in his arguments regarding why charity is the greatest virtue and why there is no true virtue, in the full sense, without charity. He underscores that love "never ends," insofar as our love for God and neighbor is already, even now, the love that we will have in eternal life, even though it is not perfected. By contrast to our knowledge of God through created things, we can love God immediately. Our love of God inspires our love of creatures. This is the opposite of our knowledge of God, which derives from our knowledge of creatures. Aquinas distinguishes between selfish self-love, which would violate the description of charity in 1 Corinthians 13, and true self-love, which includes desire for union with God.

In addition, as we have seen, Aquinas employs 1 Corinthians 13 to explore contemplation. Just as prophecy and miracles are a central part of

Christian faith—from the prophets of Israel (including Moses) and the miracles they worked, through Christ's role as a prophet and miracle-worker, and the teaching and miracles of his apostles and his followers over the centuries—so also contemplation is a central part of Christian faith. To be a Christian means to desire to contemplate God out of love for him. When charity is weak, so will be the desire to know God. Aquinas therefore makes use of 1 Corinthians 13 to explore the imperfect (but delightful) contemplation that we can experience in this life and to reflect upon the continuity and discontinuity between our contemplation in this life and our contemplation in the life to come. Lastly, 1 Corinthians 13 plays a role in Aquinas's discussion of how the religious life belongs to the state of perfection. At issue is whether it is possible to seek perfect charity in this life and how the religious life's quest for charity fosters the other virtues.

Today, the common good, martyrdom, ambition as a sin, patience, prophecy, miracle-working, mystical rapture, contemplation, the quest to be perfect in charity, and the religious life might appear to be less central than they were to Aquinas. But Aquinas's reflections in the *secunda secundae*, assisted by 1 Corinthians 13, shows the centrality of these aspects of Christianity. We also benefit from Aquinas's reflections on the contours of faith: it differs from vision and from demonstrative knowledge, it is in the intellect, and it can exist without charity. His citations of 1 Corinthians 13 tend to apply Paul's statements to speculative issues that Paul could not have anticipated. But even so, the portrait of Christian life developed in the *secunda secundae* fits well with the emphases of 1 Corinthians 13.

1 CORINTHIANS 13 IN THE *TERTIA PARS*

In the *tertia pars*, which explores Christ and the sacraments, 1 Corinthians 13 is cited only six times.[7] Interestingly, it only appears once in Aquinas's theology of Christ and his saving work (questions 1–59), namely in question nine, article three, on whether Christ had infused knowledge.

---

7. I have not included the "Supplement" to the *tertia pars*, because this supplement was pieced together after Aquinas's death from material in his *Commentary on the Sentences*.

It follows that 1 Corinthians 13 has a marginal role in Aquinas's treatise on Christ, just as it had a marginal role in Aquinas's theology of the triune God. First Corinthians 13 appears five times in questions 61–89, but it does not appear in Aquinas's theology of the eucharist (questions 73–83). Instead it appears in his general theory of the sacraments, his theology of baptism and confirmation, and his theology of penance. What role does 1 Corinthians 13 have in these questions? Indeed, why does Aquinas cite it at all in the *tertia pars*, given that there are a number of other Pauline texts (including many passages from 1 Corinthians itself) that bear more directly upon Christ and the sacraments?

The article on Christ's infused knowledge comes after an article in which Aquinas holds that Christ possessed beatific knowledge during his earthly life. Both of these articles seek to ensure the intimacy of Christ, in his human mind, with his divine Father—an intimacy whose purpose is our salvation. Christ's infused knowledge, unlike his beatific knowledge, is conceptual and therefore can be communicated to those whom Christ teaches. Yet as Aquinas observes in the first objection—citing 1 Corinthians 13:10 and 13:12—it would seem that the perfect knowledge provided by beatific vision would deprive Christ of the need (or capacity) for any imperfect mode of knowledge. In reply, Aquinas states that although Christ has vision rather than faith, he nonetheless retains the ability to know in a variety of modes, one of which is through infused concepts. By the divine power, Christ prevents his human mind from being glorified by the beatific vision, and he thereby retains the ability to communicate conceptual knowledge of God and of the plan of salvation. Like the prophets, he receives this knowledge through infusion.

The fourth article of question sixty-one asks why, after Christ's coming, there was still a need for corporeal sacraments. Before Christ's coming, the future reality of Christ was signified by sacramental signs. After his coming, now that he has ascended to the right hand of the Father, the past reality of Christ is signified by new sacramental signs. In both cases—before and after his coming—Christ stands at the center of the worship offered by the people of God. In the reply to the third objection, Aquinas adds that just as the Mosaic law is figurative, so also the new law is figurative of the state of glory. Until the state of glory is revealed, we will need corporeal sacraments to signify spiritual realities. As evidence of this, he quotes 1 Corinthians 13:12, "For now we see in a mirror dimly."

In the eleventh article of question sixty-six, Aquinas distinguishes three kinds of baptism: of water (the sacrament itself), of blood (by martyrdom), and of the Spirit (by infused charity). In the twelfth article, he seeks to establish that baptism of blood is the greatest of these. The second objection, however, proposes that baptism of the Spirit is greater, because without charity, martyrdom has no salvific efficacy. Along these lines the objection quotes 1 Corinthians 13:3, "If I deliver my body to be burned, but have not love, I gain nothing." In his *respondeo*, Aquinas explains that the effect of baptism is caused by Christ's passion and by the Holy Spirit, and that these two causes act most powerfully in baptism of blood. This is so because baptism of blood directly imitates Christ's passion and involves supreme love (see John 15:13). In reply to the second objection, Aquinas points out that martyrdom can only be a "baptism" if it is done with charity. Baptism of blood is always, therefore, a baptism of the Spirit. Since the converse is not true, one can see why baptism of blood is superior.

Question seventy-two, article one discusses the sacramental status of confirmation. First Corinthians 13 appears in the *respondeo*. Arguing that confirmation is indeed a sacrament, Aquinas notes that the sacramental organism is parallel to the human bodily organism. In bodily life, we move from childhood to maturity, as Aquinas confirms through a citation of verse eleven: "When I was a child, I spoke like a child, I thought like a child, I reasoned like a child; when I became a man, I gave up childish ways." Just as baptism provides a grace that parallels being born, confirmation provides a grace that parallels arriving at maturity.

In question eighty-five, article two Aquinas treats the virtue of penance as part of his discussion of the sacrament of penance. This article asks in particular whether penance is a special virtue rather than simply an emotion that a charitable person always feels when remembering his or her sins. The first objection argues that penance is simply an emotion linked to recollection of sins, just as joy is an emotion linked to recollection of good things. In testimony to the latter, the objection cites 1 Corinthians 13:6, where Paul says that love "does not rejoice at wrong, but rejoices in the right." In his reply to this objection, Aquinas notes that charity automatically elicits joy about good things and grief about evil things, whereas charity has to command particular acts of virtue such as those that penitentially seek to expiate sin. In this latter sense, penance is a virtue.

The last appearance of 1 Corinthians 13 in the *Summa theologiae* occurs in question eighty-nine, article six. This article asks whether subsequent penance can give charity to works that were done without charity. If a person lacking charity nonetheless frequently honored his parents, for example, would subsequent penance (and the infusion of charity) retroactively enable this good work to be meritorious? Aquinas answers no, on the grounds that acts cannot be redone. In support of this view, the *sed contra* cites 1 Corinthians 13:3, "If I give away all I have, and if I deliver my body to be burned, but have not love, I gain nothing." As Aquinas says, if subsequent penance were able to make a difference, then Paul would have written differently: he would still be able to gain something, by means of subsequent penance, from giving away all that he had. This technical point was no doubt not in Paul's mind either to affirm or to deny, but even so, one can see Aquinas's point that if penance were able to change the character of previous acts, Paul would likely have mentioned this somewhere—or at least Paul's argument in verse three would have a large loophole.

In sum, in the *tertia pars* 1 Corinthians 13 plays a small role, largely if not entirely unrelated to Paul's own purposes in 1 Corinthians 13. The first reference to 1 Corinthians 13 in the *tertia pars* has to do with the distinction between perfect and imperfect that has appeared so frequently in Aquinas's theology of faith and knowledge, and that here appears in his christology. The next two references are connected with our corporeality, both insofar as we do not yet see spiritual realities directly and insofar as we can imitate Christ bodily by martyrdom. The fourth reference belongs to the connection Aquinas makes between our corporeality and corporeal sacraments. These latter three references are united by Aquinas's emphasis that sacramental life, like Christ's incarnation, befits our nature. Lastly, the fifth and sixth references draw out something of what penance is and what it accomplishes. Christ's knowledge, the sacramental life, martyrdom and charity, Christian maturity, and penance: these are not marginal topics in Aquinas's theology. They express crucial elements, especially regarding our configuration to Christ's suffering. Yet it would not do to press overly much the importance of 1 Corinthians 13 in the *tertia pars*. Without minimizing the contributions 1 Corinthians 13 makes, each of which has value, it is clear that Aquinas's major arguments here rely on other sources.

CONCLUSION

In the *Summa theologiae*, Aquinas quotes 1 Corinthians 13 a total of sixty-nine times, and thirty-nine of these references appear in the objections. This is not surprising, since as we have seen throughout this book, many of Aquinas's biblical references in the *Summa* are used to formulate objections to the theological conclusions he draws in his *respondeo*. Fifteen of the sixty-nine references to 1 Corinthians 13 are found in the *sed contra*. Thus fifty-four of the sixty-nine references are either in the authoritative turning point of the argument, or in the objections that help Aquinas show the validity of his position against possible biblical and theological counter-arguments. But does this make for a significant impact of 1 Corinthians 13 upon Aquinas's theology?

In answer, I would identify the relationship of perfect and imperfect knowledge, of faith and vision, as a particularly important theme that benefits in the *Summa* from 1 Corinthians 13. As we saw, Aquinas also uses 1 Corinthians 13 to distinguish human knowledge from angelic knowledge, and to distinguish Christ's knowledge from that of other humans. Another frequent theme that Aquinas develops in light of 1 Corinthians 13 has to do with the immediacy, greatness, and necessity of charity, not least for giving form or "life" to faith. Charity is shown to be necessary for the other virtues as well. The relationship of faith and charity, intellect and will, is another recurring theme in Aquinas's use of 1 Corinthians 13. Central aspects of the Christian life such as prophecy, mystical union with God, contemplation, miracle-working, the three vows that characterize consecrated religious life, the gifts of the Holy Spirit, prudence for the common good, pleasure in the good actions of others, almsgiving, and charity's prompting of other virtuous acts are also elucidated by Aquinas through some relation to 1 Corinthians 13. These areas of Aquinas's theology display the significant influence of the way in which Paul elucidates the Christian life in 1 Corinthians 13.

We have also seen that Aquinas often reads the verses of 1 Corinthians 13 as principles that possess a wide application. This is most notable, perhaps, in the case of verse 10, "When the perfect comes, the imperfect will pass away." In this regard, Aquinas's use of 1 Corinthians 13 often moves away from Paul's own context, but not entirely so. After all, Paul too appeals to the relationship between imperfect and perfect in order to distinguish between faith and face-to-face knowledge, and Paul's presentation of faith and love presents the former only as life-giving in union with the latter. Even in cases where Aquinas applies verses in ways that Paul could not have anticipated, a case can still be made for the relation of his arguments to Paul's. For example, when Aquinas distinguishes between the effects of baptism and confirmation in terms of childhood and maturity (verse 11), he builds upon the distinction between imperfect and perfect that is present in verse 10. Here the main point for Paul, as for Aquinas, is that Christian life involves an ascent toward perfection in eternal union with God, an ascent that begins even now in faith and prophetic knowledge, and that is fueled by love. Indeed, it is because of 1 Corinthians 13's ability to evoke and describe this pattern of ascent in a manner that proves fruitful for a wide variety of theological themes that the *Summa theologiae* cites this very short chapter more than almost any other chapter in the Pauline corpus.

CHAPTER 9

PHILIPPIANS 2:5–11 IN THE
Summa Theologiae

D ISCUSSING Aquinas's commentary on Philippians, Francesca Aran Murphy points out that beginning with Hilary of Poitiers, "interpreters of Philippians had spoken of the 'two states' of Christ, the 'state of obedience' (*status obedientis*) and the 'state of glory' (*status gloriae*)."[1] For these two states, Philippians 2:5:11 is obviously of prime importance. Paul here describes the *kenosis* of Christ:

Have this mind among yourselves, which was in Christ Jesus, who, though he was in the form of God, did not count equality with God a thing to be grasped, but emptied himself, taking the form of a servant, being born in the likeness of men. And being found in human form he humbled himself and became obedient unto death, even death on a cross. Therefore God has highly exalted him and bestowed on him the name which is above every name, that at the name of Jesus every knee should bow, in heaven and on earth and under the earth, and every tongue confess that Jesus Christ is Lord, to the glory of God the Father.

---

1. Francesca Aran Murphy, "Thomas' Commentaries on Philemon, 1 and 2 Thessalonians and Philippians," in *Aquinas on Scripture: An Introduction to His Biblical Commentaries*, ed. Thomas G. Weinandy, OFM Cap., Daniel A. Keating, and John P. Yocum (London: T. and T. Clark International, 2005), 185. See also Jeremy Holmes, "St. Thomas's Commentary on Philippians 2:5–11: A New Translation with Introduction and Notes," in *Wisdom and Holiness, Science and Scholarship: Essays in Honor of Matthew L. Lamb*, ed. Michael Dauphinais and Matthew Levering (Naples, Fla.: Sapientia Press, 2007), 109–41.

In the *Summa theologiae*, Aquinas quotes from this passage twenty-seven times. The bulk of the quotations come from verses 7–8, where Paul says that Christ, although in the form of God, "emptied himself, taking the form of a servant, being born in the likeness of men. And being found in human form he humbled himself and became obedient unto death, even death on a cross." This emphasis on verses 7–8 is somewhat surprising given how important the distinction between "form of God" (verse 6) and "form of a servant" (verse 7) is for Augustine; one might have expected more reflection on Christ's being in the "form of God," although such reflection is certainly present.

Not surprisingly, Philippians 2:5–11 appears predominantly in the *tertia pars* of the *Summa*, specifically in the treatise on Christ's person and work (questions 1–59). Twenty-two of the twenty-seven citations of Philippians 2:5–11 are in this section of the *Summa*. Significantly, Aquinas quotes from Philippians 2:5–11 throughout the treatise on Christ's person and work rather than solely in his discussion of Christ's passion. Eighteen of the fifty-nine questions in this treatise have a quotation of Philippians 2:5–11. Three citations of Philippians 2:5–11 are found in the *prima pars* along with two citations in the *secunda-secundae pars*.

Aquinas's emphasis on Christ's humility and obedience "in the likeness of men" may be expected to differ from the approaches taken by modern kenotic Christologies.[2] In his commentary on Philippians, Aquinas does not suppose that the self-emptying of the Son involves a renunciation of his divine attributes. Instead, in his commentary Aquinas envisions the *kenosis* as consisting in the humility of the Son in taking on human nature, even unto the humiliation of death on a cross, rather than standing upon his prerogatives as the Son of God.[3] We can anticipate that Aquinas will follow the same path in the *Summa theologiae*. Our task, then, is to seek to understand how Aquinas in the *Summa* employs Philippians 2:5–11's testimony to Christ's divinity, humanity, humility, obedience, and exaltation.

---

2. For discussion see Thomas Joseph White, OP, "Kenoticism and the Divinity of Christ Crucified," *The Thomist* 75 (2011): 1–41; *Exploring Kenotic Christology: The Self-Emptying of God*, ed. C. Stephen Evans (Vancouver, British Columbia: Regent College Publishing, 2006); and *Divine Impassibility and the Mystery of Human Suffering*, ed. James F. Keating and Thomas Joseph White, OP (Grand Rapids, Mich.: Eerdmans, 2009).

3. See White, "Kenoticism and the Divinity of Christ Crucified," 8n21.

THE *PRIMA PARS* AND *SECUNDA-SECUNDAE PARS*

In question forty-two, article four of the *prima pars*, Aquinas takes up the issue of whether the Son is equal to the Father in greatness. This issue arises especially from Jesus's statement in John 14:28 (quoted in Aquinas's first objection), "The Father is greater than I." It also has roots in 1 Corinthians 15:28, which also implies the subordination of the Son. Both of these texts were employed, for obvious reasons, by Arian and semi-Arian authors in the trinitarian controversies of the fourth century. The pivotal *sed contra* quotes Philippians 2:6, where Paul says that "though he was in the form of God, [Christ] did not count equality with God a thing to be grasped." Aquinas interprets this as a statement of the Son's pre-existence, the Son's possession of full divinity. On this view, Philippians 2:6 points to the Son's will to take flesh, and in this way, in his human nature, to become less than the Father—even while remaining perfectly equal to the Father in his Godhead. This reading of Philippians 2:6 remains exegetically defensible today.

In question seventy-three, article one, Aquinas asks whether the seventh day of creation marked the completion of the divine works. Aquinas argues in accord with Genesis 2:2 that God does complete his work on the seventh day. He distinguishes, however, between a first perfection and a second perfection. The perfection for which God creates is the perfect beatitude of the saints at the consummation of cosmic history. This is the second perfection. The first perfection is the giving of form to the whole cosmos, which is what God completes on the seventh day. Thus even on the seventh day God is at work in moving his creatures toward the second perfection of the cosmos. The third objection poses the difficulty that God is still creating new things, such as new souls and even new species. In his reply, Aquinas notes that nothing entirely new is created now, because everything in the cosmos existed in some way by the seventh day—whether materially, or in its causes, or by way of likeness. By way of likeness, says Aquinas, even the work of the Incarnation was foreshadowed. He defends this position by quoting Philippians 2:7, where Christ is described as "being born in the likeness of men." The Incarnation does not create a new kind of creature, because Christ is fully human.

Having used Philippians 2 to make a point about the Son's equality in divinity and about the Son's full humanity, Aquinas in the *prima pars* turns once more to Philippians 2. In question 113, article four, under the broad rubric of God's government of the cosmos, he asks whether each human being has a guardian angel. The first objection builds upon Philippians 2:7's description of Christ as "being born in the likeness of men." It seems that Christ would not need a guardian angel, because he is superior to the angels; and therefore it would seem that not every human has a guardian angel. In reply, Aquinas answers that since Christ in his human nature was guided by the Word, he did not need a guardian angel. Yet Christ too needed in the assistance of angels, since he was mortal and faced the dangers that we all face. In his case, however, he needed and received a ministering angel rather than a guardian angel.

In sum, the *prima pars* places Philippians 2 in three contexts: Christ's full divinity (in relation to the Father), Christ's full humanity (in relation to the cosmos), and Christ's relation to the angels during his earthly life. Already in the *prima pars*, then, Philippians 2 plays a role in sketching the various dimensions of christology. Since Christ is "in the form of God," he is equal to God. Since he is "in the likeness of men," he is truly human, a creature like other creatures. As the incarnate Son, he has certain prerogatives that other humans do not have, including superiority to the angels. He is like all humans in some ways, and unlike them in others.

The first time that Philippians 2 appears in the *secunda pars* occurs in question 124 of the *secunda-secundae pars*, a question devoted to martyrdom. The third article asks whether martyrdom is an act of the greatest perfection, and of course the answer is yes. Aquinas nonetheless comes up with some good objections, among them the view that giving up one's soul through obedience is of greater perfection than giving up one's body. In his *respondeo*, Aquinas notes that martyrdom shows the greatest perfection because it demonstrates one's possession of perfect charity, insofar as one is willing to undergo death out of love for Christ. Answering the objection regarding obedience, Aquinas points out that martyrdom is an act of perfect obedience to the will of God, which mandates that we be willing to give up our bodily lives out of love rather than abandoning Christ when our lives are imperiled. Quoting Philippians 2:8, Aquinas observes that Christ himself gave up his life in perfect obedience: "He humbled himself and become obedient unto death, even death on a cross." Christ's obedience manifests his perfect charity, by which he is obedient in his human nature to his divine Father.

The second and final citation of Philippians 2 in the *secunda pars* is found in question 186, article five, on whether obedience belongs to religious perfection. Aquinas depicts the religious state as a "state of perfection," because the purpose of the religious state is to free the person, inasmuch as this is possible, from all worldly things that might be a hindrance to serving God alone. The goal of the religious state, in other words, consists in the attainment of the spiritual perfection that is perfect charity. In article five, Aquinas argues that voluntary obedience to a superior belongs to the religious state as a state of perfection. The objections include both that all religious do not seem to have to obey (for example, the superior of the community does not seem to be under obedience), and that good works are best loved by God when they are done freely rather than out of compulsion. In the *sed contra*, Aquinas quotes Philippians 2:8, "He humbled himself and became obedient unto death." If Christ became obedient, then it is clear that obedience belongs to the state of perfection, since the requirements of this state are knowable in terms of the imitation of Christ. Christ embraced poverty, chastity, and obedience for the sake of perfect love. Aquinas explains that "by the vow of obedience a man lays himself under the necessity of doing for God's sake certain things that are not pleasing in themselves."[4] In our fallen condition, we do not want to be guided by others, but in the spiritual life above all we need the guidance of those who are proficient. Those who enter religious life freely give up their self-will in order to seek the guidance of God through the direction of their religious superior who is under the direction of the bishop. Christ, for his part, was directly obedient to his Father and thereby showed the necessity of relinquishing self-will.

The two citations of Philippians 2 in the *secunda pars*, then, both have to do with Christ becoming obedient unto death. Both are interested in how we should imitate this obedience. If we are to be fully configured to

---

4. *ST* II-II, q. 186, a. 5, ad 5.

Christ, we will need to embrace martyrdom and the renunciation of self-will. We have to be willing to give up our bodily lives and to give up being in charge. These sacrifices demonstrate perfect love because they show that we love God's will more than the worldly goods to which we tend to cling most firmly, namely our lives and our autonomy. In martyrdom, we love God's will more than bodily life; in obedience, we love God's will more than our own. Indeed, as Aquinas makes clear, martyrdom is a form—the highest form—of obedience. Aquinas's use of Philippians 2 in the *secunda pars* thus expands upon the more ontological use that we found in the *prima pars*, where Aquinas was concerned with Christ's status as God, as human, and as a human in relation to the angels. Here Aquinas is concerned with how Christ became obedient and how we should imitate it. That Christ became obedient belongs to his taking on human nature, for which obedience is a perfection. Thus the moral and the ontological elements of Philippians 2 are related.

THE *TERTIA PARS*

So far we have treated five references to Philippians 2. As we have seen, they are significant both for Aquinas's christology and for our life in imitation of Christ. The focus of the *tertia pars* on Christ's person and work means that the number of references to Philippians 2 is greatly expanded. The first quotation of Philippians 2 in the *tertia pars* occurs in question two, article five, which asks whether Christ possesses the union of body and soul that characterizes other humans. It seems obvious that in order to be fully human, he must possess the union of body and soul. But the problem is that the union of body and soul produces a distinct human hypostasis or person, and Aquinas has already shown that Christ has two natures but only one person, the person of the Word. If he were not one person but two, then there would be no real unity of his divine and human natures, and thus no real incarnation. The unity of his personhood ensures that all his acts are attributable to the Word as their subject. Aquinas begins his *respondeo* by insisting that Christ is fully human, and by quoting Philippians 2:7 in support of Christ's full humanity. As fully human, Christ has a soul that is united to his body. Aquinas explains that this body-soul union does not constitute a distinct human personhood in Christ, because the soul and body are united in Christ not as subsisting in themselves, but as subsisting in the Word. Thus Christ's full humanity does not require that he subsist in exactly the same way that we do. His human nature does not stand on its own, as does ours, but rather his human nature always belongs to the divine Word.

The next two occurrences of Philippians 2 are found in question five, article one. The first objection quotes Philippians 2:7, "being born in the likeness of men," which is the same passage that we have already repeatedly seen quoted. The objection, however, proceeds in a new direction. Instead of presuming that "in the likeness of men" means that Christ is fully human, the objection argues that the Son of God did not assume a true body because his body was only in the likeness of humanity, rather than being human in truth. This position, as Aquinas knows, was that of the Docetists, who denied that Christ had a true body. They also denied that Christ truly suffered and died on the cross. For this reason, in his reply to the objection, Aquinas holds both that "likeness" here means a true human nature (just as to be like in species means to share the same species) and that the validity of this interpretation becomes apparent when Paul continues by saying that Christ endured "death on a cross" (Phil 2:8). Had Christ not possessed a true human body, he could not have undergone bodily death on the cross.

Philippians 2 next appears in question seven, article three, on whether Christ had faith. Aquinas answers that Christ possessed the beatific vision, although this non-conceptual vision did not prevent him from also possessing, in his lower reason, acquired and infused knowledge. Since Christ possessed vision, and since he taught others the content of faith, he had knowledge (rather than faith) about the things that we believe. The second objection, however, argues that Christ had faith both on the grounds that he only taught virtues that he possessed and that Hebrews 12:2 calls him "the pioneer and perfecter of our faith." Aquinas replies by arguing that faith, as a meritorious action, consists in an obedient assent to realities that we do not see. He then draws upon Philippians 2:8, which praises Christ's obedience, to show that Christ had complete obedience and therefore fulfilled perfectly the meritorious aspect of faith, even though he had vision rather than faith.

In question eleven, article two, Aquinas treats an issue related to Christ's infused knowledge. In order to know conceptually the truths he was sent to reveal, Christ needed knowledge that was infused by God. Article two asks whether Christ could know, without turning to phantasms (sense images), the truths that he received by infusion. The key issue is Christ's ability, while on earth, to know angels and the glorified souls in heaven. In the New Testament, Christ shows a knowledge of the angels that far exceeds ours. The second objection, however, quotes Philippians 2:7, "in the likeness of men," and argues that Christ's full humanity means that he, like us, could in his earthly life only know by turning to phantasms. Aquinas replies that because Christ had already received the privilege of beatific vision, his mind could know by turning to phantasms but did not have to do so. Once again, his full humanity does not mean that he is exactly the same as us. In his earthly life, he was able to know by a mode that we will not possess until we see God in eternal life.

Question fourteen, article one contains a reference to Philippians 2:7 in the *respondeo*. The topic of this article is whether the Son should have taken on a human nature with bodily "defects," that is to say with a body possessed of any of the penalties of sin, such as mortality (and even hunger and thirst). Aquinas argues that it was fitting that the incarnate Son endure these penalties for us as part of conquering sin, and furthermore that otherwise it would have seemed as though Christ was not fully human. Along these lines Aquinas quotes Paul's statement that Christ "emptied himself, taking the form of a servant, being born in the likeness of men" (Phil 2:7). In "taking the form of a servant," Christ took on some of the bodily penalties of sin, including bodily vulnerability and mortality. Had he not done so, he could not have been wounded by the nails or died on the cross. Although Christ's humanity is not entirely like ours, therefore, it must be like enough to ours so that he can accomplish his mission and be believable as truly incarnate.

Question sixteen, article one asks whether we can truly say, after the incarnation, that "God is man." The objections argue against it on four grounds: God is the infinite creator whereas a human is a finite creature; the Father and the Son are more united than are the divine and human natures in Christ, yet we do not say that "the Father is the Son"; the soul and body are united in one man, yet we do not say that "the soul is the body"; and since the Father, Son, and Holy Spirit are "God," if we say "God is man" this means that the Father and the Holy Spirit are man, which is untrue. I will not repeat all of Aquinas's replies to these objections, but instead I simply note that Aquinas sets up his answer by quoting in the *sed contra* Philippians 2:6–7, "Though he was in the form of God, [Christ] did not count equality with God a thing to be grasped, but emptied himself, taking the form of a servant, being born in the likeness of man." Christ was both "in the form of God" and in "the form of a servant." He was both God and man. Therefore we can truthfully say that in Christ, God is man. The divine nature is united to a human nature in the person of the divine Son. This expresses things in a way that Paul does not, but that nonetheless is a plausible extension of Paul's words.

The twelfth article of question sixteen addresses a similar topic: whether we can truly say that "Christ, as man, is a person." The first objection points out that all humans are persons. Quoting Philippians 2:7, "being born in the likeness of men," the objection remarks that Christ is a human. Therefore, it seems that he must be a human person. In reply, Aquinas notes that Christ is one person, the divine Word. It would, however, be correct to say "Christ as man is a person" if by this one means that he is the divine person, the Son. Christ is certainly no less a person because he is the person of the Son. Like all humans, he is a person, but he is a divine person. He does not have a distinct temporal personhood arising from his human union of body and soul. "Person" here means acting subject, and Philippians 2:5–11 does indeed depend upon the unity of the acting subject, the divine Son who became flesh.

The next reference to Philippians 2 comes in question nineteen, article three, on whether Christ's human action is meritorious. Question nineteen treats the unity of Christ's operation or action. He has two wills and two operations (human and divine), but these wills/operations are united (even though twofold), rather than being in conflict with each other. It might seem that since Christ is the Son of God, he cannot merit anything for himself by his human actions; all is already due to him. Furthermore, according to Aquinas, Christ already had a beatified soul so that he could intimately know his Father. Thus there hardly seems anything left for him to merit for himself by his actions. In the *sed contra*, however, Aquinas quotes Philippians 2:8–9 in order to show that Christ did indeed merit his own exaltation by his obedient death on a cross: "And being found in human form he humbled himself and became obedient unto death, even death on a cross. Therefore God has highly exalted him and bestowed on him the name which is above every name." Aquinas explains that Christ's obedient love merited for him the reward of bodily glorification, ascension to the right hand of the Father, veneration by all generations, and judiciary power.

The first article of question twenty asks whether Christ is subject to the Father, as is indicated by John 14:28 and 1 Corinthians 15:28. Aquinas answers by drawing upon Augustine's *De Trinitate*, where Augustine contrasts what we can say about Christ "in the form of God" with what we can say about Christ in "the form of a servant." This language comes from Philippians 2:6–7, and so after quoting Augustine in his *sed contra*, Aquinas quotes Philippians 2:7 in his *respondeo*. In his humanity—"the form of a servant"—Christ is indeed subject to the Father. For that matter, in his human nature Christ is also subject to himself (the divine Son), so long as we recognize that Christ's human nature is not a distinct person from the divine Son. Christ's subjection consists in his obedience unto death. In this regard Aquinas, still in the *respondeo*, quotes Philippians 2:8: "He humbled himself and became obedient unto death, even death on the cross." In his human obedience, Christ is subject to the Father.

Aquinas refers again to Philippians 2:7 in the *sed contra* of question twenty-one, article two. This article asks whether Christ prays not only through his human will, but also through his human sensuality (*sensualitas*). Aquinas answers that strictly speaking, no one can pray through their sensuality, since the movement of sensuality does not by itself transcend sensible things. Yet if all that is meant is that Christ's prayer expresses what he desires in his sensuality, then Christ does pray in this way. The reference to Philippians 2:7 serves simply to affirm that Christ, since he shares "in the likeness of men," is fully human and therefore can pray only through his soul, not through the movements of his sensuality.

Philippians 2:7 appears for the same purpose in the fourth objection of question twenty-eight, article one. This article asks whether Mary virginally conceived Christ. Predictably, the fourth objection argues that since Christ is fully human, "in the likeness of men," it follows that he must have been begotten in a fully human way, namely through the intercourse of male and female. Aquinas replies that by God's power, Christ's flesh could be miraculously begotten in Mary without intercourse with a male.

Question thirty-nine, article six treats the descending of the Holy Spirit in the form of a dove at Christ's baptism. The second objection argues that "to descend" implies the mystery of the incarnation, and so the term should not be used of the Holy Spirit's action, because the Holy Spirit did not become incarnate. The objection quotes Philippians 2:7 to sum up Christ's incarnation: the Son "emptied himself, taking the form of a servant." Since the Holy Spirit did not empty himself in this way, it seems inappropriate to describe as a "descent" the Holy Spirit's action at Christ's baptism. In reply, Aquinas emphasizes that the Holy Spirit certainly was not united with the dove in any kind of incarnation, but the description of the Holy Spirit as descending upon Christ in the form of a dove is nonetheless appropriate insofar as the dove symbolized the Holy Spirit coming upon Christ and insofar as grace can be said to descend upon creatures, since grace comes from above.

In question forty-two, article one, Aquinas inquires into whether Christ should have preached to the gentiles, rather than solely to the Jews. In his *respondeo* Aquinas gives four reasons for why it was fitting that Christ preach solely to the Jewish people. The fourth reason is of interest to us, because Aquinas here refers to Philippians 2:8–11. The fourth reason is that Christ, as man, merited power and lordship over the gentiles through his triumphant pasch. Prior to his pasch, he had not yet been exalted in his human nature over all nations, and so he preached only to his own people (with a few exceptions, as Aquinas recognizes). Christ's exaltation over all nations appears clearly in Philippians 2:8–11, where Paul states that because of Christ's obedience unto death, "God has highly exalted him and bestowed on him the name which is above every name, that at the name of Jesus every knee should bow, in heaven and on earth and under the earth, and every tongue confess that Jesus Christ is Lord, to the glory of God the Father." Now that Christ has been exalted so that all nations should worship him, it is fitting that his gospel be preached to the gentiles.

The next five citations of Philippians 2 are ones that I treated above in my chapter on Christ's passion, and so I will only briefly examine them here. In question forty-six, article four, on whether Christ should have suffered on a cross (rather than dying by fire or some other mode of suffering), Aquinas in the *sed contra* quotes Philippians 2:8 as biblical evidence for the fittingness of Christ's dying on a cross. In question forty-seven, article two, on whether Christ died out of obedience, Aquinas again quotes Philippians 2:8 in the *sed contra*, as this passage states precisely that Christ died out of obedience. In question forty-eight, article one, on whether Christ merited our salvation, the *sed contra* cites Philippians 2:9, because Paul here pairs Christ's "obedience unto death" (Phil 2:8) with God's rewarding Christ by exalting him and bestowing "on him the name which is above every name." This *sed contra* goes on to quote Augustine's comments on Philippians 2:9. Lastly, in question forty-nine, article six, Aquinas asks whether Christ, by his passion, merited his own exaltation. Quoting Philippians 2:8 (and 9) in the *sed contra* and in the *respondeo*, Aquinas answers in the affirmative.

In the *tertia pars*, Aquinas quotes Philippians 2 only two more times. The first article of question fifty-two asks whether it was fitting for Christ to descend, at the moment of his death, into hell (*ad infernum*). Aquinas thinks so, because Christ's mission was to free us from all penalty. Prior to Christ's victory over sin on the cross, all souls were in "hell" (including the hell of the just), because only Christ could pay the penalty owed for original sin. At the moment of his death, Christ entered the realm of the dead and freed all souls who only owed the penalty for original sin, thereby drawing them into beatific vision. In this regard Aquinas quotes Philippians 2:10, "That at the name of Jesus every knee should bow, in heaven and on earth and under the earth [*ut in nomine Iesu omne genu flectat caelestium et terrestrium et infernorum*]." The word *infernorum* (under the earth) is taken by Aquinas to signify "hell." It seems possible that Paul meant this as well, insofar as "under the earth" indicates both the realm of the dead and those who are not in heaven. Now that Jesus has become "obedient unto death," he has been exalted and recognized as Lord not only in heaven and on earth, but also in hell, the realm of those dead persons who are separated from God by their sins.

The next and final citation of Philippians 2 occurs in question fifty-nine, article six. The topic of this article is whether Christ's judiciary power extends to the angels. Aquinas answers yes, particularly because Paul tells the Corinthians, "Do you not know that we [Christians] are to judge angels?" (1 Cor 6:3). If mere Christians will judge angels, then certainly Christ must judge angels. In his *respondeo*, Aquinas argues that the humility and obedience of Christ's passion merited the exaltation of Christ's human nature above the angels. He quotes Philippians 2:10 and interprets it to mean that every rational creature will worship Jesus Christ, the incarnate Son. This certainly includes the angels, who will be judged by Christ with regard to the things that they have done in human history. The divine Word judged the angels at the beginning of creation, when some angels chose God and others fell through pride. At the end of time, Jesus Christ, the incarnate Word, will judge both the good angels and the fallen angels a second time, giving them extra rewards or extra punishments for their acts of ministering to humans or tempting humans.

Generally speaking, then, the quotations of Philippians 2:5–11 in the *tertia pars* begin in the early questions with the seventh verse, on Christ being "in the likeness of men," and move in the later questions to verses 8–10.[5] This ordering of the quotations makes good sense, because Philippians 2:7 pertains most closely to Christ's incarnation, which is the topic of the early questions of the *tertia pars*, while verses 8–11 pertain to Christ's cross and exaltation, which are topics found in the later questions of the *tertia pars*'s treatise on Christ. Aquinas uses Philippians 2 to emphasize Christ's true humanity, even though Aquinas also argues that Christ's true humanity differs in certain ways from ours (for example, his personhood is divine, since he is the Word incarnate). Like Augustine, Aquinas makes good use of the distinction in Christ between "form of God" and "form of a servant." He emphasizes that Christ died out of obedience, and that in his human obedience he was subject to the Father. He also observes that he merited both our salvation and his own exaltation. Lastly, he employs Philippians 2 in tracing Christ's descent into hell and exaltation above the angels.

---

5. Verse 2:7 appears in questions 2, 5, 11, 14, 16, 20, 21, 28, and 39, while verses 2:8–10 appear in questions 7, 19, 20, 42, 46, 47, 48, 52, and 59.

CONCLUSION

When Aquinas reads Philippians 2:5–11 in the *Summa theologiae*, he thinks first of Christ's true divinity: Christ "was in the form of God" (Phil 2:6). This is the point made by Aquinas's first reference to Philippians 2:5–11. However, it does not come up much more. Instead Aquinas turns his attention to Christ's true humanity as seen through the prism of Christ's divinity. At least eight times by my count, Aquinas employs Philippians 2:5–11 to investigate Christ's true humanity ("born in the likeness of men"). Not surprisingly, Christ's true humanity does not lend itself to easy understanding. Since Christ is not merely another human being, but rather is the sinless incarnate Word, his humanity differs in important ways from ours. For example, he was virginally conceived, he does not have a distinct human personhood, and he knows the angels in a manner that we cannot in this life. Arguably this is what we should expect of one who "was in the form of God" but "did not count equality with God a thing to be grasped."

At least ten of the references have to do with Christ's human obedience unto death and the exaltation merited by his obedience. Even more than Christ's true divinity and true humanity, the arc of obedience and exaltation—passion and resurrection—is what interests Aquinas about Philippians 2:5–11. Certainly, for Aquinas Christ's *kenosis* is not an abandoning of divine attributes in order to become incarnate. Yet Christ's *kenosis* does involve an obedience to the Father that constitutes a free subjection of himself, in his humanity. Christ's self-emptying goes all the way to martyrdom, to a perfect sacrificial obedience to God out of love for God and neighbor. By this obedience, Christ does not reveal that his eternal condition, as the Son, is one of obedience, let alone of any form of abandonment or alienation. Rather, Christ shares our human condition, including the mortality that we endure as a consequence of original sin, so as to heal us from within and to merit his own exaltation and ours. He renounces self-will in favor of following the will of God. He descends into death and hell so as to lead us out of death and hell and to enable us to share in the divine life. His exaltation reveals his glory as the incarnate Son, a glory of perfect love, and he becomes for us the path to eternal life.

His *kenosis* is indeed a stunning one: the eternal Son takes on flesh, subjection, mortality, suffering, and death. Yet, as Aquinas reads it, this self-emptying would be misunderstood if we failed to interpret it in light of his meritorious exaltation, which show us the eternal form of *kenotic* love. With all nations and with the angels, let us worship him as Lord of love and merciful Judge, hastening to confess joyfully that "Jesus Christ is Lord, to the glory of God the Father" (Phil 2:11).

CONCLUSION

BOTH as a wisdom derived from God's teaching and as a body of truth "acquired by study,"[1] sacred doctrine involves the teaching of Paul. In the chapters of this book, we have asked exactly how Paul's inspired teaching informs the sacred doctrine or "sacred science" that Aquinas sets forth in the *Summa theologiae*.[2] By this point, we can say that to read the *Summa theologiae* means to have the words of Paul ringing in one's ears. Even when Aquinas's use of Paul seems minor, for example when most of his Pauline citations serve to formulate objections, examination of a whole treatise consistently shows that Aquinas succeeds in including the Pauline texts most theologically relevant to that treatise. Although there are a few areas within the *Summa* in which Paul's voice is absent, nonetheless his voice can be rightly said to resonate throughout the whole work.

Just to give some examples taken from our chapters, Paul's voice drives the *sacra doctrina* about God's knowledge, will, and predestination; about our knowledge of God in glory; about the Son as image of the Father; about the missions of the Son and Spirit; about goodness of the Mosaic law and its fulfillment by Christ (and by charity); about the election of Israel; about the Decalogue and the natural law; about our knowledge of sin; about biblical typology; about the role of the angels; about the timing of the Mosaic law; about priesthood and sacrifice; about the love of God that comes through the Holy Spirit; about God's grace as causing eternal life; about the ongoing presence of concupiscence; about grace's

---

1. *ST* I, q. 1, a. 6, ad 3; cf. *ST* I, q. 1, a. 6, ad 1.
2. For "sacred science," see *ST* I, q. 1, a. 7; cf. *ST* I, q. 1, aa. 2, 8.

justifying and sanctifying effects; about the diversity of graces received by the members of Christ's body; about grace as sheer gift rather than based upon our merit; about our knowledge of whether we are in a state of grace; about grace and free will; about the merited reward of graced actions; about prayer and interior sacrifice; about the worship that we owe to God; about the Lord's prayer; about the suitability of vows and oaths; about tithing; about the redemptive and reconciling power of Jesus's passion; about God's manifestation of his mercy, love, and humility through Jesus's passion; about the timing of Jesus's passion; about whether God suffered on the cross; about whether Jesus suffered freely out of obedient love; about whether the Father delivered his innocent Son to die; about the relationship of Jesus's cross to his resurrection and ascension; about whether Jesus's cross delivers us from Satan and from the punishment of sin; about baptism's relationship to Christ's passion and to faith; about the trinitarian formula of baptism; about the unity of baptism; about whether anyone can be saved without baptism; about whether baptism cleanses us from all sins and incorporates us into Christ's body; and about why we suffer and die after baptism.

We have demonstrated, then, that Paul deeply informs the *Summa theologiae*'s exposition of *sacra doctrina*, both in terms of the realities that Aquinas treats and in terms of how he understands these realities. Yet Aquinas does not seek to retrieve the historical Paul. Aquinas freely employs Paul to address doctrinal questions and ecclesial practices that arose long after Paul's day. As an ecclesial reality rooted in divine revelation, *sacra doctrina* requires this engagement with the church's ongoing mediation of the realities revealed in scripture. It is thus appropriate that Aquinas uses Paul to help him engage post-Pauline ecclesial and theological debates.

My first chapter focused on Aquinas's use of Paul in his treatise on the triune God. The forty-two questions of this treatise contain ninety-three citations of Paul, fifty-two of which come from Romans and 1 Corinthians. As we saw, certain questions possess an especially Pauline flavor: most notably, question twenty-three on predestination has nineteen Pauline citations, and question twelve on our knowledge of God's essence has nine Pauline citations. Rather than seeking to understand how Paul understood the triune God, Aquinas reads Paul's words along the doctrinal lines formulated by the early church councils. Yet the Paul whose presence is felt is nonetheless, I think, the historical Paul. Aquinas employs Paul most extensively in the areas that concerned Paul himself: God's knowledge and will, predestination, our orientation toward glorified knowledge of God, adoptive filiation, the Son as the Father's image, and the missions of the Son and Holy Spirit.

Aquinas's four questions on Christ's passion are best known for his enumeration of the ways in which Christ's passion causes our salvation: by merit (or love), satisfaction, sacrifice, and redemption. Aquinas also examines issues such as whether the Father delivered up his incarnate Son to death and the relationship of Christ's passion to his resurrection. In these four questions of the *Summa*, Aquinas quotes Paul fifty-nine times. Certain passages have a particularly important role, such as Romans 3:24–25 and Philippians 2:8–10. Guided by Paul, Aquinas emphasizes that the Son of God freely and lovingly fulfilled God's covenants with Israel by paying the penalty of sin on the cross. United to Christ by faith and charity, we share not only in his cross but also in his resurrection. These four questions arguably represent Aquinas at his most Pauline.

The four questions on baptism contain eighty-nine Pauline citations, including thirty-seven citations of Romans. Again, the questions that Aquinas asks derive almost entirely from the controversies and debates of later times rather than from Paul. The relationship of the water to the words, and what words ought to be pronounced in baptism, were not Pauline issues, even though Paul certainly insisted on both water and words. Similarly, rebaptism does not seem to have been an issue in Paul's communities, although one can understand why it soon became an issue. Paul did not have canon law with its regulations about who can baptize and when, nor did Paul articulate a distinction between *sacramentum*, *res*, and *sacramentum et res*. Aquinas's labor therefore consists largely in drawing out the implications of Paul's teaching about baptism for the purpose of answering later controversies and concerns. For this task, he relies heavily upon certain pivotal verses, such as Ephesians 4:5 and 5:26, Romans 6:3–4, and Galatians 3:27–28. Like Paul, Aquinas presents baptism as an incorporation into Christ's death and resurrection. Baptism frees us from sin and gives us new life in Christ.

The seven questions of Aquinas's treatment of the Mosaic law quote Paul a total of 116 times. Drawing especially from Romans 7–8, Aquinas nicely balances Paul's emphasis on the goodness of the Mosaic law with Paul's insistence that Christ has brought the Mosaic law to the end or goal for which God gave the law. The largest number of Pauline quotations in any of the questions on the Mosaic law occurs in the question on reasons for the ceremonial precepts. Aquinas employs Paul repeatedly to underscore the typological character of the Mosaic law: in this regard, 1 Corinthians 9–10, Colossians 2, and Hebrews 10 come to the fore. The community of the messiah is organized not by the Torah but by the fulfillment of the Torah in Christ and by the sending of the Holy Spirit. Along these lines, Aquinas interprets such passages as 2 Corinthians 3:6, "the written code kills, but the Spirit gives life," and Ephesians 2:15, "by abolishing in his flesh the law of commandments and ordinances, that he might create in himself one new man in place of two." By making a careful study of the precepts of the Mosaic law, Aquinas shows that the law retains its value for Christian reflection on Jesus Christ and the requirements of holiness.

In the six questions of Aquinas's exposition of grace, Pauline citations appear seventy times. Not surprisingly, almost half of the citations—thirty-four out of seventy—are from Romans. The questions that Aquinas asks—whether grace puts something new in the soul, whether grace is a quality of the soul, and so forth—are speculative questions proper to sacred doctrine rather than to Paul's letters. Yet, like Paul, Aquinas emphasizes that the life of grace in us is God's sheer gift and that God's grace justifies us and gives us eternal life. Relying especially upon Romans 5 and 8, Aquinas shows that grace superabundantly flows to us from the work of Jesus Christ and the outpouring of the Holy Spirit into our hearts. Indebted to 2 Timothy 4:8, 1 Corinthians 3:8, and Galatians 5:6, Aquinas makes clear that grace makes us into a new creation so that, by the Holy Spirit working in us, we can merit the reward that God freely wills to give us. Thus Aquinas's exposition clarifies post-Pauline discussions of grace without muting Paul's voice.

The virtue of religion might seem at first glance to be almost an anti-Pauline concept. Its roots are in the Greek and Roman philosophers rather than in Paul. For Paul, nonetheless, certain actions should characterize the relationship of all human beings to God. Among these actions are prayer, adoration, sacrifice, vows, tithes, and oaths. In his nine questions on the virtue of religion, Aquinas treats these actions and cites Paul fifty-six times. Fourteen of these citations come in the question on prayer: Paul's exhortation to "pray constantly" (1 Thess 5:17) and Paul's requests that his churches pray for him are especially important for Aquinas. Likewise, in his question on tithing, Aquinas emphasizes Paul's requirement in 1 Corinthians 9 that churches meet the material needs of their pastors. The Corinthian correspondence also assists Aquinas's treatment of vows, and Hebrews 6:16 provides the foundation for Aquinas's theology of oaths. Neither Paul nor Aquinas envisions an extant natural religion. Indeed, the opposite is the case: people have failed to pray to the true God, refused to offer interior and external sacrifice in gratitude to God, made and kept evil vows, failed to support materially the worship of God, and broken their oaths.

When Aquinas takes up Romans 1:20 in the *Summa theologiae*, the verse speaks not only to the question of whether we can know God from created things, but indeed to the very character of human knowing through sensible things and to the goodness of this human mode of knowing. Of the sixteen citations of this verse that we find in the *Summa*, seven appear in the *prima pars*, seven in the *secunda pars*, and two in the *tertia pars*. Especially in the *prima pars*, Aquinas employs the verse to make clear that the source of our alienation from God is not our material constitution. The angels know God without sensible signs, but they are not thereby less prone than we are to rebel against God. The *secunda pars* highlights the fact that faith, contemplation, and even rapture require knowing God through created things. Lastly, in the *tertia pars*, Aquinas uses Romans 1:20 to show how fitting it is that God redeems us through the incarnation of the Son of God and through sacramental signs. The fact that we can know God through sensible things, even if we often cleave to these sensible things rather than rising to God, makes sense of why God comes to us indirectly as the incarnate Son and through material sacraments, rather than simply awakening us "directly" to his invisible presence. Tracking Romans 1:20 through the *Summa theologiae* reveals its importance not only as a warrant for the demonstration of God's existence, but also as a guide to the very pattern of salvation.

First Corinthians 13 famously has much to teach about faith and love, and Aquinas employs its teachings extensively within his speculative exposition. The thirteen verses of this chapter appear a total of sixty-nine times in the *Summa theologiae*, including fifty-four times in the *secunda pars*. Aquinas uses 1 Corinthians 13 to identify the three "theological virtues," to reflect on how angels can be said to "speak," to contrast the imperfection of this life with the perfection that we will experience in the life to come, and to explore the relationship of faith and charity. First Corinthians 13 also helps Aquinas to reflect upon the fact that the new law itself will pass away; not in the sense of being discarded, but in the sense of being fulfilled by the fullness of the state of glory. Similarly, 1 Corinthians 13 contributes to reflection on the differences between faith, prophecy, and contemplation. Even as Aquinas's speculative thought addresses post-Pauline concerns, it remains rooted in the teachings of Paul regarding faith, charity, and the perfection of both that we will experience in eternal life.

Philippians 2:5–11 is central to contemporary christology. It appears twenty-seven times in the *Summa theologiae*, and the great majority of Aquinas's quotations of this passage appear in the *tertia pars*, indicating its value for Aquinas's christology. Aquinas, like the church fathers, uses the passage to confirm Christ's full humanity and full divinity rather than to argue (as is sometimes the case today) that the Son kenotically strips himself of divine attributes in order to become human. Aquinas most often cites verses 7–8, which he uses to explore Christ's equality with God, Christ's human "form of a servant," and Christ's obedience unto death, an obedience that consists in perfect charity rather than intra-divine subjection. Drawing on verses 9–11, Aquinas also emphasizes that Christ's obedience merited the reward of exaltation. Aquinas's speculative reflection takes its bearings from Paul's portrait of the pre-existent divine Son who took on flesh, died on the cross out of obedience, and was raised from the dead and exalted to the right hand of the Father.

Beyond generalizations about the biblical richness of Aquinas's theology, I hope that these chapters have shown how sacred doctrine can be both profoundly Pauline and profoundly attuned to post-Pauline discussions. Although some of the *Summa*'s treatises have less Pauline influence than the treatises we have surveyed, it remains the case that 322 of the 393

Conclusion

questions contained in the *secunda* and *tertia pars* cite Paul (as do 67 of the 119 questions in the *prima pars*). The characteristic Pauline emphases are fully present in Aquinas's *Summa theologiae*. I have also argued that sacred doctrine requires that Paul be read in light of the theological and ecclesial debates of the centuries that come after Paul. These debates belong to the lived reality of the development of doctrine and practice in the church, the very context in which the historical Paul would have expected his voice to be heard. Aquinas thereby reads Paul in a Pauline manner, committed to the presence of the Holy Spirit guiding the church. Aquinas's Paul is not cut off from the witness of the fathers, the liturgy, and even canon law.

Nonetheless, if Paul's words are often employed in debates that were unknown to Paul, how is it that we still have Paul's voice? If the appeal to Paul pays almost no attention to historical questions about what Paul himself actually thought or to the contexts behind Paul's own letters, would it not seem that the layers of the theological tradition have muted Paul? This problem seems exacerbated by the fact that I have not differentiated (since Aquinas did not differentiate) between "authentic" and "inauthentic" Pauline letters, even including Hebrews.

My research on Paul in the *Summa theologiae* cannot resolve the familiar concerns about whether the church's creedal and theological traditions obscure the voices of scripture.[3] Much depends upon whether one thinks that one properly hears the Holy Spirit speaking through Paul in the context of the living church about which Paul taught so beautifully, and to which he devoted his life in Christ. Nonetheless, I have tried to show that Paul's voice does in fact emerge in the *Summa theologiae* as Paul's, even if some elements specific to the Second Temple period are obscured. Aqui-

---

3. For such concerns see, e.g., N. T. Wright, "Response to Richard Hays," in *Jesus, Paul and the People of God: A Theological Dialogue with N. T. Wright*, ed. Nicholas Perrin and Richard B. Hays (Downers Grove, Ill.: IVP Academic, 2011), 63; Ben Witherington III, *The Problem with Evangelical Theology: Testing the Exegetical Foundations of Calvinism, Dispensationalism and Wesleyanism* (Waco, Tex.: Baylor University Press, 2005); James F. McGrath, *The Only True God: Early Christian Monotheism in Its Jewish Context* (Chicago: University of Illinois Press, 2009); and James L. Kugel, *How to Read the Bible: A Guide to Scripture, Then and Now* (New York: Free Press, 2007). See also, from a different perspective, Michael C. Legaspi, *The Death of Scripture and the Rise of Biblical Studies* (Oxford: Oxford University Press, 2010).

nas's Paul has received "the Spirit which is from God, that we might understand the gifts bestowed on us by God" (1 Cor 2:12). This Paul confesses God's "invisible nature, namely, his eternal power and deity" (Rom 1:20). For this Paul, the Son "is the image of the invisible God, the first-born of all creation; for in him all things were created … all things were created through him and for him" (Col 1:15–16). The Paul of Aquinas holds that "the law is holy, and the commandment is holy and just and good" (Rom 7:12), that "all who rely on works of the law are under a curse" (Gal 3:10), and that "neither circumcision nor uncircumcision counts for anything, but a new creation" (Gal 6:15). This Paul explains eschatologically that we "are justified by his grace as a gift, through the redemption which is in Christ Jesus" (Rom 3:24) and notes that "if it is by grace, it is no longer on the basis of works; otherwise grace would no longer be grace" (Rom 11:6). The graces that we receive in the Church show that "grace was given to each of us according to the measure of Christ's gift" (Eph 4:7). This Paul urges the cultivation of prayer by means of "supplications, prayers, intercessions, and thanksgivings" (1 Tim 2:1), exhorts us to "pray constantly" (1 Thess 5:17), and asks that "you also must help us by prayer, so that many will give thanks on our behalf for the blessing granted us in answer to many prayers" (2 Cor 1:11). This Paul emphasizes that the ministers of the gospel deserve to earn their living by their ministry: "If we have sown spiritual good among you, is it too much if we reap your material benefits?" (1 Cor 9:11). This Paul requires believers "to present your bodies as a living sacrifice, holy and acceptable to God, which is your spiritual worship" (Rom 12:1). He recognizes a special place for those who intentionally remain unmarried so as to devote themselves to "the affairs of the Lord, how to be holy in body and spirit" (1 Cor 7:34) and he recognizes that humans "swear by a greater than themselves" (Heb 6:16). This Paul gives thanks that "God shows his love for us in that while we were yet sinners Christ died for us" (Rom 5:8). As he says, "Christ redeemed us from the curse of the law, having become a curse for us" (Gal 3:13); Christ "humbled himself and became obedient unto death, even death on a cross" (Phil 2:8); Christ "endured the cross, despising the shame, and is seated at the right hand of God" (Heb 12:2). This Paul confesses "one Lord, one faith, one baptism" (Eph 4:5) and teaches that "all of us who have been baptized into Christ

Conclusion

Jesus were baptized into his death" (Rom 6:3). He states, "For as many of you as were baptized into Christ have put on Christ" (Gal 3:27).

Aquinas does not think that Paul's words can be rightly understood outside the critical context of the church's faith and practice, a context that he engages at the same time as he reflects speculatively upon the realities proclaimed by Paul. Like Paul, Aquinas awaits the perfection of *sacra doctrina* in the final consummation. It thus seems appropriate to end this study with Paul's words of eschatological expectation, so meaningful to Aquinas: "For now we see in a mirror dimly, but then face to face. Now I know in part; then I shall understand fully, even as I have been fully understood. So faith, hope, love abide, these three; but the greatest of these is love" (1 Cor 13:12–13).

WORKS CITED

Aquinas, Thomas. *Summa Theologica*. Translated by the Fathers of the English Dominican Province. 5 vols. Westminster, Md.: Christian Classics, 1981.
Armitage, J. Mark. "Why Didn't Jesus Write a Book? Aquinas on the Teaching of Christ." *New Blackfriars* 89 (2008): 337–53.
Augustine. *Confessions*. Translated by Henry Chadwick. Oxford: Oxford University Press, 1991.
Babcock, William S., ed. *Paul and the Legacies of Paul*. Dallas, Tex.: Southern Methodist University Press, 1990.
Baglow, Christopher T. "*Modus et Forma*": *A New Approach to the Exegesis of Saint Thomas Aquinas with an Application to the* Lectura super Epistolam ad Ephesios. Rome: Pontifical Biblical Institute Press, 2002.
———. "Sacred Scripture and Sacred Doctrine in Saint Thomas Aquinas." In *Aquinas on Doctrine: A Critical Introduction*, edited by Thomas Weinandy, OFM. Cap., Daniel Keating, and John Yocum, 1–25. New York: T. and T. Clark, 2004.
Bird, Michael F. *Are You the One Who Is to Come? The Historical Jesus and the Messianic Question*. Grand Rapids, Mich.: Baker Academic, 2009.
Blankenhorn, Bernhard. "The Instrumental Causality of the Sacraments: Thomas Aquinas and Louis-Marie Chauvet." *Nova et Vetera* 4 (2006): 255–93.
———. "The Place of Romans 6 in Aquinas's Doctrine of Sacramental Causality." In *Ressourcement Thomism: Sacred Doctrine, the Sacraments, and the Moral Life*, edited by Reinhard Hütter and Matthew Levering, 136–49. Washington, D.C.: The Catholic University of America Press, 2010.
Boda, Mark J. *A Severe Mercy: Sin and Its Remedy in the Old Testament*. Winona Lake, Ind.: Eisenbrauns, 2009.
Boguslawski, Steven. "Thomas Aquinas." In *Reading Romans through the Centuries: From the Early Church to Karl Barth*, edited by Jeffrey P. Greenman and Timothy Larsen, 81–99. Grand Rapids, Mich.: Brazos Press, 2005.
———. *Thomas Aquinas on the Jews: Insights into His Commentary on Romans 9–11*. New York: Paulist Press, 2008.
Boyle, John F. "On the Relation of St. Thomas's Commentary on Romans to the *Summa*

theologiae." In *Reading Paul with St. Thomas Aquinas*, edited by Matthew Levering and Michael Dauphinais, 75–81. Washington, D.C.: The Catholic University of America Press, 2012.

———. "St. Thomas Aquinas and Sacred Scripture." *Pro Ecclesia* 4 (1995): 92–104.

———. "The Twofold Division of St. Thomas's Christology in the *Tertia Pars*." *The Thomist* 60 (1996): 439–47.

Callan, Charles J. "The Bible in the *Summa Theologica* of St. Thomas Aquinas." *Catholic Biblical Quarterly* 9 (1947): 33–47.

Campbell, Douglas A. *The Deliverance of God: An Apocalyptic Rereading of Justification in Paul.* Grand Rapids, Mich.: Eerdmans, 2009.

Candler, Peter M., Jr. "Reading Immemorially: The *Quaestio* and the Paragraph in the Summa Theologiae." *American Catholic Philosophical Quarterly* 78 (2004): 531–57.

Cessario, Romanus. "Aquinas on Christian Salvation." In *Aquinas on Doctrine: A Critical Introduction*, edited by Thomas G. Weinandy, OFM Cap., Daniel A. Keating, and John P. Yocum, 117–37. London: T. and T. Clark International, 2004.

———. *Christian Faith and the Theological Life.* Washington, D.C.: The Catholic University of America Press, 1996.

———. *The Godly Image: Christ and Salvation in Catholic Thought from Anselm to Aquinas.* Petersham, Mass.: St. Bede's Publications, 1990.

———. *Introduction to Moral Theology.* Washington, D.C.: The Catholic University of America Press, 2001.

———. "Is Aquinas's *Summa* Only about Grace?" In *Ordo Sapientiae et Amoris*, edited by C.-J. Pinto de Oliveira, OP, 197–209. Fribourg: Éditions universitaires, 1993.

Chenu, M.-D. *Toward Understanding Saint Thomas.* Translated by A.-M. Landry, OP, and D. Hughes, OP. Chicago: Henry Regnery, 1964.

Congar, Yves. *I Believe in the Holy Spirit.* Translated by David Smith. New York: Crossroad, 1997.

Cooper, Adam G. "Degrading the Body, Suppressing the Truth: Aquinas on Romans 1:18–25." In *Reading Romans with St. Thomas Aquinas*, edited by Matthew Levering and Michael Dauphinais, 113–26. Washington, D.C.: The Catholic University of America Press, 2012.

Cottier, Georges. "La vertu de religion." *Revue Thomiste* 106 (2006): 335–52.

Cousar, Charles B. *A Theology of the Cross: The Death of Jesus in the Pauline Letters.* Minneapolis, Minn.: Fortress Press, 1990.

Crowe, Frederick E. and Robert M, eds. Doran. *Grace and Freedom: Operative Grace in the Thought of St. Thomas Aquinas.* Toronto: University of Toronto Press, 2000.

Curran, John W. "The Thomistic Concept of Devotion." *The Thomist* 2 (1940): 410–43.

Dauphinais, Michael. "Christ and the Metaphysics of Baptism in the *Summa Theologiae* and the Commentary on John." In *Rediscovering Aquinas and the Sacraments: Studies in Sacramental Theology*, edited by Matthew Levering and Michael Dauphinais, 14–27. Chicago: Hillenbrand Books, 2009.

Dauphinais, Michael, Barry David, and Matthew Levering, eds. *Aquinas the Augustinian*. Washington, D.C.: The Catholic University of America Press, 2007.

Domanyi, Thomas. *Der Römerbriefkommentar des Thomas von Aquin: Ein Beitrag zur Untersuchung seiner Auslegungsmethoden*. Bern: Lang, 1979.

Donneaud, Henry. *Théologie et intelligence de la foi au XIIIe siècle*. Les Plans, Switzerland: Parole et Silence, 2006.

Donohoo, Lawrence J. "The Nature and Grace of *Sacra Doctrina* in St. Thomas's *Super Boetium de Trinitate*." *The Thomist* 63 (1999): 343–402.

Elders, Leo J. *Sur les traces de saint Thomas d'Aquin théologien. Étude de ses commentaires bibliques. Thèmes théologiques*. Translated by Véronique Pommeret. Paris: Parole et Silence, 2009.

———. "Aquinas on Holy Scripture as the Medium of Divine Revelation." In *La doctrine de la revelation divine de saint Thomas d'Aquin*, edited by Leo J. Elders, 132–52. Vatican City: Libreria Editrice Vaticana, 1990.

Emery, Gilles. "Biblical Exegesis and the Speculative Doctrine of the Trinity in St. Thomas Aquinas's *Commentary on John*." In *Reading John with St. Thomas Aquinas: Theological Exegesis and Speculative Theology*, edited by Michael Dauphinais and Matthew Levering, 23–61. Washington, D.C.: The Catholic University of America Press, 2005.

———. "Contemporary Questions about God." *Nova et Vetera* 8 (2010): 799–811.

———. "The Holy Spirit in Aquinas's Commentary on Romans." In *Reading Romans with St. Thomas Aquinas*, edited by Matthew Levering and Michael Dauphinais, 127–62. Washington, D.C.: The Catholic University of America Press, 2012.

———. *The Trinitarian Theology of Saint Thomas Aquinas*. Translated by Francesca Aran Murphy. Oxford: Oxford University Press, 2007.

———. *The Trinity: An Introduction to Catholic Doctrine on the Triune God*. Translated by Matthew Levering. Washington, D.C.: The Catholic University of America Press, 2011.

———. *Trinity, Church, and the Human Person: Thomistic Essays*. Naples, Fla.: Sapientia Press, 2007.

———. *Trinity in Aquinas*. Ypsilanti, Mich.: Sapientia Press, 2003.

Ernst, Cornelius. "Metaphor and Ontology in *Sacra Doctrina*." *The Thomist* 38 (1974): 403–25.

Evans, C. Stephen, ed. *Exploring Kenotic Christology: The Self-Emptying of God*. Vancouver, British Columbia: Regent College Publishing, 2006.

Fee, Gordon D. *God's Empowering Presence: The Holy Spirit in the Letters of Paul*. Peabody, Mass.: Hendrickson, 1994.

Feser, Edward. *Aquinas: A Beginner's Guide*. Oxford: Oneworld, 2009.

Fitzmyer, Joseph A. *The One Who Is to Come*. Grand Rapids, Mich.: Eerdmans, 2007.

Friedman, Richard Elliott. *Who Wrote the Bible?* 2nd edition. New York: HarperCollins, 1997.

Gilby, Thomas. "Appendix II. The *Summa* and the Bible." In St. Thomas Aquinas, *Summa theologiae*. Volume 1 (Ia.1): *Christian Theology*, 133–39. Cambridge: Cambridge University Press, 2006.

Goris, Harm. "Theology and Theory of the Word in Aquinas: Understanding Augustine by Innovating Aristotle." In *Aquinas the Augustinian*, edited by Michael Dauphinais, Barry David, and Matthew Levering, 62–78. Washington, D.C.: The Catholic University of America Press, 2007.

Gorman, Michael J. *Cruciformity: Paul's Narrative Spirituality of the Cross*. Grand Rapids, Mich.: Eerdmans, 2001.

Greenman, Jeffrey P., and Timothy Larsen, eds. *Reading Romans through the Centuries: From the Early Church to Karl Barth*. Grand Rapids, Mich.: Brazos Press, 2005.

Guggenheim, Antoine. *Jésus Christ, grand prêtre de l'ancienne et de la nouvelle Alliance. Étude du Commentaire de saint Thomas d'Aquin sur l'Épître aux Hébreux*. Paris: Parole et Silence, 2004.

Harkins, Franklin T. "*Primus Doctor Iudaeorum*: Moses as Theological Master in the *Summa Theologiae* of Thomas Aquinas." *The Thomist* 75 (2011): 65–94.

Hankey, W. J. *God in Himself: Aquinas' Doctrine of God as Expounded in the Summa Theologiae*. Oxford: Oxford University Press, 1987.

Hayen, André. *Saint Thomas d'Aquin et la vie de l'église*. Louvain: Publications Universitaires, 1952.

Hays, Richard B. *Echoes of the Scripture in the Letters of Paul*. New Haven, Conn.: Yale University Press, 1989.

———. *The Moral Vision of the New Testament: Community, Cross, New Creation: A Contemporary Introduction to New Testament Ethics*. New York: HarperCollins, 1996.

Hegel, Georg W. F. *The Philosophy of History*. Translated by J. Sibree. Buffalo, N.Y.: Prometheus Books, 1991.

Hertling, Georg Graf von. "Augustinus-citate bei Thomas von Aquin." In *Sitzungsberichte der philosophisch-philologischen und der historischen Klasse der Königlichen Bayerischen Akademie der Wissenschaften zu München*, 535–602. Munich: 1904.

Holmes, Jeremy. "St. Thomas's Commentary on Philippians 2:5–11: A New Translation with Introduction and Notes." In *Wisdom and Holiness, Science and Scholarship: Essays in Honor of Matthew L. Lamb*, edited by Michael Dauphinais and Matthew Levering, 109–41. Naples, Fla.: Sapientia Press, 2007.

Hood, John Y. B. *Aquinas and the Jews*. Philadelphia: University of Pennsylvania Press, 1995.

Huizenga, Leroy A. *The New Isaac: Tradition and Intertextuality in the Gospel of Matthew*. Leiden: Brill, 2009.

Hütter, Reinhard. "St. Thomas on Grace and Free Will in the *Initium Fidei*: The Surpassing Augustinian Synthesis." *Nova et Vetera* 5 (2007): 521–53.

———. "Transubstantiation Revisited: *Sacra Doctrina*, Dogma, and Metaphysics." In *Ressourcement Thomism: Sacred Doctrine, the Sacraments, and the Moral Life*, edited by Reinhard Hütter and Matthew Levering, 21–79. Washington, D.C.: The Catholic University of America Press, 2010.

Hütter, Reinhard, and Matthew Levering, eds. *Ressourcement Thomism: Sacred Doctrine, the Sacraments, and the Moral Life*. Washington, D.C.: The Catholic University of America Press, 2010.

Janowski, Bernd, and Peter Stuhlmacher, eds. *The Suffering Servant: Isaiah 53 in Jewish and Christian Sources*. Translated by Daniel P. Bailey. Grand Rapids, Mich.: Eerdmans, 2004.

Jenkins, Allan K., and Patrick Preston. *Biblical Scholarship and the Church: A Sixteenth-Century Crisis of Authority*. Aldershot: Ashgate, 2007.

John Paul II. *Fides et Ratio*. In *The Encyclicals of John Paul II*, edited by J. Michael Miller, CSB, 849–913. Huntington, Ind.: Our Sunday Visitor, 2001.

Johnson, Luke Timothy. *The Writings of the New Testament: An Interpretation*. Philadelphia: Fortress Press, 1986.

Johnson, Mark F., "God's Knowledge in Our Frail Mind: The Thomistic Model of Theology." *Angelicum* 76 (1999): 25–45.

Kaminsky, Joel S. *Yet I Loved Jacob: Reclaiming the Biblical Concept of Election*. Nashville, Tenn.: Abingdon Press, 2007.

Kass, Leon R. *The Beginning of Wisdom: Reading Genesis*. New York: Free Press, 2003.

Keating, James F., and Thomas Joseph White, eds. *Divine Impassibility and the Mystery of Human Suffering*. Grand Rapids, Mich.: Eerdmans, 2009.

Keaty, Anthony. "The Demands of Sacred Doctrine on 'Beginners.'" *New Blackfriars* 84 (2003): 500–509.

Kries, Douglas. "Thomas Aquinas and the Politics of Moses." *Review of Politics* 52 (1990): 84–104.

Kugel, James L. *How to Read the Bible: A Guide to Scripture, Then and Now*. New York: Free Press, 2007.

Kühn, Ulrich. *Via caritatis: Theologie des Gesetzes bei Thomas von Aquin*. Göttingen: Vandenhoeck and Ruprecht, 1965.

Legaspi, Michael C. *The Death of Scripture and the Rise of Biblical Studies*. Oxford: Oxford University Press, 2010.

Levenson, Jon D. *The Death and Resurrection of the Beloved Son: The Transformation of Child Sacrifice in Judaism and Christianity*. New Haven, Conn.: Yale University Press, 1993.

Levering, Matthew. "Aquinas." In *The Blackwell Companion to Paul*, edited by Stephen Westerholm, 361–74. Oxford: Wiley-Blackwell, 2011.

———. *The Betrayal of Charity: The Sins that Sabotage Divine Love*. Waco, Tex.: Baylor University Press, 2011.

———. *Christ's Fulfillment of Torah and Temple: Salvation according to Thomas Aquinas*. Notre Dame, Ind.: University of Notre Dame Press, 2002.

———. "God and Greek Philosophy in Contemporary Biblical Scholarship." *Journal of Theological Interpretation* 4 (2010): 169–85.

———. "A Note on Scripture in the *Summa Theologiae*." *New Blackfriars* 90 (2009): 652–58.

———. "Ordering Wisdom: Aquinas, the Old Testament, and *Sacra Doctrina*." In *Ressourcement Thomism: Sacred Doctrine, the Sacraments, and the Moral Life*, edited by

Reinhard Hütter and Matthew Levering, 80–91. Washington, D.C.: The Catholic University of America Press, 2010.

———. *Sacrifice and Community: Jewish Offering and Christian Eucharist*. Oxford: Blackwell, 2005.

———. *Scripture and Metaphysics: Aquinas and the Renewal of Trinitarian Theology*. Oxford: Blackwell, 2004.

Levering, Matthew, and Michael Dauphinais, eds. *Reading John with St. Thomas Aquinas: Theological Exegesis and Speculative Theology*. Washington, D.C.: The Catholic University of America Press, 2005.

———. *Reading Paul with St. Thomas Aquinas*. Washington, D.C.: The Catholic University of America Press, 2012.

———. *Rediscovering Aquinas and the Sacraments: Studies in Sacramental Theology*. Chicago: Hillenbrand Books, 2009.

Lonergan, Bernard. *Grace and Freedom: Operative Grace in the Thought of St. Thomas Aquinas*, edited by Frederick E. Crowe and Robert M. Doran. Toronto: University of Toronto Press, 2000.

Lottin, Odon. *L'âme du culture. La vertu de religion d'après s. Thomas d'Aquin*. Louvain: Bureau des oeuvres liturgiques, 1920.

MacDonald, Margaret Y. *Colossians and Ephesians*. Collegeville, Minn.: Liturgical Press, 2000.

Madigan, Kevin. *The Passions of Christ in High-Medieval Thought: An Essay on Christological Development*. Oxford: Oxford University Press, 2007.

Malloy, Christopher J. "Thomas on the Order of Love and Desire: A Development of Doctrine." *The Thomist* 71 (2007): 65–87.

Mandrella, Isabelle. *Das Isaac-Opfer: Historisch-systematische Untersuchung zu Rationalität und Wandelbarkeit des Naturrechts in der mittelalterlichen Lehre vom natürlichen Gesetz*. Münster: Aschendorff Verlag, 2002.

Marshall, Bruce D. "Aquinas the Augustinian? On the Uses of Augustine in Aquinas's Trinitarian Theology." In *Aquinas the Augustinian*, edited by Michael Dauphinais, Barry David, and Matthew Levering, 41–61. Washington, D.C.: The Catholic University of America Press, 2007.

———. "*Beatus vir*: Aquinas, Romans 4, and the Role of 'Reckoning' in Justification." In *Reading Romans with St. Thomas Aquinas*, edited by Matthew Levering and Michael Dauphinais, 216–37. Washington, D.C.: The Catholic University of America Press, 2012.

———. "What Does the Spirit Have to Do?" In *Reading John with St. Thomas Aquinas: Theological Exegesis and Speculative Theology*, edited by Michael Dauphinais and Matthew Levering, 62–77. Washington, D.C.: The Catholic University of America Press, 2005.

Martin, R. Francis. "*Sacra Doctrina* and the Authority of Its *Sacra Scriptura*." *Pro Ecclesia* 10 (2001): 84–102.

Maurer, Armand. *St. Thomas Aquinas 1274–1974: Commemorative Studies*, vol. 2. Toronto: Pontifical Institute of Mediaeval Studies, 1974.

McGrath, James F. *The Only True God: Early Christian Monotheism in Its Jewish Context.* Chicago: University of Illinois Press, 2009.

McInerny, Ralph. *Praeambula Fidei: Thomism and the God of the Philosophers.* Washington, D.C.: The Catholic University of America Press, 2006.

Moreland, Anna Bonta. *Known by Nature: Thomas Aquinas on Natural Knowledge of God.* New York: Crossroad, 2010.

Murphy, Francesca Aran. *God Is Not a Story.* Oxford: Oxford University Press, 2007.

———. "Thomas' Commentaries on Philemon, 1 and 2 Thessalonians and Philippians." In *Aquinas on Scripture: An Introduction to His Biblical Commentaries,* edited by Thomas G. Weinandy, OFM Cap., Daniel A. Keating, and John P. Yocum, 167–96. London: T. and T. Clark International, 2005.

Nieuwenhove, Rik Van, "'Bearing the Marks of Christ's Passion': Aquinas' Soteriology." In *The Theology of Thomas Aquinas,* edited by Rik Van Nieuwenhove and Joseph Wawrykow, 277–302. Notre Dame, Ind.: University of Notre Dame Press, 2005.

Nieuwenhove, Rik Van, and Joseph Wawrykow, eds. *The Theology of Thomas Aquinas.* Notre Dame, Ind.: University of Notre Dame Press, 2005.

O'Brien, T. C. "'Sacra Doctrina' Revisited: The Context of Medieval Education." *The Thomist* 41 (1977): 475–509.

O'Neill, Colman E. *Sacramental Realism: A General Theory of the Sacraments.* Chicago: Midwest Theological Forum, 1998.

Oliveira, C.-J. Pinto de, ed. *Ordo Sapientiae et Amoris.* Fribourg: Éditions universitaires, 1993.

Osborne, Thomas M., Jr. *Love of Self and Love of God in Thirteenth-Century Ethics.* Notre Dame, Ind.: University of Notre Dame Press, 2005.

Paddison, Angus. *Theological Hermeneutics and 1 Thessalonians.* Cambridge: Cambridge University Press, 2005.

Paretzky, A. "The Influence of Thomas the Exegete on Thomas the Theologian: The Tract on Law (Ia-IIae, qq. 90–108) as a Test Case." *Angelicum* 71 (1994): 549–78.

Persson, Per Erik. *Sacra Doctrina: Reason and Revelation in Aquinas.* Translated by J. A. R. Mackenzie. Oxford: Blackwell, 1970.

Pesch, Otto Hermann. "Paul as Professor of Theology: The Image of the Apostle in St. Thomas's Theology." *The Thomist* 38 (1974): 584–605.

Perrin, Nicholas, and Richard B. Hays. *Jesus, Paul and the People of God: A Theological Dialogue with N. T. Wright.* Downers Grove, Ill.: IVP Academic, 2011.

Pieper, Josef. *Faith, Hope, Love.* Translated by Richard and Clara Winston. San Francisco: Ignatius Press, 1997.

Pope, Stephen J., ed. *The Ethics of Aquinas.* Washington, D.C.: Georgetown University Press, 2002.

Porter, Jean. "The Virtue of Justice (IIa IIae, qq. 58–122)." In *The Ethics of Aquinas,* edited by Stephen J. Pope, 272–86. Washington, D.C.: Georgetown University Press, 2002.

Prügl, Thomas. "Thomas Aquinas as Interpreter of Scripture." Translated by Albert K.

Wimmer. In *The Theology of Thomas Aquinas*, edited by Rik Van Nieuwenhove and Joseph Wawrykow, 386–415. Notre Dame, Ind.: University of Notre Dame Press, 2005.

Raith, Charles. "Abraham and the Reformation: Romans 4 and the Theological Interpretation of Aquinas and Calvin." *Journal of Theological Interpretation* 5 (2011): 280–300.

———. "Theology and Interpretation: The Case of Aquinas and Calvin on Romans." *International Journal of Systematic Theology* 14 (2012): 310–26.

Reno, R. R. *Genesis*. Grand Rapids, Mich.: Brazos Press, 2010.

Rocca, Gregory. *Speaking the Incomprehensible God: Thomas Aquinas on the Interplay of Positive and Negative Theology*. Washington, D.C.: The Catholic University of America Press, 2004.

Rogers, Eugene F., Jr. *Thomas Aquinas and Karl Barth: Sacred Doctrine and the Natural Knowledge of God*. Notre Dame, Ind.: University of Notre Dame Press, 1995.

Ryan, Thomas F. "The Love of Learning and the Desire for God in Thomas Aquinas's *Commentary on Romans*." In *Medieval Readings of Romans*, edited by William S. Campbell, Peter S. Hawkins, and Brenda Deen Schildgen, 101–14. New York: T. and T. Clark International, 2007.

Schleiermacher, Friedrich. *The Christian Faith*. Edited by H. R. Mackintosh and J. S. Stewart. Translated by D. M. Baillie et al. Edinburgh: T. and T. Clark, 1989.

Schmithals, Walter. *Der Römerbrief*. Gütersloh: Gerd Mohn, 1988.

Schnackenburg, Rudolf. *The Epistle to the Ephesians: A Commentary*. Translated by Helen Heron. Edinburgh: T. and T. Clark, 1991.

Shanley, Brian J. "*Sacra Doctrina* and the Theology of Disclosure." *The Thomist* 61 (1997): 163–88.

Sheets, J. R. "The Scriptural Dimension of St. Thomas." *American Ecclesiastical Review* 144 (1961): 154–73.

Sherwin, Michael S. "Aquinas, Augustine, and the Medieval Scholastic Crisis concerning Charity." In *Aquinas the Augustinian*, edited by Michael Dauphinais, Barry David, and Matthew Levering, 181–204. Washington, D.C.: The Catholic University of America Press, 2007.

———. *By Knowledge and By Love: Charity and Knowledge in the Moral Theology of St. Thomas Aquinas*. Washington, D.C.: The Catholic University of America Press, 2005.

Smalley, Beryl. "William of Auvergne, John of La Rochelle and St. Thomas Aquinas on the Old Law." In *St. Thomas Aquinas 1274–1974: Commemorative Studies*, vol. 2, edited by Armand Maurer, 11–71. Toronto: Pontifical Institute of Mediaeval Studies, 1974.

Smith, Mark S. *The Early History of God: Yahweh and Other Deities in Ancient Israel*. 2nd edition. Grand Rapids, Mich.: Eerdmans, 2002.

Sommer, Benjamin D. *The Bodies of God and the World of Ancient Israel*. Cambridge: Cambridge University Press, 2009.

Staudt, R. Jared. "Sin as an Offense against God: Aquinas on the Relation of Sin and Religion." *Nova et Vetera* 9 (2011): 195–207.

Stump, Eleonore. *Aquinas*. New York: Routledge, 2003.
Torrell, Jean-Pierre. *Aquinas's Summa: Background, Structure, and Reception*. Translated by Benedict M. Guevin, OSB. Washington, D.C.: The Catholic University of America Press, 2005.
———. *Christ and Spirituality in St. Thomas Aquinas*. Translated by Bernhard Blankenhorn, OP, et al. Washington, D.C.: The Catholic University of America Press, 2011.
———. "Le savoir théologique chez saint Thomas." *Revue Thomiste* 96 (1996): 355–96.
Turner, Denys. *Faith, Reason and the Existence of God*. Cambridge: Cambridge University Press, 2004.
Valkenberg, Wilhelmus G. B. M. *Words of the Living God: Place and Function of Holy Scripture in the Theology of St. Thomas Aquinas*. Leuven: Peeters, 2000.
Van Ackeren, G. F. *Sacra Doctrina: The Subject of the First Question of the Summa Theologica of St. Thomas Aquinas*. Rome: Catholic Book Agency, 1952.
Van der Ploeg, J. "The Place of Holy Scripture in the Theology of St. Thomas." *The Thomist* 10 (1947): 398–422.
Vazquez, Rodolfo. "La religion segun Santo Tomas de Aquino." *Revista de Filosofía* 16 (1983): 245–84.
Velde, Rudi A. Te. *Aquinas on God: The 'Divine Science' of the Summa Theologiae*. London: Ashgate, 2006.
Vosté, Jacobus-M. "Exegesis Novi Testamenti et Sancti Thomae Summa theologica." *Angelicum* 24 (1947): 3–19.
Wagner, J. Ross. *Heralds of the Good News: Isaiah and Paul in Concert in the Letter to the Romans*. Leiden: Brill, 2003.
Waldstein, Michael M. "On Scripture in the *Summa Theologiae*." *Aquinas Review* 1 (1994): 73–94.
Walsh, Liam G. "The Divine and the Human in St. Thomas's Theology of Sacraments." In *Ordo sapientiae et amoris*, edited by C.-J. Pinto de Oliveira, 231–52. Fribourg: Éditions universitaires, 1993.
———. "Sacraments." In *The Theology of Thomas Aquinas*, edited by Rik Van Nieuwenhove and Joseph Wawrykow, 326–64. Notre Dame, Ind.: University of Notre Dame Press, 2005.
Watson, Francis. *Paul and the Hermeneutics of Faith*. London: T. and T. Clark International, 2004.
Wawrykow, Joseph. *God's Grace and Human Action: "Merit" in the Theology of Thomas Aquinas*. Notre Dame, Ind.: University of Notre Dame Press, 1995.
Webb, Stephen H. *Jesus Christ, Eternal God: Heavenly Flesh and the Metaphysics of Matter*. Oxford: Oxford University Press, 2012.
Weinandy, Thomas G., Daniel A. Keating, and John P. Yocum, eds. *Aquinas on Doctrine: A Critical Introduction*. New York: T. and T. Clark, 2004.
———. *Aquinas on Scripture: An Introduction to His Biblical Commentaries*. London: T. and T. Clark International, 2005.

Weisheipl, James A. "The Meaning of *Sacra Doctrina* in *Summa Theologiae* I, q. 1." *The Thomist* 38 (1974): 49–80.
Westerholm, Stephen, ed. *The Blackwell Companion to Paul*. Oxford: Wiley-Blackwell, 2011.
White, Thomas Joseph. "Engaging the Thomistic Tradition and Contemporary Culture Simultaneously: A Response to Burrell, Healy, and Schindler." *Nova et Vetera* 10 (2012): 605–23.
———. "Jesus' Cry on the Cross and His Beatific Vision." *Nova et Vetera* 5 (2007): 555–81.
———. "Kenoticism and the Divinity of Christ Crucified." *The Thomist* 75 (2011): 1–41.
———. *Wisdom in the Face of Modernity: A Study in Thomistic Natural Theology*. Ave Maria, Fla.: Sapientia Press, 2009.
White, Victor. *Holy Teaching: The Idea of Theology according to St. Thomas Aquinas*. Oxford: Blackfriars, 1958.
Williams, A. N. "Argument to Bliss: The Epistemology of the *Summa Theologiae*." *Modern Theology* 20 (2004): 505–26.
———. *The Divine Sense: The Intellect in Patristic Theology*. Cambridge: Cambridge University Press, 2007.
———. *The Ground of Union: Deification in Aquinas and Palamas*. Oxford: Oxford University Press, 1999.
Witherington, Ben, III. *The Problem with Evangelical Theology: Testing the Exegetical Foundations of Calvinism, Dispensationalism and Wesleyanism*. Waco, Tex.: Baylor University Press, 2005.
Wright, N. T. *Justification: God's Plan and Paul's Vision*. Downers Grove, Ill.: IVP Academic, 2009.
———. *The Letter to the Romans: Introduction, Commentary, and Reflections*. In *The New Interpreter's Bible*, vol. X: *Acts, Romans, 1 Corinthians*. Nashville, Tenn.: Abingdon Press, 2002.
———. "Response to Richard Hays." In *Jesus, Paul and the People of God: A Theological Dialogue with N. T. Wright*, edited by Nicholas Perrin and Richard B. Hays, 62–65. Downers Grove, Ill.: IVP Academic, 2011.
Yocum, John P. "Sacraments in Aquinas." In *Aquinas on Doctrine: A Critical Introduction*, edited by Thomas G. Weinandy, OFM Cap., Daniel A. Keating, and John P. Yocum, 159–81. London: T. and T. Clark, 2004.

INDEX

Abel, 71
Abelard, Peter, xxiii, 64
Abraham, 19, 71, 81, 90, 117, 120, 122, 127–29, 132, 139, 159, 188
Adam, xxi, 60–62, 92–94, 96, 103, 105, 161, 187
Ambrose, 30, 91, 96
analogy, 5, 22–23, 26, 38, 223–24, 234
angels, xxi, 11, 19, 24, 31, 128, 145, 147, 191, 211, 224, 234, 239–42, 250, 270, 272, 274, 279–81, 283, 287–88
Anselm, 31
Aquinas, Thomas, writings of: biblical commentaries, xii–xiii, xvi, xxiii, 3; *Commentary on . . . Romans*, 3; *Commentary on the Sentences*, xix; *Compendium theologiae*, xix n16; *lectura* on John's Gospel, xix n16; *Summa contra Gentiles*, xiv
Aristotle, xvii, xxi, 4, 7, 17, 38, 74, 120, 174, 189, 245, 257
ark of the covenant, 145, 147
Athanasius, 60
Augustine, xvii, xxiii, 4, 10, 12–13, 38, 41–42, 56, 92, 119, 129, 132–33, 149, 155, 157–58, 222n9, 225–26, 228–29, 231n24, 256–57, 268, 276, 278–79

Baglow, Christopher, xixn26
baptism, xx, 70, 76–106, 131, 138–39, 143, 151, 262–63, 266, 284–85, 290–91; of blood, 83–86, 263; character of, 78, 91–92, 99, 101–3, 106, 143; form of, 79, 80, 84–86, 88, 104–5, 284; grace of, 80, 84, 92, 96, 100–102, 106, 143; by immersion, 80–81, 85–86, 104; minister of, 79–81, 87–88, 93, 104, 285; by sprinkling, 81
Basil, 39

beatific vision, 10–12, 15, 34, 58, 228, 238–39, 243, 248–49, 255–56, 260, 262, 273–74, 278
book of life, 32, 34–35

Cessario, Romanus, 49, 153, 236–37
charity, 11, 27, 44, 63–64, 66, 68, 71–74, 84–85, 87, 90, 100, 102, 114, 123, 133–36, 140, 157–58, 160–61, 168–71, 174, 177, 180–82, 193, 199, 207, 210, 212–13, 216, 234, 236, 238, 240, 242–48, 250–61, 263–65, 270–71, 283, 285, 288
Chenu, Marie-Dominique, xiv, xviii, xixn16
Christ. *See* Jesus Christ
church, xi, xiii, xxiii, 33, 42, 45, 50, 66, 72, 76–77, 79, 81–88, 92–93, 100, 102, 104–5, 125–26, 135, 138–39, 148, 150, 170–71, 175, 177–80, 183–84, 186, 196–98, 202–4, 206, 209–10, 214, 216, 233, 284–85, 287, 289–91
Cicero, 189
circumcision, 81, 90, 93, 105, 116, 122, 124, 129–30, 138–39, 142, 151, 174–75, 290
concupiscence, 96–97, 101, 113–15, 131, 161, 163, 165, 182, 283
Congar, Yves, xxiii
Cousar, Charles B., 4n4, 50, 74–75
creation, xviii, xxi, 6, 8, 13–15, 18, 38, 46, 53, 70, 144, 167, 174–76, 183, 185, 189, 192–93, 219–20, 231–32, 237n4, 269, 279, 286, 290

David, 117, 252
day of atonement, 59, 144–46
Decalogue, 119–20, 132–33, 140–41, 147, 149, 152, 283
demons, 9, 13, 16
devil, 68–69, 73, 284
Dillard, Annie, 234

303

Index

Emery, Gilles, xxn30, 3, 4n3
eschatology, 76
eternal life, 5, 10–12, 14–15, 30, 35, 48, 52, 69, 71, 74, 89, 97, 100, 102–3, 105, 115, 123, 130, 145, 161–64, 167–68, 172, 176, 182, 184, 244–45, 247–49, 252, 255–57, 259–60, 274, 280, 283, 286, 288
eucharist, 75–77, 82, 87, 104, 111, 126, 131, 138, 146, 151, 199, 262
Eve, xxi, 60, 62, 187
expiation, 53, 64, 68, 121, 264

faith, xi–xiii, xviii, 8, 13–14, 37, 41, 44, 47, 50, 53, 55–58, 60, 64, 67–68, 70–71, 73–74, 77–82, 85–86, 88–95, 98–104, 113, 122, 127–31, 133, 139–40, 149, 151, 153–54, 158–61, 168, 170, 174, 181, 184, 206, 208, 212, 214, 216, 221n8, 223, 226–29, 234, 236–40, 242–44, 246–51, 256–57, 259–62, 264–66, 273, 284–85, 287–88, 290–91
fortitude, xxi, 247, 249, 254–55

Gelasius I, Pope, 87, 94
Gentiles, 21, 61, 65, 98, 116, 119–20, 129, 141, 152, 157, 182, 219n1, 220, 277
God: attributes of, xxi, 4n4, 7–8, 20–21, 38, 219, 268, 280, 288; existence of, 6–7, 10, 18, 190, 219, 223, 287; as infinite, 6–7, 9, 11–13, 24, 34, 54, 174–75, 179, 224, 246, 274; justice, 5, 19–21, 24–26, 29, 31, 35, 53–54, 141; knowledge, xviiin24, 5, 16–18, 23–25, 32, 35–36, 46, 283, 285; love, 19, 24–26, 28–30, 40, 42–43, 46–47, 50, 54–56, 60–61, 63–64, 68, 73, 114, 155, 158, 175, 192, 284; mercy, 5, 15, 19–21, 24–26, 29–31, 34–35, 53–55, 61, 72, 87, 97, 115, 154–55, 166, 284; names of, 5, 15–16, 23, 41, 223–24; perfection of, 8, 34; power, 4n4, 5–7, 13–15, 17, 32–35, 41–42, 45, 47, 49, 66–67, 73, 92, 190, 219–20, 223, 225, 229, 232, 234, 262, 277, 290; predestination, 5, 25–32, 34–36, 39, 46–47, 64, 175–76, 283, 285; providence, 5, 21–22, 24–28, 31, 35, 52, 66, 195; will, 5–6, 16–20, 23–25, 29–30, 35–36, 42, 46, 53, 191, 196, 204, 270, 272, 280, 283, 285; wisdom of, xviii, 4n4, 16, 20–21, 23–24, 29, 33, 37, 41–42, 45–46, 148, 204, 228, 232, 248; wrath of, 63
Gorman, Michael J., 4n4, 50
grace: xv, xx, 11, 13–14, 19, 27–28, 33, 39, 43–45, 50, 53–54, 64–66, 80, 84, 90, 92, 94–103, 106, 114–16, 118, 120, 124, 129, 132–33, 143–44, 153–85, 194, 201, 210, 221n8, 222n9, 223, 231, 238–40, 243, 247–49, 255–57, 259–60, 263, 277, 283–84, 286, 290; cause of, 155–56, 169; co-operating, 155–56, 166–67, 173, 185; effects of, 155; gratuitous, 43, 155, 158, 166–67, 170–71, 176, 183, 248–49, 255; habitual, 156, 159, 161, 163–64, 169, 182; operating, 156, 166, 173, 185; sanctifying, 43–44, 99–100, 155, 158–60, 166–73, 175–79, 181, 183, 238

Hays, Richard, 110, 237n4, 289n3
hell, 278–80
Hilary of Poitiers, 267
Holy Spirit, xi, 3–5, 11, 13–14, 16, 23, 27, 30, 32–33, 36–48, 60, 64, 66, 69, 76, 79–80, 83–85, 87, 90, 97, 99, 102, 105, 111, 114–18, 124, 127, 132, 134, 136, 142, 144, 150–53, 160, 162, 164–65, 168–74, 177, 180–84, 191, 193–94, 203, 215, 221n8, 229, 234, 238–40, 242–43, 245, 263, 265, 275, 277, 283, 285–86, 289–90
Hugh of St. Victor, 78

image of God, 7, 40, 45, 47, 224
incarnation. *See* Jesus Christ
Isaac, 29, 32, 128, 188
Isidore, 94, 104
Israel, 21, 23, 25, 59, 61, 73, 83, 104, 109–10, 113–14, 116–19, 124–26, 128–29, 136, 151, 153–54, 186–87, 189, 191, 194–95, 197, 214, 261, 283, 285

Jephthah, 212–13
Jerome, 81, 129
Jerusalem, 58–59, 65, 141
Jesus Christ, xvi, xviii–xx, xxiii, 9–11, 14–15, 18, 21, 24–28, 30, 33–34, 36–37, 39, 41–105, 109, 111, 114–18, 120–22, 124–31, 133–40, 142–53, 155, 157–60, 162, 164–65, 170, 172–74, 176–84, 188–90, 192–96, 198, 202–3, 205, 207, 209–10, 212–13, 215, 219, 221, 227, 229–30, 232–35, 237, 243, 247, 249, 259–65, 267–81, 283–91; ascension, 68, 71, 262, 276, 284; baptism, xx, 44–45, 78, 83, 85–86, 277; cross, 4n4, 49–53, 56–58, 60–62, 64–65, 67, 69, 71–72, 74–75, 85, 99, 135–36, 142, 148, 267–68, 270–71, 273–74, 276, 278–79, 284–85, 288, 290; exaltation of, 50, 65,

68–69, 71–74, 268, 276–81, 288; as incarnate, 19, 45, 50, 52–53, 60, 62, 64, 66–67, 73, 222, 232–34, 264, 269–70, 272, 274, 277, 279–80, 285, 287; *kenosis*, 267–68, 280–81, 288; mysteries of, xviii; as paschal lamb, 58, 82, 126, 131, 135; Passion, xx, xxiii, 50–59, 61–75, 78–79, 81–86, 91, 95–96, 120, 129, 263, 268, 278–80, 284–85; as redeemer, 53, 66–67, 73–74, 116; resurrection, xvi, xix, 50, 53, 55–56, 67–68, 71, 73–75, 86, 280, 284–85; at right hand of Father, 54, 57, 68, 70–72, 151, 215, 262, 276, 288, 290
John of Damascus, 18, 26, 57, 78, 83
John the Baptist, 79, 93
Judas, 64–65
justification, 53, 71, 75, 95, 120, 129, 157n7, 158–60, 164, 171, 173, 178–79, 181–82, 184

kingdom, 15, 42, 45, 47, 68, 70–71, 73–74, 196

last supper, 58
Levenson, Jon D., 112, 188n4
Lord's Prayer, 196, 284
Luther, Martin, 112

Maimonides, 22, 121, 136, 223
Manichees, 112
Mary, mother of Jesus, 276–77
Melchizedek, 125, 143, 147, 188
mercy. *See* God
mercy seat, 147
Moreland, Anna, 221
Mosaic law, xx, 59, 63, 72–73, 95, 109–19, 121–52, 187, 190–91, 194, 203, 207, 209, 211, 246–48, 262, 283, 286
Moses, 83, 109, 117, 127, 140, 148, 153–54, 203, 261
Murphy, Francesca Aran, 221n7, 267

Neoplatonism, 38
Noah, 124, 187

oaths, 147, 190, 195, 199, 201, 205–6, 208–9, 211, 213–14, 216, 284, 287
O'Neill, Colman, 76–77
Origen, 17, 26
original sin, 30, 71, 81–82, 95, 99, 103, 120–21, 185, 278, 280

Passover, 58, 137
Pentecost, 44–45, 111
penance, 57, 70, 91, 94, 262–64
people of God, 50, 74, 109, 144, 197–98, 262
perseverance, xxi, 161
Peter, 129
Peter Lombard, xxiii, 78
Plato, 226
Pilate, 61, 64–65
Porter, Jean, 186
predestination. *See* God
providence. *See* God
purgatory, 90
Pseudo-Dionysius, 12, 87

Rebecca, 29, 32
redemption, xviiin24, 18, 53–54, 59, 63, 66–68, 71–74, 116, 136, 144, 158, 194, 285, 290
resurrection, 15, 46, 50, 56, 76, 83, 86, 97, 102, 240
resurrection of Christ. *See* Jesus Christ

sacra doctrina, xi, xiii, xviii, xix n26, xxiii, 283–84, 286, 289, 291
sacrament, xx, 68, 73, 75–80, 82, 84–88, 90–95, 98, 101, 103–5, 111, 121, 126, 131, 135, 138–39, 143, 145, 147, 151, 210, 222, 230, 232–34, 261–64, 287
sacred history, xviii
sacrifice, 50, 58–59, 61, 63, 65, 72–74, 95, 113, 121, 123–26, 135–38, 144–49, 151, 187–88, 190–95, 198, 204, 206, 210, 212–14, 272, 280, 283–85, 287, 290
Saul, 63
sanctifying grace. *See* grace
Satan. *See* devil
satisfaction, 53, 57–58, 61, 64–66, 69, 72, 74, 91, 105, 113, 285
scapegoat, 59, 146
Schleiermacher, Friedrich, 112
Sherwin, Michael, 236
semi-Arians, 42, 269
semi-Pelagians, 29
sermon on the mount, 203
sin, 6, 9–10, 12–13, 19, 24, 28, 30, 33, 47, 50, 52–62, 64–66, 68–71, 73–74, 79, 90–92, 94–97, 100–103, 105, 113–15, 117–18, 120–21, 123, 127, 129, 134, 139, 144–45, 147–48, 150–53, 154n2, 157–66, 169, 172–74, 178–79, 182,

sin (*cont.*)
   184, 187, 194, 196, 204, 206, 210, 221n5, 222, 235, 245–46, 248, 250, 252, 259, 261, 263–64, 274, 278, 283–285
speaking in tongues, 170, 200, 205, 215, 258
Spirit. *See* Holy Spirit
Sommer, Benjamin D., 7
Summa fratris Alexandri, xxiii

Teilhard de Chardin, Pierre, 234
temperance, xxi, 254
temple, 36, 45, 47, 58–59, 70, 136–38, 144–45, 154n4, 169, 198, 204, 289
tongues. *See* speaking in tongues
Torrell, Jean-Pierre, xiin2, xiv, xv, 49n1
Trinity, xviii n24, xx, xxi, xxiii, 3–5, 13, 26, 35–39, 41, 43–45, 47, 66, 77, 79–81, 229, 238–39, 262, 284
triune God. *See* Trinity

Valkenberg, Wilhelmus, xvi–ix
Van Nieuwenhove, Rik, 49
virtue of religion, xx, 186–90, 192–95, 198–99, 204, 206–8, 212–14, 216, 230, 286–87
von Hertling, Georg Graf, xvii
vows, 192–93, 195–97, 202–6, 212–16, 259, 265, 271, 284, 287
Vulgate, xx, 245, 253

Wagner, Ross, 110
Walsh, Liam, 76
Watson, Francis, 110
Webb, Stephen H., 7
White, Thomas Joseph, 49, 221n7, 268n2
will of God. *See* God
wisdom of God. *See* God
Wright, N. T., 155n6, 220–21, 289n3

Paul in the 'Summa Theologiae' was designed in
Garamond and composed by Kachergis Book Design
of Pittsboro, North Carolina. It was printed on
60-pound Sebago Cream and bound by
Maple Press of York, Pennsylvania.

www.ingramcontent.com/pod-product-compliance
Lightning Source LLC
Chambersburg PA
CBHW031233290426
44109CB00012B/278